McGRAW–HILL SERIES IN EDUCATION

HAROLD BENJAMIN, *Consulting Editor*

FOUNDATIONS OF METHOD FOR SECONDARY SCHOOLS

FOUNDATIONS OF METHOD
FOR SECONDARY SCHOOLS

by

I. N. THUT
Associate Professor of Education
The University of Connecticut

and

J. RAYMOND GERBERICH
Professor of Education
The University of Connecticut

With special contributions by: Vernon E. Anderson, Associate Professor of Education; P. Roy Brammell, Dean and Professor of Education; DWane R. Collins, Assistant Professor of Education; William T. Gruhn, Professor of Education; Arthur L. Knoblauch, Professor of Education and Director of Extension—all of the School of Education of the University of Connecticut; and David E. Strom, Utilization Specialist, Text-film Department, McGraw-Hill Book Company, Inc.

FIRST EDITION

McGRAW–HILL BOOK COMPANY, INC.
NEW YORK   TORONTO   LONDON · 1949

FOUNDATIONS OF METHOD FOR SECONDARY SCHOOLS

PREFACE

The first quarter of the present century witnessed widespread interest on the part of educators in the problem of method. New techniques, plans, and procedures appeared in great profusion, each designed and recommended for teaching better the subjects already offered in the schools. This was the era in which teachers and laymen alike looked for a better world through the wider diffusion of knowledge. Accordingly, the educational offering was extended year by year, laws were passed to compel parents to give their children an opportunity to attend school, special training programs were established to increase the efficiency of the teaching staff, and assembly-line operational procedures characteristic of the new mass production industries were imitated widely, all to make the old knowledge more accessible to a larger number.

The drive to improve method was somewhere near its peak when John Dewey published *Democracy and Education*. Not least among the many challenges Dewey threw down to the educational world in that epochal volume was the observation that the search for a better method will not bear fruit in the form of a more democratic citizenry unless it goes hand in hand with the search for a better content. It is not claimed, of course, that this statement alone touched off the curriculum movement which followed, but it is quite clear that during the second quarter of the century large segments of the educational world have directed much thought and effort to the search for a more appropriate content for democracy's schools and have subordinated thereby the former interest in the problem of method. It is equally clear that today the balance between the emphases on method and content is not everywhere the same. In fact, the balance varies from system to system, from school to school, and from classroom to classroom. The beginning teacher thus can seldom be sure whether he will be judged by his stock of techniques and devices, by the insights his pupils develop while under his supervision, or by some other standard.

The dilemma of the beginning teacher is further compounded by the fact that his pre-service education very likely did not prepare him either to expect a diversity of practices in the schools or to make a constructive start in whatever situation he might find himself. Although teacher education programs generally devote much time to giving the student a method "which will help him through his first year," very little time is given to the development of philosophical and psychological perspective on method. Thus, it frequently happens that the inference is encouraged, either directly or indirectly, that the method which is encountered in the training program is the only one that can be accepted by right-thinking people. The one-method outlook receives further encouragement from a number of the textbooks which are encountered in general methods courses.

This text has been developed over a period of years in response to a need for new perspective on educational method. Under the influence of the curriculum movement the purposes of the school and the objectives of teaching have undergone some serious revision and redirection. A new content has been introduced to supplement rather than to replace the old. A variety of methods is now called for, and teaching procedures must be adapted to the particular goals that are sought. This text, therefore, seeks to provide the needed perspective and to bring about a closer coordination between method and content.

Although much cooperative effort has gone into its preparation, this text is not a symposium. The basic plan for the book as a whole and for each chapter in some detail has been developed by the senior author in connection with his undergraduate classes. He has written 10 of the developmental chapters (Chaps. 1, 2, 3, 6, 7, 9, 10, 12, 13, and 15) which form the central core of this book. The junior author wrote Chaps. 5, 8, 11, 14, and 16 which deal with the appraisal of pupil progress. Auxiliary chapters were prepared by colleagues, each of whom was qualified to make a unique contribution in a given area. These auxiliary contributions are as follows: Chap. 4, Vernon E. Anderson; Chap. 17, DWane R. Collins; Chap. 18, William T. Gruhn; Chap. 19, David E. Strom; Chap. 20, Arthur L. Knoblauch.

The authors express their appreciation to the individuals and publishers who have given them permission to quote from copyrighted materials. Further recognition of such permission is given throughout the text in appropriate footnotes indicating the original sources. Special thanks are due Mrs. Joanne Inglis and Miss Louise Patros for their help in preparing the manuscript for publication. Finally, but not least, are the thanks due Dean P. Roy Brammell who read the manuscript and contributed many suggestions which have helped to make this an integrated book.

I. N. THUT

J. RAYMOND GERBERICH

STORRS, CONN.

September, 1949

CONTENTS

Division C

Method Based on the Experience Unit

CHAPTER

PART THREE

SOME SPECIAL ASPECTS OF SECONDARY-SCHOOL TEACHING

Part 1. SOME FACTORS THAT AFFECT

SECONDARY-SCHOOL TEACHING

Chapter 1. THE PURPOSE OF AMERICAN SECONDARY EDUCATION AND ITS IMPLICATIONS FOR METHOD

The professional teacher knows how to answer three questions: What shall I teach? How are the pupils going to learn what I teach? How shall I teach so that the pupils will learn most easily and effectively?

The professional education of the modern teacher is concerned with finding answers to these three questions. Courses in educational theory, history of education, comparative education, and the curriculum try to answer the question of what shall be taught. Courses in educational psychology deal with the question of how pupils learn. Courses in administration, supervision, guidance, and method discuss various aspects of the question of how the teaching is to be done.

In this book special attention will be given to that part of education in which the teacher deals directly with the pupils for the purpose of instruction. This is the area of study known as methodology.

AN APPROACH TO THE STUDY OF METHOD

A study of method, whether of instruction or of any other activity, should give the student increased power to select and to use procedures most likely to bring about the ends that are sought. That is, the student as a result of his study should grow in his ability to modify and adapt his attack upon a given problem in keeping with the specific objectives in view and in line with the unique conditions under which the problem is encountered. Such ability to modify his attack grows out of a knowledge of the alternative methods available and of the merits and limitations of each. Mere competence in the use of a single teaching method does not guarantee that an individual can deal intelligently with all the problems in an area of instruction any more than competence in

3

the use of an automobile guarantees that an individual can deal effectively with all the problems in the area of transportation. The modern automobile serves many purposes, but there are some destinations and traffic conditions that call for railroads, ships, airplanes, pack horses, or one of the many other forms of transportation at man's disposal today. The competent traffic manager is familiar with many of these and knows the unique characteristics of each. He will ship a bridge from Pittsburgh to Chicago by rail, a locomotive from New York to Antwerp by boat, and carry injured plane passengers from the scene of a crash to the base of the rescue expedition by helicopter. He is competent because he is able to use more than one method and to select the most appropriate one for each situation.

Modern education also affords many different approaches to the problems encountered in the classroom. There is no one approach that excels all the others in every respect. To know but one type of teaching technique or to be restricted to the use of this or that "teaching method" places an unnecessary limitation on the efficiency of the teacher and, therefore, on the educational opportunities of the pupils. Thus a study of method in education should lead to several very definite outcomes. First, the student should acquire a clear, unmistakable idea of the goals to be achieved through instruction. Just as the traffic manager must know whether a given item is destined for Chicago or Antwerp before he can select the appropriate method of transportation, so also must the algebra teacher know if his pupils are to come away from a given learning activity with proficiency in a particular operation, with an understanding of the relation of algebra to modern industrial life, or with some other outcome before he can select an instructional procedure that will fit the situation. Second, the student should become acquainted with the several types of instructional procedures that are available. Such knowledge should include a familiarity with the main characteristics of each type, as well as the conditions under which each is likely to operate with the greatest promise of success. Finally, the student should grow in his ability to anticipate the conditions that are likely to be encountered while the teaching activity is in progress. In the case of the traffic manager it is not enough to know that ships are effective over long water routes and that a given shipment must cross an ocean. He must also know the weight of the shipment, the loading and unloading facilities at the several ports, and the hazards likely to be encountered en route before the item can be delivered safely at its destination. In like fashion the teacher must be acquainted with the learning process, the likes and dislikes of the pupils, the social and educational background of the pupils, the types of procedures used by the other teachers with whom the pupils have come in contact, and the general philosophy that determines the over-all school and community environment. Until this is achieved by the teacher he cannot deal with the problem of method wisely, and the pupils in his classroom are not likely to be given effective help in realizing their potentialities to the full.

It is perhaps unfortunate that students sometimes approach the study of educational methods with the comfortable belief that all the major problems have been solved. Some prospective teachers doubtlessly hope that the best method is now known and established in practice and that it is necessary only to learn it in much the same manner that one can learn to make a bed or bake a chocolate cake. This belief about method is reflected in the fact that few students are aware of the changes in theory and practice that took place in their own schools while they were enrolled as pupils. Lasting changes in American schools usually have been introduced so slowly that the pupils and the parents were unaware of them and missed their significance. Furthermore, at any given time there are only a few individuals who openly advocate radical changes in the conventional program of instruction. Most students in colleges today attended elementary and secondary schools that bore at least superficial resemblances. They enrolled in courses with similar titles, the selection of subjects was restricted by a strikingly similar list of offerings, the methods of instruction tended to be alike, and such variations as were noted came to be associated with differences in the subject matter. It is possible that some studied the same subjects, taught by the same teachers, in the same schools as did one or both of their parents. Hence, the personal experiences of those who are beginning their study of method may furnish no substantial basis for suspecting that the history of the American school system has been marked by conflict and dissension and that even now educational theory and practice are in a stage of transition.

Students frequently approach the study of education with the idea that they will get final answers to their problems; consequently, they may react with a feeling of futility when they discover the diversity of theory and practice which characterizes the field. Education, they may say, is an area of confusion wherein persons of apparently equal authority seem to advocate widely differing practices and points of view. Such students have been known to emerge from their program of professional studies resolved to forget all they have learned and to settle down to teaching in the manner they themselves were taught. This resolution of the problem, of course, is recognized by those who have studied psychology as one that is neither good pedagogy nor good mental hygiene.

Method should be judged in terms of purpose. A study of methods of organizing and directing learning activities is particularly prone to confuse beginning students because of the multiplicity of practices to which they are introduced. Although methods may have the appearance of uniformity in a given school or system, these local similarities are soon lost in the diversity of practice revealed by an inquiry conducted on a larger scale. This study hopes to forestall confusion and to provide the student with certain educational moorings by directing attention at the very beginning to the purposes for which secondary schools are maintained. If an agreement can be reached on the purpose of education, a common standard will be available for appraising the various practices that will be encountered in this study and elsewhere, as well as for directing the invention of new practices to meet situations in which existing ones are judged to be inadequate. Armed with a definite standard for appraising them, students may find that in a given situation one method of procedure may offer advantages over other methods. It does not follow, however, that this method is "the best" and is always to be preferred, or that all teachers can learn to use it with equal success. On the contrary, it may mean that variation in educational practice is as natural and no more diverse than is a difference of opinion regarding fishing equipment, wearing apparel, or good restaurants.

A definition of method. Confusion may also arise from the fact that the books and articles written on the subject do not agree on a common definition of a teaching method. To some writers any established technique or device such as the socialized recitation, supervised study, individualized assignments, or even the thought question is acceptable as a method. Others think a method is a well-defined pattern of procedures within which a variety of techniques and devices may appear as circumstances may require. The laboratory method, the Winnetka Plan, the project method, and other well-known plans and patterns of procedure are of this nature.

In this study a method is defined as a general plan of action formulated to achieve a particular type of educational outcome. That outcome may be the mastery of a prescribed body of subject matter; the exploration of large areas of knowledge with mastery to be determined, in part at least, by pupil interests and needs; or the development of power to cope satisfactorily with the physical and social environment. It is the outcome sought that determines the operational plan, whereas it is the particular circumstances encountered in carrying through that plan which suggest the particular techniques, devices, and aids to be used.

Since three distinctive types of educational outcomes are sought by secondary schools today, three distinctive types of operational plans or methods have been developed. These three have already been identified and described by experts in the curriculum area.[1] They are the daily-assignment or "recitation" method, the subject-matter unit method, and the experience-unit method. In discussing these, the major emphasis will be upon describing (a) the type of outcomes each method has been designed to yield, (b) the general nature of the method, and (c) the kind of procedures, techniques, and devices that usually are employed within the framework of each method. No attempt will be made to list or describe all the specific teaching techniques and devices in use to-day. Their number and variety alone are enough to bewilder even experienced teachers.

It is recognized that the classification and treatment of methods presented here do not follow the conventional treatment given them in the professional literature. The simplicity of this presentation, it is hoped, will lend itself well to an initial study of method.

THE PURPOSE OF SECONDARY EDUCATION IN A DEMOCRACY

All peoples seek to transmit their way of life through some form of education. In common with all teachers, those who work on the level of the

---

[1] See in particular Hollis L. Caswell and Doak S. Campbell, *Curriculum Development*, American Book Company, New York, 1935. Also, William H. Burton, *The Guidance of Learning Activities*, D. Appleton-Century Company, Inc., New York, 1943.

secondary school must accept responsibility for helping children become contributing members of the adult community. That community will be made up of many individuals with differing interests and many groups which, because of geographical proximity and social interdependence, have developed some common interests and concerns. That is to say, the individuals who make up such a community are held together by the belief that they possess some knowledge, skills, or social arrangements which make life in their community richer and more secure than in any other. In the interests of the individual *and* the community these bodies of knowledge, skills, and social arrangements must be absorbed, lived, and if necessary modified by each child during the period that he is growing into adulthood.

Historically, the knowledge, skills, and social arrangements in some communities have been limited and simple. Frequently they could be mastered by observation and direct participation alone. These communities maintained no schools because their children could be "educated" without the aid of a special agency created for that purpose. Ceremonial dances, for example, were regarded by the primitive American Indians as a definite contribution to their well-being. Their children did not learn these dances in schools or special classes, but by watching their elders and by imitating them. They learned in a similar manner to plant corn, to hunt, to build shelters, to participate in the councils of the tribe, to value eagle feathers, and to give expression to their emotions in ways that were approved.

Modern Indian children, unlike their ancestors, have social experiences which transcend tribal boundaries. They are members, voluntary or involuntary, of a larger community that includes not only members of their own tribe, but also people of other tribes, races, and cultural backgrounds. These children cannot become effective participants in the larger community until they have learned to read, write, and speak the common language, to observe the accepted customs, and to participate in the established institutions. However, one does not learn to read or write by watching someone else. These accomplishments, and numerous others, required of the modern child, cannot be acquired by the methods of observation and direct participation alone. Special instructional activities are called for and in the case of the Indian children are now being provided in schools maintained and controlled by a number of public and private agencies.

The children in all communities employ the method of observation and direct participation to some degree. They learn to speak, play, dress, and to regulate personal habits by imitating the people around them. Many attitudes and skills are acquired in like manner. For example, a course of driving lessons was part of the contract covering the sale of an automobile a generation ago. Now many boys and girls "pick up" this skill long before they have reached the legal age for obtaining an operator's license. Some vocational skills and understandings are acquired in a similar fashion. Thus, the farmer's son usually can "turn his hand" to a variety of jobs by the time he is old enough to leave home.

It is unfortunate, perhaps, that the demands of modern industry have made it necessary to locate many crafts and trades in places to which children have no access. When isolated, these occupations cannot be mastered by the direct method, and it is necessary for the learners to seek out the craftsmen and to arrange to work with them for a period of time. The primary purpose of the apprentice system of education is to make it possible for the learner and the master craftsman to be brought together.

Modern industry is based upon so many technological developments that many workers are needed who have a knowledge of the basic sciences. Even though children were not excluded from the factories and commercial establishments, this knowledge could not be taught by the methods of observation and direct participation alone without impairing the efficiency and adaptability of the industrial system. Better results are secured by establishing and maintaining vocational, technological, and professional schools and departments. By concentrating on the process of developing the desired knowledge and skills, these agencies prepare individuals for industrial employment more quickly and with greater satisfaction than is possible by the direct method.

Modern social and political life has become equally complex and difficult to place under direct observation. In the colonial period of American history the social and political activities of adults in the main were confined to the geographical area represented by the pioneer settlement with its surrounding lands. Here these activities could readily be observed by those too young to engage in them directly. Formidable obstacles hindered ready communication with other settlements. This forced isolation together with the system of colonial government which concentrated nonlocal authority in the hands of the Crown, stimulated each community to develop a high degree of self-sufficiency. In New England where the outer forms of this local self-sufficiency have survived, children even to this day acquire their understanding of adult political affairs by attending the annual town meetings.

The simple agrarian period in the political and social life of America, like the hand production period in industry, has been replaced by a period of greatly expanded and vastly more complicated institutions and processes. The transformation has been marked by a corresponding expansion of the geographical area over which the individual is now called upon to function. Individual opportunities and responsibilities have multiplied as a result of these changes. The advantages to the individual cannot be realized, however, unless those who would enjoy them are as well prepared to exercise the functions of citizenship in the expanded communities as were the citizens of the pioneer communities prepared to meet the needs of their day. The understanding and skills basic to such competence are no more to be mastered by the methods of direct observation and participation than are the technological skills and understanding essential to competence in the modern industrial world. Just as schools are now expected to develop industrial competence, so also must they provide social and political competence. Since the responsibilities of citizenship rest upon virtually every adult in America today, social and political competence have become almost a universal requirement, and the responsibility of providing such competence is rapidly devolving upon the secondary schools. This statement in no way is meant to relieve the elementary schools and the institutions of higher education of their share of responsibility. For the majority of American young people, however, the interval between attendance at some secondary school and the assumption of the responsibilities of citizenship is marked by no other formal education.

American secondary schools should acquaint pupils with the democratic way of life. This, then, is the primary function of secondary education in America: To prepare the individual for effective participation with his contemporaries in carrying on the activities that constitute their common life. The fact that such participation is based in part on wholesome individual development serves to include that aspect of education in the process.

If democratic education were nothing more than the process of passing on a way of life or a body of valuable information, it would not of necessity differ from the kind of education provided in a non-democratic community. The adjective "democratic" when used with education, therefore, would have no meaning. All education is concerned with a way of life, and to speak of "democratic" education would appear to indicate that this "democratic" way of life has certain distinguishing characteristics.

The very nature of a community as a social unit implies that the lives of the individual members will be thrown into intimate contact. There is much to be gained from the shared interests and cooperative action which membership in a community affords. But there is also inherent in that relationship the possibility of uncertainties and conflicts with reference to opinions and actions. Sooner or later two individuals will want to use the same facility or will desire the same objective at the same time. These are simple examples of conflicts, but they serve to illustrate the need communities have for a way to settle disputes and to arrive at common agreements. That is to say, the community must acquire some principle for resolving conflicts or be destroyed by dissension. The principle employed is likely to determine not only the institutions and agencies of the community, but also its ideals, aspirations, and general nature.

The history of human societies reveals the fact that mankind has tried a number of ways of resolving conflicts and of arriving at decisions that commit the group. In some cases this is done by establishing prior rights and privileges among individuals. The rule of the jungle is a good example. There are still some communities in which conflicts are resolved by an appeal to force. Might makes right, and the stronger, more ruthless, more clever individual takes what he wants from or imposes his will upon the weaker individual. The community of nations has not yet succeeded in abandoning this principle in favor of a better one, although the desire to do so has been expressed time and again.

In other communities rights and privileges are distributed on a caste basis. That is, members of the community have a definite rank on an established scale and the higher rank always takes precedence over a lower rank. This principle is employed in most military organizations. Hence, there is never a question as to whether the captain or the major shall have the first choice of quarters. Sometimes rank is determined by heredity, as in certain oriental communities and in aristocratic societies.

The literature of medieval Europe provides numerous instances in which noblemen, traveling through the country and desiring quarters, thought nothing of putting a peasant and his family out of their house for the night. Sometimes the individual's age or length of service determines his rank, as in the case of some families, labor unions, and the United States Congress. Again, rank may be determined on the basis of material wealth, and an individual's position may fluctuate with his fortunes.

A different type of principle is based on the authority of a person, a position, or a document. Contestants for the right to run for office are selected far too frequently by the political boss. Very definite authority to arbitrate differences of opinion is given to umpires and referees in sports, while clergymen decide issues of theology by turning to the articles of faith that were set forth by the founders of their sect. In each case the parties to the dispute appeal to an authority whose judgment is assumed to be better than their own. The judgments rendered will be accepted without question as long as the individuals of the community give allegiance to the guiding principle by which those judgments are determined.

The democratic way of life is based on respect for the dignity and freedom of the individual. The distinctive quality of the democratic principle seems to reside in the emphasis that is given to individual freedom.[2] The American citizen is famed for his impatience with restrictions and for the value he places upon his own freedom of action. He likes to think that any man who grows tired of human contacts is free to go to any spot that promises to provide him with the desired degree of isolation. Similarly, anyone who thinks a trip to the moon would add to the enjoyment of life is free to exploit all the resources at his command to speed his departure. Some may argue that if photography, fishing, attending a motion picture, going to church, playing bridge, or studying to become a teacher will increase the measure of individual happiness, then nothing other than the lack of personal resources should be allowed to interfere with the fulfillment of that desire.

The principle of individual freedom touches upon every aspect of life in a democracy. Democratic institutions and arrangements are designed to extend that freedom. They exist only for the purpose of

[2] Joseph A. Leighton, *Social Philosophies in Conflict*, p. 358, D. Appleton-Century Company, Inc., New York, 1937.

serving the individual. When they cease to further the end for which they have been created, they have outlived their period of usefulness and need to be modified or discarded. In America a bureau of vital statistics is maintained as a recording agency and as a source of information which may be useful and interesting. The birth rate may move up or down, but the bureau has no responsibility other than to register and report the facts. The bearing of children is regarded as a strictly personal matter in which the state has no authority to interfere.

This is not necessarily true among undemocratic peoples. Whenever the perpetuation of a particular form of government becomes the controlling principle, a declining birth rate may cause those in authority to decide to exercise corrective measures. By one means or another, women may be persuaded to perform the function of motherhood. Even the institution of marriage may be swept aside when it appears to interfere with the desired end. Were the United States of America to become a dictatorship tomorrow, it is entirely possible that before many months had passed some of those who, under a democracy, have freely elected to prepare for teaching, would be ordered to engage in other activities judged by those in authority to be of greater value to the government. Individuals accustomed to freedom would not be likely to enjoy this state of servility.

Individual freedom is increased through respect for the rights of others. At first glance one might conclude that democracy places no restrictions upon the individual. Adolf Hitler made this error when he derided democracies for their lack of discipline and compared the people to chickens on a poultry range which engage in constant, uncoordinated activity that does not change the status of the flock. Were Hitler's observations correct, perhaps *license* would be a better word than *freedom* to describe the democratic principle. However, it has already been shown that where many individuals are involved, each with his own purposes, interests, and desires, conflicts will arise. If no better solution is provided, such conflicts will be solved on the basis of the survival of the fittest. Experience has shown, however, that the law of the jungle is prejudiced in favor of the strong and that it serves to lessen rather than to increase the measure of freedom enjoyed by the individual. This is well illustrated whenever an audience is thrown into a state of panic by a theater fire and the weak and unfortunate are trampled in the struggle to gain the exits. The mad scramble of shoppers at a bargain counter differs from the panic principally in the degree of violence that is committed. In both cases, activity that is directed on a strictly selfish basis serves to destroy freedom, for such action adds to the dangers inherent in the situation by arousing the hostility, active or potential, of every other individual. This point may be further illustrated in the case of a fisherman who has energy enough to be the first to reach a promising location on the banks of a popular river. On the basis of unlimited competition, he cannot exploit his advantage unless he is willing—and able—to defend it against all competition. If it is a particularly desirable spot, there might not be much time left for fishing if he must fight with all who would dislodge him.

Part of the knowledge which democratic peoples have developed over long years of experience is the principle that more freedom results when individuals respect the rights of others. When this principle is utilized in solving conflicts, the results differ markedly from those obtained by the principle of mob rule. Observe, for example, the relative efficiency and orderliness of registration day on a well-regulated college campus. There is no physical injury or property damage, as is frequently the case on bargain days in large centers of population. By the simple expedient of standing in line, large numbers of students can be accommodated quickly and with a minimum of inconvenience to all individuals concerned. This system operates smoothly when each individual recognizes the rights of every other individual and takes his turn at the end of the line.

When the principle of respect for others is applied to other potential areas of conflict, it is found that the fisherman referred to in a previous illustration, is now free to fish without interference at the spot he has appropriated. On the other hand, his movements up or down the banks of the river are restricted by the degree to which such activity may encroach upon the territories that other fishermen may have appropriated for themselves. Similarly, the adventurous soul who aspires to reach the moon is free to develop his rocket apparatus as long as his activities do not become a nuisance or a source of danger to others. Because of the potentialities of his rockets, it is the part of discretion for him to conduct his experiments in an isolated place. The case of the would-be hermit differs only in detail. If his longing for the primitive life is motivated by a distaste for the responsibilities that are the lot of the family man, freedom for him through flight may reduce his dependents to the point of destitution. Have they no rights to develop their potentialities and to enjoy the good life? Shall the many suffer restrictions in order that he may discard circumstances of his own creation with which he is now displeased? The principle of respect for the rights of others limits his freedom of action for the moment, but in doing so it extends freedom to those who would otherwise be deprived. Perhaps the man merely needs a vacation from which he can return without prejudice to his social position and privileges.

Individual freedom is increased through cooperation on common problems. There is a second way in which democratic peoples have learned to extend their individual opportunities for development. This method is based upon the principle of cooperation on common problems.[3] It, too, was developed to a marked degree in the social and physical environment of the pioneer community. The literature of that era is replete with descriptions of logrollings, house-raisings, husking bees, and threshing parties. By working together as a team, the settlers accomplished for each member those tasks which were too difficult to be mastered alone. To provide increased protection against the common enemy, they built community stockades and sent out scouts to keep the Indians under observation. These arrangements provided greater freedom to the many to till their land and to go about the multitudinous tasks of pioneer life. The principle of cooperation was ultimately applied to the problem of providing transportation. Roads were constructed and bridges built by the simple expedient of having each settler contribute his services and those of his oxen to the common enterprise.

The modern form of cooperation on these community problems consists of paying taxes. The funds collected are then used to employ individuals who make it their business to provide the desired facilities. In this manner, individuals need no longer neglect their own affairs to participate in the affairs of the community, and they gain thereby greater freedom to pursue their own interests. Fire and police departments, hospitals, schools, insurance companies, and the public utilities also represent cooperative efforts to solve common problems. In spite of the criticisms to which they are frequently subjected, these community agencies are maintained because individuals enjoy greater

[3] Boyd H. Bode, *Democracy as a Way of Life*, p. 52, The Macmillan Company, New York, 1937.

freedom of action as a result of the services they render than would be possible if they were abandoned.

Individual freedom is increased when action is determined by the processes of intelligence. A third principle for extending individual freedom was discovered when reason replaced tradition and other forms of authority as the basis for solving conflicts. This principle is based on a recognition of the changing nature of the universe and the assumption that present problems, no matter how much they may resemble problems of the past, are different in detail and in their human implications. The human race was periodically plagued with epidemics until someone refused to accept as their cause the reasons advanced by tradition. From that point on, a search was instituted for the real causes. The microscope, test tube, hypodermic needle, the science of immunization, and of electronics have each in its turn contributed a measure of relief. The search continues for new data which, when discovered, will be utilized in further extending control over the forces of nature. The significance of this progress lies in the fact that so long as man regarded epidemics as having a supernatural origin and, hence, having causes beyond his control, no efforts were made to control them. Progress resulted only after it was assumed that the problems would yield to well-directed efforts and that the time had come to launch the attack.

The invention of the log house was a distinct break with tradition. It represented one solution to the universal need for shelter and was worked out under a certain set of circumstances—the forest wilderness of early America. The problem called first for an appraisal of those conditions and then a tentative solution based on that appraisal. When the structure of rough logs, which could be prepared with the aid of the ever-present ax, was invented, the pioneers, as a result of their ability to appraise and adjust, had an instrument that enabled them to settle in the new world at will. Nor did the treeless prairies stop them, for they merely substituted strips of sod for logs and continued their march across the continent. Had they depended upon the traditional forms of shelter—upon the development of stone quarries, sawmills, and the metal industries—their progress would have been painfully slow in comparison.

The process of reason and the resulting invention of new combinations of facts or materials to meet new conditions or purposes is sometimes referred to as the process of intelligence. In the field of material things where it has helped bring about the technological wonders that characterize modern living, this process is called the scientific method. Social problems, however, have not been so freely submitted to its processes, and the frequently deplored lag of social development behind the developments in the technological field has been the consequence. Wars and recurring periods of inflation and depression with their train of human misery continue to be regarded in some quarters as inevitable. The process of reason relegates them to the realm of natural phenomena and, hence, subject to human control. If individuals are to rid themselves of these curses, attention must be given to their causes and new arrangements invented to prevent their periodic visitations.

If the process of intelligence is to be applied to social problems, many persons may need to learn a new method for determining and appraising social action. Appeals to tradition will no longer be accepted. The value of employment and old-age insurance, of public works programs, of the regulation of the markets by governmental agencies, or kindred innovations will need to be determined not on the basis of who proposed them or whether they enjoy established precedents, but merely on the basis of whether or not the arrangements provide the individual citizen increased opportunity to achieve his own self-development. In democratic communities it is assumed that the individual alone can be the judge in this matter. Free elections are his means for giving expression to his decisions. Progress in the social realm will be made, therefore, to the degree that individuals become proficient in analyzing their needs, and in evaluating social arrangements on the basis of their consequences.

SUMMARY

By way of summary, it is the conviction of those who choose to regulate their affairs in the light of the democratic principle, that individual freedom or opportunity for self-realization are increased as people learn to fashion their actions, institutions, and arrangements along lines suggested by their own reason rather than by accepting the reasoning of others. The process of intelligence, however, must be guided by consideration for the rights and potentialities of each individual, as well as by the possibility of securing increased individual benefits through cooperative action. This faith in the superiority of the democratic ideal over any other known social principle as a guide to the good life suggests that it is the most valuable cultural possession of democratic groups. As such, the ideal must become a part of the thought and practice of the young. Schools are needed to teach the democratic ideal, and the American secondary schools have a special responsibility for fulfilling that function. The succeeding chapters will present some of the procedures by means of which secondary-school teachers devoted to the democratic principle seek to achieve this end.

SELECTED REFERENCES

ALBERTY, HAROLD B.: *Reorganizing the High School Curriculum*, Chap. II, The Macmillan Company, New York, 1947.

BODE, BOYD H.: *Democracy as a Way of Life*, The Macmillan Company, New York, 1937.

————: *Progressive Education at the Crossroads*, Newson and Company, New York, 1938.

CHILDS, JOHN L.: *Education and the Philosophy of Experimentalism*, Century Company, New York, 1931.

Commission on the Secondary School Curriculum: *Science in General Education*, Chap. II, Appleton-Century Inc., New York, 1938.

Commission on Teacher Education: *Teachers for Our Times*, American Council on Education, Washington, D.C., 1944.

Committee on Philosophy of Education: *Progressive Education: Its Philosophy and Challenge*, Progressive Education Association, May, 1940.

DEWEY, JOHN: *Democracy and Education*, particularly Chaps. I and III, The Macmillan Company, New York, 1916.

————: *Experience and Education*, Chap. I, The Macmillan Company, New York.

Educational Policies Commission: *The Purposes of Education in American Democracy*, National Education Association, Washington, D.C., 1938.

LEIGHTON, JOSEPH A.: *Social Philosophies in Conflict*, D. Appleton-Century Company, Inc., New York, 1937.

QUILLEN, JAMES: "Education for Democratic Living," *Utilization of Community Resources in the Social Studies*, Part I, Ninth Yearbook of the National Council for the Social Studies, Cambridge, Mass., 1938.

RUGG, HAROLD (Ed.): *Democracy and the Curriculum*, Third Yearbook of the John Dewey Society, D. Appleton-Century Company, Inc., New York, 1939.

SCHNEIDEMAN, ROSE: *Democratic Education in Practice*, Chap. I, Harper & Brothers, New York, 1945.

Chapter 2. THE CONCEPT OF PUPIL NEEDS

AND ITS IMPLICATIONS FOR METHOD

Attention was directed in the preceding chapter to the variety of principles man has invented to meet his need for a way to resolve conflicts. The nature of the principle that is used in a given community gives character to its customs and institutions. Thus, the principle that might makes right is used to resolve conflicts among the animals and in certain communities of men. In other communities conflicts are decided in favor of the individual with the higher social status. This social principle has been given the name of aristocracy. In a plutocracy, the person with the most money has the right of way over others. Oligarchies and theocracies represent still different bases for resolving conflicts. Among all the known social principles, the democratic ideal stands out as the only one that seeks to preserve the freedom and integrity of the individual. This is the primary consideration in a democracy whenever a decision must be made.

There is psychological evidence to show that none of the social principles known to man is instinctive. Individuals are not born with a predisposition to one or the other. Each must be acquired by a process of education, either directly or through formally organized effort. It follows that young people in democratic communities must learn to understand the democratic principle and learn to apply it in the everyday affairs of life. To help pupils become efficient in the use of this principle is coming to be recognized as the primary objective of American secondary education.

THE CHANGING CONCEPT OF PUPIL NEEDS

The implications of this objective are not clearly recognized or uniformly interpreted by everyone who has contact with the American secondary schools today. If one were to ask the average man on the street what secondary-school pupils need to learn, his answer very likely would be that they need "to learn" Latin, algebra, geometry, and a variety of incidental subjects that are offered to fill out the pupil's class schedule. If asked why these should be studied, he might say that secondary schools always have taught Latin and mathematics and that if a school does not teach them it is, perforce, not a secondary institution.

This widely held belief that secondary-school pupils need to study a particular list of subjects has an ancient origin. It acquired its basic form in the periods of Greek and Roman domination of western political life. As early as the first Christian century, Quintilian, perhaps the best known of the Roman educators, expressed his preference for a curriculum consisting of grammar, astronomy, physics, music, geometry, and philosophy.[1]

The grammar probably included literature and composition. Quintilian certainly referred to the grammar of Latin because that was the language used by the dominant social class of his time and was the language in which the available textbooks were written. Because the Romans controlled virtually all of the social institutions of Europe, including schools, the Latin curriculum set the pattern of European education.

The schools that survived the decline of the Roman Empire perpetuated the Latin curriculum because nothing else was being written that seemed better suited to the intellectual needs of the pupils. Meanwhile, the modern European languages were evolving and, in time, Latin was no longer spoken by the common people, even though it continued to be the official language of the Church and state. Because the modern languages were learned in the home and were used by the common people, they came to be regarded as "common" or inferior. Latin, on the other hand, was used by the officials of the Church and state. This gave it social status. Furthermore, it was mastered only at the expense of a prolonged and formally directed effort. Thus, the ability to read or speak Latin became a mark of social distinction, and to the content of the Latin texts were ascribed cultural values that any literature based on the experiences of contemporary people or cast in

[1] I. L. Kandel, *History of Secondary Education*, pp. 29–30, Houghton Mifflin Company, Boston, 1930.

a "common" language was not expected to possess. Hence, culture and learning came to be associated with the past, and the people looked to a previous generation to provide the answers to their problems.

The undesirable social consequences of this tendency to look backward to an antecedent culture for the guides to contemporary thought and action are widely recognized today. The period in European history that was dominated by this point of view is now frequently referred to as "the Dark Ages." During that period an increasingly greater part of the educational effort came to be directed upon mastering the form of the language of the textbook with a proportionately lesser emphasis upon the content. The intellectual life of the people consequently tended to be confined within constantly narrowing limits, and much of the cultural heritage, particularly the works of the pre-Christian authors, was lost or neglected.

Secondary education as preparation for college. By the twelfth century there was an intellectual awakening apparent in Italy that gradually spread northward over Europe. The awakening was due to the fact that the works of neglected authors were being reexamined. In some instances it was found that the accepted Latin translations of the Greek authors were gravely misleading. These discoveries aroused a strong desire on the part of many students to read the original texts of the old masters. Copies of their works were scarce and only a few individuals had access to them. It was necessary, therefore, for students to congregate in the places where particular works were located and where they could listen to the lectures of the few scholars who had had an opportunity to master them. These congregations of students and masters developed into the European universities. The purpose of the universities was not to teach the Latin and Greek languages, but to study the ideas the Latin and Greek authors had presented in their works. Hence, a reading and speaking knowledge of these languages became a prerequisite to attendance at a university. The schools which for centuries had prepared persons for service in the Church or state, primarily by teaching the Latin language, were now ready to meet the needs of those who wished to qualify for admission to the universities. By adding Greek to their curriculum, these Latin schools became in fact college-preparatory institutions, and the pattern was set for secondary education which, particularly in Europe, is widely copied even to this day.

However bitterly the Puritans may have quarreled with the other Europeans over theological matters, they were in accord on many theories of education. It is not surprising, therefore, that the Puritans who came to America founded Harvard College on the pattern of the English universities. Nor is it surprising that individuals seeking admission to Harvard College were expected to be able to read the Latin and Greek classics. This is reflected in the admissions standards, published in 1643, which announced that:

> When any Schollar is able to understand *Tully*, or such like classical Latine author extempore, and make and speake true Latine in verse and prose, *suo ut aiunt Marte;* And decline perfectly the Paradigim's of nounes and Verbes in the *Greek* tongue; Let him then and not before be capable of admission into the college.[2]

In following the European pattern for higher education, it is logical that the Puritans also should establish Latin grammar schools to prepare boys for admission to Harvard College. Schools of this type were established throughout New England in generous number during the colonial period. They followed the pattern of their European prototypes, and as late as 1789 the curriculum of the Boston Public Latin School included nothing more than the study of Latin and Greek grammar and practice in reading some of the ancient authors.[3]

The development of commerce and industry in the American colonies which helped precipitate the War for Independence also created a demand for a new kind of secondary education. The academies appeared in response to this demand. They broke with the language tradition of the Latin schools and offered instruction in the subjects of mathematics and the physical and social sciences which had an immediate economic value. Mathematics and some forms of science had been taught in the Greek and Roman schools and, for that reason if for no other, speedily regained the prestige of academic respectability. Also, the theory of mental discipline was gaining popularity in educational circles and, on the assumption that the study of

---

[2] Emit Duncan Grizzell, *Origin and Development of the High School in New England before 1865*, p. 14, The Macmillan Company, New York, 1923. As quoted from Broome, *A Historical and Critical Discussion of College Admission Requirements*, p. 30. Italics in original.

[3] *Ibid.*, p. 13.

mathematics developed the ability to reason, many colleges began to accept achievement in mathematical studies as evidence of eligibility for admission. As a consequence, the established Latin grammar schools, which were college preparatory in purpose, altered their curricula to meet the new admission standards. By 1820, the Boston Public Latin School had added arithmetic, geometry, algebra, and geography to its list of offerings.[4] The study of Latin and mathematics has been prominent, if not dominant, in American secondary education ever since that time.

In the light of these developments, one can readily understand why the belief is widely held even today that secondary education deals with well-established and specific subjects. It is also apparent that this belief assumes that preparation for life, at least for those who attend secondary schools, is identical with preparation to pursue the traditional program of college studies. If one pauses long enough to ponder the matter, it must also be apparent that this type of secondary education has very little to do with the processes by which adolescents can learn to understand and apply in their everyday affairs the principles that give character to the institutions, customs, and values of their social group. To those who believe that secondary schools should develop social, economic, and political skills and understandings, the traditional college-preparatory curriculum is not adequate.

Secondary education as the mastery of useful knowledge. What, then, will contribute most effectively to the well-being of the individual? Herbert Spencer, a distinguished philosopher who looked upon modern science and the scientific method with great hope, suggested an answer that represents an important trend in the development of educational theory. In 1862, he wrote that:

Every one in contending for the worth of any particular order of information does so by showing its bearing upon some part of life. In reply to the Question, "Of what use is it?" the mathematician, linguist, naturalist, or philosopher, explains the way in which his learning beneficially influences action—saves from evil or secures good—conduces to happiness. When the teacher of writing has pointed out how great an aid writing is to success in business—that is, to the obtainment of sustenance—that is, to satisfactory living; he is held to have proved his case.[5]

[4] *Ibid.*, p. 290.

[5] Herbert Spencer, *Education*, p. 15, A. L. Burt Company, New York, 1862.

It was Spencer's argument that the good life is the product of knowledge. This argument assumes that the individual will do good if he knows what is good and will avoid evil if he knows what is harmful. The knowledge needed to give direction to action is secured by means of scientific inquiry. It is necessary for the schools to determine what knowledge is of most worth and to transmit this knowledge to the pupils.

Spencer went on to say that the knowledge of most worth is that which bears most directly upon the life activities of the individual. He suggested that these activities, in the order of their importance, can be classified as follows:

1. Those activities which minister directly to self-preservation;
2. Those activities which, by securing the necessities of life, indirectly minister to self-preservation;
3. Those activities which have for their end the rearing and discipline of offspring;
4. Those activities which are involved in the maintenance of proper social and political relations;
5. Those miscellaneous activities which make up the leisure part of life, devoted to the gratification of the tastes and feelings.[6]

The systems of knowledge which Spencer believed were able to make the most significant contributions in these five areas of life are physiology, mathematics, physics, chemistry, biology, the social sciences, and the science of parenthood. It was these and other practical courses that gave the early American academies their distinctive character.

In 1918 a committee of the National Education Association which had been appointed to study the matter suggested that the educational effort should consist of seven major emphases rather than the five outlined by Spencer. According to the report of the Committee, the seven aspects of life that require cultivation are:

1. Health
2. Command of the fundamental processes
3. Worthy home membership
4. Vocation
5. Citizenship
6. Worthy use of leisure
7. Ethical character [7]

[6] Ibid., pp. 18–20.
[7] Commission on the Reorganization of Secondary Education, Cardinal Principles of Secondary Education, U.S. Bureau of Education, Bulletin 35, Government Printing Office, Washington, D.C., 1918.

The effect of these seven "cardinal principles" upon educational practice closely resembled the effect produced by the Spencerian line of thought, that is, educators were encouragd to place their faith in the acquisition of knowledge as the means of achieving the good life. The effect upon the schools was one of adding to the existing list of offerings specific new courses made up of the scientific facts judged to be most important of all that was known about one or another of the seven areas. Thus courses in civics were widely introduced to develop citizenship. Courses in physiology, economics, chemistry, art, music, physical education, and so forth, made their appearance, and each was expected to develop competency in a particular area. In all of the new courses, the emphasis was placed upon the acquisition of information that would have usefulness for the individual when he became an adult. Such knowledge was not expected to have meaning or use for the pupil while he was in school. This point of view has implications for educational methods as well as for the curriculum and will be discussed again in Chap. 6.

Although Spencer and the commission of the National Education Association succeeded in arousing the interest of educators in the needs of all the pupils, regardless of their ultimate vocational objectives, there is now a growing conviction that their efforts fall short of the modern objective of providing competence in democratic living. It is claimed that merely acquiring knowledge, particularly if it is not immediately related to personal interests or needs, brings about very few changes in the conduct of the learner. For example, chemistry students in high school are expected to learn a formula describing a process for producing sulphuric acid; yet very few can repeat the formula 2 years later. Nor does the learning of that formula help them to decide whether sulphuric acid should be used for producing the goods all people want, or for creating instruments of destruction by means of which neighboring individuals or communities can be forced into submission and their possessions seized. If the educational effort is limited to the transmission of knowledge, no matter in what categories such knowledge is organized, pupils will be forced, so far as the school is concerned, to derive incidentally and haphazardly the social principle that will determine the ends to which that knowledge will be used.

Secondary education as participation in life activities. The critics of the theory that learning consists of the acquisition of knowledge offer a new concept of the needs of pupils. They argue that improvement is the result of practice and that this principle is valid whether one wishes to learn to play the piano or to participate in group action involving the establishing of a world government.

The basic characteristic . . . is that every experience enacted and undergone modifies the one who acts and undergoes, while this modification affects, whether we wish it or not, the quality of subsequent experiences. For it is a somewhat different person who enters into them.[8]

From this point of view it follows logically that secondary-school pupils need not merely to know about, but must also participate in the activities of life. Through participation, they will gradually acquire a higher degree of proficiency and improved forms of conduct. The school can speed the process of learning by giving direction to the participation.

The schools have difficulty in providing opportunities to participate in activities, however, for the reason that the existing program of instruction is based on the conventional subject-matter courses which were designed to transmit useful knowledge without reference to the life activities in which that knowledge can be used. Which subject, for example, can include in one sequence all the aspects of planning a dinner party, including the decorations and conversations? Or, in what existing course will the pupil learn to budget his income, keep his accounts, and spend his funds wisely, all of which are intimately connected with real-life activities ranging from having a date to making plans for a college education? Since the conventional subjects are poorly suited to deal with life activities in their total aspects, numerous educators have urged that instruction be organized into more fundamental or lifelike categories.

One of the most recent efforts to define such categories is reported in a work called, *The Purposes of Education in American Democracy*.[9] The members of the Commission who prepared this report concluded that those who are living and growing up in a democratic community need to become proficient in activities that have as their objective the

---

[8] John Dewey, *Experience and Education*, pp. 26–27, The Macmillan Company, New York, 1938.
[9] Educational Policies Commission, *The Purposes of Education in American Democracy*, The National Education Association, Washington, D.C., 1938.

development of the individual (*a*) as an individual, (*b*) as a member of a family and other social groups, (*c*) as an economic being, and (*d*) as a citizen. The educated individual, it would appear from the report, is one who can engage effectively in a variety of activities in each category. One may infer that the school is expected to provide opportunities to engage in a broad program of activities representing a desirable balance among the several categories, and to give direction to the pupil in order that he may achieve proficiency in some activities in each category.

It should be noted that the members of the Commission have suggested a new type of curriculum—one in which pupil needs are described in terms of the ability to carry on successfully the affairs of everyday life. This is in sharp contrast with the earlier concepts which identified pupil needs with (*a*) preparation for college, or (*b*) the acquisition of knowledge, but which ignored the life situations in which the training would ultimately be used. The newer approach is based on the theory that the nature of life situations which stimulate pupils to act, can also be used to show them the kind of information they will need to carry on the activity with satisfactory results, and to provide the specific standards by which they can judge the effectiveness of their actions. In other words, subject matter will be learned in the activity program because it is needed to reach the specific, recognized goals which the pupils establish for themselves; and discipline will result from selecting, using, and judging the actions and resources employed as they try to achieve the desired end.

Secondary education as participation in the democratic way of life. Unless one is careful, it may be assumed from the above discussion that schools can transmit the democratic way of life merely by fostering pupil activities—any activities as long as they can be classified in one or another of the four categories suggested in the report of the Commission. To avoid that error one must bear in mind that the democratic ideal points to a particular kind of activity.

It is common knowledge that pupils encounter activities that are not democratic in purpose. The expressions of intolerance and discrimination that may be heard in the home or on the street are familiar examples. There may be activities even in the school that are engaged in for nondemocratic ends. Curricular and extracurricular affairs that are dominated to excess by the professional staff are open to criticism along this line. Hence, a shift from a subject-matter mastery program to an activity program alone does not guarantee that the school will now be democratic. Nor, does a general scheme for classifying activities necessarily furnish the pupils with a basis for discriminating between democratic and nondemocratic activities. An activity is neither democratic nor nondemocratic in its own right. Thus when pupils are allowed to come in contact with both democratic and nondemocratic forms without having their attention directed to the basis for distinguishing between them, the democratic school has failed in its major function.

That schools maintained by democratic communities have an obligation to acquaint the pupils with the democratic principle as a guide to the good life is evident from the previous discussion. Pupils can acquire a knowledge of this and other social principles only by examining them and by observing their effects upon the individuals in situations in which they are used. Furthermore, it is a basic tenet of democracy that all principles, beliefs, and values must be able to stand up under examination. This applies to the democratic principle itself. Pupils have a right—should be encouraged, in fact—to examine the democratic principle together with other social principles that are urged upon them today with a view to finding out which one is the best.

Obviously, pupils cannot make an intelligent choice unless they have adequate information upon which to base their choice. It is known that many pupils have direct contacts with nondemocratic forms of living in the home and the community. Opportunities for gaining experience in democratic living, however, may not be provided to the same degree. Democracy needs a fair chance, and the school program must be so arranged that pupils will have an opportunity to gain direct experience with democratic arrangements. Let them conduct all their affairs for a period of time consciously directing their actions by the light of the democratic ideal. Then let them try other social principles in a similar manner. That is to say, the school should be a proving ground on which the pupils can try with deliberate intent this or that social principle on the level of their own everyday concerns. The school requires only that democracy be given a fair trial along with other forms. It is the firm faith of democratic peoples everywhere that given such a trial the democratic principle will demonstrate its superiority over the others. Thus, it is through participation in democratic living that schools provide pupils with the experiences needed to know and to judge intelligently the democratic way of life.

THE NEEDS OF SECONDARY–SCHOOL PUPILS IN A DEMOCRACY

The democratic way of life is a unitary process in the sense that it reaches into every aspect of human affairs. For example, what one does in search of personal satisfaction is bound sooner or later to have some implications for one's behavior in the social, civic, and economic areas as well. It is hard for an individual to direct his family life on a democratic basis but to follow a different way of life in his economic affairs. Compartmentalization of this kind is reported from time to time, but it is not recommended as a wholesome arrangement. It is important that the teacher understand the unitary nature of democracy, but for teaching purposes it is sometimes desirable to focus the learner's attention first upon one aspect of a complicated problem and then upon another in order that later he may better comprehend the whole. In keeping with this procedure, the implications of the democratic way of life for the pupil are presented here as needs distinguishable one from the other.

The first need is self-respect. As stated in the preceding chapter, the democratic social principle is finding favor in many quarters because it offers greater opportunity for the individual to secure his own well-being than do opposing social principles. Democracy is *the* way of life that places greater value upon individual freedom and opportunity than upon specific social forms or institutions. Hence, the first thing the individual in a democracy must learn is self-respect. He must be led to accept his own self-realization as a worthy and, in fact, the highest goal toward which he can direct his life's efforts. This does not imply malicious self-seeking, but rather the spirit of living and working with his equals, each of whom has a similar right.

It is not always an easy matter for the school to awaken within the pupil a sense of his own worth. Members of minority groups in particular have been expected to have natures that are inferior to the natures of the members of dominant groups. For example, people of the minorities are expected to become servants and to do whatever menial work that needs to be done in the community. Pressures are exerted to force them into these forms of employment and sometimes the pressures are defended by the argument that these individuals, because of their assumed natures, find their greatest happiness only when engaged in work of a menial character. An individual who resists the pressures is likely to encounter many unpleasant experiences. Knowing this, minority group parents sometimes try to protect their children by teaching them to accept their low status philosophically. Any attempt on the part of the children to break out of their sphere of limited opportunity is quickly punished. Thus, the children are taught "to know their place" and not to aspire to a higher station in life than is theirs by inheritance.

Class distinctions which are sharply drawn in aristocratic societies exert similar restrictions. In a recent conversation on the subject of his early education, a young British army officer of aristocratic antecedents said: "In England we think it is better for everyone concerned when each person recognizes his place and stays in it." He went on to say that as a boy he was encouraged to "go down to the village" to play cricket with the boys. After the game it was considered proper for all of them to go to the tavern for a glass of ale. At that point no further fraternization was permitted and neither he nor the villagers attempted to cross the social barriers that separated them. The social code decreed that he must attend a special secondary school and ultimately he matriculated in Oxford University. In contrast, the villagers attended the local school and upon completing the course of studies offered there found employment in keeping with their respective stations in life. When the Second World War was declared, he received an army commission while the villagers dutifully joined the ranks. Thus, every detail of their respective social lives was ordered by the prevailing class system. Parental attitudes, social customs, and the system of education were all designed for preservation of the existing class distinctions.

The aristocratic traditions that have been brought to America by the European immigrants, from the time of the Pilgrims to the present, have not been completely removed from the American educational scene. It is reported that at least one American university, in its early history, listed the students in the order of their social position. In an aristocratic environment, such as the early colleges attempted to create, this custom was a social convenience. Among other things it helped the hostess to decide in what order to seat her dinner guests. While the practice has been abandoned, the social standing of faculty members continues to be determined by academic rank on many college campuses. The families of assistant professors rank below the families of associate and full professors, respectively, with the professor of Greek heading the list by virtue of the fact that his "discipline" has the most honored tradition. In such an atmosphere it sometimes happens that a prospective student's ability to profit from the opportunity to go on to college is not necessarily the major or the only consideration in determining whether the college will admit him. Needless to say, the realization that he will be unable to attend a college of his choice for other than academic reasons can do much to destroy the self-respect of a secondary-school pupil.

There are some who argue that schools in rural areas should teach all pupils agriculture in order to keep them on the farms. There is pressure based on a similar line of reasoning to provide highly specialized vocational training for the noncollege pupils in industrial communities to prepare them for employment in the dominant local industry. This type of specialization is undemocratic, for it is likely to limit individual opportunity. It denies to the pupil the opportunity to discover other possibilities and to make his own vocational choices. The farm boy who has never known any form of profitable employment other than agriculture obviously will become a farmer. He has no alternatives. He may even become a good farmer and a reasonably happy one, but the quality of his attitude toward himself and his work will be vastly different from that of the individual who has carefully examined a number of vocations and has selected agriculture because he has found it to be the one pursuit that promises him the greatest degree of personal satisfaction.

Self-respect grows with the opportunities to choose. It is built up as the pupil comes to realize his opportunity to choose freely that which in his judgment will contribute most to his personal well-being. The school can help the pupil to choose freely and wisely in spite of restricting social pressures, limited knowledge, and inadequate personal resources. The freedom to choose is his democratic birthright, while the barriers in his way, in many instances, are nothing but rubble left by an ebbing social ice age. One must add that there is no objection to teaching agriculture, or other forms of specialized vocational education in the secondary schools of a democratic society. However, there is objection to imposing a highly specialized form of training upon any individual who has not voluntarily requested that training after he has explored freely and adequately the several alternatives before him.

It is at this point that the four categories of life activities suggested by the Educational Policies Commission may become valuable guides. The secondary school can look upon them as areas within which the pupil may be directed to search for his own unrealized potentialities. Awareness of new potentialities sometimes comes from a comparison of one's own achievements with the achievements of others. History, sociology, politics, and literature offer valuable bases for such comparisons. Similarly, a study of the attributes of well-adjusted individuals may become the means for focusing the pupil's attention upon the aspects of his own personality that can be improved through well-directed effort.

Properly directed exploratory activities, including the comparison technique, may help the pupil become aware of his unexploited opportunities as an individual, as a member of social groups, as an economic being, and as a citizen. For example, many pupils have missed carefree recreational and social opportunities because of physical defects of which they were unaware until a routine medical examination revealed them. A highly respected college professor relates that in his youth he was accused of being snobbish and hard to get along with. One day he was informed by the school physician that he needed glasses. After acting on the physician's advice, he found that he, too, could recognize friends at a distance down the hall or across the street, as others had mysteriously been able to do before. Similarly, pupils who have known only the strife-laden atmosphere of their own homes are not likely to realize that more congenial family relationships are possible. They need to be introduced to an atmosphere of gracious living, after which they may choose for themselves what manner of relationships shall govern their contacts with others.

In the economic area, the need for information prior to making a vocational commitment has already been mentioned. But wise spending and saving are also involved in economic efficiency. Good judgments in these matters can be reached only after the alternatives and their respective consequences have been given careful consideration. The alternatives may become apparent as a result of a study of the ways in which other individuals deal with their financial problems.

In civic affairs, the high-school pupil may be woefully ignorant of the influence the individual can exert in bringing about better government. Traditional-school government frequently is of, by, and for the teaching staff. The pupils may grumble but they are expected to accept without any other show of resistance whatever is decreed for them. Is it any wonder that upon becoming legal voters they accept a government of, by, and frequently for professional politicians with no other show of opposition than ineffective grumbling? What other alternatives have the schools provided? How can individuals take effective action unless they know what possibilities for action are open to them?

The second need is to acquire social consciousness. In a society where the individual is of primary concern, there may appear at first glance to be no need to develop social consciousness. This is not the case, for a more careful examination will show that the maximum development of the individual can be obtained only in a social environment. This is demonstrated in a negative way by the case histories of "lost children," a number of which are now on record. Contrary to the popular Tarzan myth, these children who apparently were separated from human contacts in early life and who grew up in the company of wild animals, developed not the characteristics of humans but those of the beasts with whom they lived. The close relationship between the development of the individual and the quality of his social environment is further demonstrated by studies of the children of the canal people of England, of the well-known Jukes and Edwards families, and numerous other studies, some of which suggest that the environment may affect even the individual's capacity to learn. In consideration of this evidence, secondary-school pupils need to be brought to the realization that individual opportunity is to be found in a social environment. Contacts with others tend not only to stimulate personal efforts, but also to provide increased opportunity for specialization in the area of one's interests, and to make possible economies of time and energy through cooperative activities.

Social consciousness may be developed out of what appears to be a natural desire for social experiences. Even very young children seem to seek the company of others. The desire for social experiences will continue as long as the resulting contacts yield personal satisfaction. Therefore, if the individual is to enjoy the benefits of community life, he must have not only a desire for social contact, but also the ability to engage with satisfaction in activities that involve his contemporaries. If he lacks the necessary knowledge, skills, and understanding, the school must help him acquire them.

The direction-giving function of social consciousness has already been mentioned. In a society where each individual is concerned primarily with his own purposes, conflicts are inevitable. The democratic social principle affords a basis for resolving the conflicts, but the success of the formula depends upon the willingness of the individuals concerned to redirect their purposes when this is necessary in the interests of the common welfare. The common welfare is interpreted here not as the preservation of an institution or custom created by common consent, but rather the preservation of freedom for all the individuals who are involved. It is the democratic faith, based upon experience, that more freedom is available to the individual in a community in which each member agrees to redirect his personal goals whenever it is shown that his intended line of action will result in a reduction of the opportunities of others. Respect for the rights of others is the price of individual freedom. Social consciousness includes the recognition of this fact and a willingness to pay the price.

The third need is to develop confidence in the authority of intelligence. The development of self-respect has been listed as a requisite to maximum individual development. However, when the individual becomes aware of new potentialities, he may find that existing institutions, customs, or attitudes stand in his way. In such cases, a conflict may arise between democratic theory and existing practice, for the welfare of the individual may appear to be accessible only at the expense of the existing arrangements. These conflicts frequently assume serious proportions because the old habits of thought and action are likely to be firmly established and strongly supported by individuals who enjoy special benefits as long as the *status quo* is maintained. When there are strong pressures to resist change, some doubt may arise as to whether it is better to forego the old ways or the new opportunities.

Examples of such conflicts are apparent in many areas of current social life. Thus, some individuals continue to oppose the practice of vaccination because the demonstrated value of immunization against epidemics of smallpox is thought to be the work of wayward and willful humans who desire to interfere with the plans of the supernatural. Similarly, social security legislation is opposed on the grounds that the removal of the threat of economic want will deprive the individual of the stimulation afforded by the rewards of unrestricted enterprise and the threat of starvation. Along the same line, there is a story told of an American of Italian birth who returned one day to visit his ancestral home. While there, he took pity on his aged mother who toiled every day carrying water from a spring on a nearby hillside for a large household of children and grandchildren. The American, a plumber by trade, bought some pipe, borrowed some tools, and installed a water system that added appreciably to the comfort and convenience of the family. His mother and other relatives, however, were furious, for the new arrangement destroyed their established manner of living and left the old lady without her traditional means of justifying her presence in the social group.

Secondary-school pupils are not free from shackling traditions. Frequently the college-preparatory courses enjoy a prestige among pupils that seems to have little foundation other than tradition, and yet it is strong enough to persuade many pupils to spurn courses that are more directly related to their needs and interests. For this reason pupils who expect to work after graduation may refuse to elect commercial subjects. Home economics and shop courses are said to be for "dumbbells" and are avoided whenever possible, even though they might be fun as well as helpful. Sometimes pupils possessing academic ability but modest means choose to forego the opportunity to attend college rather than to enroll in a "secular" state university.

Restricting attitudes and beliefs are slowly yielding ground in the face of a more intelligent attack upon individual and group problems. The new approaches are more intelligent because they create more effective ways for the individual to achieve the good life. Intelligence means the ability to fashion actions to achieve specific purposes. Thus, if a college education is the purpose, the pupil is intelligent who lists his opportunities and resources, and then selects a course of action that promises success within those limits. Similarly, if health is the objective, the individual is intelligent who avails himself of the medical skills and services that give greatest promise of health when applied to his specific case. If physical comfort is the purpose, it is intelligent to install heating, air conditioning, and plumbing systems, regardless of whether or not houses were equipped with these in the past. If security in old age is the goal, payroll deductions and special taxes to create a pension fund under governmental supervision seem to be intelligent procedures regardless of what has been the tradition. New purposes cannot always be achieved by living in the old pattern of life. New purposes may call for new arrangements and institutions. Resourcefulness, imagination, and creativeness pay dividends in individual well-being when they are used to invent better means to achieve desirable and clearly defined ends.

It follows that if pupils grasp clearly the idea that democracy has as its purpose the welfare of the individual, the process of intelligence can be presented as a necessary means to achieve that end. Tradition and other forms of authoritarianism when imposed upon the pupil restrict development, for they force upon him the habits, institutions, and customs that were designed by others living at a different time and under different conditions to achieve their own purposes. Intelligence, on the other hand, liberates the individual. It sets him free to try new forms of behavior and arrangements. This freedom, however, is not an invitation to revolution or irresponsible experimentation, for with it goes responsibility. When the pupil consciously departs from time-tested precedent and chooses a new line of action, he must also accept responsibility for the consequences. This knowledge is a sobering influence and is inclined to stimulate caution and a thorough examination of the probabilities. Only those who are inexperienced in making choices are inclined toward recklessness. Experience is a sobering influence, but it may also develop confidence in the process of intelligence as a means of building a better way of life.

The fourth need is to acquire practice in democratic living. Finally, the democratic way of life is an active, ongoing process and not a static state of being. One cannot achieve the good life simply by refraining from doing anything bad or by memorizing facts that others have found to be useful. Individual happiness is the product of creative effort. Democracy is a way of doing things. Hence, secondary-school pupils must learn to live, to work, and to play, and to do these things in a manner that will bring them nearer the goal of individual well-being.

There is a growing tendency to regard learning as, basically, the process of improving action by taking into account the results of previous actions. This is what is implied in the phrase, "learning by doing." It follows that if secondary-school pupils are to learn the ways of democracy, they must practice the democratic processes under conditions that are typical of life outside of the traditional classroom and which result in better living for them even while they are in school.

Outside of school, learning takes place in a concrete situation. Specific circumstances and conditions are present that call for definite action. Evidence that learning has taken place is found when some modification in conduct, attitude, or understanding has occurred that gives the individual better control over his physical and social environment. Learning is a single, unitary process even though it may extend over a period of time covering days, months, or years. The learner, individual or group, must run through the entire learning process even though it is probable that errors will be made and that on subsequent "runs" a different course will be taken. The process is illustrated in the case of the motorist who, on his first trip to a given destination, makes a wrong turn or two, or selects a route that has many traffic lights and is used by a large number of slow-moving vehicles. The next time he is called upon to make that trip, he will review his experiences on the previous trip, consult road maps, make inquiries in likely places, and finally act in a manner that will avoid the annoyances he previously had encountered. Thus his experiences serve as the basis for planning a new route that will get him to his destination more quickly and pleasantly than did the old one. In other words, he has learned by reconstructing his experiences, and the evidence of learning is found in his changed mode of behavior.

So, also, must the secondary-school pupil learn to deal with his personal and social problems. The learning process starts with the problems that arise as the pupil lives, works, and plays as an individual and as a social being. He learns as he acquires experiences that help him make adjustments and adaptations in his own actions and environment. The adjustments and adaptations, selected in the light of the democratic ideal, bring him progressively nearer to the goal of his own well-being. This process of finding and testing better forms of behavior and adaptation is sometimes referred to as problem solving.

In developing problem-solving ability, the particular problem before the learner is of less importance to the teacher than the nature of the attack that is made and the ends that are sought. Any concern that is vital enough to drive the pupil to seek a solution can be used as the basis of a learning situation. The problem may be to get enough money to do the things other pupils do, to learn to dance, to understand one's parents and the adult point of view, to get a new suit or a new dress, to secure admission to a college, to get better grades, to acquire a skill, or to select a vocation. Whatever the problem, the school can foster learning by helping the pupil define what his own well-being means. Thus, the first step in solving a problem is to establish specific goals which, if achieved, promise to bring about a larger measure of contentment.

Next, the school can help the pupil decide upon a good way to reach his goal or goals, and to gain whatever skills or abilities are needed to use the means selected. The ability to deal effectively with a problem depends in no small measure upon the knowledge one has to draw upon for the suggestion of possible solutions. The acquisition of knowledge, therefore, may well continue to occupy a major part of the pupil's time while he is in secondary school. Knowledge may be secured in two ways. In the first method, the learner deals directly with the materials and conditions that make up the problem situation. He then depends upon the reconstruction of his own direct experiences to furnish guides to future action. In the second method, the learner may draw upon the experiences of others which are made available to him through the printed and spoken word.

In the normal course of events, an individual when faced with a problem situation first searches his own experiences to find a likely solution. When the knowledge that has been acquired through the direct method is not adequate for the problem at hand, it is a real advantage to be able to tap other sources of knowledge. Pupils have to learn how to tap the accumulated experiences of the human race, to use the great systems of classified knowledge which are represented by the sciences, mathematics, history, and the like, for specific ends. This involves not only the methods of research but also the basic tools of learning such as reading, the number skills, and the arts of communication. The emphasis here, however, is on the method of inquiry and the use of information rather than upon piecemeal memorization. For example, the pupils need not merely to know what are the facts of chemistry or of ancient history, but also what experiences the chemists or the ancients have had with problems similar to their own, and what are the probabilities that the methods employed in dealing with such problems might now prove satisfactory under modern conditions. It follows that the acquisition of knowledge now becomes a subordinate part of the problem-solving skill. Whatever knowledge is needed will be acquired by the pupils, either from personal experience or through research, as they deal with the problems that arise.

Finally, the school can help the pupil appraise the solution which he has selected, in the light of the goal or goals he is seeking. The appraisal becomes the basis for projecting new solutions or even new goals. This is essential to the continuous reconstruction of experience and consistent growth. It occurs whenever one asks questions such as, "Which way brought about the best results," or "Are we better off now than we were before?"

The definition of purpose, the discovery and selection of appropriate means, the testing of the selected means, and the appraisal of outcomes are aspects of a single process. The process is larger than the memorization processes to which some schools continue to limit their efforts. It must be practiced in its entirety, supervised and directed by the school, if pupils are to grow in their ability to deal with problems.

Because the individual, adolescent as well as adult, lives, works, and plays in a social environment, many of his problems are likely to be of a social rather than of a personal nature; that is, more than one individual will share the concern that gives rise to the problem at hand, and for that reason others may be involved in its solution. Hence, secondary-school pupils need to acquire proficiency in working with others. They must learn to participate in group planning, in arriving at group decisions, and in carrying on group action. This, too, is an action process in which doing is the keynote of learning.

To be capable of participating in a cooperative undertaking, individuals must know how to conduct themselves in a group situation. They must know how to organize themselves in a manner that will facilitate discussion and the appraisal of opinion as a basis for formulating and carrying through a cooperative plan of action. These social skills, like any other skill, are developed through practice. A study of concerns common to secondary-school pupils will show the kinds of group activities through which the school may foster the needed development. It follows that schools must be prepared to accept the concerns of pupils as the starting points for the learning process, and that pupils must be given an opportunity to deal with the problems as a group and as a single, complete process—from purposing, through doing, to evaluating the resulting experiences.

One must not assume, however, that all problem solving and all cooperative experiences develop the capacity for democratic living. Those who are tempted to make this assumption are reminded that thieves engage in rather complicated problem-solving activities and are known to cooperate with each other in a very effective manner. Their actions are undemocratic nonetheless, for they are undertaken for the very obvious purpose of gaining personal advantages at the expense of others. Problem solving and cooperation are democratic proceedings only when they are directed by the democratic ideal. This is an important distinction and it must be made by all who wish to become intelligent in their social action and thinking. The school has a responsibility for pointing out this distinction. Pupils must be reminded of the kind of ends that are sought and must seek democratic ends consciously and willingly if their ability to use democratic procedures is to develop.

SUMMARY

By way of summarization it may be said that the democratic secondary school, like any other agency of a democratic society, derives its nature from the task it is created to perform. The secondary school in America may, therefore, be expected to help the adolescent realize his potentialities for living a life that yields greater satisfaction than would be possible if he were left to his own resources and devices. This function includes awakening the pupil to a realization of his potentialities and to a desire to achieve them; helping him explore the opportunities that a social environment affords together with the responsibilities that devolve upon him if he is to utilize them; helping him explore the advantages and the responsibilities entailed in charting his own action guided by his ability to predict and to select the consequences of his proposed action; and affording him an opportunity to live creatively with his contemporaries from day to day.

For a great many years secondary schools have selected and judged teaching methods in terms of the amount of ground covered or the number of facts memorized by the pupils. Increasingly, however, secondary schools in America, as well as in other communities that aspire to a democratic form of life, must examine their procedures in the light of the following questions:

1. Does this method build up the self-respect of the pupil?

2. Does this method develop social consciousness and sensitivity to the rights and dignity of other individuals?

3. Does this method develop faith in and the ability to use the method of intelligence?

4. Does this method provide pupils satisfactory experience in democratic living?

SELECTED REFERENCES

BLACKHURST, J. HERBERT: *Principles of Methods*, Drake University Press, Des Moines, Iowa, 1936.

BROWN, ELMER E.: *The Making of Our Middle Schools*, Longmans, Green & Co. Inc., New York, 1902.

CASWELL, HOLLIS L. (Ed.): *The American High School*, Eighth Yearbook of the John Dewey Society, Harper & Brothers, New York, 1946.

Commission on the Reorganization of Secondary Education: *Cardinal Principles of Secondary Education*, U.S. Bureau of Education, Bulletin 35, Government Printing Office, Washington, D.C., 1918.

Commission on the Secondary School Curriculum: *Science in General Education*, Chap. II, Progressive Education Association, D. Appleton-Century Company, Inc., New York, 1938.

DEWEY, JOHN: *Experience and Education*, The Macmillan Company, New York, 1938.

EARHART, LIDA B.: *Types of Teaching*, Chaps. I and III, Houghton Mifflin Company, Boston, 1914.

Educational Policies Commission: *Learning the Ways of Democracy*, National Education Association, Washington, D.C., 1940.

———: *The Purposes of Education in American Democracy*, National Education Association, Washington, D.C., 1938.

GRIZZELL, EMIT DUNCAN: *Origin and Development of the High School in New England before 1865*, The Macmillan Company, New York, 1923.

———: "The Secondary School Program as a Heritage from the Past," Chap. I in *The High School Curriculum*, The Ronald Press Company, New York, 1947.

JOHNSON, B. LAMAR (Chairman): *General Education in the American High School*, particularly Part I, North Central Association of Colleges and Secondary Schools, Scott, Foresman & Company, Chicago, 1942.

KANDEL, I. L.: *History of Secondary Education*, Houghton Mifflin Company, Boston, 1930.

KILPATRICK, WILLIAM HEARD: *Foundations of Methods*, particularly Chap. I, The Macmillan Company, New York, 1925.

SCHNEIDEMAN, ROSE: *Democratic Education in Practice*, Part I, Harper & Brothers, New York, 1945.

SPENCER, HERBERT: *Education*, Part I, A. L. Burt Company, New York, 1862.

THAYER, V. T., ZACHRY, CAROLINE B., and KOTINSKY, RUTH: *Reorganizing Secondary Education*, Part I, D. Appleton-Century Company, Inc., New York, 1939.

Chapter 3. THE SECONDARY-SCHOOL PUPIL

The intelligent worker in any walk of life plans his work to meet the particular conditions that confront him. The salesman adapts his sales talk to emphasize the features of his wares most likely to interest his client, the farmer grows the crops that promise to have a high market value, the manufacturer designs his product to comply with the wishes of his customers, and the doctor prescribes whatever medicine is likely to correct the ailment of his patient.

Teaching also must be adapted to a variety of conditions and circumstances. Among the many factors that must be taken into account are the personality of each pupil and the general characteristics of the class. It is obvious that the teacher of agriculture cannot use the same procedures and learning materials with boys and girls from the farms that are used with success with pupils from urban or suburban areas. Furthermore, not all of the farm boys intend to become farmers and for that reason not all of them can be expected to take an interest in the study of agriculture. Similarly, teachers of the sciences, of the languages, and of the practical arts cannot expect all pupils to be equally prepared or equally motivated to study their subjects. Because pupils are not alike and the reasons for providing instruction are not everywhere the same, the teacher when he plans his work must take into account such factors as the maturity, the abilities, the backgrounds, the interests, and the purposes of the particular pupils with whom he is to work. What, then, are some of the characteristics of secondary-school pupils to which instruction must be adapted?

TRADITIONAL TEACHING METHODS WERE DEVELOPED WHEN RELATIVELY FEW BOYS AND GIRLS ATTENDED SECONDARY SCHOOLS

For a great many years the pupils enrolled in American secondary schools represented a very small percentage of the boys and girls of secondary-school age. This was due in part to the belief that equality of educational opportunity meant merely that all boys should be free to take what the school has to offer or do without.[1] Thus when the first secondary school was founded in Boston in 1635, it was established as a public institution. It received support from the town funds, and admission was open to any boy living within the town who could meet the entrance requirements. Soon all towns in the Massachusetts Bay Colony with a population of one hundred families or more were required to provide similar schools. Other colonies soon followed the example of Massachusetts. However, attendance was not required, and a boy could elect to attend or not as his personal interests or circumstances dictated.

As stated in Chap. 2, these early secondary schools followed the college-preparatory patterns set by the Latin schools of Europe. Thus, the study of Latin and Greek constituted the chief occupation of the pupils. That the classical curriculum was designed primarily to serve boys who were preparing for the ministry was widely recognized, but nobody seemed to object. It was thought enough that each boy had an opportunity to attend, and if he chose instead to learn a trade, to secure employment in agriculture or some other unskilled occupation, or to seek his fortune on the frontiers to the west, he had a right to do so.

The historical data that are available show that a majority of the young men growing up in the rough environment of the pioneer communities were not attracted to the Latin grammar schools. The large majority elected other pursuits. It is also evident that those who did choose to go to school constituted a highly selected group with interests, purposes, and presumably abilities that were nearly homogeneous when judged by present-day standards. Helping this highly selected and homogeneous group of pupils to achieve their educational purposes was a relatively simple matter.

The secondary school's preoccupation with the classical studies was not seriously challenged until the colonies were ready to seek their political independence. By that time colonial trade and industry had developed to sizable proportions. Shops and factories now offered financial security and social position to young men who possessed technical knowledge and skills. Because the Latin schools did not deal with subject matter of this nature, a demand was created for a new kind of

[1] Girls were not admitted to secondary schools until later.

secondary education. The academies were introduced to satisfy this need. These new schools were not publicly supported, but in many instances were private ventures which were dependent upon tuition fees. While some of the academies were endowed, and some ultimately received public support, the fee barrier frequently was formidable enough to place a secondary education beyond the reach of many of the boys and girls living at that time.

The rise of the free high schools during the latter half of the nineteenth century did not immediately alter the general nature of the secondary-school population. Although the tuition fees were removed, it was not long before the curriculum again was dominated by the traditional college-preparatory subjects. These subjects retained their prestige due to the widespread acceptance among leading educators of the doctrine of mental discipline. According to this theory, learning is a form of mental exercise that improves the powers of the mind without reference to the subject that is studied. Since abstract subject matter was thought to require greater mental effort and, therefore, to provide more exercise than practical subject matter, the high schools retained many of the classical subjects. Thus, as long as attendance was not required, only those boys and girls who possessed high academic ability and who were attracted to the classical subjects voluntarily made their way into the high schools.

The highly selective nature of early secondary education is indicated by the fact that as late as 1880—long after the public high-school movement had been launched—only 3 per cent of the boys and girls of secondary-school age were actually enrolled. This small group represented the interested and the able who were willing to follow the program of instruction that was provided. Apparently, the interests and purposes of the pupils were sufficiently alike to make possible the use of a uniform pattern of instruction. The nature of that pattern with some of its modern adaptations will be discussed in Chaps. 6, 7, and 8.

MODERN METHODS MUST SERVE THE NEEDS OF ALL BOYS AND GIRLS

Since 1880, there has been a phenomenal increase in the number of pupils enrolled in secondary schools. Data collected and published by the U.S. Office of Education show that the number of pupils enrolled has doubled every 10 years from 1880 to 1930. By 1940, the total number enrolled was approximately 6 million. A part of the increase has been due to the rapid expansion of the total population, but an important part is due to the fact that a larger percentage of the boys and girls of secondary-school age are now going to school instead of going to work. Startling as the increase in enrollment has been, it is estimated that for the country as a whole approximately 35 per cent of those of secondary-school age are not in school today. Furthermore, it has been estimated that "the number of children attaining age 14 will increase rapidly up to 1961, when there will be almost 50 per cent more of these children than there were in 1945." [2] It is evident, therefore, that the enrollment increases are likely to continue for a number of years to come.

The problems presented to secondary schools by this expanding pupil population are many and varied. While the pupils who constituted the highly selected enrollments of 1880 were relatively homogeneous, the present population is approaching the heterogeneity of the unselected total adolescent population. In 1880, the pupils attended voluntarily except for such parental persuasion and social pressure as may have been employed in individual cases. Today, however, many pupils are forced to attend by legislation and the fact that they are excluded from gainful employment by the competition from older workers and the increased complexity of the industrial processes. In 1880, nearly every boy in secondary school ultimately went on to college. Today, only one pupil out of five continues his education in some type of post-secondary school. Now that the theory of mental discipline is generally discredited, it is apparent that the 80 per cent who do not continue their schooling beyond graduation have abilities, needs, and interests that differ from those who do go on.

In the face of the increasing diversity of the pupil population, the concept that equality of opportunity means merely the opportunity for all to study the traditional list of subjects adopted by the earlier secondary schools is due for some serious revision. Equality of educational opportunity should mean more than an opportunity to attend, tuition free, a school whose facilities and program of instruction were designed many years ago to meet the needs of a highly selected group. It should mean, among other things, that the school must make available to each pupil, regardless of his interests and abilities, the facilities that will enable him to use the time and effort spent in school in ways

[2] From a reprint from *Statistical Bulletin*, Metropolitan Life Insurance Company, 28 (6), June, 1947.

that are satisfying to him. This concept of equality of opportunity makes the consideration of individual differences a matter of paramount importance to the teacher.

Increased enrollments mean increased differences in ability to learn. Teachers probably have been aware of differences in their pupils since the instruction of the young first became a specialized function. However, the nature and extent of these differences were not studied in a scientific manner until modern psychology was developed. Early in the twentieth century, a French psychologist by the name of Binet developed what he believed to be a method for discriminating between children who could profit from instruction and those who could not. The latter group, he believed, were so meagerly endowed with the capacity to learn that any educational effort spent upon them would be wasted. For reasons of economy, therefore, he sought a method by means of which the permanently disabled ones might be recognized as a basis for separating them from the normal group before too much money had been spent in trying to educate them. Binet's search for such a method ultimately produced a crude form of the now familiar intelligence tests.

In a short time, Binet's method for discriminating between the feeble-minded and the normal was adopted quite generally by the psychologists who were attempting to reduce their field of investigation to an exact science. Binet's technique was refined and used as a device for collecting objective data about the nature and possibly the causes of human behavior. From the data these investigators gathered, it was concluded that the range of differences with reference to one trait, namely, the ability to learn, confirmed Binet's theory that there is a difference between the feeble-minded and the normal. Binet had erred, however, in assuming that these are two sharply defined groups and in implying that a given individual is either clearly feeble-minded or normal. On the contrary, it was found that the range of differences is a continuum extending from the extremely dull idiot to the extremely brilliant genius. In the total population some individuals may be found to represent each point of gradation between these two extremes. The large majority of individuals, however, have abilities that tend to cluster approximately midway between these two extremes and are said to have average or normal ability.

The range of abilities and the nature of their distribution have significance for teachers because the increase in enrollments has brought into the secondary schools more and more pupils who have average or even less than average ability to learn. A generation ago, the selection factors described earlier had discouraged all but the very able from seeking a secondary-school education. Today, however, it is not unusual to find within a given school, or even within a given classroom, a pupil whose ability to learn borders on feeble-mindedness while next to him is a pupil so able that psychologists may call him a near genius. If teaching is planned on the assumption that all pupils are alike, these two individuals, one with an IQ of 85 and the other with an IQ of 145, will be given identical assignments and expected to reach the same goals in the same period of time.

Variations in ability to profit from school experiences are revealed in other ways. The ability to read, for example, is a major factor in determining the success or failure of secondary-school pupils for the simple reason that reading activities constitute a large portion of their assigned work. In Table 1 it is shown that variations in reading ability are as great as, if actually not greater than, the variations in the ability to learn. The data in this table are expressed in terms of "grade levels" and show that among the 127 entering ninth-grade pupils who took the tests, one pupil indicated a mental development equal to the development of an average pupil in the last half of the fourth grade while another pupil in the same class indicated development comparable to that of college students.

With reference to their ability to understand or comprehend what they were reading, the range of variation is indicated by the fact that one pupil demonstrated ability equal to that of average beginning pupils in the fifth grade while the top pupil could read with comprehension equal to that of college students. Variation was slightly greater, however, with reference to speed of reading. This fact suggests the possibility that if assignments are of such a length that the average pupil in a high-school class can complete them in a comfortable manner during the time available, some pupils may be able to rush through them with time to spare for hobbies, extracurricular activities, and part-time employment, while others may not be able to do the assignments no matter how conscientiously they try.

Differences of another kind are suggested by the psychologists who argue that the ability to learn is not a general ability but a specialized

Table 1. Distribution of the Grade Scores of 127 Entering Ninth-grade Students on the Stanford-Binet Test of Intelligence and the Gates Reading Survey Test *

Grade level	Chrono-logical grade	Mental grade	Level of Compre-hension	Vocabu-lary	Speed
13.0 +		1	1		2
12.5–12.9		2	1		3
12.0–12.4		5	2	4	3
11.5–11.9		5	4	6	4
11.0–11.4		6	9	9	5
10.5–10.9	1	7	13	13	9
10.0–10.4	2	9	14	14	10
9.5– 9.9	23	14	15	13	8
9.0– 9.4	42	17	18	17	12
8.5– 8.9	51	15	17	16	13
8.0– 8.4	8	14	14	13	11
7.5– 7.9		11	10	5	10
7.0– 7.4		9	4	4	8
6.5– 6.9		5	1	2	10
6.0– 6.4		3	2	3	7
5.5– 5.9		1	1	4	6
5.0– 5.4		2	1	3	2
4.5– 4.9		1		1	1
4.0– 4.4					2
3.5– 3.9					1
High score	10.7	13.0 +	13.0 +	12.3	13.0 +
Median †	9.0	9.1	9.3	9.3	8.7
Low score	8.0	4.8	5.2	4.8	3.8

* Guy L. Bond, "Identifying the Reading Attainments and Needs of Students," *Reading in the High School and College*, Part II, Chap. V, p. 70, Forty-seventh Yearbook, National Society for the Study of Education, University of Chicago Press, Chicago, 1948. By permission of the Society.

† Calculated on ungrouped data.

one. They claim, on the basis of a considerable body of data, that there are, in fact, four distinct types of abilities—academic, social, motor, and aesthetic—and that these four are not necessarily present to the same degree in the case of a given individual. While some individuals may be fortunate enough to have above-average ability in all four areas, others may be below average in each. Still others may possess a high degree of ability in one or two areas but be merely average or even below average in the others. The student who has an excellent scholastic record but who fails miserably on the athletic field or in social situations illustrates this type of specialized ability. The same may be true of the athlete who performs brilliantly in the gymnasium but fails in the classroom.

The possible variety of individual ability patterns seems endless, but one needs merely to draw upon personal experience to realize that the instructional procedures found in secondary schools are too commonly designed to develop abilities of an academic nature with little or no attention to the other three types. Until teaching methods and learning activities are provided to accommodate all four types, equality of educational opportunity does not exist, and pupils cannot look to the schools to help them develop fully the potentialities with which they happen to be endowed.

Increased enrollments mean increased physiological and emotional differences. The ability to learn is not the only trait with reference to which a range of individual differences has been found. Boys and girls undergo definite physiological and emotional changes during the years they normally are enrolled in secondary schools. This period of change is called adolescence and is the last of four distinct periods or stages, which will be discussed later, through which the individual normally passes in the process of becoming an adult.

The onset of puberty marks the transition from the earlier stage of development to that of adolescence. This transition is brought about by a number of physiological changes which include a readjustment in the functioning of the glands of internal secretion and, hence, in the hormone balance. Everyone is familiar with the rapid physical growth that occurs at this time, but there are other changes that render the individual responsive to new aspects and conditions of his environment. New interests, purposes, and concerns appear that have a profound effect upon behavior. This is also a period of instability during which interests and purposes may shift from day to day or even from hour to hour, much to the annoyance of parents and others who may not understand what is taking place. Thus, one investigator working with a small group of high-school pupils found that 67 per cent of the boys and

37 per cent of the girls changed their vocational choices during the course of a single semester.[3]

If all individuals became adolescents at a given chronological age, secondary schools would find it a relatively easy matter to anticipate the changes in the pupil population and to make appropriate adjustments in the educational program. Unfortunately, however, the problem is not so simple as that. There is ample evidence to show that girls achieve physiological maturity from 1 to 2 years earlier, on the average, than boys. This means that in a group of students who are in their eighth year of school, many of the girls have interests and needs that are typical of adolescents in their community while many of the boys are still absorbed in activities typical of childhood. But the problem is even more complicated, for the age at which girls enter puberty varies from ten to seventeen, while for boys the range is from eleven to eighteen.[4] Thus, on nearly every level of secondary education one may find pupils who represent each of the different degrees of development between late childhood and maturity, with all the diversity of interests, purposes, and behavior that this great variation implies.

Emotional development is closely related to physiological development and in part is judged in terms of the source from which the individual draws his sense of security and well-being. Thus, in infancy, which is the first of the four stages of development to which earlier reference was made, the individual is a law unto himself. During this period, usually covering the first 2 to 4 years of his life, the individual is self-centered. Virtually all activity is undertaken for his own satisfaction. Any activity, any form of behavior is good or bad to the degree that it enhances or detracts from his physical well-being. To him there are no moral or social problems for he is in effect the king, and the king can do no wrong. Thus, he laughs and smiles when events and conditions please him, and cries when they are unpleasant. He seeks to please only himself, and all other persons are looked upon as instruments to help him attain his own ends.

[3] Claud Mitchell, "Pupils' Vocational Choices," *Occupations*, 11:363–367, May, 1933.

[4] See Robert A. Davis, *Educational Psychology*, Chap. 1, McGraw-Hill Book Company, Inc., New York, 1948. Paul H. Landis, *Adolescence and Youth*, Chaps. 2 and 3, McGraw-Hill Book Company, Inc., New York, 1945. Almost any good textbook on educational psychology will present additional data on this subject.

When the individual enters the second stage, his feeling of security is affected by a new factor. He now responds to the approval or disapproval of his immediate family and of others with whom he is in close contact. He is pleased when their approval is given and unhappy when it is withheld. In this stage the individual becomes very responsive to the wishes of his parents and immediate associates. Their praise or scorn become effective means of directing his behavior. He accepts the behavior pattern of his family and is happy in conforming to it. This attitude is evident in the affection kindergarten and primary-school pupils lavish upon and expect in return from their teachers, for at this age children are likely to extend the family group to include their teachers.

By the time the child has progressed into the second or third year of school he may give evidence of breaking away from his close family ties. His emotional attachments to his family tend to become subordinated to his attachments to a group of playmates, particularly those approximating his own age and of his own sex. This stage is marked by the tendency to form closely knit "gangs" of boys or girls, and gang life begins to dominate the behavior of the individual. Intense loyalties to the members of the gang become evident. Members develop similar standards of behavior, of dress, and of speech. Frequently, the standards are set by a particular motion-picture or comic-strip hero for whom the gang has developed profound respect. It is important to note that the standards are now set by the gang and not by the home. When the gang and the home come into conflict, the emotional security of the child depends to a marked degree upon his ability to maintain the respect and approval of his fellows. It is also important to note that the sexes segregate and only in exceptional cases are girls permitted to participate in the activities of a gang of boys, or boys in the activities of a gang of girls.

With the onset of puberty, however, the homosexual attachments show a tendency to become heterosexual. The old gang ties lose their strength, and one by one the members forsake the company of their former close associates. The gangs gradually disintegrate as the individual members are drawn into "sets" consisting of boys *and* girls. Boys who but a few months before had regarded every girl as nothing less than a nuisance now may spend many hours in a neighboring drugstore or some other gathering place frequented by the girls of their acquaintance. Mixed relationships of this kind are new for both sexes, and they seek the security that is provided by numbers. Thus, they go about at first as small mixed groups attending "movies," drinking "cokes," and dancing at some juke-box "hangout." They are uncertain and insecure in the new social environment. Their giggling, loud talk, and horseplay are mechanisms by means of which they attempt to cover up their insecurity. It should be noted that the set or crowd is an experimental social group. It affords opportunities for the inexperienced and immature to "try their wings" in mixed society and to acquire the experience that will make possible the establishment and maintenance of social stability on the adult level.

It is normal for the adolescent to derive his feeling of security from the approval of his "set." Therefore, when the standards of the set are not in agreement with family standards, serious emotional disturbances may result. Because they lack understanding, parents sometimes attempt to enforce a strict adherence to their own standards by the several coercive methods at their disposal. Excessive pressure of this kind may cause the adolescent either to break away from the set and to withdraw from normal associations with individuals of his own age, or to revolt against his parents. In extreme cases, the first alternative may result in a variety of unfortunate emotional and social maladjustments such as homosexuality or an abnormally strong attachment to the parent of the opposite sex, while the latter course may lead to rejection of the restraints imposed by the adult society and end in a career of fanatical anarchy or crime. It follows that if the home fails to help the pupil make a satisfactory adjustment to boys and girls of his own age, the school must supply the help that is needed.

Increased enrollments mean increased differences in the home background of pupils. The drive to achieve status among his peers presents the adolescent with many of his most pressing concerns. Sympathetic and understanding parents who maintain the pupil's home life on an even and steady keel and who lend a helping hand when it is needed can do much to help him make the necessary adjustments. There is evidence, however, that not all secondary-school pupils are fortunate in this respect. On the basis of data gathered from pupils in the ninth grade in two small secondary schools in Connecticut it was found:

In three-fourths of the homes, parents quarrel, although a minimum of pupils thought this bothered them; two-fifths do not go to either parent for advice on personal problems, although those who do are satisfied with the advice received; half have received no parental instruction in sex. . . . [5]

One-third or more do not have a quiet place at home in which to study.[6]

The need for spending money becomes a critical one for adolescents because "cokes," motion-pictures, and juke-box dancing call for a ready supply of nickels, dimes, and quarters. To the adult these expenditures represent a shameful waste of money, and frugal parents as well as the impoverished ones find it difficult to provide funds for such purposes. An odd job or an allowance, therefore, are valuable social assets whereas the lack of "private means" can bring about many anxious hours. In the Connecticut study it was found:

Half of these (ninth grade) pupils have a regular allowance . . . averaging fifty cents (per week) . . . about a third have bank accounts and have had them for five years or more, averaging from ten to fifty dollars; a fourth or more work at odd jobs in summer, mostly caring for children or housework or mowing lawns. . . .[7]

The Connecticut studies are limited in scope and cannot for that reason be said to present an accurate picture of national conditions. It is fair to assume that schools located in larger centers of population, particularly where there are many people of foreign birth, have a more heterogeneous pupil population than the two small schools for which data were given. The problems of adolescents brought on by the economic and social status of their parents may, therefore, be more acute in the large urban high school than in the smaller school located in a village or rural district. Yet it frequently happens that there is a closer personal relationship between teachers and pupils in the smaller schools than in the larger ones. The problem in all schools is to keep the administrative and instructional program flexible enough to make possible good teacher-pupil relationships, or even to enable teachers to learn to know their pupils as individuals.

[5] Fred Couey, "A Report on Studies of Pupil Interest in Two Small Secondary Schools," *Curriculum Laboratory Studies*, Bulletin 31, p. 16, School of Education, University of Connecticut, Storrs, Conn., September, 1942.
[6] *Ibid.*, p. 27.
[7] *Ibid.*, p. 22.

Increased enrollments mean increased differences in pupil attitudes and work habits. The pupil's reaction to school, and therefore his success in school, are dependent upon such factors as his attitudes, interests, and habits. Many of these, notably his attitudes toward religion, politics, and obedience to law and custom have their origin in the home. The importance of these for the teacher is indicated by the fact that the social sciences have taken on a different aspect since pupils began to come in large numbers from the homes of unionized workers as well as from the homes of the managers and owners of commercial and industrial establishments. There are many issues that are called controversial today which were either ignored entirely or treated in a dogmatic fashion by the textbook writers a generation ago. Today, however, so many adult points of view are reflected by the pupils that virtually every contemporary social problem becomes a controversial issue if it is brought into the classroom.

Work habits, too, are likely to reflect home conditions. Some pupils are encouraged to develop initiative and resourcefulness while others are supervised so closely that they become dependent upon members of the family and friends for leadership and direction. In a recent study in Florida more than 2,000 seventh-grade pupils in 25 schools were rated by the investigators with reference to initiative. A 5-point scale was used ranging from "Child, of his own inner urge or volition, starts or originates activities of little mental content and soon shifts his interests" to "Child is self-starting and self-propelling; high degree of ability to solve problems, to create, to persevere, to bring successful climaxes." It was found that the ratings evaluated 17 per cent of the pupils as belonging in the first group with 15 per cent in the fifth group. Groups two, three, and four had 16 per cent, 30 per cent, and 23 per cent, respectively.[8]

The same investigators rated 1,374 seventh-grade pupils in six Florida schools with reference to their work habits. They found that 24 per cent of the pupils work best alone, 32 per cent are adaptable and can work well either alone or in a group, and 44 per cent work best in a group.[9]

[8] A. R. Mead and Edith D. Glenn, "A Study of Pupil Initiative and Cooperation," Bulletin 11, p. 16, Bureau of Educational Research, University of Florida, Gainesville, Fla., July, 1939.
[9] *Ibid.*, p. 33.

These variations in attitudes and work habits suggest that it is not possible to have all members of a given class respond to their assignments in the same way. The emotions aroused by assigned readings, particularly in the social studies, vary with the economic, social, political, and religious backgrounds of the pupils. Some pupils have the initiative necessary to deal with the challenges presented by school activities while others do not. Part of the class can work well on an individual basis but the rest do their best work when working with others. Clearly, teaching methods are needed that can accommodate divergent points of view and at the same time encourage pupils to make the approaches to their work that promise the best results for them.

Increased enrollments mean increased differences in personal and social problems. As pupils from many economic and social levels enroll in secondary schools they come in contact with standards from which former generations have been shielded by their isolation in the home or on the job. Thus, the modern diversified pupil populations multiply the potentialities for conflicts between pupils and their parents, between the rich and the poor, between the able and the dull, as well as between races, creeds, and nationality groups. The nature and importance of these conflicts were not given serious attention by secondary schools until recently. Numerous research workers have been studying this area in recent years, and there is available now some evidence that can be used to give direction to the efforts of the schools.

One body of evidence has been secured through the use of the *Mooney Problem Check-list.*[10] This check list consists of 330 problems that had been reported by secondary-school pupils in preliminary studies, and is administered by having individual pupils check the particular problems that are of concern to them. The 330 items represent 11 major problem areas or concerns. They are:

1. Health and physical development.
2. Finance, living conditions, and employment.
3. Social and recreational activities.
4. Courtship, sex, and marriage.
5. Social-psychological relations.

[10] Ross L. Mooney, "Surveying High-School Students' Problems by Means of a Problem Check List," *Educational Research Bulletin*, Ohio State University, Columbus, Ohio, XXI (3): 57–69, Mar. 18, 1942.

6. Personal-psychological relations.
7. Morals and religion.
8. Home and family.
9. The future: vocational and educational.
10. Adjustment to school work.
11. Curriculum and teaching procedures.

The kind of problems and concerns found among secondary-school pupils is indicated by an analysis of the items checked by the pupils of one North Carolina high school. Of the 603 pupils in this school, 90 indicated concerns that centered very definitely in the area of "the future: vocational and educational"; 87 others were troubled by well-defined problems involving "finances, living conditions, and employment." An equal number were disturbed by their apparent lack of ability to adjust to school work. Concerns centering in the area of "personal-psychological relations" were reported by 63 pupils and each of the remaining seven problem areas were indicated by from 14 to 55 pupils per area. Furthermore, 84 cases reported multiple concerns that involved two or more areas.

It must be remembered that in this study each pupil checked a number of items that represented his concerns. In each of the cases cited above, the items checked by a given pupil were related in such a manner that they could be said to center in one or more of the 11 major areas. Many pupils checked problems in more than one area so that while only 87 cases were discovered where the concerns were clearly clustered around the problem of finances, at least 429 other pupils out of the total enrollment of 603 checked one or more items in the financial area. Thus, each of the following items in the financial area, arranged here in the order of frequency, was checked by 10 per cent or more of the total student body.

1. Want to earn some money of my own.
2. How to spend money wisely.
3. Annoyed by having to ask parents for money.
4. Learning how to save money.
5. Having no regular allowance.
6. Having no car in the family.
7. Needing a job in vacation.
8. Having less money than friends have.
9. Having too few nice clothes.

10. Living too far from school.
11. Needing to find a part-time job now.
12. Too little money for school lunches.
13. Getting money for education beyond high school.

The three most frequently reported problems in each of the other 10 areas were as follows:

I. Health and physical development
  1. Weak eyes
  2. Not as strong and healthy as I should be
  3. Frequent headaches

II. Adjustment to schoolwork
  1. Being a grade behind in school
  2. Afraid of failing in schoolwork
  3. Worrying about grades

III. Personal-psychological relations
  1. Forgetting things
  2. Not taking some things seriously enough
  3. Losing my temper

IV. Social and recreational activities
  1. So often not allowed to go out at night
  2. Taking care of clothes and other belongings
  3. Wanting to learn how to dance

V. Courtship, sex, and marriage
  1. Wondering if I'll ever find a suitable mate
  2. Wondering if I'll ever get married
  3. Not being allowed to have dates

VI. Curriculum and teaching procedures
  1. Too much work required in some subjects
  2. So often restless in class
  3. Lunch hour too short

VII. The future: vocational and educational
  1. Wondering what I'll be like 10 years from now
  2. Wondering if I'll be a success in life
  3. Deciding whether or not to go to college

VIII. Social-psychological relations
  1. Wanting a more pleasing personality
  2. Being disliked by certain persons
  3. Disliking certain persons

IX. Morals and religion
  1. Can't forget some mistakes I've made
  2. Wondering what becomes of people when they die
  3. Being punished for something I didn't do
X. Home and family
  1. Father not living
  2. Sickness in the family

With only a few exceptions each of the above items was checked by at least 100 of the 603 students in this school.

When the check lists were examined to learn if there were any qualitative differences between the problems reported by the younger pupils and the older pupils, it was found that freshmen were noticeably more concerned about their physical development and health than were the pupils of any other school year. Seniors, on the other hand, appeared to be turning toward their own personal future and were noticeably concerned about their educational and vocational problems as well as the necessity of making the personal-psychological adjustments that would enable them to fit into the adult out-of-school situation.

There were also some sex differences. The girls at all levels indicated their concern about the problem of adjusting to their status of dependency upon others which social conventions force upon them. Many of their specific concerns fell within the areas of personal-psychological and social-psychological relations, thereby reflecting a feeling of insecurity and a fear that they might not be able to attract and to please the "others" upon whom they must depend.

On the other hand, the boys expressed greater concern than did the girls about their educational and vocational future and their ability to get along well in school. This seemed to indicate that the boys, accepting the role of breadwinner which society has designated for them, were uncertain that they would be able to measure up to their responsibilities.

There is a danger that this description of one North Carolina high-school pupil population will be interpreted too broadly. It must be remembered that these data apply only to one school. Local conditions such as the degree of homogeneity of the community with reference to the social, economic, and cultural background of the pupils obviously may affect the problems in a given school.

The significance of individual differences for method. Limitations of space do not permit the presentation here of data depicting the interests, the accomplishments, the vocational choices, and other characteristics of secondary-school age youth that should be of concern to their teachers. These matters are discussed, much more thoroughly than is possible here, by those who write on educational psychology and the psychology of adolescence. Furthermore, detailed data of this nature are of greater significance in determining the specific subject matter of instruction than the method by which the instruction is to be given, that is, the individual interests, needs, and purposes present in a given class may indicate which specific learning activities are appropriate for that class, though not necessarily for any other. Curriculum making, therefore, must be carried on in the light of such detailed information, and modern textbooks on the curriculum frequently offer many valuable suggestions to the teacher for gathering the necessary information.[11]

Methods of teaching, on the other hand, are influenced chiefly by the answer to the basic question: Are pupils alike or are they different? It was stated at the beginning of this chapter that the early secondary-school teachers assumed that pupils are alike. A method of teaching that has wide acceptance, even today, was developed on the basis of that assumption.

Ample evidence has been presented here and elsewhere to show that modern secondary-school pupils are not alike. In fact, they differ so markedly with reference to a variety of traits and characteristics that it is doubtful if any two individuals living today are identical. Furthermore, it is doubtful if there ever has been or ever will be such duplication. Each individual is a unique creation. He has characteristics, abilities, and potentialities that set him off from every other individual. Because of his unique qualities, no other person can make precisely the contribution to society and the culture which he can make. Nor can any other person quite understand the purposes, problems, and conditions which drive him on and give individuality to his mode of living. It is up to the teacher to help him to resolve those influences and to

[11] See particularly Harold B. Alberty, *Reorganizing the High-School Curriculum*, Chap. III, The Macmillan Company, New York, 1947.

reach that point of human achievement of which he alone is capable. In a very real sense each pupil represents an opportunity that will never come to that teacher or any other teacher again.

In the light of the above, the traditional teaching procedures, which treat all pupils as though they were alike, must be reexamined. There is an obvious need for a method or methods, techniques, and aids that can accommodate great differences in pupil ability, development, interests, and needs. Many teachers, particularly in recent years, have recognized this need and have attempted to meet it in a constructive manner. Some of their efforts have brought about significant progress. These new developments in teaching, as well as the old, will be described in some detail in Part 2.

SUMMARY

The pupils to whom the teaching procedure must be adapted are a major factor in the selection of teaching methods for use in secondary schools. The early secondary schools had a selected pupil population and for that reason developed relatively uniform procedures. Modern secondary-school populations, however, have become heterogeneous. The pupils vary greatly with respect to ability to learn; to proficiency in the learning skills, such as reading, needed for further study; to physical development; to emotional stability and social development; to home backgrounds; to attitudes; and to work habits. These differences introduce a variety of problems and concerns for the pupils with which they must cope if their satisfactory development is to be realized. The school program in general and teaching methods in particular can be directed to provide assistance to the pupils in dealing with these concerns. New methods are needed and are now being developed which make possible the instruction of heterogeneous groups of pupils and the accommodation of a variety of problems and concerns within a given classroom.

SELECTED REFERENCES

ALBERTY, HAROLD B.: *Reorganizing the High-School Curriculum*, Chap. III, The Macmillan Company, New York, 1947.

BLOS, PETER: *The Adolescent Personality: A Study of Individual Behavior*, D. Appleton-Century Company, Inc., New York, 1941.

CASWELL, HOLLIS L. (Ed.): *The American High School,* Chap. V, Eighth Yearbook of the John Dewey Society, Harper & Brothers, New York, 1946.

COLE, LUELLA: *Psychology of Adolescence,* Farrar & Rinehart, Inc., New York, 1942.

CROW, LESTER D., and CROW, ALICE: *Our Teen Age Boys and Girls,* McGraw-Hill Book Company, Inc., New York, 1946.

DAVIS, ROBERT A.: *Educational Psychology,* Part I, McGraw-Hill Book Company, Inc., New York, 1948.

JERSILD, ARTHUR T., and others: *Child Development and the Curriculum,* Chap. VI, Bureau of Publications, Teachers College, Columbia University, New York, 1946.

JONES, HAROLD E. (Chairman): *Adolescence,* Part I, Forty-third Yearbook, National Society for the Study of Education, distributed by the Department of Education, University of Chicago, Chicago, 1944.

KELIHER, ALICE V.: *Life and Growth,* Chap. VIII, Commission on Human Relations, Progressive Education Association, D. Appleton-Century Company, Inc., New York, 1938.

LANDIS, PAUL H.: *Adolescence and Youth,* McGraw-Hill Book Company, Inc., New York, 1947.

MEEK, LOIS HAYDEN (Chairman): *The Personal-social Development of Boys and Girls with Implications for Secondary Education,* Committee on Workshops, Progressive Education Association, 1940.

STRANG, RUTH: *Behavior and Background of Students in College and Secondary School,* 2d ed., Harper & Brothers, New York, 1937.

THOM, D. A.: *Guiding the Adolescent,* Children's Bureau, U.S. Department of Labor, Government Printing Office, Washington, D.C., 1933.

WILLIAMS, CORNELIA T.: *These We Teach: A Study of General College Students,* University of Minnesota Press, Minneapolis, 1943.

Chapter 4. THE ORGANIZATION OF THE SCHOOL AND THE CURRICULUM

Learning may be directed effectively by superior teachers under many kinds of circumstances, but few people would advocate poor buildings, meager equipment, and outmoded books for their children in the schools. It is well to remember that the school's facilities and its organization in terms of grades, size, schedule of classes, and arrangement of the program of studies have a direct bearing on the effectiveness with which learning can be promoted. Moreover, the manner in which the experiences that constitute the curriculum are organized in a class or subject, or during the various activities that make up the school day for the pupil, will definitely affect the kinds of outcomes that will result from school attendance. A school that is organized for effective learning is in a better position to implement educational goals than one that is not.

What kind of setting best provides the experiences that adolescents in a democracy need to have? There is certainly no cut-and-dried answer to this question. This chapter will examine the organizational setting of the curriculum in secondary schools of this country. Brief consideration will be given first to the size and type of secondary schools and how they affect the experiences that pupils have in the school. Next, the kinds of curriculum organization, broadly conceived as the framework within which the curriculum develops, will be examined. This section will be followed by an attempt to appraise these curriculum arrangements. Finally, some forward-looking practices which seem to give genuine help in realizing democratic educational goals will be discussed.

SIZE AND TYPE OF SECONDARY SCHOOLS

Size. In 1938, the average enrollment in the high schools of the United States was slightly over 100 pupils.[1] It is in the numerous small towns and villages and in the rural areas of America where this typical high school, small in size, is found. An enrollment of 200 or fewer pupils, as found in 65 per cent of all high schools, is rather small when compared with an enrollment of 5,000 or more, found in about 50 high schools in the nation. About 40 per cent of our high schools have fewer than 100 pupils.

It is important to realize that approximately 40 per cent of all high-school pupils are enrolled in schools having 1,000 or more pupils, even though these schools are relatively few in number. In the subsequent discussion of kinds of curriculum organization, relationships between the size of the school and the proportion of pupils who are having different kinds of experiences will be of interest.

It would be difficult to establish any proved relationship between size and quality of a high school. There are too many other, more important, factors involved in determining the success with which democratic goals are achieved. However, a certain size may provide a more favorable setting for attaining such ends.

The small high school of 100 or fewer pupils has generally been regarded with disfavor. There is a growing feeling among educators that the large high school may have just as many disadvantages. Both the small and the large high school need to be critically examined to determine what obstacles to democratic education are presented.

In what size high school does a curriculum that is concerned with problems of youth and provides democratic experiences related to real-life needs have a better chance to develop? The small high school enrolling approximately 100 pupils will more than likely have these characteristics that relate definitely to pupil experiences in the curriculum:

1. A small staff of relatively inexperienced, younger teachers, whose period of tenure in the school will be brief.

2. A principal whose time is largely taken up with teaching or directing extraclass activities, with little time left for supervision.

[1] The figures in this section are taken from the *Biennial Survey of Education, 1936–38*, Bulletin 2, U.S. Office of Education, Washington, D.C., 1939.

3. A schedule in which teachers often teach in more than one subject field and have the same pupils in classes more than one period.

4. Few books, meager classroom equipment, and inadequate facilities for physical education, shop, assembly, and other activities demanding special rooms.

5. Few electives to provide for specialized needs or individual interests.

6. A relatively small number of pupils in classes.

7. A limited number of extraclass activities.

8. A rather close relationship to the community which it serves.

The large high school of 1,000 or more pupils, usually found in larger cities, is more likely to have the following characteristics that relate to the effectiveness of the curriculum:

1. A staff of mature teachers with long periods of tenure, specialists in their subject fields who usually teach only one subject, such as English I or American history.

2. A full-time principal who has little opportunity to supervise the staff of 50 or more teachers.

3. A staff that is too large to work effectively as one group.

4. Departmental organization of the staff for supervisory and administrative purposes.

5. A schedule in which each teacher meets around 150 different pupils each day.

6. Rooms equipped for instruction in shop, art, music, and other special areas.

7. Relatively up-to-date instructional materials.

8. Offerings that include commercial subjects, music, art, shop, home economics, and other specialized courses, but which are often closed to large numbers of college-preparatory students.

9. More impersonal relations between staff and pupils because of the size of the student body.

10. A varied program of extraclass activities.

11. Little opportunity to serve the community as a neighborhood center.

Although the dangers of generalization are recognized, these are characteristics of the majority of small and large high schools. Both pro and con arguments can be selected from each of these lists depending on the point of view of the individual. The tendency is to regard the large school, with its wealth of equipment and enriched course offerings, as the most desirable school for the community. One can hardly contend that the large high school is adequately meeting the needs of pupils in our democracy. Mere bigness is not a virtue. Stratification of practices can easily result in the school whose size is more likely to promote the factory type rather than the family type of human relationships.

It would seem that a middle ground between these two extremes is the best size high school in which to build a program for youth, one close enough to the community to be cognizant of its needs and to serve out-of-school young people and adults as well. A high school of 250 to 750 pupils would probably be the optimum size.

Yardsticks for evaluation of the size of a school need to have their orientation in human relations. The following criteria are consistent with the philosophy of democratic education:

1. Does the school serve as a community center for adult and youth education and year-round activities?
2. Is there a friendly, personal relationship among the staff and students?
3. Is there an opportunity for principal, teachers, and community to work together effectively for the improvement of the instructional program?
4. Are there rich and varied experiences to provide for a well-balanced general education of the pupil and for specialized interests and skills?
5. Does the situation promote knowledge of the pupil and his needs?

It is doubtful whether either a school with insufficient funds and inadequately prepared teachers, or one in which the individual personality is lost and mass production is prevalent, can fulfill these criteria.

Type. Secondary schools can be classified conveniently in two ways: first, according to the grades included in the school organization, and second, according to the general nature of the work offered by the school.

In so far as the first classification goes, the most common type of high school in this country is the four-year high school composed of grades nine to twelve, inclusive. These four grades, added to the traditional eight grades of the elementary school, constitute the so-called 8–4 plan. Other grade combinations which are becoming quite common are the junior high school (grades 7, 8, and 9); the junior-senior high school (grades 7 to 12, inclusive); and the junior college (grades 13 and 14). These "reorganized" secondary schools, those breaking away from the old 8–4 pattern, now enroll over half of all the high-school pupils. The grades indicated here for each of the types of schools are the ones most commonly found. Various other combinations exist. Some junior high schools include grades 7 to 10, for example, and some junior colleges, grades 11 to 14.

One of the most important reasons for the development of the junior high school was to provide an educational program suited to early adolescents. Gruhn and Douglass include, in their summary of evidence regarding advantages of the junior high school, the following points dealing with the curriculum:

> The instructional and extra class program of the junior high school on the whole is broader and richer and is better adapted to the needs of adolescents than in the traditional secondary schools, especially in such respects as (a) the organization and content of the curriculum, (b) teaching methods, (c) extra class activities, (d) guidance, (e) instructional materials, and (f) provision for individual differences.[2]

They also conclude that in junior high schools, generally speaking, there are more adequate housing and libraries and better instructional facilities and equipment than in the upper grades of the traditional eight-year elementary school.[3]

While the junior high school has undoubtedly provided a better program of education for early adolescents in many communities, it does not guarantee an improved curriculum or teaching methods. Many junior high schools, for example, have departmentalized their work to such an extent that the subject-matter, daily-recitation type of teaching has crowded out any real cooperative learning between teacher and pupil. Thus, pupil needs are lost sight of as the guiding lights in determining the types of experiences the school will sponsor. These schools fall into the error of copying some of the undesirable features of curriculum organization of the four-year high school.

From the beginning of the movement for reorganization of the secondary school, the number of six-year high schools, grades 7 to 12, has been greater than the number of separate junior high schools. These six-year junior-senior high schools have been found largely in small communities where only one high-school building has been thought

---

[2] William T. Gruhn and Harl R. Douglass, *The Modern Junior High School,* p. 85, The Ronald Press Company, New York, 1947.
[3] *Ibid.,* p. 85.

feasible. The advantages for the curriculum have been the possibility of enriched offerings for seventh and eighth-grade pupils, such as industrial arts, home economics, music, and improved facilities and equipment. The disadvantages are serious ones from the standpoint of educating youth for participating in a democratic society: (*a*) pupils in the lower three grades often have meager opportunity for leadership positions, or even participation, in school activities; (*b*) the practice of departmentalization and the subject-matter philosophy of the senior high-school grades often dominate the lower three grades.

Separate senior high schools have no particular advantage other than grouping pupils of somewhat similar interests. They have resulted naturally from the development of the junior high school. They are relatively few in number, constituting less than 4 per cent of the total number of high schools in this country. Many of them are large institutions with all the attendant disadvantages and advantages previously cited.

The junior colleges of this country were also organized to provide more adequately for the needs of youth. Most of these institutions are 2 years in length, although some have absorbed part of the senior high-school years, as in the 6–4–4 plan, in which the junior college constitutes the eleventh through the fourteenth grades. It is entirely conceivable that this may become the prevailing pattern for the American secondary school, eliminating the senior high school as a separate organization. Again, when these schools ape the senior colleges, and organize their curricula along traditional lines, real needs of young people may be lost sight of.

Some of the promising features of the junior college, sometimes termed the "community college" or "community institute," present a rather bright outlook for the future educational program for older youth. These are some of the practices of forward-looking junior colleges:

1. They run an all-day program, with late afternoon and evening classes for youth and adults.

2. Terminal curricula are developed especially for youth not going on to senior college.

3. Community interests and needs are served through adult classes, short courses, forums, cultural activities, semiprofessional vocational training, guidance, and other services.

4. Curricula planned for individuals are flexible in length: either 2 years, 1 year, or shorter, depending on the needs.

5. The curriculum is constantly evaluated and replanned through community-school cooperation.

There are few traditions to hamper the junior college that desires to develop a real educational program for the majority of its youth, those who will not take professional or other courses in four-year colleges and universities.

The second convenient classification of secondary schools deals with their general nature or purpose. Here we encounter such schools as the vocational school, the trade school, the technical high school, the commercial high school, the academic high school, and the comprehensive high school. The first four of these types obviously are intended to provide specialized types of vocational training; the academic high school, to provide the general and college-preparatory type of education. Diversity among these types is somewhat less at the junior-college level than at the high-school level.

The merits of specialized schools, such as the first four mentioned above, have often been cited, but it can be questioned whether they encompass the purposes of democratic secondary education as defined in this book. In critically examining the specialized high schools in the light of principles advanced in this book, the student of education should consider such questions as these:

1. Are social consciousness and high regard for the individual fostered by segregating pupils into different types of schools?

2. Is learning to work with all social and intellectual classes a part of general education?

3. Are pupil needs well enough defined, or are pupils mature enough, for making a vocational choice before the ninth or tenth grade?

Criticisms of special schools to the effect that they develop economic and social class consciousness might also, to a lesser extent, be leveled at comprehensive high schools that have specialized curricula into which pupils are divided. The exaggeration of social differences and the emotional effect on the individual are serious problems of the special school that cannot be ignored.

The comprehensive high school, replacing the specialized type of high schools such as vocational, commercial, and technical schools, is a pattern of organization that more nearly complies with the democratic objectives of secondary education. Instead of the class distinctions which sometimes become associated with the specialized high schools, there is an opportunity within the comprehensive school for a pupil to make choices of elective courses cutting through the various types of studies within the one school. He may take shopwork, commercial training, art, part-time cooperative education for distributive types of business occupations; specialize in the sciences; take extensive work in mathematics; or pursue some other program consistent with his needs, all within the same school.

KINDS OF CURRICULUM ORGANIZATION

The program of studies. Secondary schools in the nation have varied practices as to how the curriculum experiences are organized for learning during the year and the day, and in terms of subject-matter relationships. The term "curriculum organization" is used here to refer to these types of organization, some of which pertain more definitely to administrative arrangements. Included are the program of studies, the schedule of classes, and the relationships of subject fields or smaller subject-matter areas—the organization or setting provided for the experiences.

The usual pattern of subjects pursued by a pupil in one of the 10,000 small high schools would probably include 4 years of English, 2 years of mathematics, 2 years of science, 2 years of a foreign language, 2 years of social studies, and 4 years of work selected from agriculture, industrial arts, home economics, physical education, and business education—if offered—or more courses in the above academic fields. Ordinarily, high schools with enrollments of 100 or fewer have but little choice of electives to offer pupils. Since the number of subjects that can be offered by a small high school is limited, the college-preparatory pattern remains dominant.

In most of the small high schools, the program of studies for the 4 years lists the required and elective subjects open to all students each year, freshman through senior. This is the "constants-with-electives" type of organization.

Pupils in large city high schools have a greater number of subjects from which to choose in making out their own programs, but the choice may be more restricted than appears on the surface. One is likely to find in many larger high schools that the program of studies is divided into several strands, either called "curricula" or "courses" depending upon the section of the country. This type of combination of courses in the total program of studies is known as the "multiple-curriculum" type of organization.

There are some regional differences that can be noted in regard to organization of the program of studies. The multiple-curriculum pattern is more prominent in high schools of all sizes in New England and some other areas in the East than in the South, the Middle West, or the West.

The most common types of curricula found in the multiple-curriculum plan are the college-preparatory or academic, the commercial, the general, and the industrial or the technical, each intended to group courses that will serve future educational or vocational goals of the pupils. Some schools even go further and break down the academic curricula into classical, scientific, and other divisions. In each of these types, the organization or pattern of courses composing the 3 or 4 years of work is somewhat different. One result of this differentiation is that, since the pupils are guided into different curricula on the basis of academic ability more than on the basis of other factors, it represents a form of ability grouping.

Since the lines between the curricula are often difficult to cross, the actual choices that pupils have are really limited in nature. A pupil in a college-preparatory curriculum in some schools, for example, is not allowed to take any work in home economics or in typewriting, even though the course may serve his needs and particular interests better than other courses that he is required to take. There is fundamentally no choice in a situation where a pupil must choose between French and Spanish, or chemistry and physics, if neither of the two choices are in accord with his needs, or if both offer as much of an authoritative and recitation-drill type of classroom atmosphere.

In spite of the fact that only about one-fourth of the high-school graduates continue their education in college, the enrollments in the different types of college-preparatory curricula will often equal or exceed those in all the other curricula combined. The result has been that, as a guidance device, the multiple-curriculum plan has failed to accomplish what it was intended to do.

Some high schools are changing or have changed to the constants-with-variables type of organization of the program of studies to avoid the stigma and the ill effects on pupils' mental health caused by the multiple-track plan. They are depending upon a well-organized system of guidance to assist pupils in planning individual programs, rather than upon a preconceived pattern expected to fit all cases within large groupings.

When the curriculum is being revised, it is not uncommon to find that a good deal of emphasis is placed on preserving or expanding the required subjects for each field, rather than on a fundamental revision in terms of youth needs. This is true no matter what the pattern of organization of the program of studies might be.

The day's schedule. We are likely to find that the schedule in secondary schools of all sizes consists of either eight periods of 45 minutes in length or six periods of an hour in length. Although there is some variation in these figures because of the length of time used in passing from one class to another, the 55- to 60-minute period is usually referred to as the "hour" period.

In small high schools, the teacher will more often than not be scheduled for classes in more than one subject field. Very seldom, however, has any attempt been made to fuse two subjects in such a situation that provides a rather ideal setting, especially if it is possible to schedule two identical groups with the same teacher. Undoubtedly, such an arrangement would demand some planning ahead by the teachers and the administrator. It is even difficult to find effective correlation between two subjects taught by one teacher to the same group of pupils. The preoccupation with the recitation-type method, with so much subject matter to be covered, has obscured these possibilities for a better learning situation.

The schedule of the high schools, both in the small and in the somewhat larger group, is usually built with the thought in mind of avoiding conflicts for students. It is a relatively simple pattern in the small school because, with almost all students taking the same subjects for a particular grade, there is little chance for conflicts to occur. As the school grows larger, the schedule becomes more of an intricate mosaic of many sections and varieties of classes that is a puzzle to the uninitiated, but represents a great deal of effort on the part of the administrator to produce a smooth-running schedule. Too often, once it is built, it becomes a sacred work that must not be tampered with from year to year.

In secondary schools in general the trend is toward the hour period. A few have gone beyond that length. Although the lengthening of the period may have the effect of increasing the length of the school day, there are still too many places, notably the Northeastern section of the country, where the school day is short and pupils are expected to do their study as regularly assigned homework outside of school time. High schools that end the school day at 2:00 P.M. will increasingly have a more difficult time explaining to a homework-ridden public why such a practice is continued.

Subject-matter relationships. The idea of covering a certain amount of subject matter in a course has exerted its influence in keeping subjects in their respective compartments into which they are typically divided. Teachers have feared to intrude on other teachers' subject areas. In such a situation the experience-unit approach to teaching has had a hard time getting a foothold.

In the large high schools, this separateness becomes even more emphasized, with department heads or city supervisors of subject areas supervising the work of the teachers. Here the dividing lines between subjects are usually rigid, and it is only in rare instances that the teacher has classes in more than one field. Rather, he is apt to teach only certain subjects such as tenth-grade English or modern world history.

Field trips are sometimes troublesome for a teacher to arrange because of this situation. All-school projects such as an operetta may run into difficulty because some teachers are concerned largely with the outcomes of learning subject matter, and insist on having pupils present in classes, penalizing them for staying out to participate in the legitimate school activity. "Extracurricular" activities are segregated from class activities. Pupils come to regard the latter as one of the main reasons why they enjoy and stay in school. They justifiably object to the bell ringing at brief intervals while they jump from one activity to another, from one end of the building to the other, without a real opportunity to carry through what they are doing or may wish to do. As one student remarked, "Living isn't getting up at seven, discussing current affairs from eight to nine, and writing out formulas from nine to ten. Living is all of these things mixed together in a day."

Junior high schools whose daily schedule places pupils under the same teacher for half a day get away from many of the evils of extreme departmentalization. The core-curriculum organization and other promising attempts to make the school day into one or more integrated experiences for pupils are discussed at length later on in this chapter.

APPRAISAL OF THE CURRICULUM ORGANIZATION

Factors in the development of the present organization. Changes in administrative provisions for organization of the curriculum have come about slowly. Many practices are still not too different from those of the early academy. There are certain factors that account for the development of present patterns, as well as for the crystallization of old patterns and the apparent unwillingness to change. In addition to the human factors—the ideals and points of view of the teachers and administrators concerned and the psychological reasons for resistance to change—five other pertinent ones are cited here.

1. *The traditions established throughout the history of the secondary school in the United States.* The program of studies of the Latin grammar school was the same for all pupils, with no electives. Its emphasis was distinctly college preparatory and its curriculum classical in nature. With the coming of the academy, and its stress on scientific studies and practical preparation for business life in the early stages of its development, the electives began to multiply in encyclopedic fashion.

The early academy, too, began the practice of dividing the program of studies into more than one sequence of courses to meet the demands for different types of education. In some cases these divisions were "schools"; in others, departments. Franklin's Academy had a Latin school, an English school, a mathematical school, and a philosophical school. The Phillips Academy at Andover operated an English department and a classical department, a differentiated organization destined to become popular with both the academy and the early high school.[4] The Latin curriculum of the academy was copied from the classical emphasis of the Latin grammar school, and the English and other curricula were developed to meet the new social needs of the day.

---

[4] James William Norman, *A Comparison of Tendencies in Secondary Education in England and the United States*, Contributions to Education, No. 19, p. 65, Teachers College, Columbia University, New York, 1922.

Departmental specialization resulting from the multiple-teacher school was also a practice in which the academy pioneered.[5]

With the middle classes increasing in political strength and demanding a wider opportunity in secondary education for their children, and the national feeling growing, the high school came into being to serve a changing society. The Boston English Classical School stressed the English program alone, intended to serve those who were not going on to college. It was not long, however, until the college-preparatory function again became dominant and the classical curriculum occupied a prominent place.

Multiple curricula grew, merging many ideas developed in the academy and the Latin grammar school. In the period 1860 to 1865, 7 separate curricula were listed in an investigation by Stout in the North Central states, and 36 different titles of curricula were found in the period 1895 to 1900.[6]

From 1925 to 1930 there was a decrease in the number of curricula offered and an increase in the constants-with-electives type of organization. The multiple-curriculum plan, which had started out as a means of providing for different needs of pupils, and later was also used as a means of guidance in an era when guidance in high schools was poorly developed, often became too inflexible to serve these functions. Moreover, the prestige of college preparation and the traditional value of a college education were powerful motives that operated in the choices of curricula made by pupils.

2. *The emphasis on subject learnings.* There is little doubt that the curriculum of the high schools of today is typically subject centered. There is so much material to be covered, judged to be desirable by teachers, administrators, supervisors, and textbook writers, often influenced by pressure from the community groups and state legislatures. The subject is the focal point around which the activities of the classroom revolve. It is evident in the assignments written on the board, the single textbook, the review lessons, the make-up work, the homework under whose burden pupils often literally stagger, the recitation method, and the subject-matter unit. Evaluation consists largely of

[5] Harl R. Douglass (Ed.), *The High School Curriculum*, p. 17, The Ronald Press Company, New York, 1947.

[6] I. L. Kandel, *History of Secondary Education*, p. 458, Houghton Mifflin Company, Boston, 1930.

determining how much information or what degree of skills involved in the particular subject have been learned. It is still not uncommon for United States history or modern world history classes to reach the last two decades during the latter part of May, if at all.

The inclusion of new developments in the subject means adding another unit or section at the expense of some of the time devoted to other sections. Faith in the accretion method of changing the curriculum is unbounded. More subjects are added, but little thought is given to the type of experiences pupils have in those subjects, for example, the part pupils have in learning democratic skills through participation in planning, executing, and evaluating, or the opportunity they have to develop values.

The departmentalized type of subject offerings and class schedule is well suited to the point of view of the subject-centered curriculum. Groups need to meet for a period of time each day to be checked on the information or skills acquired and to be assigned further materials to be learned. It is only when teachers begin to think in terms of developing children as well-adjusted individuals, when they feel the need for knowing their pupils intimately, when time is needed for planning and investigating, that the rigid schedules, compartmentalization, and ability grouping are questioned.

3. *The belief that certain patterns of subjects constitute the best college preparation.* The domination of the colleges over the high-school curriculum, coupled with the inertia of high-school administrators in doing anything about the situation, has long operated to keep the organizational pattern of the high-school curriculum at a *status quo.* The early secondary school, the Latin grammar school, built its curriculum entirely on the needs for college preparation. The academy soon became imbued with the same purposes.

It was probably not too strange that the high school before the twentieth century emphasized college preparation, since a majority of its graduates went on to college. But that emphasis has continued and the "respectable" one of the multiple curricula, the college-preparatory curriculum, has attracted pupils in numbers far out of proportion to the true situation. The very fact that a college-preparatory curriculum exists indicates the persistence of the belief that the usual academic or "solid" subjects serve as the best preparation for college.

The Committee of Ten of the National Council of Education, which made its report in 1893, helped to retain the emphasis on the usual college-preparatory subjects for years to come. In its report, it made no distinction as to curriculum needs of the college and noncollege students. It stated that "every subject which is taught in a secondary school shall be taught in the same way and to the same extent to every pupil so long as he pursues it, no matter what the probable destination of the pupil may be, or at what point his education is to cease." [7] The report gave further impetus to the differentiation of curricula into multiple types through its recommendation that the program of studies be divided into one or more of four types of curricula: Latin-scientific, classical, modern languages, and English, each of which was to prepare students to enter college.

The belief that the usual pattern of English–mathematics–foreign-language–laboratory-science subjects best equips the student for success in college still persists in spite of scientific studies such as the Eight-year Study of the Progressive Education Association. This one, and a host of other studies of the relationship of the pattern of subjects pursued in high school to subsequent college success, have found no significant differences in favor of the hallowed few. The slowness of colleges and universities to change their practices, in spite of the overwhelming evidence against them, has left its mark on the organization of the curriculum in the American secondary school.

4. *The method of accounting for high-school experiences.* The Carnegie unit, so called because the Carnegie Foundation for the Advancement of Teaching defined the unit as a course of five periods weekly throughout the academic year, has been a convenient device for accounting for the work in courses where the amount of subject matter covered was the foremost aim.[8] Throughout the past four decades it has remained as a powerful determiner of the length of class periods and the amount of time per week or year devoted to any particular course.

Colleges use this accounting system; state departments of education and school systems perpetuate it in setting requirements for graduation. It has served as an obstacle to newer developments in teaching

[7] National Education Association, *Journal of Proceedings and Addresses,* p. 749, Washington, D.C., 1894.
[8] Carnegie Foundation for the Advancement of Teaching, *Annual Report,* p. 38, 1906.

methods and experiences of a more democratic nature, because teachers and administrators have often hesitated to change the accepted class organization for the day and the year.

5. *The emphasis on the business type of management in administration.* The efficiency idea, which up until recent times has been the ruling concept in school administration, has advocated precision schedules, a timesaving device of accounting for students' progress through school, and convenient administrative devices, at the expense of a setting in which learning experiences can be directed most effectively.

The familiar example of the principal who feels that he has a good school if the schedule runs like a clock and there are few interruptions can still be seen in high schools. Authoritarian methods used by business have not promoted the democratic principles for which American education stands. Teacher education institutions must assume a good deal of responsibility for this condition.

Other conditions not elaborated on here have undoubtedly been contributing factors to maintaining the type of organizational pattern within which the curriculum develops. Policies of state departments of education and accrediting agencies, lack of cooperation between school and community, the type of teacher education, and the type of leadership in schools are just a few that might be mentioned.

Bases for evaluation of the present situation. The discussion of factors in the development of the typical organizational patterns for the curriculum has raised a number of questions about the desirability of present practices. What is a desirable organization? In what kind of a setting does learning take place most effectively? How can we arrive at some tentative answers? It is an area in which no categorical answers can be found in research studies. Certainly, studies in which learning is measured by progress in learning facts and skills alone does not suit our purpose.

There are certain basic principles in line with research in the field of learning and understanding the adolescent, and based on the democratic way of life, that can be applied as a yardstick to present practices.

1. *The setting for those experiences of youth that constitute the curriculum should be planned for conformity with those conditions which underlie effective learning.* The emphasis upon drill and formal exercises, and the imposition of learning upon unwilling scholars, based on an outmoded psychology, can scarcely be used to

gauge present-day practices. When learning is understood as a change in behavior through experience, there is an entirely different orientation from which to plan.

We must look to the most recent information on how effective learning takes place. Does the organization of the curriculum permit the development of learning experiences that are lifelike for the learners? Does it allow learning experiences to be unified around some central purpose? Is there time to develop goals that are clearly seen and accepted by the learner? A type of setting that does not give a pupil the opportunity to draw upon many areas of information to solve problems important to him, that gives him no sense of unification of learnings, and that gives him no opportunity to participate in planning, executing, and evaluating his experiences hardly measures up to these criteria. Does an important field trip or a dramatic production that takes time and effort upset the "schedule" and everyone else? If it does, there is a serious question as to what types of learning the school has as its goal.

2. *In organizing the high school for learning experiences, the nature of the adolescent and his needs for physical, social, mental, and emotional development should receive primary consideration.* Research in the field of child and adolescent psychology has produced a wealth of information to assist the teacher in understanding pupils.[9] Knowledge of these findings must be accompanied, however, by constant observation and a study of adolescents themselves. It is doubtful if a 45- to 60-minute period a day provides adequate opportunity for such study. When the number of pupils a high-school teacher must meet in classes during the day is totaled, it becomes quite obvious that very few of them can be understood as individual personalities.

We must consider whether the organization of the schedule and the program of studies provide the best possible kind of conditions for helping adolescents solve their adjustment problems. Do they furnish a setting for social development and getting along with one's age mates? Do they encourage the types of experiences that build self-control? Is a situation in which a number of courses·are required of all, but designed for 20 per cent, conducive to meeting adolescent needs? Is there likely

[9] Arthur T. Jersild, *Child Development and the Curriculum*, Bureau of Publications, Teachers College, Columbia University, New York, 1946. A useful summary.

to be a chance to achieve success, or will the tasks set by someone for the mythical "average" pupil be too difficult for many? Does the multiple-curriculum plan, in which about 50 per cent enroll in the college-preparatory curriculum, and in which groups are segregated according to academic ability, provide for the adolescent's finding security and making other emotional adjustments?

Other questions that need to be answered in evaluating the organization of the curriculum might include these: Does the plan of organization permit pupils to gain valuable work experience when the opportunity presents itself? Can pupils explore the community and secure assistance from the school in finding their place in the community? It is in terms of those for whom the school exists that curriculum organization must be evaluated.

3. *Administrative provisions for the curriculum should make it possible for each student to have the richest possible experiences in democratic living.* The democratic objectives of secondary education should be primary factors in any decisions as to the type of administrative provisions to be made for the curriculum. Is there opportunity for making choices? Do pupils participate in making decisions about matters that affect them in and outside the classroom and in taking responsibility for those decisions? Is there a common concern for others and responsibility for one's own actions as they affect others? Do pupils participate in group planning? Is there a high regard for individuals and a value placed on the differences among those individuals?

Unless there is an opportunity for carrying out these objectives in classes and extraclass activities, the existing organization should come under close scrutiny. There are infinitely greater possibilities of carrying on investigation, group planning, and other cooperative activities in a flexible schedule that extends over a larger period of time. The differentiation of curricula, with its attendant segregation of those with high academic ability from those not thus endowed, does not live up to democratic objectives if there is a distinction made as to respectability of different curricula. It has been a common experience that students in general or vocational curricula are not considered "so good" as other students.

Tentative conclusions. On the basis of these three general criteria some tentative conclusions are presented with regard to organizational provisions for curriculum experiences.

1. The inflexible departmentalization and compartmentalization of subject fields that exist in the majority of high schools are suited to a subject-centered approach to learning rather than to one that considers the individual's development through carefully planned experiences as most important.

2. Bell-ringing schedules that herd pupils from room to room on each hour or three-quarters of an hour are not particularly conducive to integrated and unified learning experiences.

3. The measurement of learning in terms of units, either for progress in high school or for graduation, has retarded other changes in curriculum organization that would provide for more desirable types of learning experiences.

4. The differentiated or multiple-curriculum plan of organizing the program of studies for guidance purposes, based on a subject-matter approach to curriculum development, has failed to promote the democratic objectives of secondary education.

5. On the other hand, adding more electives to the required constants in the constants-with-electives organization of a program of studies has not necessarily meant that individual differences among pupils—social, emotional, and physical, as well as mental differences—were taken care of.

SOME FORWARD–LOOKING PRACTICES

There is a growing recognition that traditional programs and organizations have not provided the best conditions for effective learning experiences designed to promote the democratic objectives of secondary education. Evidence of this can be found in the different types of efforts being made to improve the organization of schools for learning. Throughout the country, high schools can be found that are moving ahead of outmoded practices. School administrators and teachers with vision are experimenting to find better solutions than the ones that have been used all too frequently.

All of these changes are aimed at providing an enriched educational opportunity for youth. Some basically stress more effective use of subject matter through breaking down the fixed dividing lines between fields; others, the knowledge and understanding of the adolescent and his needs for balanced development as a member of a democratic society.

Changes emphasizing clearer relationships among subjects. Three common ways of improving the high-school curriculum through reorganization of materials and arrangement of subject matter are correlation, fusion, and a combination of subjects into broad fields. The idea behind all of them is the recognition of the fact that subject fields are interrelated in actual life. Consequently, an attempt is made to create a more lifelike situation for pupils.

1. *Correlation.* One of the first steps taken in many schools to provide more unified learning experiences is to correlate the work in two subject fields, or to show relationship between departments without disturbing each department as a separate unit. The emphasis is on the subject matter. The teaching of projects in art classes to supplement units in American literature, or the teaching of American literature and American history so that the chronological periods coincide, are examples of the usual type of correlation attempted. The basic administrative arrangements for the curriculum are not changed, but the organization of subject matter within a course may be changed.

2. *Fusion.* A fused course represents changes in the organization of the curriculum in that two or more courses may be replaced by a single subject of one period in length, combining the subject matter included in the former courses. For example, biology is a fusion of zoology and botany; social studies, a fusion of history, geography, and civics. One of the typical kinds of fusion is a combination of English literature and composition in a 2-semester course, where the two phases of English are interwoven rather than taught separately as different semester courses. Obviously, certain administrative changes are involved in this transition.

This synthesis of a field of study is another way of combining subject matter in order that pupils might see relationships and learn more effectively. The emphasis is also a subject-centered one.

3. *Broad fields.* Another organization of curriculum experiences that emphasizes the subject matter is one that is termed the "broad-fields curriculum." However, it is a rather confusing label to the inexperienced student because it also represents fusion of subject matter and is used in a number of different ways by different authors.

Probably it may be best to confine the term to the survey type of course at the college level, a rather common usage. The junior college, which may be regarded as a type of extended secondary school, frequently offers survey courses in science, literature, the arts, and social sciences. Such courses involve a transition from several separate elective courses in order to give the student a perspective of the whole field of study. Considerable change is often involved from fewer electives to a more common program for all. It represents a forward step toward breaking down compartments between conventional subjects.

Changes emphasizing the adolescent and his needs. More promising than the changes which emphasize subject matter are efforts through administrative provisions and organization of experiences to provide for the basic needs of young people. The concern here is not so much the subject content as it is the kinds of experiences pupils have with the content. The core curriculum is discussed here somewhat more extensively in order to clarify its meaning and indicate its possibilities.

1. *The homeroom.* In the elementary school the teacher has his pupils in the room during the entire day or the major portion of the day. Those schools that departmentalized under the platoon movement or other influences are tending toward a change to the self-contained classroom. In some upper grade classes, the group is together under one teacher for half the day in its "homeroom."

The homeroom concept has been carried into the high school, largely for guidance purposes, in order to enable a teacher to become better acquainted with a small group of pupils, and in order that a teacher might have definite responsibility for the guidance of a small group. Where the homeroom is not just a 10-minute period at the beginning of the day for roll and announcement purposes, it has possibilities for development of a worth-while contribution to the curriculum experiences that pupils have in a school.

In cases where the homeroom has two or more full periods per week devoted to it, the type of a curriculum that has been developed is often like that found in classes of forward-looking high schools that stress the experience approach. A study of problems really vital to the life of pupils is carried on, such as personal grooming, selection of an occupation, school traditions, what school activities offer, problems before the student council, social events, and conduct in school.

These types of experiences are more in line with principles of learning than the cut-and-dried subject matter often presented in regular classes in the same school. Moreover, the pupils in homerooms usually have a greater opportunity for democratic participation in group living. Somehow or other, since the homeroom has not gained "respect" through credit offered, a number of teachers have come to the interesting but tragic conclusion that democratic participation might be carried on in homerooms but has no place in the regular subjects.

One main advantage of the homeroom is that it offers a better opportunity for the teacher to know his pupils as individuals, to study them, and to give them assistance in their numerous adjustment problems. As an organizational device, it attempts to compensate for the fact that the school day has been compartmentalized to such an extent that no teacher can expect to know all the 100 to 150 pupils with whom he works.

2. *An extended class period, school day, or school year.* The trend in secondary schools is toward a 55- to 60-minute period. A few have extended the period even further. Accompanying the emphasis on supervised study has been a tendency to work toward the hour period. In some of the large cities and sections in the East, where the school day often ends around 2:00 or 2:30 P.M., there is developing a realization of a need for extension of the school day in order to furnish pupils with shop and laboratory experiences, time for study, and well-organized activities within the school day. The extended day in junior colleges that includes late afternoon and evening classes is in line with this tendency.

The 12-month school year is still largely theoretical, although many educators are convinced of its desirability. Some trend in this direction can be noticed in the greater frequency with which schools are employing some members of the teaching staff for the full year, particularly for summer recreational programs. A few schools such as Glencoe, Illinois, for all teachers, and Portland, Oregon, for principals, are employing school personnel for 12 months with a month's vacation.

All of these efforts to extend the time in which pupils may be served by the school indicate an increasingly clearer understanding that, in a changing society, youth need further opportunity to develop recreational interests and skills, and that the whole development of the adolescent is of importance. The rapid-changing period with its intervening study halls, suited to a recitation procedure based on a subject-matter philosophy, is not adequate for full growth of the individual.

3. *Block scheduling.* Another method of compensating for departmentalization of subjects, used by high schools where the concern for pupils is apparent, is the block type of schedule. This schedule is applicable to large high schools where pupils can be divided into sections that

remain together for the required courses. For example, a ninth-grade class of 30 pupils, in which English, social studies, and science are common subjects, is scheduled together to work with Teachers A, B, and C. These pupils also will be taking art, music, industrial arts, home economics, mathematics, or some other electives with teachers of special subjects.

The three teachers, sometimes known as the general education teachers, meet together to plan experiences and discuss ways and means of assisting their pupils in adjustment problems. The teacher designated as the homeroom or guidance teacher may serve as chairman of this group. As frequently as possible, they meet with the other teachers of this particular group of pupils.

In some larger high schools, "a school within a school" has been established successfully. In such cases, the entire corps of teachers of required and elective subjects for a group of 200 or 300, or some other arbitrary number of pupils, works together under a director of instruction in planning for the needs of the particular group.

These plans of organization make it possible for a group of teachers to know certain pupils in the school more intimately and to create a situation within which it will be possible for adolescents to become acquainted with fellow classmates and find greater security.

4. *The core curriculum.* One of the more recent changes in the organization of the curriculum in forward-looking high schools is the core curriculum. It departs somewhat radically from the traditional plan of organization in more than one respect. An examination of its characteristics will reveal that it indicates unusual promise in providing a setting for the experience-unit method and the principles of democratic education discussed in Chaps. 1 and 2.

The core curriculum is not just a grouping of the common required subjects. It has distinct characteristics of its own which distinguish it from other plans of curriculum organization: [10]

1. The core utilizes more time of the school day than the traditional organization, usually from two periods to half a day.

[10] Further explanation and examples of the core curriculum can be found in Harold Alberty, *Reorganizing the High-School Curriculum*, Chap. VI, The Macmillan Company, New York, 1947; and Educational Policies Commission, *Education for All American Youth*, National Education Association, Washington, D.C., 1944. Also see Chap. 15 of this book.

2. The subject matter is drawn from several areas of the conventional subjects as information or skills are needed to solve problems of concern to the learner.

3. The experiences in the core curriculum are those which represent common types of experiences needed to participate effectively in a democratic society. Pupils work on common problems of personal and social concern to all youth.

4. Provision is made for individual differences within the framework of the core, supplemented, of course, by elective courses which meet individual needs.

5. The approach within the core is experience centered rather than subject centered, with the use of larger units of work.

6. The guidance function occupies an important place in the core, and responsibility for the guidance of a certain group of pupils is placed on the core teacher.

Obviously, the reorganization of the daily schedule to include two or more periods under one teacher does not necessarily guarantee the experience-unit method. The difference between the experience and subject approach is one of degree, and all teachers include in their procedure some characteristics of both.

There are certain types of developments in accord with principles of learning, democratic objectives, and concern for the adolescent that are more easily carried out in the core organization, and there is considerable indication that the following developments are occurring in schools that use this organization of curriculum experiences.

1. There is more concern for the individual and his adjustment problems and for adjusting the work to his interests and abilities. The unit method makes it possible for pupils to be doing different things at the same time as an outgrowth of problems of common concern. The teacher lives with his pupils in the core class long enough each day to become acquainted with them and their needs.

2. Social action through cooperation on common problems gives pupils experience in group control and social responsibility. Problems are such that they help pupils acquire social consciousness since they are more apt to be of real concern to pupils; for example, developing rules and regulations by which the group will live, studying the problems of discrimination among racial and ethnic groups as they touch the lives of the pupils in the community, or clearing up a bad lunchroom situation in the school.

3. Complementary to the above, is the opportunity for pupils to par-

ticipate in planning, organizing, and evaluating their experiences in the class, the opportunity to gain proficiency in democratic procedures.

4. The problem-solving technique used in investigating problems in the unit procedure is the essence of the method of intelligence. If a problem faces the group, data must be gathered from all available sources—books, people, institutions, experience—to help arrive at a solution. In a situation where there is time for planning and cooperative work without emphasis on "covering the ground," the method of inquiry has a chance to grow.

5. There is more use made of the field trip, community facilities, and community study since the larger block of time more readily permits excursions outside of the school without disturbing the schedule or annoying other teachers.

This plan of curriculum organization might be termed a variation of the constants-with-electives plan since all pupils are together in the core. There is no need for differentiating among students according to ability since the very nature of the core curriculum provides for individual differences within the core class, where different activities can go on at the same time and cooperative planning is prominent. Different vocational objectives are provided for in the electives outside the core, chosen intelligently through the core class. Multiple curricula are not needed in such a situation.

5. *Part-time cooperative education.* The plan of cooperative education between business establishments and the school, in which the pupil attends school part of the time and obtains work experience part of the time, is another plan of organization that is relatively new. Large and small high schools, junior colleges, and senior colleges have used it successfully. It has some features similar to the core in that the work on the job, and often in school, is arranged in larger blocks of time.

The experience approach is predominant. In related classes at school, work is planned cooperatively to fit into the needs of the job. If the work in a grocery store calls for show-card lettering, the student is given that training. The evidence of cutting across conventional subject lines can also be noted in such related courses, where the work is planned in line with the requirements of the job.

SUMMARY

This chapter has presented the conditions as to the organization of the curriculum that are most typical in the high schools of this country today. It has examined what those high schools are like in respect to size and general organization, for the manner in which young people are thrown together or kept apart in school has tremendous significance for a democratic society. The way in which the school day is organized for them and how well they can get to know their teachers and fellow pupils affect their learning. These patterns as well as those of groupings of subjects in the program of studies were examined.

Basic principles by which curriculum organization may be evaluated were presented to serve as a yardstick by which to measure practices. The student himself is urged to appraise the traditional patterns and the forward-looking practices discussed, using these principles in such a manner.

Although some tentative conclusions were presented, it has not been the intent of this chapter to furnish any ready-made answers for the reader. Instead, it is hoped that the analysis of present practices, along with the principles set forth, will furnish a clearer basis for evaluation of the current situation and help to indicate the direction in which secondary schools should move. Each individual must make the decisions for himself based on the kind of school he wants in a democratic society.

SELECTED REFERENCES

ALBERTY, HAROLD: *Reorganizing the High-School Curriculum*, The Macmillan Company, New York, 1947.

Biennial Survey of Education, 1936–38: Bulletin 2, Chap. V, U.S. Office of Education, Washington, D.C., 1939.

CASWELL, HOLLIS L. (Ed.): *The American High School: Its Responsibility and Opportunity*, Chap. VII, Harper & Brothers, New York, 1946.

DOUGLASS, HARL R.: *Organization and Administration of Secondary Schools*, Chaps. I, III, and VI, Ginn & Company, Boston, 1945.

—— (Ed.): *The High School Curriculum*, Chaps. II, IX, XIV, and XVIII, The Ronald Press Company, New York, 1947.

Educational Policies Commission: *Education for All American Youth*, National Education Association, Washington, D.C., 1944.

GRUHN, WILLIAM T., and DOUGLASS, HARL R.: *The Modern Junior High School*, The Macmillan Company, New York, 1947.

JERSILD, ARTHUR T.: *Child Development and the Curriculum*, Bureau of Publications, Teachers College, Columbia University, New York, 1946.

KANDEL, I. L.: *History of Secondary Education*, Chap. IX, Houghton Mifflin Company, Boston, 1930.

LEONARD, J. PAUL: *Developing the Secondary School Curriculum*, Rinehart & Company, Inc., New York, 1946.

NORMAN, JAMES WILLIAM: *A Comparison of Tendencies in Secondary Education in England and the United States*, Contributions to Education, No. 19, Chap. III, Teachers College, Columbia University, New York, 1922.

North Central Association of Colleges and Secondary Schools: *General Education in the American High School*, Chaps. II and VI, Scott, Foresman & Company, Chicago, 1942.

PARKER, J. CECIL, et al.: *The First Five Years of the Michigan Study of the Secondary-school Curriculum*, Michigan Study of the Secondary-school Curriculum, State Board of Education, Lansing, 1942.

SPEARS, HAROLD: *The Emerging High-school Curriculum*, American Book Company, New York, 1948.

Chapter 5. THE CURRENT BASES FOR

APPRAISING PUPIL PROGRESS

The tendency of man to classify and to catalogue objects, events, and forms of life is not new, and fortunately so. One criterion of the advancement attained in a given field of human knowledge is based on the methods whereby its leading exponents classify what is known about the field. Man has been known to recognize individual differences and to classify individuals in terms of those differences as far back in history as records have been authenticated. Even the lower forms of animal life distinguish among their members in terms of function and ability. It is, therefore, not strange that man has devised and long used methods whereby he can estimate the success of his children in mastering the learning tasks set before them, whether such tasks were posed in the hunt by a father to his son, in the shop by a master to his apprentice, or in the school by a teacher to his pupil.

Most of the individual differences among school pupils which are important to the teacher, and they run almost the gamut of possible differences, have been objectively measurable only during the last half century or so. Exceptions are found in certain physical measurements and in measurements of such tangible behavior as skills and knowledges. The development of the aspect of psychology known as individual differences and of objective methods for measuring many such differences has opened up vast new fields to the psychologist, the educational psychologist, and the teacher. Not least among the areas to which the new understandings and techniques are applicable is the evaluation of pupil behavior in the school.

Numerous aspects of pupil growth and progress are subject to measurement. Among these are physical, anatomical, physiological, motor, social, emotional, intellectual, and educational. Some are of more direct concern to teachers than are others. Those to be dealt with in this chapter pertain directly to those changes in pupil behavior which result in large measure from pupil experiences in the school. Others of these types of growth and development will receive consideration in Chap. 16.

BASES FOR PUPIL EVALUATION

In most school systems today, pupils in each grade differ widely in their general intelligence and aptitudes. This means that they differ widely in their potentialities for learning from their school experiences. They also differ widely in their educational achievement, as evidenced both by teachers' marks and by results obtained from objective testing. Their differences in physical and social characteristics, interests, and attitudes are no less marked. The existence of a wide degree of such differences within a class of pupils taught by one teacher, in the main by group methods of instruction, has long been recognized as causing a problem in the evaluation of pupil success. No one solution to this problem has been, or is likely in the near future to be, widely accepted.

Three distinguishable approaches to the solution of this problem are in use today. They are based on quite different philosophies concerning such fundamental questions as the nature of successful pupil performances, the purposes of education, and even the nature of the good life. In the accounts following, more attention is given to the methods and procedures involved in each than to their philosophical bases.

Comparison with standard. Educators in the early schools were prone to uphold certain standards, often intangible and subjective in nature, which pupils were expected to attain before they entered the next grade or level of the school system. This procedure, which had its origins at a time when education was the privilege of only the select few, has come to be accepted practice in many schools today where education is provided for the relatively unselected many.

Educational standards are analagous to hurdles of varying and somewhat regularly increasing heights which pupils are expected to jump successively on their routes toward graduation from the elementary and secondary school. Pupils who fail to jump the hurdle which is their task for a given school year are often retained in the same grade a second year in the attempt to develop their hurdle-jumping proficiency. Pupils who knock the hurdle down in attempting to jump it are often promoted to the next grade conditionally or on probation. However, pupils with excellent hurdle-jumping aptitude, who could easily jump two hurdles in 1 year, are often restrained from attempting a second, and are thereby held to the rate of hurdle-jumping progress character-istic of the average pupil. The educational equivalent to this analogy is known as the grade-standard theory of pupil progress.

Standards of educational progress are even more intangible and sub-jective today than they probably were under the more traditional edu-cational system which placed major emphasis upon knowledge and skill outcomes. The problem of measuring pupil learnings would be very simple if educational standards were stated, for example, in terms of such tangible knowledges as those concerning the dates of certain his-torical events and skills involved in finding the roots of certain types of quadratic equations. It is much more difficult to establish and objectify standards when the emphasis is upon such less tangible outcomes as understandings concerning historical cause-and-effect relationships and abilities to solve practical problems by the establishment and solution of quadratic equations.

Relatively few objective and tangible educational standards have been widely accepted in the schools of today. Standards vary from school to school and from teacher to teacher within the same school, except for the very few which are widely accepted by educators. Problems of evaluating pupil attainments are vastly complicated, and it is unreason-able to expect that standards of sufficiently objective types can be set and agreed upon to warrant the belief that status in a certain school grade represents the same level of achievement in all schools.

Comparison with norm. Increasingly since standardized achievement tests first appeared in the first decade of this century, test norms have come into use as a basis for the evaluation of educational attainments of pupils. Norms represent what pupils in different school grades or of different ages have actually done on standardized achievement tests.[1] Norms are most often stated in terms of age equivalents and grade equivalents for elementary-school tests and as percentile ranks by grade levels and subjects for secondary-school tests.

---

[1] Such tests would be better characterized if they were called normalized tests rather than standardized tests. A norm is an objective statement of average (usually median) performance, whereas a standard represents a subjective placement of a performance often too intangible for ready objective evaluation.

It is possible to compare objectively the score of any pupil on a standardized achievement test with the scores made by pupils in the same grade, of the same age, or who are taking the same school subject. For example, it can be learned that John's score of 83 on a standardized reading comprehension test represents reading comprehension ability characteristic of pupils having grade equivalents of 7.6, *i.e.*, characteristic of the average pupil who has attended the seventh grade for 6 months. Similarly, Sally's score of 117 on a test in social studies may represent typical achievement in the social studies of pupils whose age equivalents of 14–5 indicate that they are fourteen years and five months of age. Again, Henry's percentile rank of 33, based on a score of 71 on a standardized plane geometry test, indicates that he scored higher on the test than did 33 per cent of the plane geometry pupils upon whose scores the test was standardized. That John, actually starting the ninth grade, is below the norm of achievement for his grade in reading comprehension can readily be inferred. That Sally, who is celebrating her thirteenth birthday anniversary today, is superior to many pupils of her age in the social studies can be inferred. Henry's standing among plane geometry pupils can readily be assigned to the upper end of the lowest third.

It is obvious that not all pupils can surpass the norm of achievement. By its nature the norm of the age or grade type demands that approximately half of the pupils be above it and half of them be below it. Similarly, not more than half of the pupils can have percentile ranks higher than the median, or 50. It is, consequently, futile to attempt to bring all pupils up to the norm. It is undesirable, moreover, to think of the norm as a standard, for a norm cannot be thought of as a standard unless satisfactory performance is expected from only about half of the pupils.

Comparison with previous status. The belief that pupils should be evaluated in educational achievement in relation to their potentialities for learning prompts those who advocate comparisons with previous status as the basis for marking and promoting pupils. This theory is based on the recognized facts that the frustrations and failures of pupils unable to meet standards often result in serious emotional disturbances and maladjustments, that the ease with which superior pupils meet standards often results in slovenly work habits and unwarranted self-satisfaction, but that if every pupil is kept busy at his highest level of natural achievement he will be "successful, happy and good." [2]

If attainments are evaluated in terms of the potentialities for learning possessed by individual pupils, it is thought by exponents of this method that both the adjustment and the education of pupils will be improved. Amounts of pupil progress can be judged objectively from standardized test results by determining the amount of growth attained in a known period of time, such as 1 year or 2 years. Direct and exact evidence concerning how much an individual pupil should progress under optimum conditions is not available, however, although the achievement quotient and other similar devices have been designed and sometimes used for this purpose. In each such attempt, some measure of the pupil's achievement level or educational attainment is divided by some similarly stated measure of his intelligence or aptitude, or of his potentialities for achievement, in order to obtain an index of how well he is using and developing the abilities he possesses.

Just where in the educational ladder or exactly how these three bases for pupil elevation and promotion should function is far from clear. If the procedure based on previous status were followed rigidly throughout the entire school system from the primary grades through professional schools, standards embodied in state bar examinations, for graduation from medical schools, and for licensed pharmacists could not be maintained. If the grade-standard procedure were followed rigidly, and without special classes for certain types of deficient pupils, it would not be uncommon to find some children retarded by as many as four or more grades by the time they are legally eligible to leave school and to find other pupils receiving their high-school diplomas at fourteen, thirteen, and even at younger ages.

Although neither of these extremes is acceptable, it is far from simple to attain a satisfactory compromise or an acceptable alternative method. Educators have devised methods of ability grouping or homogeneous grouping for classifying pupils. They have evolved plans providing for different rates of pupil progress through the school grades. A solution widely acceptable to educators has yet to be found, however.

[2] C. E. Seashore, "The Talented Child," *Journal of Educational Psychology*, 7:241–242, April, 1916.

TYPES OF EVALUATION INSTRUMENTS AND TECHNIQUES

With the advent of standardized tests early in this century, of the informal objective test in the early twenties, and of the still newer evaluative tools and techniques about 15 years ago, the educator's concept concerning effective methods of evaluating pupil achievement has necessarily undergone a thorough revision. Developments of at least three distinguishable types have occurred during the twentieth century in the scientific study of instructional outcomes as evidenced in the behavior of pupils. Greene, Jorgensen, and Gerberich [3] distinguish these periods in terms of primary emphasis upon: (1) testing, (2) measuring, and (3) evaluating.

The shift of emphasis is borne out in changes observable in tools and techniques and in titles of books published during the three periods. The first period, characterized by testing, lasted until perhaps the early or middle twenties; it may be considered as having its origins as late as 1908, or even as far back in history as education was practiced by human beings. The second period covered the 10 or 15 years from the early or middle twenties to the middle or late thirties, and the third period has been in effect for the past 10 or 15 years.

Testing. The modern testing movement probably originated with the introduction of the comparative test by J. M. Rice [4] in 1894, although other significant dates which may be considered as starting points are 1904, when Thorndike [5] brought out the first book dealing mainly with mental and educational measurements; 1905, when Binet and Simon inaugurated the intelligence-testing movement by the publication of the first intelligence scale; and 1908, when Stone [6] published his arithmetic reasoning test—the first standardized test.

[3] Harry A. Greene, Albert N. Jorgensen, and J. Raymond Gerberich, *Measurement and Evaluation in the Secondary School,* pp. 6–7, Longmans, Green & Co., Inc., New York, 1943.

[4] Leonard P. Ayres, "History and Present Status of Educational Measurements," *The Measurement of Educational Products,* Seventeenth Yearbook of the National Society for the Study of Education, Part II, Chap. I, p. 11, Public School Publishing Company, Bloomington, Ill., 1918.

[5] Edward L. Thorndike, *An Introduction to the Theory of Mental and Social Measurements,* Teachers College, Columbia University, New York, 1904.

[6] Cliff W. Stone, *Arithmetical Abilities and Some Factors Determining Them,* Contributions to Education, No. 19, Teachers College, Columbia University, New York, 1908.

It was during this period, particularly for a few years after 1908, that many educators looked to the objective test as a panacea for all educational ailments. The objective test was constructed only by specialists, and there was a tendency to emphasize the test and its development rather than the use of test results.

Measuring. The second or measurement aspect in the scientific study of learning outcomes probably had its inception with the suggestion of McCall [7] in 1920 that objective tests very similar in form to standardized tests can be constructed by the teacher for classroom use. Unfortunately, the teacher-made objective test came to be known as the new-type examination; preferred now is the term, informal objective test. Ruch, with the publication in 1924 of the first book entirely devoted to the teacher-made objective test, [8] furnished major impetus for the measurement movement.

Although the production of new standardized tests continued, particularly during the early part of this period, the twenties were marked by increasing attention to the use of test results and to the measurement of the less tangible types of instructional outcomes. This was the period during which measurement ceased to be the province of the specialist solely and during which the teacher began to assume his rightful place in the assessment of pupil performance.

Evaluating. The modern phase of this movement, characterized by the evaluation or appraisal of pupil behavior, was probably introduced by Tyler [9] when he outlined steps for objective test construction based on the objectives of instruction and the changes in behavior of pupils who had attained the desired instructional outcomes. The Eight-year Study of schools of the Progressive Education Association, in which the approach proposed by Tyler was basic, [10] contributed significantly to further development of this procedure in achievement measurement and evaluation.

Much broader in its scope than either the testing or the measuring

[7] William A. McCall, "A New Kind of School Examination," *Journal of Educational Research*, 1:33–46, January, 1920.

[8] G. M. Ruch, *The Improvement of the Written Examination*, Scott, Foresman & Company, Chicago, 1924.

[9] Ralph W. Tyler, "A Generalized Technique for Constructing Achievement Tests," *Educational Research Bulletin*, 8:199–208, Apr. 15, 1931.

[10] Eugene R. Smith, Ralph W. Tyler, *et al.*, *Appraising and Recording Student Progress*, Harper & Brothers, New York, 1942.

movements, the evaluative approach makes use not only of paper-and-pencil tests but also of many non-test procedures and tools, such as objective types of observations, ratings, questionnaires, the profile, and the cumulative record. The testing, measuring, and evaluating periods are characterized by an increasingly broad conception concerning the nature of the child. This trend in the direction of appraising the whole child is doubtless one result of the theories propounded by modern behavioral psychologists of the Gestalt and organismic schools.

Consideration will be given in three later chapters of this volume to testing, measuring, and evaluating pupils to determine their attainment of desired instructional outcomes when they have been taught under the daily-assignment method (Chap. 8), the subject-matter unit method (Chap. 11), and the experience unit method (Chap. 14). Although no definite parallelism exists among the three periods in the appraisal of pupil behavior discussed above, and the three instructional methods treated in Part 2 of this volume, it seems appropriate here to mention and briefly outline such parallelism as does exist.

Some but not all of the methods basic to testing and measuring are appropriately used with the daily-assignment method of instruction. Testing and measuring procedures of wider scope are fundamental in the subject-matter unit method, including most of those properly used in the daily-assignment or recitation plan. Instructional outcomes of the experience unit method can best be assessed by a combination of the newer evaluating techniques with many of the procedures developed during the testing and measuring periods. The plan which will be followed in Chaps. 8, 11, and 14 is to discuss the methods which seem most appropriate for the daily-assignment method in Chap. 8, to discuss in Chap. 11 the additional procedures of significant value for the subject-matter unit method, with occasional reference to the techniques previously treated in Chap. 8, and to devote greatest attention in Chap. 14 to evaluative techniques, but again with occasional reference to the pertinent content of Chaps. 8 and 11.

Subject-centered tools and techniques. Tests today represent the most widely used means of measuring the school attainment of pupils, as was doubtless true of ancient schools as well. Included here must be not only the written test, first known to enter into educational testing in the medieval universities of the eighteenth century, but also the oral examination or quiz and the performance or skill test.

Would-be scholars of ancient Greece "stood" oral examinations at which they were required to defend certain theses, and Spartan youths underwent tests of physical skill and endurance. The oral examination or quiz is still widely used by many teachers as a measurement technique, although it better serves a teaching than a measuring purpose. The first written tests used in American schools were probably those inspired by Horace Mann in the Boston of 1845. Performance tests are most commonly used for measurement in such fields as physical education, commercial education, home economics, and industrial arts, and they are also used in some aspects of the more academic subjects.

Written tests are of two major types—standardized and teacher-made. Informal objective tests are teacher-made or classroom objective tests similar in types of items to standardized tests, which are also objective in form. The still widely used essay or traditional examination is also a teacher-made or classroom test.

Written tests may be classified by type as objective, which includes the standardized and the informal objective classroom examinations, and as subjective, which is represented by the essay or traditional examination. Again they may be classified by source as standardized and as teacher-made, the last mentioned including both the essay and the informal objective examinations.

Standardized tests are either general or specific in their functions. General in function are the survey tests, which measure achievement in major curricular areas by means of a test battery or which measure achievement in one subject field or one subject by means of a single test. Also general in function are the prognostic tests, which measure background preparation necessary for success in a more advanced field of study or course. Much more specific in function are diagnostic and analytic tests, the purposes of which are to diagnose or analyze pupil abilities in particular subject areas.

Whereas the standardized test is available only in published form, and the user is faced with the necessity of finding a test which satisfactorily meets his needs, the teacher-made or classroom instruments, whether essay or informal objective in nature, may be devised to meet the particular purposes in mind. Some performance tests are available in standardized form, also, but such tests can quite readily be constructed by the teacher for measuring certain outcomes of skill types.

Another type of subject-centered instrument is found in the quality

99

and product scales which have important uses in some subject areas. An important distinction between tests and scales is that the former are ordinarily put into the hands of the pupils whereas the latter are used only by the teacher. Quality scales in handwriting consist of scaled and numbered samples ranging from an almost illegible to an excellent specimen of handwriting. The teacher is able to assign quality scores to samples of pupil handwriting by comparing them with the scale samples. Product scales in spelling consist of words listed in terms of their difficulty for pupils in various school grades. The teacher can prepare his own test at a particular grade level and of the desired level of difficulty by selecting words appropriately from such a product scale.

Two other non-test measurement devices—check lists and profiles—are primarily of the subject-centered type. Check lists are often used in measuring pupil ability in laboratory or other skills. Such an instrument often consists of a list of possible operations or manipulations of apparatus, on which the teacher checks the manner in which the pupil performs the operations, whether right or wrong, whether in the correct order or not, in the attempt to solve his problem. Profiles are used to show levels of pupil attainments in several areas of knowledge or in several aspects of one area of knowledge in such comparable terms as age equivalents, grade equivalents, or percentile ranks.

An aspect of evaluation which cannot be overlooked is that of teachers' marks [11] based on pupil achievements. Teachers' marks, usually subject centered, have become such an integral part of American education, and so much dependence is placed upon them by pupils, parents, school officials and prospective employers, that attention must be devoted to them.

In a recent survey of marking practices with primary emphasis upon the secondary-school level, Wrinkle listed the following as typical of methods in use or which have been tried experimentally: (a) manipulating the symbols, (b) supplementing the symbols, (c) parent-teacher conferences, (d) informal letters to parents, (e) check forms, (f) pupil self-evaluation and reporting, and (g) parents' reports to the school.[12]

[11] Although often referred to as "grades," the term "grades" is more properly used to designate the pupil's placement on the educational ladder.
[12] William L. Wrinkle, *Improving Marking and Reporting Practices*, Chap. 8, Rinehart & Company, Inc., New York, 1947.

As Wrinkle pointed out, manipulating the symbols by changing the traditional 100-point percentage scale to a 5-point scale of A, B, C, D, F or comparable marks and even to a 2-point scale of S and U, meaning satisfactory and unsatisfactory, has been quite common. The 5-point scale is doubtless most typical in present marking practice. Some schools have supplemented such letter symbols by providing teacher evaluations of significant and well-defined pupil traits of personality.

Although various ones of the other five procedures Wrinkle listed have been tried out or adopted by certain schools, more often at the elementary than at the secondary level, none has yet gained wide acceptance in practice. Such factors as excessive time demands upon teachers and other members of the school staff, incomplete cooperation by parents of the pupils, dependence upon a teacher-grade plan of school organization, unreadiness of teachers, and inadequate provision of data deemed necessary for permanent school records have been powerful deterrants to the wide acceptance of any of these newer procedures.

A type of teachers' report and of a parallel report to the home was devised by the staff of the Eight-year Study.[13] Major characteristics of the report to the home are provision for: (a) teachers' judgments concerning pupil performances in five areas of instructional outcomes common to all school subjects, (b) teachers' judgments concerning weaknesses pupils should particularly attempt to eradicate, (c) teachers' reports by subject areas on likely success of pupils in further secondary-school and college work, and (d) teachers' general comments to parents of the pupils. The five types of instructional outcomes set apart are success in achieving specific course objectives, progress in learning how to think, effectiveness in the oral and written communication of ideas, active concern for group welfare, and general work habits. The eight points on which pupil weaknesses may be reported have to do primarily with work-study habits and related personality traits.

Activity-centered tools and techniques. Prominent among the devices used in evaluating the behavioral outcomes of an activity-centered curriculum are the interview and several observational techniques. Interviews with pupils, whether informal and spontaneous or pre-

[13] Eugene R. Smith, Ralph W. Tyler, *et al., Appraising and Recording Student Progress,* Chap. 11, Harper & Brothers, New York. 1942.

arranged, permit the teacher to learn much concerning the pupil's progress and his difficulties in learning. The teacher can also learn much about the pupil by observing him in his classroom and playground behavior, and can add much of value to cumulative records by noting outstandingly significant or revealing acts in the form of anecdotal records. The projective techniques, which involve observation of pupil behavior in controlled situations, often of a play or recreational nature, also reveal much to the trained observer concerning pupil characteristics and progress.

Rating scales to be filled out by the teacher or even by the pupil himself are often useful in measuring pupil progress and methods of work. Such scales provide for each of several important characteristics listed on separate lines of the instrument places for indicating performance of differing degrees of merit. Furthermore, and by no means least important, some standardized tests and various informal objective testing techniques make possible the measurement of such activity-centered learnings as ability to interpret data, ability to locate information, ability to make appropriate generalizations, and ability to draw appropriate inferences.

Two other broad evaluative devices are of value in measuring activity-centered instructional outcomes. They are the cumulative record and the case study. The cumulative record should include such information concerning the pupil's home background and environment, health history, scholastic history, results from intelligence and achievement tests, anecdotal records, rating scales, etc., as will enable the teacher to survey his school progress and history readily and quickly. When a case study is made, most often for a pupil who is not well adjusted in the school, the cumulative record and results from further investigation of his case are utilized in the attempt to determine the sources of his difficulties and then to furnish needed remediation.

CRITERIA OF A GOOD EXAMINATION

Workers in any field where quantitative measurement is used must give careful consideration to the characteristics or criteria of their evaluative instruments and techniques. It matters not whether the field of work is education, sociology, chemistry, zoology, or astronomy, whether it is a social science, a physical science, or a biological science; similar although not identical criteria must be satisfied by the satisfactory measuring instrument or technique. It matters not whether the purpose is to determine the incidence of substandard housing in a given city, the quantity of a given element in a chemical compound, or the knowledge of school pupils about the French Revolution; similar although not identical criteria are applicable in evaluating the instrument or technique to be used.

The criteria of a good examination or technique designed for use in the measurement of pupil behavior [14] can be viewed under two headings—those which depend directly upon the nature of the test or the technique itself, and those which depend in some manner upon the use to which the test or technique is put. In each of the two following sections, the criteria are listed and discussed approximately in ascending order of importance. Hence, the criteria of greatest significance appear last.

Criteria dependent upon the nature of the instrument or technique. Certain of the characteristics of a good examination or evaluative technique are relatively independent of the use to which the measuring instrument or tool is put. They may, therefore, be looked upon as general rather than as specific characteristics or criteria. Of the six general characteristics—economy, administrability, scorability, adequacy, objectivity, and reliability—the three last named are aspects of, and are essential to, one of the specific characteristics in the absence of which no examination or technique can serve a worth-while purpose.

These six characteristics depend in large measure upon the test author and publisher, whether the test is standardized and published commercially or whether it is prepared by a teacher or group of teachers and mimeographed for local use only.

Economy. An evaluative instrument or technique is economical if its time requirements and financial costs are reasonable. A test which requires 1 hour of testing time and costs 10 cents per booklet is less economical than a test which requires 40 minutes of testing time and costs 7 cents per booklet. Economies can be effected by the use of gelatin plate or mimeograph machines in reproducing test materials, by the use of printed or otherwise reproduced answer sheets, and even by oral presentation of certain types of objective test materials.

[14] For a more extensive treatment of these criteria, see Harry A. Greene, Albert N. Jorgensen, and J. Raymond Gerberich, *Measurement and Evaluation in the Secondary School*, Chap. 4, Longmans, Green & Co., Inc., New York, 1943.

Administrability. A good examination or evaluative technique should ordinarily be easy to administer. To rate high on administrability, any test or procedure, whether standardized or teacher-made, should provide the examiner with complete instructions for testing the pupils and should provide pupils with complete instructions for taking the test. Nothing should be left so indefinite that the examiner is called upon to improvise hastily conceived instructions or that the pupil is required to decide for himself what course of action to pursue in attacking the test.

For all written examinations, the examiner should understand clearly the procedure to follow in passing out testing materials, giving necessary oral instructions, timing the test, and collecting materials when the test has been completed. The pupil should know how he is to record his answers, whether or not he should guess on items for which he does not know the answers, the length of time he will be allowed, and probably also the total possible score he can attain and how the test results will be scored. If the test consists of two or more timed parts, directions to the pupil should appear at the bottom of each page and at the beginning and end of each part. If the task to be performed by the pupil is complex or if the types of test items used are new to the pupil, sample items should supplement the directions and a few practice exercises may even be necessary.

For any performance or skill test to be given with oral instructions only, the statement to be made to the pupil at the beginning should embody as many of these characteristics as are applicable and should be framed in advance with as great care as if it were to be used in a printed or mimeographed test. Each pupil should have the necessary equipment in good working order and should know exactly what task he is to perform or what problem he is to solve.

Scorability. Scores or results stated in terms other than numbers should ordinarily be easy to obtain if an evaluative instrument or technique is to possess a desirable degree of scorability. An instrument for which results may be obtained by an accurate clerical worker or even by an electrical test-scoring machine possesses a higher degree of scorability than one which demands that the teacher do the scoring. An instrument which can be scored in 1 minute possesses a higher degree of scorability than one which will require 2 minutes for scoring.

Instructions to the scorer should be clear and definite concerning how the scoring key is to be used, the amount of credit to be given for each correct answer, whether or not to correct for chance and if so how, and the method of obtaining and recording total scores and any necessary part scores.

Adequacy. To possess a satisfactory degree of adequacy, a test or technique must be of reasonable length and must sample rather widely the skills or abilities to be tested. Narrow and specific skills can be tested adequately in a shorter time or by use of a shorter test than a test of more complex skills or abilities will require. As it is usually if not always impossible to measure educational outcomes in their entirety, the sample chosen for testing should be broad enough to make certain that it is quite representative of the total skill or ability.

A test or technique adequate in length and in sampling of behaviors to be measured should deal mainly with important knowledges, skills, understandings, and other types of outcomes. Highly detailed and unimportant knowledges, skills, and understandings contribute little to the attainment of adequacy in a test.

Objectivity. A test or technique is objective when the subjective factor of personal judgment or opinion is ruled out in obtaining the score or result. In an objective test, therefore, two or more scorers will obtain exactly the same results unless clerical errors have been made in obtaining one or more of the scores.

Objectivity can be attained in written examinations by the use of such objective item types as the true-false, multiple-choice, matching, simple recall, and their adaptations. It is important that each item be so constructed that there is only one correct answer or, in recall types, that there is only one idea which would correctly complete the meaning.

Reliability. The most important general characteristic of a good test or technique, general in the sense that it is independent of the use to which the instrument or tool is put, is reliability. Reliability may be defined as the degree to which an evaluation instrument measures whatever it *does* measure or in terms of its consistency in measurement. Thus, a well-calibrated, *i.e.*, reliable, thermometer would be reliable even if it were mistakenly used in the attempt to measure atmospheric pressure, and a well-constructed, *i.e.*, reliable, test of basic skills in arithmetic computation would be reliable when mistakenly used in the measurement of ability in arithmetic reasoning. However, neither the thermometer nor the basic skills test in arithmetic would satisfactorily accomplish the purpose for which it was here used.

If a test is to be reliable, it must possess satisfactory degrees of adequacy and objectivity. Thus, adequacy and objectivity may be looked upon as aspects of reliability and as prerequisite to reliability. A satisfactory degree of reliability in a test will be insured if the test is so constructed that it possesses satisfactory degrees of adequacy and objectivity, *i.e.*, if it samples broadly enough and if it is scorable in a highly objective fashion. By this token, neither a 10-item true-false test nor a 3-hour essay examination would possess a satisfactory degree of reliability. The true-false test would be objective but inadequate. The essay examination would be adequate but subjective.

Criteria dependent upon the use of the instrument or technique. The remaining characteristics of a good examination or evaluative technique are specific rather than general, for they depend upon the use to which the test is put and the manner by which results from the test are given meaning. The three criteria appropriately listed here—comparability, validity, and utility—occur relatively in increasing order of importance. However, validity is doubtless the most important criterion, and utility depends upon the use to which results are put rather than to the potentialities of the test if properly used.

Comparability. The characteristic of a test or technique which permits the interpretation of scores or other results on a continuum which has natural or accepted meaning is known as comparability. As raw scores on tests have no meaning until they are converted into some form of derived scores, it is the responsibility of the test maker to provide for the type of derived scores best calculated to meet the needs for each test. Such provision for derived scores cannot be made until the standardized test has been administered to a representative group of pupils, often referred to as the normative group, or until the informal objective test has been used with a pupil group.

Such derived scores or measures as age norms, grade norms, percentile ranks, certain types of quotients, and certain types of standard scores are most common in the attainment of comparability in standardized tests. Two or more equivalent forms, commonly provided for the better standardized tests, are further evidence of test comparability. For informal objective tests available in only one form and not accompanied by norms, comparability may be established quite simply by a method presented in Chap. 11.

Validity. The most important specific criterion of a good test or evaluative tool is validity. An instrument is valid only if it is used in measuring those types and those levels of behavior for which it is designed. Hence, a test is valid to the degree in which it measures what and where it is *supposed to* measure.

A reliable thermometer will furnish a valid result only if it is used to measure temperature and a reliable test of basic arithmetic skills will be valid only if it is used in measuring basic skills in arithmetic. But a thermometer having a temperature range from − 20 degrees to 120 degrees Fahrenheit will not be valid for temperature measurement either in a blast furnace or at the North Pole in winter. Neither will a test of basic arithmetic skills for the second grade be valid for measuring basic arithmetic skills of sixth-grade pupils. It follows, therefore, that a test to be valid must be used for the appropriate purpose and at the appropriate level of advancement.

The validity of a test depends upon its reliability in much the same manner as the reliability of a test depends upon its adequacy and objectivity. A test cannot measure what it is supposed to measure unless it measures what it does measure, so a test cannot be valid unless it is also reliable. A test which has a title and description indicating that it was designed for measuring functional grammar or grammatical usage but which actually measures formal grammar will be reliable regardless of how it is used, if its adequacy and objectivity are high. It will lack validity, however, for the measurement of functional grammar, even though it will possess both reliability and validity if used, contrary to its avowed purpose, in measuring formal grammar.

Utility. The utility of an examination or evaluative technique is all-important, for the test or technique serves no useful major purpose unless the results are put to good use. Even if a test has been well chosen for a given purpose and properly administered to an appropriate group of pupils and if the results have been properly scored and interpreted, the educational gains will be small if the results are not used in the guidance of pupils. Tests which, once given and scored, are filed on the top shelf of a closet to accumulate dust, possess little if any degree of utility. It is only when the teacher follows through to the ultimate stage of testing—use of results in pupil guidance—that the test can be said to possess utility. The day is fortunately far in the past when educators saw fit to test pupils for the mere satisfaction of curiosity.

As other criteria are not always equal in the evaluation of a test or other educational measuring device, to paraphrase negatively the well-known "other things being equal," an excellent test more often attains its quality by means of an optimum balance among the criteria listed above than through the maximum possible satisfaction of each criterion singly. Thus, a test which is economical in both financial and time costs may accomplish so little or even be so harmful because of weaknesses elsewhere that its apparent cheapness may well be a misrepresentation, whereas a more expensive test may so well serve its purpose as to warrant its cost. The *Stanford Revision of the Binet-Simon Intelligence Scale* requires a highly skilled technician in its administration and scoring, and yet it is recognized as the most reliable and valid test of intelligence so far produced. A test may possess high degrees of economy, administrability, scorability, adequacy, objectivity, reliability, and comparability without satisfying the ultimate criteria of validity and utility, if it is incorrectly or carelessly used. It may even be satisfactory in all major respects other than utility. However, the major values of testing have been lost if results are not well used."

The accompanying rating scale has been found useful in evaluating examinations, whether standardized or teacher-made, as well as other instruments and techniques of appraisal. The arbitrarily assigned weightings for the nine criteria represent what is believed to be appropriate emphasis for each criterion. In the use of this scale, it is recommended that the same person rate the two or more tests or techniques which may at any time be receiving consideration for a particular purpose, rather than to use ratings of two or more persons for comparison, in order to hold constant the tendency toward high, average, or low ratings which may characterize three different persons. Care should be taken that only instruments or techniques designed for accomplishing the same purpose are compared by means of this rating scale. It is only when an instrument is evaluated in terms of the purpose for which it is designed that the results have real meaning.

OUTCOMES OF INSTRUCTION

It seems evident that a teacher who wishes to evaluate instructional outcomes in pupils should possess an understanding of considerable

STANDARDIZED ACHIEVEMENT TEST RATING SCALE

Criteria	Maximum ratings	Test_____		Test_____	
		Ratings	Reasons	Ratings	Reasons
1. Validity	20				
2. Reliability	15				
3. Adequacy	10				
4. Objectivity	10				
5. Administrability	10				
6. Scorability	10				
7. Comparability	15				
8. Economy	5				
9. Utility	5				
Totals	100				

Summary statement of major reasons for preference.

depth concerning the types of pupil behavior which result from school instruction and from out-of-school experiences. The final stage in the complete teaching process is evaluation, and it is difficult to believe that appropriate evaluation can occur unless the behavioral changes brought about in pupils in the form of instructional outcomes are well understood. Furthermore, such earlier stages of the instructional process as planning and providing learning experiences for pupils cannot be integrated into a unified whole most effectively unless the teacher has a clear conception of the instructional outcomes.

The instructional outcomes classified and discussed by major types below have been adapted from Woodruff [15] and will serve as the basis for discussion of evaluation in later chapters. The objectives of science instruction presented in a recent yearbook of the National Society for the Study of Education [16] are based on a similar classification of instructional outcomes.

Skills. Among the most tangible and readily observable instructional outcomes are skills of the sensory-motor and perceptual-motor types. Sensory-motor skills, often repetitive in nature, ordinarily become automatic after they have once been learned. They are represented by walking, skating, standing, and eating. Perceptual-motor skills, usually unique rather than repetitive, are directed even though they may be independent of conscious control. Such skills as typewriting, playing a cornet, and writing illustrate the need for selective rather than for purely repetitive behavior.

Of these types of skills, the perceptual-motor are of greater consequence to the secondary-school teacher than are the sensory-motor, for most of the important sensory-motor skills have been developed in pupils to a rather high degree before they enter the secondary school. Improvement may well be sought in the performance of such skills by high-school pupils, but there is seldom need for teaching them directly. On the other hand, many perceptual-motor skills of significant value have not been developed in children before they enter the high school, and hence become appropriate concerns of the high school and college.

[15] Asahel D. Woodruff, *The Psychology of Teaching* 2d ed., Chap. 8, Longmans, Green & Co., Inc., New York, 1948.
[16] Victor H. Noll (Chairman), *Science Education in American Schools*, Part I, Chap. 3, Forty-sixth Yearbook of the National Society for the Study of Education, University of Chicago Press, Chicago, 1947.

Knowledges. When a person acquires knowledge, he establishes such mental associations as that between a certain object and the name by which it is ordinarily known, between a term and the color or other characteristic it represents, between a date and an event or a person, and among numbers in a situation involving addition or some other arithmetic process. A person has knowledge if he associates the date of May 8, 1945, with the surrender of the German armies in the Second World War, if he knows how to perform the operation 6 − 2, or if he has learned that certain foods are rich with vitamin A or vitamin B_1.

Concepts. The development of concepts is closely allied with if not paralleled by the emphasis in modern schools on the development of meanings in pupil learning. Concepts are illustrated by the ability to give definitions of words; to discriminate among types or qualities of color; to use abstract terms in thinking, speaking, and writing; and to reach a generalized conclusion or idea.

Concepts are necessarily based on knowledges and frequently also on certain types of skills. Although knowledges can be learned so completely that they will not be forgotten, and although basic knowledges are not usually subject to any modification after they are learned, concepts are often modified many times and acquire enlarged meanings as the learner has further experiences contributing to them. For example, the time concepts of children are quite narrowly restricted to their experiences and the immediate future; it is only when children reach the age of about ten years that historical time assumes much meaning.

Understandings. The truism that "knowledge is power" has been supplanted in the thinking of modern educators by the psychologically sound generalization that "understanding passeth knowledge." Knowledge without power is evidenced in the "idiot savants," whose phenomenal ability to memorize facts was not accompanied by ability to apply or to see the use of those facts. Knowledge organized at the level generally referred to as understandings becomes functional in the life of the individual. It is those intermediate levels of knowledge referred to above as concepts and those higher levels of knowledge referred to here as understandings which the school should seek to develop in its pupils.

An understanding perhaps represents only a higher level of outcome than a concept, so the two terms are not mutually exclusive. Meanings are necessarily present in both. Understandings perhaps more often than concepts demand abstract in contrast with concrete thinking. A person who has a concept of man, for example, may be primarily aware of man's physical characteristics, his usual behaviors, and the environment within which he lives. An understanding of man, however, seems to demand an awareness of his psychological as well as of his physical organization, an awareness of causal factors lying behind his behavior, and an awareness of the interaction between man and his environment.

Tastes and Preferences. Many types of behavior are based on personal liking for a color, type of music, architectural style, or author rather than on any objective evaluation of the quality preferred. The feelings and emotions of the individual are important in the formation of his tastes and preferences, whereas his knowledges, concepts, and understandings are founded more largely on his intellectual processes.

Tastes and preferences may be classified into three not entirely distinguishable types. Attitudes indicate how a person feels about certain practices, issues, and persons or groups of persons. He may, for example, have an attitude of any degree between extremely favorable and extremely unfavorable toward such a practice as capital punishment, on such an issue as high tariffs, and toward such a group as orientals. Interests may vary from negligible to very intense in certain forms of recreation, types of reading, vocations, and types of persons. Appreciations, those inner feelings of varying degrees of satisfaction obtained from different experiences which are difficult if not impossible to convey to another person, are particularly important in such fine arts as music, drama, and literature, although they are by no means restricted to the fine arts alone.

Applications. The ability to think logically and to solve problems represents the type of instructional outcome here designated as applications. This type of outcome represents an end product or ultimate goal of teaching. Unless an individual has acquired skills, knowledges, concepts, and understandings of types and of degrees which contribute to his effectiveness in logical thinking and in the solution of problems, his learnings lack functional value and contribute little to his success in life. Unless his attitudes, interests, and appreciations are based upon reality rather than upon wishful thinking, he will be hampered in logical thinking and problem solving.

Problem-solving behavior certainly is not limited to the fields of mathematics and science, where the term has been most widely used. It occurs in any area where problems exist and decisions are to be made, whether social, economic, political, mathematical, or scientific.

Adjustment. Much consideration is given by the modern school to the attainment of adjustment on the part of pupils to the type of society in which they live. Whether adjustment should be listed as a type of instructional outcome or whether it should be considered as a desirable over-all result from the attainment of the more specific types of outcomes listed above is not entirely clear. It is certainly true that many forms of antisocial behavior, such as criminality, extreme forms of "rugged individualism," and various forms of mental disease, occur in persons who are maladjusted and apparently are a result of their lack of adjustment. It is also true, however, that our society is not perfect, and that the attainment of adjustment to society as it exists is not the sole and ultimate desideratum.

The school should doubtless aid the pupil in attainment of adjustment to modern society. However, it should not do so with the purpose of developing in him a blind acceptance of conditions as they exist. Man's adjustment to his environment includes not only the adaptation of himself to the facts of nature but also the adaptation of nature to his welfare. It seems implicit that responsibilities of the school, therefore, are to aid the pupil in his adaptation to his environment and to develop in him abilities and desires to accept and to aid in bringing about change along socially desirable lines.

SUMMARY

Historically, the assessment of pupil attainments in the school has passed through three recognizable stages in terms of the techniques used by teachers—testing, measuring, and evaluating. The trend has been toward an increasingly broad interpretation of the behavioral changes sought in pupils, and each stage has created demands for improved and more broadly conceived techniques of pupil appraisal than were previously deemed adequate.

Somewhat similarly, bases for interpreting results from appraisal of pupils for purposes of marking and promotion may be distinguished as of three types. In the most traditional method, pupil learnings are compared with what are thought to be rather definite standards of achievement. In the transitional stage, pupil attainments are compared with norms of performance, *i.e.*, with quantified designations of what similar pupils have actually accomplished on standardized achievement tests. In the emerging stage, pupil attainments are evaluated in terms of the varying abilities to succeed with which they, as individuals, come to the school.

Three instructional methods may be considered in rough parallel to the trends noted above. The daily-assignment method is often accompanied by testing as a technique and by the grade-standard theory of marking and promotion. Pupils taught under the subject-matter unit method are more often measured and have their attainments rated by the use of norms of attainment. Under the experience unit method of instruction, pupils are more often evaluated in terms of their capacities for achievement or in terms of progress made in relation to progress reasonably expected from them as individuals. Various types of tests, techniques, and tools are employed, ranging from those closely related to the subject matter or content of instruction to those based more definitely upon the activities in which pupils learn to engage as a result of instruction.

The teacher should be familiar with the characteristics or criteria of a good examination if he is to attain optimum values from testing, measuring, and evaluating. Criteria dependent upon the test or technique itself are economy, administrability, scorability, adequacy, objectivity, and reliability, while those dependent on the use of the instrument or technique are comparability, validity, and utility. Quality in a good examination results from an optimum degree of each of these criteria.

The teacher should also be conversant with the types of behavioral changes which are brought about in pupils by their school and out-of-school experiences. Knowledges and skills are the most tangible and easily measurable of these outcomes. Somewhat less tangible are concepts, understandings, and applications, which are higher level outcomes of a functional nature. Such tastes and preferences as attitudes, interests, and appreciations are not only intangible but also highly personalized. Adjustment to self and society is a type of over-all behavior extremely desirable in an individual, whether or not it is properly considered as an instructional outcome. The teacher should have an understanding of the behavioral changes represented by this outcome which will not only aid him in appraising pupil achievement but which will also enrich his contribution to pupil welfare in all aspects of the teaching process.

SELECTED REFERENCES

GREENE, EDWARD B.: *Measurements of Human Behavior*, Chaps. 1–2, The Odyssey Press, Inc., New York, 1941.

GREENE, HARRY A., JORGENSEN, ALBERT N., and GERBERICH, J. RAYMOND: *Measurement and Evaluation in the Secondary School*, Chaps. 1–4, Longmans, Green & Co., Inc., New York, 1943.

LANG, ALBERT R.: *Modern Methods in Written Examinations*, Chaps. 2–3, Houghton Mifflin Company, Boston, 1930.

LEE, J. MURRAY: *A Guide to Measurement in Secondary Schools*, Chap. 1, D. Appleton-Century Company, Inc., New York, 1936.

McCALL, WILLIAM A.: *Measurement*, Chap. 1, The Macmillan Company, New York, 1939.

ORLEANS, JACOB S.: *Measurement in Education*, Chaps. 1–2, Thomas Nelson & Sons, New York, 1937.

REMMERS, H. H., and GAGE, N. L.: *Educational Measurement and Evaluation*, Chaps. 1–2, Harper & Brothers, New York, 1943.

ROSS, C. C.: *Measurement in Today's Schools*, 2d ed., Chaps. 1–3, Prentice-Hall, Inc., New York, 1947.

RUSSELL, CHARLES: *Standard Tests*, Chaps. 2–4, Ginn & Company, Boston, 1930.

SYMONDS, PERCIVAL M.: *Measurement in Secondary Education*, Chaps. 1–2, The Macmillan Company, New York, 1927.

TIEGS, ERNEST W.: *Tests and Measurements for Teachers*, Chap. 1, Houghton Mifflin Company, Boston, 1931.

WOODRUFF, ASAHEL D.: *The Psychology of Teaching*, 2d ed., Chap. 8, Longmans, Green & Co., Inc., New York, 1948.

WRINKLE, WILLIAM L.: *Improving Marking and Reporting Practices*, Chaps. 1–4, Rinehart & Company, Inc., New York, 1947.

Part 2. METHODS USED BY SECONDARY-

SCHOOL TEACHERS TODAY

METHOD BASED ON DAILY ASSIGNMENTS

Chapter 6. THE ORIGIN AND THEORY OF

THE DAILY–ASSIGNMENT METHOD

The daily assignment with its retinue of techniques and devices constitutes a distinctive pattern of classroom procedures. Under the name of "the recitation method," this pattern is familiar to all who have struggled through innumerable repetitions of the assign-study-recite sequence that forms its basic outline. For reasons that will be discussed later, this pattern has fallen into disfavor in recent years among those who speak and write about pedagogical matters. In spite of this formidable opposition, teaching based on the daily assignment continues to dominate the secondary schools to this day, and a teacher who is not familiar with either the major purpose for which it is undertaken or the principles which govern its use is likely to encounter serious difficulties.

EVOLUTION OF THE DAILY–ASSIGNMENT PATTERN

The procedures associated with daily assignments are the products of distinct lines of development that cover the span of a great many centuries. At the time each line emerged, it was thought to be revolutionary in nature and incompatible with the prevailing theories and practices. As time went on, the basic differences were disregarded with the result that the three lines now seem to have converged into a single pattern of thought and action. The major concern here is to describe the nature and purpose of the common pattern rather than to emphasize the differences out of which it has emerged. However, each of the three lines of development will be reviewed briefly to draw attention to the specific characteristics each has contributed to the common pattern.

Contributions from the classical tradition. The first line of development to be considered here began with the educational doctrines of Plato.

His basic ideas have been perpetuated in the writings of some of the most famous philosophers and educators of Europe and America. For that reason, this line of influence is generally referred to as "the classical tradition."

In answer to the question of what it is that man needs in order to achieve his own self-realization, Plato said that one must know what is true, what is good, and what is beautiful. Only when armed with such knowledge is man able to move in the direction of perfection. Plato taught that the ideals of truth, goodness, and beauty have an independent existence in a realm unrelated to the physical universe. Perhaps the best illustration of this supermundane world of absolute perfection is the Christian's idea of heaven where nothing is believed to exist except in a state of perfection. Just as the Christian believes that life on this earth improves as the conditions and arrangements here are made to duplicate the conditions and arrangements in heaven, so also did Plato urge mankind to strive to learn what forms truth, goodness, and beauty have in the realm of ideals.

Plato thought of the human mind as a tool by means of which man may look into the supermundane realm and thereby get ideas of what to do to improve himself and his environment. Like any other tool, the mind cannot function well unless it is of good quality and in good working condition. Education was looked upon as the process of improving the mind, a "disciplining" process accomplished by means of appropriate mental exercises.

Plato reasoned further that not all human minds are of equal quality. The minds of some groups, notably of slaves, are of such inferior quality that effort expended in attempting to put them in good working condition is largely wasted. These people, it was argued, are intended by nature to be concerned only with mundane interests and activities. Hence, all they need is some form of vocational training that will fit them for practical pursuits but not for directing the affairs of the community. A few males, on the other hand, can generally be counted upon to have minds of good quality that need only the discipline of a good education to put them in excellent working condition. A wise society, therefore, will seek out these few able individuals, educate them, and then turn over to them the responsibility for formulating and directing all policies affecting the welfare of the community.

From Plato's theory, it follows logically that education has a twofold task. First, it must isolate the few great minds from among the many inferior ones; and second, it must condition these few for their great social responsibilities. The system of education outlined by Plato was designed to accomplish both purposes with one procedure. On the theory that the mind of the learner must be conditioned through practice in seeking perfection, he suggested a curriculum consisting of the best exercise materials with which he was acquainted. It included, among several others, the disciplines of grammar, logic, arithmetic, and geometry which, all together, are now known as the liberal arts. These studies were recommended not to fill the mind of the learner, but to exercise it and to provide a foretaste of that perfection which man should pursue throughout his stay on earth. Inasmuch as the only purpose of education is to enable the individual to seek ideas of perfection, and since the perfection sought has only one form, all students were expected to follow the same curriculum. It was thought that those who have the necessary endowments and persist to the end of the prescribed studies would emerge qualified to be the social leaders. The others would find the offering so repulsive that they would withdraw voluntarily as soon as they had reached the limits of their capacity for development.

Judged by modern standards, the teaching procedures employed by those who followed the Platonic pattern appear quite simple. Because the content of the study was not as important as the mental exercise it provided, there were few curricular changes made in the span of several centuries, and the course offerings in the main were restricted to the few subjects recommended by Plato in *The Republic*. The textbooks constituted the courses of study. Thus under the name of geometry or of grammar, pupils actually studied a work by one of the great masters, starting at the beginning and proceeding through to the end line by line or exercise by exercise. Changes in textbooks were infrequent. For example, almost every boy who studied Latin grammar from the decline of the Roman Empire to the middle of the eighteenth century did so by laboring through either the *Ars Minor*, written by Donatus in the fourth century A.D., or *Lily's Grammar*, written early in the sixteenth century by Colet and Lily, with the aid of Erasmus.

Before the art of printing was practiced widely, a school might have only one copy of a given textbook. For this reason it was necessary for the teacher to dictate the lesson by reading from the available copy.

When he had dictated a portion sufficient for an assignment, he would comment upon its meaning, point out and explain unusual examples of style or forms of grammar, and expound in general upon the nature and virtues of the passage under consideration. Having received their assignment, the pupils would study the portion of the textbook they had copied, together with the instructor's comments, in order to be prepared to expound and explain in like manner at the next class meeting. This teaching method is described in part in the following quotation:

. . . . We may picture to ourselves a group of lads seated on the floor, which was strewn with clean straw, their waxen tablets in their hands, and busily engaged in noting down the words read by the *scholasticus* from his manuscript volume. So rarely did the pupils, in those days, gain access to a book, that to *read* (*legere*) became synonymous with to *teach*. The scholars traced the words on the tablets, and afterwards, when their notes had been corrected by the master, transferred them to a little parchment volume, the treasured depository, with many, of nearly all the learning they managed to acquire in life. . . .[1]

When textbooks became plentiful and cheap, the teacher was able to dispense with the unpleasant task of dictating the study materials. The textbook in the hands of the pupil became a book of exercises from which the teacher needed merely to measure out for the pupil the amount of work to be done before their next meeting, to explain any new features that would be encountered in the assignment, and then to set the pupil to work according to his own devices. In due time, the teacher was expected to call upon the pupil to "recite" his lesson. The recitation was a testing device to determine if the pupil was ready for a new assignment or required punishment to spur him on to greater effort in mastering the old one. The familiar assign-study-recite pattern of teaching is apparent even at this early stage.

In this type of education pupil progress came to be judged in terms of the amount and the difficulty of the exercise undergone rather than in terms of the knowledge gained or the understandings acquired. The accepted studies were arranged by experience and tradition in a particular sequence, for example, the familiar sequence of Latin grammar,

[1] J. B. Mullinger, *The Schools of Charles the Great*, p. 131, G. E. Steckert & Company, New York, 1932. Also E. P. Cubberly, *Readings in the History of Education*, p. 102, Houghton Mifflin Company, Boston, 1920.

Caesar, Cicero, and Virgil. Thus, the achievement of a given pupil could be appraised in a moment by asking him to show the place in the sequence to which he had progressed. There was, apparently, no need for the modern elaborate system of credits and marks, for as late as 1734 a boy might demonstrate his eligibility for admission to Harvard College by appearing before the examining committee and translating extemporaneously whatever passage from Tully [2] or Virgil the examiners set before him.

From the foregoing description, it is clear that the classical tradition in education is based on the assumption that there is but one good type of education. There is only one curriculum and one method suitable for making the mind a proper instrument to guide man in his search for perfection. The accepted system of education has been designed to provide the maximum amount of mental exercise possible in the time that is available. The learning activities engaged in by the pupil preferably consist of the diligent study of Latin, Greek, mathematics, and other classical subjects, without reference to the ultimate vocational and social needs of the pupil. Long experience has demonstrated the most effective order in which these subjects are to be pursued. It is admitted that these studies are not intended for everyone, for most pupils are expected to find them uninteresting and difficult. Failure or lack of interest are taken as evidence that such pupils should be allowed to drop out of school or to transfer to a division that provides "training" [3] for a specific vocational field. Thus only the best minds will be left to complete their education and to emerge in due time as the true leaders of society.

It follows that teaching method consists of the techniques and procedures by which the pupils can be put through the standard sequence of studies with the best results obtainable. It is the teacher's responsibility to measure out the work and to see that it is done. Two considerations guide the teacher in accomplishing that end. First, the pupil must do the work, otherwise he will not receive the benefits of the mental exercise the assignment provides; and second, failure is evidence that the learner lacks the mental equipment necessary to profit from further study. There is no room for sentiment or "soft pedagogy." A power greater than the teacher has determined the place the pupil is to fill

[2] Cicero.
[3] As distinguished from "education."

in life, and education can do no more than help the pupil recognize his predestined role and to prepare him for it.

Contributions from the theories of Herbart. The classical tradition in education with its emphasis on mental discipline was not seriously challenged until the nineteenth century. By that time, a line of educational reformers that includes Amos Comenius, John Locke, J. J. Rousseau, Henri Pestalozzi, and many others, had despaired of securing the social reforms they sought through the prevailing system of education which disregarded practical considerations. At the same time, there was a corresponding shift of interest in philosophical matters that marked a growing concern for success in this life rather than in a life to come. Modern science was making a bid for recognition and a few philosophers, who had studied the methods of scientific research and their fruits, now suggested that truth, goodness, and beauty might be found through the observation of physical phenomena just as readily as through the processes of the mind. That is to say, knowledge gained through observation and experimentation is worth seeking because it can help man build the better world he has been seeking through the study of the classical subjects. There is an implication here that man will voluntarily live the good life if he has adequate knowledge from which to draw his ideas of what is good. This theory is in conflict with the classical doctrines which held that man will do good only when his mind has been properly disciplined, and that right action is determined without direct reference to any specific knowledge.

The new emphasis in education upon the acquisition of knowledge, as opposed to the older emphasis on mental discipline, led to a number of interesting developments. The academy movement in America is an example. Through the efforts of men like Benjamin Franklin, who had an interest in practical affairs, a new form of secondary education was introduced to provide young men—and later young women, too—with the practical knowledge that would enable them to make a good living and to find a useful occupation in the growing business community. When writing of the curriculum of the early academies, Monroe [4] stated that it was the natural sciences that gave these schools their popular appeal. Astronomy, natural philosophy, physics including new sections on electricity and magnetism, chemistry, and the biological

[4] Paul Monroe, *Founding of the American Public School System*, Vol. I, p. 404, The Macmillan Company, New York, 1940.

sciences were among the courses offered in this group. In addition, there were courses offered in bookkeeping, business law, navigation, surveying, the modern languages useful in foreign trade, and apparently in any other subjects that represented a body of knowledge useful in making a living and for which there was a popular demand. This new form of education was so well received that in the period between the American War for Independence and the War between the States, the academies nearly drove the Latin grammar schools out of existence.

However, old habits of thought and action are as difficult to displace in education as in any other walk of life. The academies soon demonstrated a tendency to take over some of the forms and teaching methods of the Latin schools. It appears, for example, that the new courses in English and other modern languages were taught in a manner similar to that used in the old Latin courses. The grammar textbooks were little more than translations of the standard Latin grammars. The new science textbooks were mastered item by item and from beginning to end in a manner reminiscent of the mental discipline methods and there appeared to be little regard for the relative merit of the various items of subject matter. Faith in the value of committing the textbooks to memory continued to be expressed by both parents and teachers. It is difficult to judge whether this emphasis on *memoriter* methods was due to a faith in the future value of the knowledge mastered or to a vestigial faith in the mental development the memorizing activities were thought to produce. It is well known, however, that ultimately such subjects as astronomy and navigation were found in schools far removed in time and space from any opportunity to put the knowledge to practical use.

A second development in education that made possible the instruction of large numbers of pupils in the elements of learning was introduced in Europe and America shortly after the War for Independence by Joseph Lancaster and Andrew Bell. These men were searching for an inexpensive method for bringing education to the masses. Although they worked independently, each hit upon the idea of dividing the subject matter into very small segments and of arranging these segments into a course of study in the order of their difficulty and complexity. A master might then teach the first item of the course to a group of monitors, who were usually older pupils. Each monitor, in turn, would take a group of uninstructed pupils and teach them what he had learned. By repeating the process with each item in the course, one master could instruct hundreds of pupils almost as easily as a dozen.[5]

As a mass production scheme, these monitorial systems have few more ingenious rivals. They dramatized the new hope in the acquisition of knowledge. The systems enjoyed a wide, though brief, popularity in America chiefly because they promised for the moment to put schooling within the reach of everyone. Although this democratic hope was not to be realized immediately, the monitorial methods popularized the idea of group instruction as opposed to individual instruction, and paved the way for the graded schools that followed. Thayer described this influence as the desire ". . . to have ten little voices chirrup where one chirruped before."[6]

It was in this atmosphere of new hope for a better world through the acquisition of knowledge that John Frederick Herbart preached his theory of education. Instead of the mental discipline advocated by the classicists, Herbart's doctrines placed major emphasis upon the development of moral ideas through the acquisition of knowledge. He was led to deny the mental discipline theory by his observation that an individual may employ his mental powers in markedly different ways in different situations.

Many pupils reveal a curious contrast. In their own sphere they display a good memory, a lively imagination, a keen understanding; by the teacher they are credited with little of all these. They rule perhaps over their playmates because of their superior intelligence, or possess at least the respect of the latter, while in their classes they show only incapacity. Such experience suggests the difficulty of making instruction take proper hold of the inner growth of the pupil. It is evident, at the same time, that what is customarily ascribed to the action of the various mental faculties takes place in certain groups of ideas. . . . The boy has one set of ideas for his school, another for the family circle, still another for the playground, etc. This fact explains better than intentional reserve the observation that a boy is one being at home or at school and quite another among strangers.[7]

[5] For a vivid description of the monitorial system, see Samuel Chester Parker, *A Textbook in the History of Modern Elementary Education*, pp. 101–107, Ginn & Company, Boston, 1912.

[6] V. T. Thayer, *The Passing of the Recitation*, p. 5, D. C. Heath and Company, Boston, 1928.

[7] John Frederick Herbart, *Outline of Educational Doctrine*, trans. by Alexis F. Lange, pp. 18–19, The Macmillan Company, New York, 1904.

Herbart concluded that the ideas that give direction to behavior are built up through sensory experiences. Thus, when a child sees a tree, the experience leaves a trace in his mind called a percept. Touching, tasting, hearing the tree in the wind, and smelling it also provide "tree" percepts as do subsequent experiences with this tree or with other trees. From these percepts there may then come a general idea that serves to direct the child in its future relations with trees. This general idea that gives direction to action is called a concept. Ideas or concepts can be derived either from direct sensory contacts or from the written and spoken word. Hence, the way to improve the individual, and through him society, is to provide him with an abundance of percepts, which in turn are to be generalized into the moral ideas needed to guide his future conduct along approved lines.

Ideas spring from two main sources,—experience and social intercourse. Knowledge of nature—incomplete and crude—is derived from the former; the latter furnishes the sentiments entertained toward our fellowmen. . . . Hence, we have two main branches of instruction,—the historical and the scientific. The former embraces not only history proper, but language study as well; the latter includes, besides natural science, mathematics.[8]

The above quotation makes very clear Herbart's answer to the question of what to teach. His recommendations on this score were in keeping with the general trend of thought current in his day. His theory of how the pupil learns, however, was a definite innovation and deserves special consideration because of the influence the procedures he recommended have had upon subsequent practice.

Herbart's theory of teaching grew directly from his theory of learning. His view that each sensory experience leaves a trace upon the learner's mind to which related traces, subsequently received, are added until a mass of sufficient size has accumulated to form a generalization or idea, suggested several specific teaching practices. In the first place, the teacher must select the experiences to which the learner is to be exposed. Herbart provided for this in a general way in the curriculum suggested in the above quotation. Within each branch of the sciences and the social sciences, however, it is necessary for the teacher to isolate each item in order that it may be grasped clearly. Second, care must be exercised to insure that a new trace is added to the proper existing

[8] *Ibid.*, p. 24.

mass of accumulated traces, or it will make no satisfactory contribution to the development of general ideas. Third, the generalization process must be directed to insure the emergence of the desired moral ideas. Finally, it must be assured through practice that the idea developed through instruction will be applied in the learner's everyday affairs.

From these considerations, Herbart developed his well-known steps in teaching. His four-step pattern, namely: (a) clearness, (b) association, (c) system, and (d) method, has undergone some modification in the hands of his followers, but its essential features still stand. Perhaps the best known modification is the five-step pattern[9] outlined by Bagley as follows:

> First step .... Preparation
> Sub step .... Statement of aim
> Second step .... Presentation
> Third step .... Comparison and abstraction
> Fourth step .... Generalization
> Fifth step .... Application

Space does not permit a detailed account of how this pattern should be used in the classroom. In general, however, the preparation step is intended to make the learner aware of the information he had previously acquired and which is related to the new material about to be taught. When every pupil in the class is attentive to the subject under consideration, the new fact or process is presented, or taught, by the teacher. This constitutes the presentation step. In the third phase, the information newly acquired is compared with the old body of knowledge; similarities and differences are pointed out, and the various relationships are noted. All this is in preparation for the fourth step, the formulation of a generalization or general idea. This must take into account all the old information as well as the new item or items presented in the second step. The generalization thus formed is now ready to be applied to a variety of situations in the fifth step. After a few preliminary applications made in class under the watchful eye of the teacher, an out-of-class assignment—frequently some form of homework—is made to provide additional practice.

Strictly speaking, the above pattern is intended only for teaching

[9] William C. Bagley, *The Educative Process*, p. 287, The Macmillan Company, New York, 1907.

ideas *inductively*. In addition to this inductive method, Herbart also suggested a pattern of procedures for teaching ideas *deductively*, or preformed. The inductive pattern, however, seems to have received more favorable attention and is the better known of the two. In fact, some teacher training institutions became so enthusiastic about the new method that they seem to have directed a major share of their efforts to the task of winning their students to the use of this method to the exclusion of all others. These institutions provided practice in the preparation of detailed daily lesson plans, each one of which ran through every one of the five steps. Learning was identified with the activities of the teacher, and pupil failure was therefore interpreted as an indication of faulty teaching. The importance attached to these techniques led to the employment of master teachers to supervise the less skillful in the use of the proper procedures. This system of supervision, together with the emphasis in the normal schools on a single pattern of teaching, soon gave teaching a uniformity of practice and rigidity of form that is apparent in many places even to this day.

Although the Herbartian movement was directed against the memoriter methods then prevalent in the schools, it helped to perpetuate teaching based on daily assignments and group instruction which since have become such prominent features of the recitation method. Furthermore, it strengthened the prevailing respect for the textbook as the unfailing authority and source of knowledge. Although new textbooks were prepared for the new content courses, the systematic organization of knowledge which the textbooks in history and the natural sciences presented, appealed to teachers as material to be mastered bit by bit.[10] Although McMurry states that, "In recent years a better class of teachers has required pupils to memorize only the substance of the thought, neglecting the form of expression in the book,"[11] the mastery of the textbook continued, nevertheless, to be for the pupils no less than for the teacher, the major objective of their daily activities.

There is little evidence that the formal Herbartian pattern of teaching was widely adopted by teachers on the secondary-school level. Its general popularity on the elementary level and the prominence it received in the professional literature nevertheless exerted considerable

[10] Charles A. McMurry and Frank M. McMurry, *The Method of the Recitation*, p. 298, The Macmillan Company, New York, 1909.
[11] *Ibid.*, pp. 120–121.

pressure in bringing about some modifications of the classical influence in the upper schools. Among other things, there was an increased emphasis on the content of the lessons assigned, which was in keeping with the newer value placed on knowledge. Second, the importance of sound instructional procedures was recognized and ultimately this led to better planning and consequently to better teaching. There was also a marked tendency to identify learning with what the teacher did, particularly during the recitation period. Thus the importance of reviewing materials previously learned, of the form of the questions asked, and of the nature of the assignments made gained new significance in the eyes of the teachers. Lesson planning became an accepted teacher activity, and each day's work in a given course came to be looked upon as a discrete segment of subject matter which called for a separate teaching plan.

Contributions from the scientific movement in education. The third great influence in the development of the daily-assignment method has been the rise of what may here be called scientific psychology as distinguished from the earlier speculation psychologies. The success of scientific research on other areas had stimulated certain individuals to look for quantitative data, which could be verified objectively, in the study of human behavior including mental activity.

One of the men most prominent in this scientific movement in educational psychology is E. L. Thorndike. He did not, as did some others, make a sharp break at the outset with the educational aims of the Herbartians, but devoted himself to determining by experimental methods the means by which those aims might be more quickly and effectively realized. As a result of his investigation, he soon came to reject the Herbartian description of the learning process. His own conclusions on the subject indicate that "the basis of a mind's action,— the starting point of intellect, feeling, and conduct,—is thus its equipment of instincts and capacities, its native or unlearned tendencies." [12] These he attributes to neural connections in the central nervous system which are present at birth. The number of such connections, called native reflexes, is rather small, but they account for all the responses to stimuli of which the infant is capable. By a process of substituting one type of neural connection for another, these native patterns are gradu-

[12] Edward L. Thorndike, The Elements of Psychology, p. 185, A. G. Seiler, New York, 1907.

THE METHODS WE USE

ally modified until the complex behavior of the educated adult is produced.

Learning—that is the modification of the native reflexes—occurs whenever the response given to a stimulus no longer produces a satisfactory adjustment. Hence, the stimulus will persist, and the learner will try at random other responses of which he is capable until a satisfactory adjustment is achieved. Under repeated presentations of the stimulus, all unsuccessful responses will tend to drop out until finally none but the successful response remains. When this occurs, a new neural connection will have been established so that when the stimulus is presented in the future only the successful response will be given, that is, learning will have occurred.

In describing the nature of the teaching process based on this theory of learning, Thorndike states:

The work of teaching is to produce and to prevent changes in human beings; to preserve and increase the desirable qualities of body, intellect, and character; and to get rid of the undesirable. To thus control human nature, the teacher needs to know it. To change what is into what ought to be, we need to know the law by which the changes occur.[13]

This means simply that the teacher's work is to present or to withhold stimuli in such a way as to produce desirable responses or to prevent undesirable ones from occurring. In elaborating upon the teaching process, Thorndike stated that learning can be managed or directed on the basis of the following three principles:

1. Some activity is essential before learning can be directed. Hence, the individual to be taught, if he is not already an active, responding organism, must be stimulated to such activity.

2. The teacher must arrange the instructional situation so that the individual undergoing training is likely to make the right response.

3. The teacher must arrange the situation so that when undesirable responses are given, dissatisfaction will result for the learner, and when the right response is made, satisfaction will result for the learner.[14]

It is evident that the teacher occupies the position of central importance in this teaching process no less than in the Herbartian and the

[13] Edward L. Thorndike, *The Principles of Teaching*, p. 7, A. G. Seiler, New York, 1906.

[14] *Op. cit.*, pp. 209–210.

disciplinary procedures previously discussed. It is the teacher who must select and arrange the stimuli that are to initiate and control the learning activities of the pupils. Furthermore, he must be ready to reward or to punish whatever responses the stimuli induce. It is the teacher who sets the stage and controls the direction of the learning outcomes. Hence, the teaching process begins with the selection of the particular outcomes desired and the most promising combination of environmental factors, or teaching techniques, for producing them. Carefully controlled experiments have thrown considerable light on the relative merits of a large range of techniques, devices, and procedures.

The data produced by the scientific movement in education did not, in its early stages, call for a break with the Herbartians on the question of what is to be taught. The textbooks developed by the Herbartians for transmitting useful knowledge continued to be viewed with favor and to occupy the dominant position in the list of study materials used in the schools. As late as 1926, one prominent writer associated with the scientific movement stated:

Textbooks may be employed in such a variety of ways that a complete discussion of the technique of using the textbook would involve a discussion of almost all the various methods of teaching, assignments, class discussions, reviews, and, in fact, little short of a complete discussion of teaching methods.[15]

The efforts of the research workers were confined, for the most part, to seeking new ways to teach the old content. Carefully controlled experiments were made to learn what kind of procedures would enable the largest number of pupils to learn to spell correctly a given list of words or to master the largest number of facts about a given subject in the shortest possible period of time. Through similar inquiries, data were gathered to guide teachers in breaking down subject matter and complicated skills and processes into segments or steps best suited to easy mastery. Their arrangement into levels of progressively greater difficulty was also determined experimentally, as were the conditions under which each item should be presented to reduce the obstacles to learning most frequently encountered. It was discovered, for example,

[15] Harl R. Douglass, *Modern Methods in High School Teaching*, p. 12, Houghton Mifflin Company, Boston, 1926.

that learning takes place more readily if the pupil is required to focus his attention upon only one new item at a time and if the attention span is short. This conclusion also served to reenforce the prevailing practice of planning instruction on the basis of the activities that might engage the attention of the pupil with profit for one class period per day.

It follows logically that the daily planning of his activities is one of the most important aspects of the teacher's work. The planning must begin with the selection of the aim or objective for the day inasmuch as the aim determines the kind of activities that will be employed to achieve it. Three types of outcomes are recognized. They are ". . . the imparting of information, as in teaching the structure of living organism; the development of some interest or attitude, as the appreciation of a bit of literature or music; (and) the development of some skill, as in typewriting." [16] Each type calls for its own pattern of teaching techniques and devices. Without reference to type, however, all daily planning must provide for (a) acquainting the pupil with the aim to be achieved, (b) a learning activity or activities that will engage the pupil's efforts until mastery is achieved, and (c) appraising the degree of mastery achieved as a basis for planning the next teaching situation. These three provisions fall readily within the already familiar teaching pattern which consists of an assignment, a study period, and a recitation.

The major emphasis in teacher planning is on the recitation. The importance of the recitation in the daily plan is indicated in the following quotation:

> The plan should first of all consider the ground to be covered in the recitation period. This naturally falls into three parts,—namely, *the review, the advance, and the assignment.*[17]

There is evidence here of a recitation pattern that lends itself quite readily to repetition from day to day. Thus the pattern of the daily-assignment method seems, if anything, to have become even more firmly entrenched in secondary-school practice through the influence of the early scientific investigations in education. Admittedly, however,

[16] *Ibid.,* p. 3.
[17] S. S. Colvin, *An Introduction to High School Teaching,* p. 334, The Macmillan Company, New York, 1922. Italics in the original.

the procedures were richly augmented by the new practices and devices discovered through the efforts of hundreds of research workers.

THE NATURE OF TEACHING BASED ON DAILY ASSIGNMENTS

Whether or not one is in sympathy with the kind of teaching that is based on daily assignments, there is sound logic in the reasoning underlying such procedures. If a school is convinced that it has a specific body of facts, ideas, habits, skills, and attitudes which represent the very best of all that is known by mankind, then that school will look with favor upon any teaching method that promises to transmit that body of subject matter to each pupil in the shortest time possible. For many years schools have regarded their curricula in exactly that exalted light. Their need for a mass production teaching method has stimulated the development of the now familiar pattern based on the daily assignment and its seemingly inseparable companion, the recitation.

The basic pattern. Given a specific content to be taught, there is good reason, supported by experience, for breaking up that content into small segments to facilitate mastery. The size of the segment is governed by the amount of subject matter the pupil can master between the time the assignment is made and the time he is called upon to recite what he has studied. The effectiveness of the daily assignment as the determining factor in controlling the size of the segments of subject matter has been accepted by many teachers on the basis of their own experiences. Furthermore, it is highly probable that one segment in a given subject-matter area is similar in nature to the others and that a method that is effective in teaching one will be equally effective in the case of the others. The daily repetition of the assign-study-recite pattern of teaching, therefore, has the argument of consistency on its side.

If one grants the assumption that the school must teach a specific content, there is also good reason for assigning the teacher responsibility for setting up and controlling the learning situation. The teacher becomes, in effect, the custodian of the storehouse of knowledge and is, therefore, responsible for preserving the cultural heritage as well as for supervising its use. Learning results from activities engaged in by the teacher, and it is entirely proper that he should be the center of action in any learning situation.

It follows with equal logic that the content of learning is of equal value to all, that is, whatever is regarded as indispensable for one pupil is also indispensable for the others. Where the demand for education is so great that pupils must be taught in groups, it follows that all members of the group may be held responsible for identical achievements in a given period of time. That some will apply themselves more diligently than others and for that reason will profit more from the time spent in study is to be expected. The school must, therefore, prod along the laggards for their own good.

Some modern modifications. The basic assign-study-recite pattern developed by the classicists and modified by the Herbartians and the scientific psychologists has undergone some further revision at the hands of the scientific educators. One innovation is the departmentalization of instruction. On the theory that each subject-matter area presents unique obstacles to learning, it is thought that a given teacher can learn to deal effectively with the problems of teaching met in one or two subjects but not in all subjects. Hence, the practice of assigning a given teacher responsibility for only one or two subjects has been introduced widely. The platoon system, which was popular a few years ago, was an extension of the departmentalization idea.

A second innovation is that of homogeneous grouping. This is an administrative device invented to make assignments fit the abilities of pupils. The need for a device of this nature was made apparent by the differences in the backgrounds and abilities of pupils in a given class or grade which soon came to the attention of the research workers. The difficulties presented by these differences, when pupils were expected to achieve identical mastery of their assignments, brought about a movement to group pupils in a manner that would eliminate the differences. Tests were developed to determine pupil achievement and their probable rate of learning in advance of teaching. On the basis of the test data, teaching groups were formed in which the obstacles to learning presented by the pupils were made as nearly identical as possible. Thus, sixteen-year-old pupils might find themselves in a group composed largely of twelve-year-olds because all of them had approximately the same level of mastery. When segregated in this manner, one group in elementary algebra might demonstrate an ability to master daily assignments of such a length that they could readily cover the entire course in 1 semester. Another group, however, might require 3 semesters to achieve the same goal. Some schools, therefore, found it desirable to promote pupils at the end of every half year. Thus homogeneous grouping and midyear promotions made it possible to reduce the range of individual differences present in a given class.

Schools have also assumed a larger measure of responsibility for supervising the pupil's study activity. There is evidence to show that in many instances failure to master subject matter is due to ineffective study habits. Pupils left to their own devices, in the traditional manner, simply do not happen to develop good study techniques. This fact, together with the change in the home conditions of the modern secondary-school population, have forced the schools to provide study facilities in school and under school supervision. A common device used is to provide study periods in the pupil's daily program. Less frequently, special rooms are provided and supervised by teachers who are trained in the development of good study techniques. In other cases, special study guides are provided by the subject-matter teacher as part of the assignment. Less frequently, the recitation period has been lengthened in order that the teacher may use part of the period to guide the attack the pupils are to make on the assignment that has been given.

There are innovations, too, affecting the recitation phase of the daily-assignment pattern. Improved forms of checking on the pupils through questions have been developed. The shift from fact questions to thought questions is indicative of this modern trend. Also, better drill techniques have been developed and audio-visual aids have come to occupy an important place among the recitation activities. Teachers are showing a tendency to withdraw into the background as the pupils assume a larger share of responsibility for both planning and conducting their learning activities. Finally, the appraisal of pupil progress, formerly a major purpose of the "recitation," is being relegated to the position of a special function. Its nature in relation to the daily-assignment procedures will be given special treatment in Chap. 8.

SUMMARY

Teaching procedures based upon the daily assignment were developed, in the main, as a result of three major movements in education. The first movement, known as the classical tradition, sought to develop the mind as a tool to aid man in his search for the good life. This development was to be achieved by means of the mental exercise afforded by the study of a list of subjects made up chiefly of languages and mathematics. The teacher prescribed amounts of study materials for the learner in quantities commensurate with his ability. These the learner mastered as best he could against the time when he would be called upon to recite what he had learned.

The second movement sought to educate by transmitting to the learner the knowledge which, it was thought, would lead to right action. A nineteenth-century philosopher and educator, John Frederick Herbart, devised procedures by means of which he thought the transmission operation might best be accomplished. In the hands of some of his followers in America, this procedure was developed into a formal, five-step teaching pattern by means of which segments of subject matter, each one small enough to be mastered in one lesson, were introduced into the mind of the learner. This pattern was repeated day after day until the prescribed body of knowledge had been acquired by the learner.

The third influence came from the scientific movement in psychology and education. On the theory that learning consists of establishing new neural pathways in the central nervous system, teaching became a process of presenting selected sensory stimuli and of controlling the responses to be fixed by means of rewards and punishment. This procedure also called for the subdivision of curricular materials into small fragments, only one of which would occupy the learner's attention at a given time. The necessity of drilling what had previously been learned, for the sake of retention; the need to set the stage for the new learning; and the need for a technique for establishing the desired response led to the development of a pattern of teaching that was frequently used again and again.

From these three movements there has emerged a pattern of teaching consisting of three basic steps—the assignment, the study period, and the recitation. This pattern has been fitted into the conventional class period in such a way that its repetition each day is an accepted practice in many secondary schools today. The adaptations and refinements that have been made in this pattern in recent years have been concerned, in the main, with improving the devices used in one or another of the three basic steps. Thus, assignments may now be "individualized" and "motivated"; the study activities of pupils may be "supervised"; and the recitation may be featured by the "thought" question and by various forms of "socialized" techniques.

SELECTED REFERENCES

BAGLEY, WILLIAM C.: *The Educative Process*, The Macmillan Company, New York, 1907.

COLVIN, S. S.: *An Introduction to High School Teaching*, The Macmillan Company, New York, 1922.

CUBBERLY, E. P.: *Readings in the History of Education*, Houghton Mifflin Company, Boston, 1920.

DEWEY, JOHN: *Democracy and Education*, Chap. V, The Macmillan Company, New York, 1916.

DOUGLASS, HARL R.: *Modern Methods in High School Teaching*, Houghton Mifflin Company, Boston, 1926.

HERBART, JOHN FREDERICK: *Outline of Educational Doctrine*, trans. by Alexis F. Lange, The Macmillan Company, New York, 1904.

MCMURRY, CHARLES A., and MCMURRY, FRANK M.: *The Method of the Recitation*, The Macmillan Company, New York, 1909.

MONROE, PAUL: *Founding of the American Public School System*, Vol. I, The Macmillan Company, New York, 1940.

PARKER, SAMUEL CHESTER: *A Textbook in the History of Modern Elementary Education*, Ginn & Company, Boston, 1912.

SANDWICH, RICHARD L.: *How to Study*, D. C. Heath and Company, Boston, 1915.

STORMIZAND, MARTIN J.: *Progressive Methods of Teaching*, Houghton Mifflin Company, Boston, 1924.

STRAYER, GEORGE D., and NORSWORTHY, NAOMI: *How to Teach*, The Macmillan Company, New York, 1917.

THAYER, V. T.: *The Passing of the Recitation*, D. C. Heath and Company, Boston, 1928.

THORNDIKE, EDWARD L.: *The Elements of Psychology*, A. G. Seiler, New York, 1907.

———: *The Principles of Teaching*, A. G. Seiler, New York, 1906.

WAPLES, DOUGLAS: *Procedures in High School Teaching*, The Macmillan Company, New York, 1924.

WHITNEY, WILLIAM T.: *The Socialized Recitation*, A. S. Barnes and Company, New York, 1915.

WILSON, H. B., and WILSON, G. M.: *The Motivation of School Work*, Houghton Mifflin Company, Boston, 1916.

Chapter 7. THE DAILY–ASSIGNMENT
METHOD IN ACTION

A modern critic has referred to teaching based on the daily assignment and its familiar corollary, the recitation, as a type of instruction "which was characterized by assignments in daily installments, identical demands upon all pupils, identification of ground covered with genuine learning, and docility and passivity in reproducing for the teacher the information contained 'in the book.' " [1] Out of consideration for the many conscientious teachers who use what is known as "the recitation method" with good results today, it must be added that Thayer was referring specifically to the teaching of one hundred years ago. Furthermore, if one assumes that education is undertaken to develop the powers or facilities of the mind, it is only reasonable to look upon learning materials as a series of mental gymnastics through which the learner must progress exercise by exercise. Or if education is regarded as the acquisition of a particular body of facts and skills thought necessary for successful living, then textbooks and courses of study can be expected to arrange those materials in clearly defined series to facilitate their mastery in a systematic and efficient manner, presumably in easy installments. Either view leads quite logically to a second assumption, namely, that the educational needs of all pupils are served by a curriculum and a method that are identical for all.

Whenever the daily-assignment method is used, the various subject-matter sequences that constitute the curriculum are arranged in the order of the difficulty of the component parts, proceeding from the simple to the complex. This makes it possible for pupils to move up the educational ladder until they have achieved to the limits of their abil-

[1] V. T. Thayer, *The Passing of the Recitation*, p. 27, D. C. Heath and Company, Boston, 1928.

ity. The attack upon the subject matter is by groups of pupils rather than by individuals, and for that reason learning is frequently competitive with the rewards going to the most able. Learning is an individual matter only in the sense that the progress of a given pupil is measured in terms of the ground he personally has covered.

Characteristics of the daily-assignment method. The familiar assign-study-recite pattern followed by those who seek to educate by leading the pupil through a specific body of subject matter, whether it consists of exercise materials or of scientific facts, lends certain distinctive characteristics to the teaching process. For example, there is a tendency for the teaching pattern to be repeated in its entirety from class meeting to class meeting. This usually means that the pattern is repeated each day, on the secondary-school level, even though it is begun on one day and concluded on the next. The work for each day in each subject is started by a teacher-made assignment, followed by a period of independent work by the pupils, and concluded with some form of recitation of the lesson assigned.

A second characteristic is observed in the school's preoccupation with subject matter rather than with the well-being and contentment of the pupils. This does not mean that the teachers are inhuman but rather that teaching success is measured by the speed and thoroughness with which the pupils cover the ground designated for them. Courses of study, textbooks, achievement tests, and other devices are prepared and used on the assumption that all pupils are to master the same body of subject matter. A group of pupils which has progressed to a given point in the curriculum will be expected to move on to the next item of subject matter as a group and not as individuals each with a different need.

Finally, the learning activities associated with the daily assignment center rather closely around the person of the teacher. The teacher is regarded as the custodian of the cultural heritage. It is he who is responsible for measuring out the new lesson and seeing to it that each pupil does the work. He is in charge of the learning situation and is responsible for setting up conditions that will insure the best pupil progress.

Good teaching, as judged by the above considerations, will of necessity be organized around the three major parts of the daily-assignment method. That is, teaching consists of planning and making the assignment, providing suitable conditions for study, and conducting the recitation in such a way that a reliable estimate of the progress made by the group may be secured. The three parts of this basic pattern are considered separately in the discussion that follows.

THE ASSIGNMENT

Planning the assignment. Inasmuch as daily-assignment procedures are used to help the learner cover a definite body of subject matter, the planning of instruction must begin with the curricula, courses of study, and textbooks that point out the materials to be studied. If teachers were free to take up whatever subject matter has greatest appeal at the moment, the educative process might lack unity. If the educational effort is to yield maximum returns to the pupil and to society, the work of all the teachers with whom a given pupil has contact must be coordinated. A particular lesson is merely a small part of the total educational effort made in behalf of a given pupil, and the teacher must approach the task of planning the assignment properly oriented to the larger school program. This orientation is achieved, in part, by means of curricula, which list the subjects that contribute to the achievement of a particular educational or vocational objective; courses of study, which list the items of subject matter to be taken up in each of the several subjects in a curriculum; and basic textbooks which contain the study materials with which the pupils are to deal.

In large school systems, the classroom teacher normally plays a minor role in planning the curriculum, the courses of study, or in selecting the textbooks to be used. Specially appointed curriculum committees generally are assigned these functions. The committees may work directly under the supervision of the superintendent or of a curriculum expert employed by the school system on either a permanent or a temporary basis. In a few states, New York for example, curricula and courses of study are planned for state-wide use. Texas and a number of other states specify the textbooks that are to be used in each approved subject. California provides both course outlines and textbooks with some provisions for local autonomy. Many states, however, leave curricular matters in the hands of the county or local school district, and in the smaller schools the teacher may have nothing more tangible to guide his planning than the textbooks used by his predecessor. In such cases, the textbook is the course of study, and the pupils will be expected to "cover the book" unless the teacher can justify desired omissions or additions in the eyes of the school authorities, the parents, and the pupils.

A teacher may expect a limited degree of freedom from the prescribed course outlines or textbooks in almost every school. The amount of deviation permitted will depend upon the attitude of the school authorities and the confidence the teacher has inspired through the exercise of good judgment in the past. The inclination to disregard curricular restrictions, which may tempt new teachers rather strongly, should be tempered by the consideration that the activities of a given teacher represent a definite part of a larger coordinated effort. Failure on the part of any one teacher to cover the ground that has been assigned to him may work hardships on the pupils and the other teachers for as long as that class remains in school.

Planning the Work for the Year. Planning by the classroom teacher, then, begins with the course of study or the textbook that designates the subject matter to be covered in the course. In the interest of efficiency, the materials should be divided in such a way that the work will be distributed evenly over the semester or the year. If a basic textbook is to be used in a rather mechanical fashion, the distribution may be made by counting the number of pages in the textbook and dividing by the number of class meetings. In the 36-week school year, there are, theoretically, 180 class periods provided for a given subject. The experienced teacher knows, however, that from 10 to 20 will be lost due to examinations, holidays, and a variety of other causes, and these will reduce the total number of class meetings accordingly. By a process of simple division it is seen that a class can be expected to proceed through an 800-page textbook at the rate of from four to six pages per lesson. It does not follow that this number of pages must be assigned for each lesson, but assignments that include less than this daily quota of reading must be compensated for by assignments that include more pages, if the average is to be maintained. There are, of course, other forms of teaching based on daily assignments that are not merely textbook learning. Teachers who employ them must, nevertheless, consider the year's work as a whole and plan a time schedule that will provide for complete coverage and a uniform pace.

The topics in English composition recommended in the New Hampshire Program of Studies for grade 9 illustrate what is covered in a course of study. That list of topics includes:

1. Sentence work.
   Continued war on sentence fragments and the comma fault. Practice in joining short sentences into well-built longer ones. Accurate use of connectives.
2. Personal experiences, incidents, and anecdotes.
   Autobiographies.
3. Simple explanations.
4. Letter writing.
   a. Requests and excuses connected with school life.
   b. Explaining mistakes or difficulties in a business transaction.
5. Precise writing, based on simple expository paragraphs.
6. Paragraph themes, developing the conception of the paragraph as a structural unit. War on the babyish sentence paragraph.
7. Simple outlining.
8. Practice in writing simple, personal book reviews, considering the class as the audience.
9. Creative work.
   a. Guided attempts at verse writing for abler pupils.
   b. Contributions to a school or class publication.[2]

The ninth-grade English teacher in New Hampshire must decide at the beginning of the school year which of the above topics is to be studied first and the probable order in which the others will be taken up. A tentative time schedule should be formulated that provides not only for each topic, but also for examinations, tests, field trips, enrichment or special activities, and any other matters that are to be included in the course. Laying out the year's work can be done with the aid of the school calendar, a copy of which usually can be secured from the principal or superintendent before the beginning of the school year.

The Daily Lesson Plan. In laying out the work, the teacher theoretically should plan the topic to be covered or the objective to be reached in each class meeting for the entire year. However, few teachers have the fortitude to plan so long in advance, and it is the accepted practice to

[2] "English," *Program of Studies Recommended for the Public Schools of New Hampshire, Grades VII to XII*, Part II, p. 110, State Board of Education, Concord, N.H., 1938.

lay out the details of the daily assignments for only 1 or 2 weeks in advance.

Each assignment should be clearly defined if the teaching is to be effective. That is, the teacher must first decide what objective is to be reached on a given day, and then select the activities that are most likely to bring success. Hence, the plan for each day should begin with the statement of a major problem or aim of the lesson. Statements typical of such an aim or problem are: "To develop the idea of equality before the law," "To learn to bisect an angle," or "How do catalytic agents work." Next, the plan should list the activities of the teacher to be engaged in to secure the desired outcome. Under the heading of teacher activities may be included a very brief description of a demonstration to be made or an outline of related information to be given. A few questions may also be included which can be asked if needed to stimulate discussion or interest. Finally, there should be a list of pupil activities. Under pupil activities may be listed the reading to be done, the investigations to be made, the problems to be worked, or other activities that will help the pupil achieve the objective set up for him.

A skeleton plan is sufficient when laying out the daily assignments for several weeks in advance. Two skeleton plans are given below. The more detailed teaching plans can then be developed from these.

PLAN 1

Major Problem: How may heat be transferred?

Teacher Activity: Do the experiment on page 242, making sure that the terms "conduction," "connection," and "radiation" are understood. Discuss good and poor insulators.

Pupil Activity: Read pages 240–246. List examples of various kinds of heat transfer. Which is most common? Make a list of conductors and classify them as either good or bad.

PLAN 2

Major Problem: How are fires extinguished?

Teacher Activity: Stress the fact that fires are put out by either lowering the kindling temperature or by removing the supply of oxygen. Take the extinguisher from the hall and take it apart for the class. Allow some sulphuric acid to react on some baking soda. If you decide to make a model extinguisher, be sure that you have an apron and that you point the nozzle away from the pupils.

Pupil Activity: Read pages 269–276. Study the picture on page 273 and list the fire hazards. Find out what fire hazards exist in your town. List several types of fires and the methods used to fight them. What equipment does a modern fire truck carry? [3]

The teaching plans which are developed from these skeleton outlines need not be elaborate if the teacher has had ample experience and is thoroughly acquainted with the subject matter. Student teachers and other individuals, with limited experience, of course, need to plan in greater detail. For them, the daily plan should outline procedures for reviewing the previous work, motivating the class for the new work, making the assignment, conducting the recitation including key questions to be asked and important points to be discussed, the testing to be done, as well as the time budget to be followed if each activity is to receive the attention it deserves. Help in preparing the detailed teaching plans is usually given in special methods courses and in connection with the supervised teaching experience. For that reason, this aspect of planning needs no lengthy discussion here. One may say, however, that adequate preparation will prevent the embarrassing pauses that sometimes occur when the inexperienced teacher frantically searches for something to say. Secondary-school pupils are quick to seize upon these pauses not only to cover up their own embarrassment, but also to introduce some interesting distractions to relieve the boredom of a slow-moving recitation.

Making the assignment. A well-made assignment is one in which adequate attention has been given to three points. First, each pupil must understand exactly what he is expected to accomplish. Second, he must have a worth-while reason for doing the work, that is, he must accept the reason for the assignment as a justifiable one in his case. Finally, he must know how to go about doing the job that has been set before him. While many assignments are made every day which do not meet one or more of these three requirements, it is reasonable to assume that attention to them will result in more efficient learning.

When making the assignment, the pupils are told what it is they are expected to do to accomplish the day's objective. Too frequently, making the assignment has consisted merely of a statement that the

[3] These plan outlines were prepared by Stanley Sprague, Rockville High School, Rockville, Conn., and are available in *Curriculum Laboratory Studies*, Bulletin 15, p. 19, University of Connecticut, Storrs, Conn., May, 1942.

new lesson will cover the next four or six pages in the textbook and that the pupil will be held responsible for the mastery of every fact contained within those pages. Good teachers, however, have come to think of learning as something broader than mere textbook memorizing. Such teachers direct the attention of the students to special topics for investigation, opportunities for making practical use of the subject matter that is being studied, and other activities selected to develop not merely an encyclopedic knowledge but rather an understanding of the over-all objectives of the course. They recognize pupil interest as an important factor in learning. Inasmuch as interests grow out of the experiences of the learner, good teachers try to relate the lesson at hand to the background of the pupils. The process by which teachers attempt to create pupil interest in the subject matter is called "motivation."

To motivate the class to do the assignment, the teacher may choose to point out its relationship to an interest or concern the pupils may have expressed in the past. If so, it is desirable to make this relationship as immediate and direct as possible. If no direct connection can be established between the subject matter and the natural interest of the pupils, teachers sometimes resort to less desirable methods of getting them to do the work. Competition for grades, prizes for good performance, sarcasm, extra assignments are forms of reward and punishment used for this type of motivation.

When the class as a whole has accepted the teacher's objective as a necessary one, the pupils are ready to be told how that objective may be reached. Usually the teacher will indicate special topics to be investigated, problems to be solved, questions to be answered, pages read, and supplementary activities to be undertaken before the next class meeting. When necessary, the pupils should be told how to secure the information they will need, where it is located, and how to organize their findings so the information secured will be available to the class at the next meeting.

The importance of the assignment has led to long and bitter debates over the question of when it should be made. One group of teachers has argued that the assignment is the most important activity in the entire teaching pattern, and for that reason it must be unhurried. It should be made, therefore, before the recitation activities covering the assignment made on the preceding day are begun. Others argue with equal logic that the new assignment should be built upon the work that the class has done with the previous assignment. It is claimed that the teacher cannot determine what the class has done with any accuracy until the end of the recitation. For that reason the assignment should be made at the end of the hour, when it is possible to direct the study of the pupils along the particular lines that require additional attention as revealed in the recitation. Obviously, both groups have good reasons to support their points of view. It seems reasonable, therefore, to suggest that the teacher must use his own judgment and make the assignment at a time that seems most opportune in view of the progress of the class and the particular subject matter to be dealt with. When the assignment is left until the end of the hour, it is apparent that the teacher must take extra precautions to insure that interesting class discussions do not infringe upon the time that has been budgeted for the assignment.

THE STUDY PERIOD

The study phase of the daily-assignment pattern is closely related to the assignment, for it is in this stage that the pupil attempts to perform the tasks that the teacher has set for him. Study activities fall into two classes. In one group are the activities of pupils who received little in the way of direction in meeting the assignment. When teachers limit the directions they give the pupils to indicating which problems must be worked, what lines must be translated, or the kind of composition that must be prepared before the next recitation, pupils are left to their own resources to achieve the desired results. Their ingenuity in enlisting the aid of parents has been well publicized in the comic strips. Pupils have also discovered the advantages of cooperating on assignments that are supposed to be done individually. It is a common practice for pupils to exchange answers, to copy compositions, and to write translations between the lines of the language textbooks. These practices obviously are not the most profitable forms of study activities, but pupils will employ them as long as the teaching method consists merely in the setting of tasks and the subsequent checking upon the answers given the next day.

In an effort to overcome undesirable features that frequently result from undirected study, several procedures have been developed to give greater assistance to the students. It was found, for example, that many students are unable to pick out of an assignment the items that are important. This is true chiefly because they have no adequate overview or perspective that enables them to judge what is important information and what is insignificant. Thus, their only recourse is to treat each item of subject matter as though it were as important as any other and to try to memorize all items. To avoid this unnecessary waste of effort, teachers employing the daily-assignment method have found it desirable to list key topics or questions while making the assignments. The pupil can then direct his efforts to mastering the significant items with relatively little attention to the less important ones. When teachers attempt to direct the study activity of pupils, the term "supervised study" is applied to their procedures.

Pupils need a place to study. Two aspects of supervised study merit special attention. The first involves the responsibility of the school in providing the pupils with an opportunity to study. In the early history of American secondary education when the pupils came almost exclusively from homes where intellectual pursuits were an important part of the home activities, the school could ignore with reasonable success the study phase of the learning process. This can no longer be done, for the high-school population now includes pupils who come from homes where the parents are not in sympathy with the program of formal education, or who provide no physical environment within which study activities can be carried on with success. With the increase in the school enrollments, teachers have found it necessary to give greater attention to providing an opportunity for study at school. The problem is twofold, for it consists of finding time for study within a limited and crowded schedule as well as a place for study in an overcrowded building. The problem is not a simple one, for although the conventional schedule provides from two to four study periods in the pupil's daily program, school buildings have not been planned to provide suitable places where the pupils may spend these periods. This fact is demonstrated by the number of instances in which pupils must study in a classroom where a recitation is in progress, or in an auditorium that was designed for listening and not for reading.

One solution that is gaining in popularity is to increase the length of the conventional 40- or 45-minute period to 60 minutes by reducing the number of periods in the school day. While this reduces the number of study periods in the pupil's program, it does provide him with study time during each period of the day. Teachers are expected to use the extra time, not in longer recitations, but rather in helping the pupil prepare the new assignments. This arrangement has the advantage of enabling the pupil to go to work upon the new assignment while the directions given by the teacher are fresh in his mind. Furthermore, the teacher is present to give any additional help that is needed at the time it is needed. The teacher can also provide in the classroom a variety of study aids that would not be available to the pupil if he were compelled to make his preparation in the auditorium, in another classroom, or at home. Under this arrangement, it is necessary and possible for every pupil to make some preparation for each recitation. That obviously has not been true whenever pupils have been allowed to make their preparations in the study halls or outside school hours.

The most serious weakness in this plan over other procedures is the inclination of teachers to use too large a part of the period for the recitation. Teachers, who for many years have spent the entire class period in questioning their pupils on the subject matter of the previous assignment, frequently find considerable difficulty in convincing themselves that they are teaching when any other form of activity, including study, is taking place in their classroom.

Pupils need training in how to study. A second aspect of supervised study is the training that is given pupils in how to study. Numerous research studies have been conducted in recent years that demonstrate beyond question the benefit this type of help can be to the pupil. In one experiment conducted on the college level, two groups of students, doing poor work, were matched to see what effects would result from special instruction in study techniques. Before the experiment was begun only 25 per cent of group 1 were doing passing work. At the same time, 27 per cent of group 2 were doing passing work. These data show that the two groups were evenly matched at the time the experiment was begun. During the course of the experiment, group 1 received special instruction in how to study, whereas group 2 received no such help. At the end of the experiment the percentage of the students in group 1 who were doing passing work had been increased from 25 per cent to 70 per cent. In contrast, group 2, which had received no special help, increased from 27 per cent to only 34 per cent. Because of the controlled conditions under which this experiment was conducted, it is logical to conclude that the improvement made by the students in group 1 as compared with the students in group 2 was due primarily to the instruction in study techniques given them.[4]

It is impossible at this point to engage in a lengthy discussion of the manner in which teachers may improve the study habits of their pupils. Any teacher who needs help of this nature may secure it by consulting one of the several recent textbooks in general or educational psychology.[5] This problem has also received the attention of special investigators, and some textbooks and manuals have been prepared especially for the use of high-school pupils.[6] In general, study aids of this nature include helping the pupil to recognize the problem with which he is expected to deal, to locate information that is pertinent to the problem, and to draw valid conclusions from the information secured.

Helping the Pupil Recognize the Problem. The pupil's attention may be directed to the major aspects of the assignment by means of guide questions and well-selected topics. Teachers sometimes distribute guide sheets for this purpose. Obviously, as time goes on, the teacher should help the pupil develop the ability to formulate his own guides. Sometimes this can be done by directing the class to skim over the assignment for the purpose of picking out what seem to be the major topic or topics discussed. This can be followed with a more careful reading of the assignment for the purpose of gaining a more complete understanding of these major items.

Helping the Pupil Locate Information. Skill in locating information can be developed by making a variety of sources available in the classroom and study halls. Then, if the pupil is directed by the assignment to consult one or more of these sources, he will gradually learn to know where to turn for desired information. When he has become acquainted with standard sources of information, such as encyclopedias, textbooks, journals, and other standard references, it is relatively simple for him to learn to find these sources in their usual places in the library, or wherever they may be kept. The ability to locate information is a skill that grows through practice. Until schools assume responsibility for developing that skill, they will continue to graduate pupils who in later

[4] S. L. Pressey, *Research Adventures in University Teaching*, Public School Publishing Company, Bloomington, Ill., 1927.

[5] For example, see Floyd L. Ruch, *Psychology and Life*, new ed., Chap. X, Scott, Foresman & Company, Chicago, 1941.

[6] See Robert W. Frederick and others, *How to Study*, D. Appleton-Century Company, Inc., New York, 1938.

years are pitifully helpless when they need to become informed about a personal or social problem. A good teacher can and will do a great deal toward improving the quality of the civic participation and personal development of the graduates by developing habits of study and inquiry in the classroom.

Helping the Pupil Evaluate Information. In addition to learning how to locate information, the pupils need to develop the ability to evaluate the data with which they come in contact. This function has two aspects. The first aspect deals with determining which data are pertinent to the problem at hand and of ignoring data that are irrelevant. In an assignment suitable for one day's work, there is seldom time to deal with more than one or possibly two clearly defined and worthwhile aims. When the assignment is made, the pupil should be made aware of the particular goal that is to be accomplished. If the aim has been clearly stated and is fully understood, the pupil should experience little difficulty in pulling out of the materials he studies the information that relates to or illuminates the point that he seeks to understand. If difficulty is experienced, special drill may be needed to develop the ability to see logical relationships. For the purpose of drill lists of miscellaneous facts can be prepared in mimeograph form. The pupil may then be told to pick out of such a list the facts or data that relate to a given subject. By varying the length and complexity of the lists as well as the complexity of the subject matter, gradations in the difficulty of the drill may be achieved. Pupil progress in developing this skill may be measured by means of evaluation techniques perfected by Ralph W. Tyler and associates in connection with the Eighth-year Study.[7]

The second aspect of evaluation calls for discriminating between information that is in the nature of proof and that which is mere opinion. As long as pupils are directed to only one source of information and that source is treated as an authority, there will be little opportunity for pupils to develop the power to discriminate. When several sources are assigned, however, particularly if these have been well selected to present differing points of view, the pupils will be forced to weigh what they read with greater care. Subsequent class discussions should then focus attention on these differences with a view to evaluating the data and conclusions presented by the several authors. Experi-

[7] See Eugene R. Smith, Ralph W. Tyler, *et al.*, *Appraising and Recording Student Progress*, Harper & Brothers, New York, 1942.

ences of this type will encourage pupils to challenge the authority of the text whenever there is reason to doubt the validity of a statement of fact given or of a conclusion drawn.

Helping Pupils to See the Personal Value of Subject Matter. Finally, the study of pupils will be more effective if the subject matter of the assignment is related to their personal interests. Psychologists learned long ago that pupils will study harder and retain more information, if the subject with which they are dealing has a personal reference. The pupil who expects to become an aviator can be made to look upon mathematics as a useful tool. The girl who expects to become a fashion expert can hope some day to visit Paris and other fashion centers, and may wish, therefore, to learn a foreign language. The skillful teacher will learn to know the personal ambitions of the pupils and make an effort to point out by special topics for investigation whatever personal interests the assignment may hold for a given pupil.

THE RECITATION

The recitation derives its name from the practice of calling upon the pupil to repeat or to "re-cite" to the teacher the lesson previously assigned to be learned. One hundred years ago, the recitation was a formidable procedure. The textbooks frequently were nothing but lists of questions each of which was followed by the accepted answer which the teacher expected the pupil to memorize. When a suitable study time had elapsed, the teacher, with book in hand, called upon the pupil to recite verbatim what he had been told to learn. No deviation from the answer in the printed text was permitted, for the object in learning was not merely to gather information, but also to develop the mind, particularly the faculty of memory. The discipline was strict and the procedure highly formalized. There are persons living today who can repeat the "rule of three" and many other rules of arithmetic and grammar, word for word, as these appeared in their school books 50 or more years ago, even though they have had no occasion to use these rules in the meantime.

The mastery type of recitation activities. The practice of testing the pupil's mastery of the lesson by means of memory questions is, fortunately, disappearing from the educational scene. However, the recitation period continues to be a prominent aspect of the instructional pattern wherever assignments are made on a daily basis. In addition to the traditional verbal testing, the activities carried on in the recitation period may be for the purpose (*a*) of reenforcing the pupil's understanding of the subject matter, (*b*) of supplementing the knowledge which the pupil has acquired through his own efforts, (*c*) of developing through a teacher-directed drill a skill that is essential to further pupil growth, or (*d*) of enriching the pupil's experience by developing an appreciation of some phase of his physical or social environment.

Testing the Mastery of Subject Matter. The recall question, long used to test the pupil's mastery of the subject matter, is gradually being replaced by the thought question. This shift reflects the conviction, growing in educational circles, that it is more important for the pupil to understand the implications for personal-social living contained in the assignment than it is for him to memorize the specific information with which the assignment happens to deal. Thought questions serve to focus attention upon such implications. Through carefully selected questions, the pupil can be stimulated to see relationships that might not be apparent to him from even a careful reading of the assigned materials. The shift from memory to thought questions is reflected in the number of questions asked which begin with the words, *Why, Why do you think, In what way might, How, and How might* as compared with questions that begin with *Who, When,* and *What.* Supervisors have been known to rate their teachers by the ratio of thought questions to fact questions used in the recitation.

The effectiveness of a recitation is sometimes judged by the number of pupils in the class who participate. It is relatively easy for a few eager and intelligent pupils to monopolize the entire class period. When this is allowed to happen, the remainder of the class is forced by sheer boredom into daydreaming or less passive forms of rebellion. There is reason to doubt that the pupil of low intelligence should be called upon to recite as frequently as the near genius, but he should be made to feel that he has a part to play in the class activities. The teacher can check on the range of pupil participation by placing a mark by the name of each pupil as he is called upon or volunteers a contribution.

The nature of a good recitation as judged by one school of thought was described by the late Professor Bagley as follows:

There were no pumping questions put forth with the faith of the fisher-man that if one casts successively various kinds of flies one will sooner or later get a nibble. In fact, there were no questions at all. The pupils were trained to study their assignments in terms of relatively large topics. When the time for recitation came, the teacher would state one of the topics. Then he would pause, perhaps for two minutes, before calling upon a pupil. No one knew who would be called upon, and during this interval every member of the group was busily engaged in reviewing his knowledge in order to give a good account of himself if he should happen to be the victim. Finally the teacher would call upon a pupil and the latter would rise and begin the discussion. His business was to talk through that topic in a clear, straightforward fashion—not to talk over it or under it or around it in the hope that a few questions from the teacher would set him straight. Did his fellows listen to him? You may be sure that they did, for no one knew at what point the teacher would interrupt the discussion and direct someone else to proceed with the same topic. Did the first pupil now sit back with a consoling consciousness that it was all over and that he could rest on his laurels? Not if he had been a week under that teacher's instruction and dis-cipline, for by that time he would know that a minute or two minutes or five minutes after he sat down, he might be called upon to continue the discussion. Attention in that teacher's classes hovered around 100 percent from the beginning to the end of each period.[8]

Supplementing the Pupil's Knowledge. Sometimes it is desirable to supplement, during the recitation period, the information made avail-able to the pupils in the materials of the assignment. An informal talk by some member of the community, a member of the teaching staff, or even a pupil who happens to be well informed on the subject may serve this end. Audio-visual aids have special value for this purpose. The effectiveness of a class activity undertaken to provide supple-mentary information obviously depends upon the advance preparation that has been made. When it is planned to use recordings or films, the teacher must arrange, sometimes weeks in advance, for the materials to be available on the desired date. Similar arrangements must be made to have the projection or other necessary equipment reserved for the use of the class at the desired time. In some instances it is even neces-sary to arrange for someone to operate the equipment or to use a spe-

8 William C. Bagley, "The Textbook in American Education," *School and Society*, XXXIII:358–360, Mar. 14, 1931.

cially equipped room. A class activity of this type obviously cannot be undertaken on the spur of the moment.

Providing Drill. The need for drill activities in the recitation is, according to some writers, too frequently overlooked by teachers on the secondary level. The chief purpose of drill is to fix some fact or skill firmly upon each member of the class. Drill should be provided particularly when there is a need for the pupils to acquire some motor skill or system of facts and ideas before they can deal successfully with the work that is to follow. For example, pupils cannot progress in geometry until they have acquired a few fundamental construction techniques. Nor can they learn to read and write a foreign language until they have acquired a basic vocabulary. Either the construction techniques or the foreign language vocabulary can be fixed rapidly and reliably by means of well-selected, teacher-directed drill activities that are properly motivated.

The motivation of drill is necessary to secure pupil interest and attention. Progress in mastery is immeasurably accelerated when the pupil has accepted the skill or fact to be acquired as worth while and is willing to make its acquisition his primary concern for the moment. Elementary-school pupils sometimes require artificial types of motivation, but secondary-school pupils, because of their different psychological make-up and greater freedom of choice of subject matter, usually can be made to realize the intrinsic value. Showing the relationship between the fact or skill to be mastered and its future use may be adequate motivation for secondary-school pupils. If no such relationship can be demonstrated, it is very doubtful that the fact or skill in question is important enough to merit special drill. Review drills can be motivated if they are based upon the errors actually made by the pupils.

Drill should be teacher directed to insure the highest possible degree of mastery in the shortest time possible. Several guides to effective learning through drill have been formulated on the basis of experimental studies. A sizable body of literature is available on the subject. A brief though excellent discussion of practical guides for drill appears in a publication that was written for student and beginning teachers. It includes a list of techniques for securing correct responses during the drill period that has special significance at this point. The list is as follows:

a. Be sure pupils understand the exact form which they are to repeat.

b. Supervise all drill closely until the right habit is established, since this step insures correcting errors before habits become fixed.

c. Make sure that pupils have not forgotten the process since the last drill.

d. Establish one skill before introducing another.

e. Proceed slowly in the early stages of habit formation.

f. Make accuracy the main issue at first.

g. Do not attempt to change habits already formed unless you are absolutely sure they are bad.

h. Form habits in the way they are to be used.

i. Follow diagnosis with sufficient drill on the specific difficulty to overcome it.

j. Do not prolong drill on a specific difficulty to the point where pupils lose sight of the whole process of which this difficulty is a part.[9]

Developing Appreciations. Class activities may also be provided to develop an appreciation of some aspect of the physical or social environment or an attitude toward a particular pattern of behavior. A great deal has been written about the need for this kind of education but relatively little has appeared in print that is helpful in developing the kind of instruction required. Authors sometimes write derisively of the inclination of the average man to be swayed more easily by emotion and the mores than by reason. Yet the schools have assumed very little responsibility for giving direction to the pupil's expression of feelings and emotions.

Not so many years ago it was assumed that appreciations, attitudes, and ideals could be placed upon the level of strong feelings or emotions if the attempt to develop them was started from an intellectual level. Thus, the poetry of Milton, the plays of Shakespeare, the music of Beethoven, and the pictures of Rembrandt were presented in dissected form. Pupils were introduced to the techniques of literary and artistic workmanship, the variations in style, and the life and thoughts of the masters before they were permitted to have contact with the masterpieces themselves. How many pupils have had the experience of going to a music appreciation class anxious to hear a recording of a well-known symphony played by a famous orchestra, only to have the

---

[9] Raleigh Schorling, *Student Teaching*, p. 183, McGraw-Hill Book Company, Inc., New York, 1940.

teacher spend three-fourths of the class time talking about background, theme, counterpoint, and instrumentation; and, as the last straw, of having the playing interrupted by the class bell before the performance had run through the first movement? How many more high-school and college graduates are now actually repelled by Shakespeare, or even Dickens, because these authors are associated with the dullest moments spent in school?

Two guides to the appreciation lesson may be worth mentioning at this point. First, appreciation cannot be an outcome unless the learning process produces enjoyment. This means that the object of appreciation must be on a level capable of being enjoyed by the pupils. It is possible that certain aspects of Shakespeare are capable of inducing pleasant associations in the minds of high-school pupils. It is almost certain that the aspects suitable to this age group are not identical with the aspects that are pleasurable to the mature literary critics. Is it not better for pupils to be emotionally aroused in favor of acts expressing courage and social integrity even though such acts are presented in comic-strip form, than to have the pupils react unfavorably to the ideals presented by Lincoln in his Gettysburg Address? The pupil's ability to appreciate the good, the true, and the beautiful must be developed like any other ability, and instruction in this area must be adjusted to the level of the pupil's present status, just as it must in any other form of learning.

The second guide to the development of appreciations, attitudes, and ideals suggests the need for pupil activity. Personal satisfaction for the pupil frequently grows out of his opportunity to apply the desired attitude or ideal with success in his own area of operation. The Boy Scout thrives on the performance of a good deed every day. Free, expressive dancing to music provides kindergarten and even older pupils with a richer musical experience than is afforded by passive listening. Similarly, the principles of good government become live, vital things when they are encountered on the level of a homeroom organization or of a student council. Democratic processes gain value when the pupil discovers that they guarantee to *him* the right to express a dissenting opinion in class or to correct an abuse of his cafeteria privileges. The relationship of the ideal expressed in the textbook to the activities of the athletic field and auditorium is neither self-evident nor inevitable. Practice must be afforded on the teaching-learning level before thoroughgoing loyalties to desirable attitudes and ideals can be expected to show in the pupil's total behavior pattern.

The socialized recitation. The need to supplement subject-matter mastery with opportunities for pupils to experience desirable personal and social living has led to the development of a new form of recitation. This newer type of procedure has been labeled the "socialized recitation." It is undertaken primarily to give the pupils practice in dealing with the subject matter of instruction in a manner that is compatible with satisfactory personal and social living. The proponents of the socializing techniques point out the dictatorial and authoritarian nature of the older, teacher-dominated recitation procedures which too frequently treated the textbook as the infallible and sole source of knowledge. Democratic procedures, on the other hand, portray class instruction as a group effort to find the best possible solution to a common problem. In this search, each member of the group can make a contribution to the common purpose. A division of labor on the basis of a coordinated plan of study may make available a much larger body of information than is possible when all members of the group are expected to confine themselves to the same sources. The techniques of democratic group action make it possible to pool the individual contributions and thus to have a broad basis of information and experience out of which a common understanding or an intelligent conclusion can be drawn. This may bring about a solution to the initial problem that will yield greater individual and group satisfaction than would be possible through any other approach. Socialized techniques, therefore, provide not only for the mastery of subject matter desirable for satisfactory living, but also afford practice in employing the skills necessary to make the information useful.

When the socialized approach is made, the recitation activities tend to lose the characteristics of an oral examination and take on the aspects of a group discussion. Under the skillful direction of the teacher, the pupils are led to look upon the central theme of the new assignment as an issue or problem for which no entirely satisfactory solution has yet been discovered. The assignment leaves room for pupil initiative and planning in drawing upon sources of information other than the textbook. Resourcefulness, ingenuity, and energy are approved and rewarded, and plans for sharing the individual findings are made. An assignment of this nature takes more time than the 2 to 5 minutes traditionally allowed for this purpose. However, the enthusiasm and direct-ness with which at least some of the pupils approach their studies under the socialized recitation plan is ample justification for taking the time needed.

The Formal Socialized Recitation. When a socialized recitation plan is used, the activities of the recitation period itself are undertaken primarily to secure the pooling by the pupils of the information collected individually and to arrive at a common understanding of the aim or solution to the problem set forth in the assignment. The pupils need procedures and techniques that will enable them to achieve these ends through their own efforts as far as possible. They face much the same situation as any group of adults who have met to take action on a common problem and must rely upon the resources of the individuals comprising the group for the information, experience, and skill necessary to find a suitable solution.

Adults have developed a variety of techniques to serve their needs. The New England towns have their town meetings with a moderator, clerk, and a variety of formalized procedures that have been developed over the years to expedite the business at hand. It is natural that class after class has been organized in New England schools along the lines of the town meeting because this is the dominant pattern for adult group action in that area. In other areas of the country, the schools look to the town or city council, the board of aldermen, the county commission, the state legislature, or the national Congress for their pattern of organization and action. Less frequently used patterns are those of the board of directors or the stockholders of a corporation, the chamber of commerce, and the service clubs. These and a large number of other patterns developed by organizations and institutions, when copied by schools, provide a type of socialized recitation activities that is referred to as the "formal" or "institutionalized" type.[10] By means of these activities, pupils can gain skill in using adult forms of group procedures, while dealing with subject matter that is on the level of their intellectual and social development.

The Informal Socialized Recitation. The "informal" [11] types of social-ized recitations place emphasis upon pupil participation comparable, in outward form, to the pleasant exchange of ideas on topics of current

[10] Nelson L. Bossing, *Teaching in Secondary Schools*, p. 499, Houghton Mifflin Company, Boston, 1942.

[11] *Ibid.*, p. 500.

interest that occurs when neighbors meet at the home of a mutual friend on a Sunday afternoon. Whether the discussion is teacher directed or pupil directed, the recitation is conducted in an atmosphere of mutual respect and congeniality, dominated by the attitude that the topic under consideration is worth while for each member present. Informal socialization, in its simplest terms, may mean nothing more than a relaxation of the rigid disciplinary controls that formerly required pupils to "turn, stand, and face the teacher," and "answer in a complete sentence." Furthermore, it assumes that the teacher is a discussion leader rather than a medieval inquisitor bent upon convicting the pupils of evil and misdeeds.

SUMMARY

The daily-assignment method is clearly a pattern of teaching that has been developed to help pupils cover a specific body of subject matter. It consists of three parts, namely, the assignment, the study period, and the recitation. The assignment must be made in such a manner that the pupils know what they are to do, as well as how to go about the assigned tasks. Careful planning by the teacher of the work to be covered each day is necessary not only to insure properly made assignments, but also satisfactory results in the other two stages of the teaching pattern.

Due to the changes in the nature of the pupil population that have occurred in recent years, secondary schools are finding it necessary to give increased attention to the second or study phase of the daily-assignment method. In many instances it has become necessary not only to provide a place for pupils to study, but also to give them instruction in how to study. The lengthening of the class period to 60 minutes is a device that is frequently used for this purpose. Only half of the lengthened period is used for recitation activities, thus making the remaining time available for supervised study activities.

The traditional recitation activities have also undergone some changes. While the recitation phase of the assign-study-recite pattern was developed originally to test the pupil's mastery of subject matter, other objectives have given rise to a variety of activities. Recitation activities now vary with the primary objective of the lesson. While in one instance this may be the mastery of subject matter, in other cases it may be to drill facts or skills previously taught; to develop the appreciation of an object of art, an attitude, or an ideal; or to develop a social skill or understanding. The last type of objective has led to the development of the socialized recitation.

Whatever objective is sought in a given lesson, the teacher must select and direct the activities that are most likely to bring success in that particular undertaking. Learning is largely teacher centered and teacher dominated. This may be good or bad depending upon how closely the teacher's objectives correspond to the real needs of the pupils.

SELECTED REFERENCES

BAGLEY, WILLIAM C.: *The Educative Process,* The Macmillan Company, New York, 1907.

BOOK, WILLIAM F.: *Learning How to Study and Work Effectively,* Ginn & Company, Boston, 1926.

BOSSING, NELSON L.: *Teaching in Secondary Schools,* Houghton Mifflin Company, Boston, 1942.

COLVIN, S. S.: *An Introduction to High School Teaching,* The Macmillan Company, New York, 1922.

DOUGLASS, HARL R.: *Modern Methods in High School Teaching,* Houghton, Mifflin Company, Boston, 1926.

EARHART, LIDA B.: *Types of Teaching,* Houghton Mifflin Company, Boston, 1915.

FREDERICK, ROBERT W., and others: *How to Study,* D. Appleton-Century Company, Inc., New York, 1938.

RISK, THOMAS M.: *Principles and Practices of Teaching in Secondary Schools,* Chap. XVII, American Book Company, New York, 1941.

SANDWICH, RICHARD L.: *How to Study,* D. C. Heath and Company, Boston, 1915.

STORMIZAND, MARTIN J.: *Progressive Methods of Teaching,* Houghton Mifflin Company, Boston, 1924.

STRAYER, GEORGE D., and NORSWORTHY, NAOMI: *How to Teach,* The Macmillan Company, New York, 1917.

THAYER, V. T.: *The Passing of the Recitation,* D. C. Heath and Company, Boston, 1928.

WAPLES, DOUGLAS: *Procedures in High School Teaching,* The Macmillan Company, New York, 1924.

WHITNEY, WILLIAM T.: *The Socialized Recitation,* A. S. Barnes and Company, New York, 1915.

WILSON, H. B., and WILSON, G. M.: *The Motivation of School Work,* Houghton Mifflin Company, Boston, 1916.

Chapter 8. THE APPRAISAL OF PUPIL PROGRESS

IN THE DAILY–ASSIGNMENT METHOD

The point of view was developed in Chap. 5 that the measurement of pupil achievement is basically dependent for its method upon the behaviors of pupils. However, the types of behaviors sought or stressed in a particular school or classroom, as well as the instructional materials and procedures, have much to do with the measurement instruments and techniques employed. It seems desirable, therefore, to review briefly some of the outcomes of behavior sought under the recitation or daily-assignment method of instruction.

Three types of outcomes quoted from Douglass[1] were listed in Chap. 6 as of major importance under the daily-assignment method of instruction—knowledges, interests and attitudes, and skills. Elsewhere in that chapter, reference was made to the factual knowledges, ideas, habits, skills, and attitudes which the schools attempt to transmit to their pupils under the recitation plan. These indications of the behavioral changes sought are background for the treatment of testing procedures which follows.

It is worthy of note that some of the possible types of behavioral changes discussed in Chap. 5 as measurable are neither listed nor implied in the outcomes mentioned above. Although skills, knowledges, and certain tastes and preferences are listed directly, and concepts are perhaps implied, it seems certain that the remaining types of outcomes—understandings and applications—were neither listed nor implied. This is to be expected, for the reason that the philosophical and even psychological foundations of the daily-assignment method placed no emphasis upon understandings and applications as direct instructional outcomes.

[1] Harl R. Douglass, *Modern Methods in High School Teaching*, p. 3, Houghton Mifflin Company, Boston, 1926.

THE METHODS WE USE 161

Testing procedures characteristic of the daily-assignment method. Neither Herbart's four steps in teaching nor Bagley's five-step modification, both of which are referred to in Chap. 6, makes any mention of evaluation in the instructional process. The inclusion of evaluation as an integral part of the instructional process is a product of the last few decades.

The daily-assignment method requires a great degree of teacher responsibility in the evaluation of pupil achievement. Hence, the informal objective test and other less objective classroom or teacher-made tests and procedures are basically important in this instructional plan. Although the standardized test antedated the informal objective test, the methods of informal objective test construction seem to represent the testing theory of the recitation plan most appropriately.

Ruch, in the pioneer book on teacher-made tests,[2] lists the eight steps in objective test construction which are restated and somewhat condensed below:

1. Decide upon the exact scope of the proposed examination, by making a list of the most important topics.
2. Think out very carefully the most significant facts falling under each topic.
3. Arrange the questions falling under each topic in your estimate of their order of importance.
4. Turn the questions into the most appropriate objective test item forms.
5. Decide upon the length of the examination.
6. Select the items under each topic for inclusion in the examination.
7. Arrange the items in ascending order of difficulty according to your best judgment.
8. Check upon the reliability of the examination.

Although Ruch's concern was with the written objective test constructed by the teacher, many of the principles involved in this list may be extended to the traditional or essay examination, the oral examination, and other testing procedures ordinarily used in the daily-assignment method. Admittedly, however, Ruch's steps of procedure are typically embodied very imperfectly in such testing techniques. These

[2] G. M. Ruch, *The Improvement of the Written Examination*, pp. 96–98, Scott, Foresman & Company, Chicago, 1924.

procedures seem to emphasize factual knowledge outcomes above all others and to depend upon course content quite strongly.

Treated in some detail below are the major testing techniques and instruments typically used in the recitation or daily-assignment plan of instruction—oral quizzes, the essay or traditional examination, short written quizzes, the informal objective test, and other types of written work. The last section of the chapter is devoted to teachers' marking practices under the daily-assignment method of instruction.

ORAL QUIZZES

The oral quiz has doubtless been used in education as a means of measuring pupil attainments for centuries. Despite this fact, it serves functions other than that of measurement or very limited measurement functions only, and does not justify the dependence many teachers have placed upon it. The oral quiz as a group measurement technique usually is restricted almost entirely to factual outcomes, which undesirably narrows its usefulness. Moreover, it suffers seriously in reliability and economy of time if its scope is extended beyond the knowledge outcomes. It is highly subjective and lacking in comparability unless examiners are carefully trained in the construction of questions and in the evaluation of the oral responses. In any event, the oral language proficiency and fluency of the pupil and his adjustment to group examination situations largely influence his reactions to oral quizzing.

Horace Mann sounded the death knell of the group oral examination as a satisfactory measuring instrument more than a century ago, when he compared the oral and written examinations for use in the Boston schools.[3] He contrasted the two examining procedures by making the following points in favor of the written examination:

1. It is impartial.
2. It is just to the pupils.
3. It is more thorough than older forms of examinations.
4. It prevents the "officious interference" of the teacher.
5. It "determines beyond appeal or gainsaying, whether the pupils have been faithfully and competently taught."

[3] Otis W. Caldwell and Stuart A. Courtis, *Then and Now in Education: 1845–1923*, Chaps. 1, 3, World Book Company, Yonkers, New York, 1923.

6. It takes away "all possibility of favoritism."
7. It makes the information obtained available to all.
8. It enables all to appraise the ease or difficulty of the questions.

Major ideas presented by Horace Mann in these statements are that the oral examination of groups: (*a*) makes impossible the testing of all pupils with the same questions, (*b*) is very uneconomical of time, (*c*) permits of teacher interference and favoritism, (*d*) fails to show whether or not teaching has been well done, (*e*) leaves no permanent record of results, and (*f*) fails to control ease or difficulty of questions.

Even when the oral examination is considered for use with only one pupil at a time, it is a weak measurement device. Barnes and Pressey [4] found the oral examination of individuals to be seriously lacking in reliability and validity, and findings in other studies have been similar in nature.

Despite Horace Mann's foresighted views presented in 1845 and the evidence of more recent objective studies, the oral quiz has persisted in American schools. However, the oral quiz serves very imperfectly as a tool for the measurement of factual knowledges. If advance preparations are carefully made by the examiners, if examinations are conducted in a consistent manner, and if scoring and rating methods are carefully worked out, oral examinations may be administered satisfactorily to individuals. It is doubtful, however, whether oral examining of groups for purposes of measurement can be satisfactory.

There are, it is true, some situations in which oral questioning leads to significant responses. Socratic questioning is a teaching device by means of which pupils may be led to reach new conclusions and understandings. Responses to searching questions directed at pupils individually on detailed aspects of their school performances may well be of diagnostic value to the teacher. Fact-finding questions in an interview elicit useful information. Oral responses are the only means whereby such instructional outcomes as those involved in oral expression in English and pronunciation in the foreign languages can be tested. This is also true of group performances in debates and glee club contests. Finally, oral examinations may properly be used with individuals to supplement written examinations, but such use has largely been limited,

[4] Elinor J. Barnes and S. L. Pressey, "The Reliability and Validity of Oral Examinations," *School and Society*, 30:719–722, Nov. 23, 1929.

and probably with justification, to comprehensive and honors examinations in colleges and to civil service examinations.

ESSAY OR TRADITIONAL EXAMINATIONS

The essay form of examination was in use in the civil service system of China as early as 2000 B.C., and was introduced into medieval universities of Europe by 1702. However, it was not until the pressure of oral examining upon the Boston School Committee became too great, as Boston grew in size, that Horace Mann made his pronouncements and that the written examination was introduced into American schools. As the twentieth century dawned, essay examinations were unquestionably the most widely used measurement devices in American schools.

It was not until late in the nineteenth century and early in the twentieth century that the essay examination was critically scrutinized. Starch and Elliott [5] precipitated a controversy in 1912 when they reported that the marks assigned to an examination paper in English by 142 teachers ranged from 50 to 98 on a percentage scale of 100. Other studies by these authors and by other research workers shortly thereafter bore out the conclusion that the essay examination is typically very subjective and hence very unreliable. In 1914, however, Kelly [6] published a report showing that the use of a definite set of rules resulted in a material reduction in the degree of variation found when marks were assigned to essay test papers by usual methods. Stalnaker [7] in a more recent study found that experienced teachers marked essay examinations in a variety of high-school subjects with quite high reliability when scoring rules were applied.

The two criticisms which have rightly been made of the traditional examination are that it lacks objectivity and adequacy. Stated positively rather than negatively, it is highly subjective and limited in sampling or breadth. As it has typically been given, it often consists of 5 or 10 questions on which pupils are expected to write for a class period. It has been demonstrated that so few questions do not adequately cover the content the examination is expected to encompass. In many studies

[5] Daniel Starch and Edward C. Elliott, "Reliability of Grading High School Work in English," *School Review*, 20:442–457, September, 1912.

[6] Fred J. Kelly, *Teachers' Marks*, Contributions to Education, No. 66, p. 83, Teachers College, Columbia University, New York, 1914.

[7] John M. Stalnaker, "Essay Examinations Reliably Read," *School and Society*, 46:671–672, Nov. 20, 1937.

comparable to that made by Starch and Elliott, the objectivity of scoring essay test results was shown to be low. Some of the factors which are known to influence teachers' judgments of essay test results are length of the paper, shifting standards of expectancy, neatness and grammatical correctness of the writing, and unconscious influence by the "halo" effect, which is a tendency to overrate papers of pupils having created favorable impressions on the teacher. The essay test also is thought by many to encourage bluffing by the pupil and to place an undue emphasis upon factual answers.

Several advantages which have been claimed for the essay examination are worthy of mention. The essay test is undoubtedly easy to construct and to administer. It is quite readily adaptable to testing needs in the various fields of subject matter. It can be useful in the measurement of certain higher mental abilities. Other advantages which have sometimes been claimed for the essay test are training in the use of written English and motivation of desirable review methods on the part of the pupils. Although the first three of these advantages may be accepted with minor qualifications, the two last mentioned are highly questionable. An examination is hardly the appropriate place to seek training in the use of English, for the measurement purpose of the examination precludes any real emphasis upon such a secondary purpose. Moreover, training in the use of English should doubtless receive adequate attention elsewhere in the activities of pupils. As essay tests have typically been constructed, emphasis in study upon factual knowledges of a detailed nature rather than upon broad understandings seems to be appropriate pupil procedure. Educators are in quite general agreement, however, that broad understandings are more important instructional outcomes than are detailed and often unintegrated factual knowledges.

What has been said above may give the impression that the essay examination is both unsatisfactory and satisfactory as a measuring instrument. Such is actually the case, a seeming ambiguity which is not true alone of this type of test. An essay test casually prepared and administered, followed by careless evaluation of the results, may well produce highly unreliable scores. On the other hand, answers evaluated by carefully thought out scoring rules and procedures to questions thoughtfully prepared and carefully administered may well produce quite reliable scores. Much depends upon the ability of the teacher to use this examination type satisfactorily and upon his willingness to devote the necessary care to his examination procedures. Most of the recommendations for improvement of the essay or traditional examination center about the (*a*) selection of content and preparation of questions, and (*b*) scoring of obtained results.

Constructing the essay examination. Sims[8] divided essay-type questions into three groups on the basis of their objectivity. The first type, simple recall in nature and demand, are usually introduced by such words as *what, who, when, where, how many*, and *name*. They are designed to elicit such factual information as an event, a name, a date, a number, a place, or a list. The second type, short-answer questions, often have such key words as *define, identify, find, list*, and *state*. Both these and questions of the first type elicit answers subject to quite objective evaluation. The third type, discussion questions, are characterized by such introductory words as *why, how, discuss, describe, compare, explain*, and *outline*. Responses to such discussion questions are not subject to objective marking unless scoring rules and other procedures designed for the improvement of objectivity are observed.

Another meaningful classification of essay-type questions is that of Monroe and Carter,[9] who distinguished 20 types of thought questions. The list below gives Odell's adaptation and supplementation[10] of the original classification.

1. Selective recall—basis given. (Name the presidents of the United States who had been in military life before they were elected.)

2. Evaluating recall—basis given. (Name the three statesmen who have had the greatest influence on economic legislation in the United States.)

3. Comparison of two things—on a single designated basis. (Compare Eliot and Thackeray as to ability in character delineation.)

4. Comparison of two things—in general. (Contrast the life of Silas Marner in Raveloe with his life in Lantern Yard.)

5. Decision—for or against. (In which in your opinion can you do better, oral or written examinations? Why?)

[8] Verner M. Sims, "Essay Examination Questions Classified on the Basis of Objectivity," *School and Society*, 35:100–102, Jan. 16, 1932.

[9] Walter S. Monroe and R. E. Carter, *The Use of Different Types of Thought Questions in Secondary Schools and Their Relative Difficulty for Students*, University of Illinois Bulletin, Vol. XX, No. 34, University of Illinois, Urbana, Ill., 1923.

[10] C. W. Odell, *Traditional Examinations and New-Type Tests*, pp. 207–210, Century Company, New York, 1928.

6. Causes or effects. (Why has the Senate become a much more powerful body than the House of Representatives?)

7. Explanation of the use or exact meaning of some phrase or statement in a passage. (Explain the meaning of the expression "Sinais climb" in the line: "We Sinais climb and know it not.")

8. Summary of some unit of the text or of some article read. (Summarize in about one hundred words the advantages of the hot-air furnace.)

9. Analysis. (Mention several qualities of leadership.)

10. Statement of relationships. (Tell the relation of exercise to good health.)

11. Illustrations or examples (your own) of principles in science, construction in language, etc. (Give an original sentence in Latin illustrating the use of the infinitive in indirect discourse.)

12. Classification—usually the converse of No. 11. (To what group of plants do the mosses and liverworts belong?)

13. Application of rules or principles in new situations. (In what countries other than Brazil would you expect to find rubber plantations?)

14. Discussion. (Discuss the Monroe Doctrine.)

15. Statement of aim—author's purpose in his selection or organization of material. (What was the purpose of the author in having Athelstane return to life after he was apparently dead?)

16. Criticism—as to the adequacy, correctness, or relevancy of a printed statement, or a classmate's answer to a question on the lesson. (Criticize "Macbeth was wholly indifferent to the superstitions of his time.")

17. Outline. (Outline in not more than one page the chief events of the French and Indian Wars.)

18. Reorganization of facts. (Select the incidents which characterize Portia in *The Merchant of Venice*.)

19. Formulation of new questions—problems and questions raised. (If you were asked to state how much you could trust the viewpoint of a particular historian about whom you know little or nothing, what questions would you want to have answered concerning him?)

20. New methods of procedure. (How might the plot of *Julius Caesar* be changed to make it a comedy rather than a tragedy?)

The practice of allowing pupils options on the questions to be answered is probably responsible for some of the subjectivity often observed, for by so doing the examination is not held constant for all pupils. Moreover, essay examinations are often constructed without clear ideas concerning the aspects of instruction they are supposed to measure. If each examination is limited to one major type of instructional outcome, if optional questions are not included, and if questions are carefully framed in terms of the implications of the key words, the first step has been taken toward objectifying the test.

A device which has been found valuable in the construction of essay-type questions is an informal score card designed by Greene, Jorgensen, and Gerberich.[11] They recommend that no question be considered satisfactory unless affirmative answers can be given to at least 7 of the 10 questions.

TENTATIVE SCORE CARD FOR RATING ESSAY-TYPE EXAMINATION QUESTIONS

	Yes	Slightly	No
1. Is the question concerned with important phases of the subject?			
2. If the question emphasizes minor details, are they useful in linking up other facts, ideas, theories, involved in the subject?			
3. Does the question give emphasis to evaluation and to relational thinking?			
4. Is the question apparently of a suitable degree of difficulty in relation to the other questions in the test?			
5. Is the question stated in such a way as to stimulate thought, to challenge interest of pupils?			
6. Does the question force the pupil to integrate his ideas around certain interest-centers?			
7. Is the question stated in such form as to force the pupil to sample widely into his background of fact?			
8. Does the question call for any originality of thought organization and expression?			
9. Does the question call for the pupil to integrate facts gained from different sources?			
10. Is the question limited sufficiently that the pupil has some chance of writing what he really knows about it in a reasonable time?			

[11] Harry A. Greene, Albert N. Jorgensen, and J. Raymond Gerberich, *Measurement and Evaluation in the Secondary School*, p. 148, Longmans, Green & Co., Inc., New York, 1943.

Scoring the essay examination. Two alternative procedures have been suggested for scoring the results of the essay test. One involves the reading of each examination in its entirety and its placement in one of five piles representing different degrees of merit. The other involves the reading of one question on all papers and the assignment to each of a score based on a predetermined total for the question.

The first of these procedures, recommended by Sims,[12] is briefly outlined below. Sims suggested that acceptable answers worked out in advance by the readers serve as guides for the classification of papers.

a. Quickly read through the papers and on the basis of your opinion of their worth sort them into five groups as follows: (*a*) very superior papers, (*b*) superior papers, (*c*) average papers, (*d*) inferior papers, (*e*) very inferior papers. (Remember that in a normal group you would expect to have approximately 10 percent of *very superior* and 10 percent of *very inferior* papers, 20 percent of *superior* and 20 percent of *inferior* papers, and 40 percent of *average* papers. Do not, however, try to conform rigidly to this rule. Your group may not be a normal one.)

b. Re-read the papers in each group and shift any that you feel have been misplaced.

c. Make no attempt to give numerical grades or to evaluate each question. Place each paper on the basis of your general impression of the total.

d. Assign letter grades to each group; beginning with *A* for the very superior group, *B* for the superior group, etc.

Greene, Jorgensen, and Gerberich [13] incorporated the second plan for evaluating essay-type responses into a list of five suggestions for improving the traditional examination. Also included are recommendations designed to obviate some of the deficiencies often found in this type of test and suggestions concerning the establishment of certain types of scoring rules.

1. Examinations should be scored by the one who makes out the questions. He should know exactly what responses are desired, and should write out his answers to the questions in advance.

[12] Verner M. Sims, "The Objectivity, Reliability, and Validity of an Essay Examination Graded by Rating," *Journal of Educational Research*, 24:216–223, October, 1931.

[13] Greene, Jorgensen, and Gerberich, *op. cit.*, pp. 146–147.

2. Each pupil taking the test should write his name on the back of the test paper and the scorer should disregard the name until the test is scored. This eliminates the subjective factor of being influenced or biased in judgment because of former contacts with the pupil, insofar as the teacher does not become aware through handwriting, manner of expression, etc., of the writer's identity.

3. The scorer should not mark off for misspelled words or poor sentence structure, paragraphing, handwriting, etc. Similarly, he should not increase the score for excellence in these things. However, such factors may be indicated or checked on the examination. The reason for this lies in the fact that the function of the examination is to measure the pupil's abilities in a course and not his ability to write or to spell. If it is desirable to test his ability to write, spell, or use correct written English, suitable tests can be obtained for these purposes.

4. Each separate item should be scored in all of the papers consecutively. This is preferable to the correction of each entire test as a unit, for it permits the scorer to concentrate on the answer to a single test exercise and better to judge the merits of the several pupil responses to the same question.

5. Each question should be rated on a scale of ten, twenty, or a given number of scoring points. The total score should be obtained for each pupil by adding the scores on the different questions only after all of the scoring has been done.

If precautions such as those outlined above are observed by teachers, the essay examination may be expected to fulfill an important function in the measurement of behavioral changes in pupils resulting from the daily-assignment method of instruction.

SHORT WRITTEN QUIZZES

Written quizzes 5 or 10 minutes in length are often used to measure achievement in a daily-assignment or recitation plan of instruction. Questions asked in such quizzes frequently fall somewhere between the essay test and the informal objective test in their scope and degree of objectivity. If the questions are rather narrow in scope and demand only brief answers, the results can be evaluated with reasonable objectivity. The tendency of such questions toward a high degree of factuality can be obviated when desired by the use of problem situations and of other types of questions which require the pupil to project his learnings beyond the knowledge and simple skill areas into areas of application.

Suggestions for appraising essay test results seem to apply quite directly to the marking of answers to questions in short written quizzes. The emphasis should be upon the real merits of answers rather than upon such outcomes as are represented in handwriting, spelling, and neatness, which admittedly are desirable outcomes but which are not fundamental in many subjects of instruction. Only those answers or parts of answers directly to the point of a question should receive credit, in order to objectify the scoring and to minimize the importance of length in the pupils' answers. A point system of scoring, whereby each question may be assigned a maximum value of from two to five points, is a further aid in objectifying the scoring procedure.

INFORMAL OBJECTIVE TESTS

Informal objective tests made their debut early in 1920, when McCall[14] first publicly suggested that teachers could construct their own objective tests for classroom use. These instruments were at first referred to as new-type tests or even as objective tests, but both designations were at least unfortunate. No test type can remain a new type for very many years. Furthermore, standardized tests and informal objective tests both possess the characteristic of objectivity. The modern designation of this objective form of teacher-made or classroom tests as an informal objective test is much to be preferred. It is a form of test well adapted to the content and instructional procedures common in the daily-assignment method.

The essay or traditional examination and the informal objective test are designed to serve the same classroom functions, although they do so in a very different manner and with varying degrees of success. The informal objective test consists of items to which responses must be clear and unambiguous, and hence is objective, whereas the essay test is usually characterized by subjectivity in the evaluation of results. The informal objective test samples much more widely than does the essay examination, by virtue of the many items which can be given in a relatively short period of time, and hence rates higher in adequacy. Economy of time eventually results from the use of informal objective rather than essay test procedures. The informal objective test is initially very time consuming in its construction, but time demands for scoring the results are not great and test items constructed and demonstrated to

[14] William A. McCall, "A New Kind of School Examination," *Journal of Educational Research*, 1:33–46, January, 1920.

be good can be used many times over a period of years. Essay tests are relatively easy to prepare, but time requirements are great in scoring the results. The bluffing easily possible by pupils taking essay tests is entirely eliminated in the objective type of classroom test.

Several disadvantages have been pointed out for the informal objective test. Admittedly it does not typically provide training in the organization and expression of thought, although some of the newer adaptations permit measurement of the organization of thoughts. Moreover, it is probable that development of ability to express thought should come from school activities other than the examination. The over-emphasis upon factual knowledge claimed by some to characterize the informal objective test seems to be more apparent than real, for two major reasons. The deluding simplicity and brevity of objective item types and the mere fact of their objectivity imply factuality which may, but need not, exist. Furthermore, poorly constructed tests of this type tend toward factual emphases because the teachers constructing them emphasize factual knowledge in their teaching, or at least in their testing, or because factual items are more readily and easily constructed than are thought items.

Encouragement of guessing has been advanced by some as a weakness of this test type, but guesses are seldom pure guesses and correction-for-chance formulas counteract the influence of such guessing as may occur. Furthermore, many life situations demand that evidence be weighed and decisions be made without certainty of correctness. Although informal objective tests may be somewhat more expensive to prepare for classroom use than are essay tests, reproducing by mimeograph or gelatin plate processes is not very costly. Some objective item forms can even be given orally or reproduced, somewhat laboriously, on a blackboard.

Major types of objective test items. Two major types of objective test items may be distinguished—recall and recognition. Recall items are those which place the burden upon the pupil for recalling or by other means indirectly determining the correct answers. Recognition items are those in which the material is presented to the pupil for his evaluation or for his selection of the correct answers.

Although there are probably 50 or more distinguishable objective item forms, all except a few represent modifications or combinations of four or five simple and basic forms. It is to these few basic item forms that attention will be directed here. As it is possible only to discuss and illustrate the basic item types briefly,[15] a few samples from standardized tests are interspersed through the discussion following to illustrate the simple item types.

Recall Forms. The two simplest and most widely used recall item types are the simple recall and completion. Differences between them

EXCERPT FROM KNISS WORLD HISTORY TEST

DIRECTIONS. Read each statement and decide what word or name should be placed in the blank at the right to make the statement true and complete. Study the sample.

SAMPLE. America was discovered by ——..

Columbus

1. The Protestant Revolution was begun by a German monk and university professor by the name of —— 1

2. Without much doubt modern Germany was created mainly by the efforts of that famous statesman —— 2
3. The great revival and new interest in learning, art, etc., which took place in the late Middle Ages is called the ——..3

Source: F. Roscoe Kniss, *Kniss World History Test,* Form A, World Book Company, Yonkers, N. Y., 1940.

are primarily in complexity and length, for fundamentally they are very similar. The simple recall is the item in which a single word, number, symbol, or short phrase is to be given by the pupil in response to a question or to complete a statement. The completion item, if item it may be called, is represented by one blank in a unified paragraph from which the pupil is expected to gain the idea enabling him to fill each blank with the appropriate word, number, symbol, or short phrase.

EXCERPT FROM HUNDRED-PROBLEM ARITHMETIC TEST

Complete the following:

76. 75% of 160 = ☐ (76)   **78.** 130% of 30 = ☐ (78)

77. 3.2% of 60 = ☐ (77)   **79.** $\frac{2}{3}$% of 6000 = ☐ (79)

Source: Raleigh Schorling, John R. Clark, and Mary A. Potter, *Hundred-Problem Arithmetic Test,* Form W, World Book Company, Yonkers, N. Y., 1942.

[15] For more extensive treatments of objective test item construction, see Harry A. Greene, Albert N. Jorgensen, and J. Raymond Gerberich, *Measurement and Evaluation in the Secondary School,* Chap. 8, Longmans. Green & Co., Inc., New York, 1943; C. C. Ross, *Measurement in Today's Schools,* 2d ed., Chap. 5, Prentice-Hall, Inc., New York, 1947; and J. Murray Lee, *A Guide to Measurement in Secondary Schools,* Chap. 11, D. Appleton-Century Company, Inc., New York, 1936.

Although the simple recall item stands alone as a separate test element and requires only one answer, several blanks requiring as many completions often occur in a completion exercise. It can be said more accurately that several completions may be required in one completion exercise, which is itself a unit. Consistency demands that a completion exercise be considered to merit as many scoring points as there are blanks in the exercise. This is in harmony with the usual practice of awarding one scoring point to each simple recall item that is answered correctly.

The simple recall item is not dissimilar to a short-answer question form used by many teachers in essay tests, but there may well be a difference in the degree of objectivity possessed by the two methods. Factual questions of the *what, who, when, where, how many,* and *name* variety are most easily measured by this item type, although it may be used in many other significant ways. When used to measure ability to identify objects pictured or ideas described, when used with maps or charts as part of an identification exercise, when used to measure spelling ability or vocabulary, and when used in computational problem situations, to mention only a few of its applications, its values go beyond those of factual tests. There is danger that simple recall items will tend to be used largely in the measurement of highly factual outcomes, however, and their usefulness is somewhat restricted for this reason.

EXCERPT FROM RUCH-COSSMAN BIOLOGY TEST

DIRECTIONS. In each of the paragraphs below write in the words that have been left out. Try to find the word for each blank that makes the best sense. The sample has been filled in correctly.

SAMPLE.   The ... *public* ... ... *drinking* ... cup often spreads ... *disease* ...

---

2. Study of the structure of the fish reveals many adaptations for locomotion in water: the general shape of the body, the secretion of............by certain cells of the skin, the............of the scales, the possession of a............which tends to make the fish nearly the same density as the water, and the possession of............and............as balancing and swimming organs.   [5]

Source: Giles M. Ruch and Leo H. Cossman, *Ruch-Cossman Biology Test,* Form A, World Book Company, Yonkers, N. Y., 1924.

The completion exercise is similar to the simple recall item in its major characteristics and uses, but it is based on longer thought units and requires more integration of ideas than does its simpler counterpart. Good completion paragraphs should be well unified and of summary nature, and blanks should not be so numerous that the general meaning of the paragraphs is obscured.

Recognition Forms. The most widely used, basic recognition item types are the alternate-response, the multiple-choice, and the matching. Alternate-response items, of which the true-false is the best known type, present the pupil with two possible answers. The answers may indicate

EXCERPT FROM DENNY-NELSON AMERICAN HISTORY TEST

B. DIRECTIONS. Draw a line under "True" after each true statement and a line under "False" after each false statement.

26. The United States Senate failed to ratify the League of Nations............... True   False

27. Our city population has increased faster than our rural population since 1860.... True   False

Source: E. C. Denny and M. J. Nelson, *Denny-Nelson American History Test*, Form A, World Book Company, Yonkers, N. Y., 1928.

the truth or falsity of a statement, an affirmation or denial of a question, or the one of two alternative answers which correctly completes a statement. Multiple-choice items consist of an initial statement or question and from three to five alternatives, one of which correctly or best completes the statement or answers the question. The pupil is expected to select and designate the correct answer. Matching exercises consist of two lists of facts or ideas related in a consistent manner throughout. The pupil is expected to pair the facts or ideas in the two lists. Matching items do not exist as entities, for a matching exercise or unit has embedded in it anywhere from 3 to 10 or even more correct pairings, and each correct pairing is ordinarily accorded one scoring point of credit. Alternate-response and multiple-choice items, however, are distinct entities, and each ordinarily carries one scoring point toward the total test score.

The true-false item and the essentially equivalent yes-no and plus-minus variations are the most widely used and broadly applicable of

EXCERPT FROM BROWN-WOODY CIVICS TEST

DIRECTIONS. Draw a line under the right answer to each question.

Begin here.
1. Is the United States a democracy?   Yes   No   1
2. Is the Constitution of the United States the highest law of the land?   Yes   No   2
3. May any adult become a candidate for office, local or national?   Yes   No   3

Source: Arold W. Brown and Clifford Woody, *Brown-Woody Civics Test*, Form A, World Book Company, Yonkers, N. Y., 1926.

the alternate-response forms. Although this item type is often highly factual, it can well be used in measuring instructional outcomes of less tangible types than knowledges. It is delusively simple in its construction, and is probably more subject to ambiguity than any other objective item form unless it is constructed with great care. However, its apparent simplicity, ease of construction, and wide range of applicability have made it the most widely used item type in informal objective tests, although it is seldom used in its pure form for standardized tests.

EXCERPT FROM COOPERATIVE CHEMISTRY TEST

Directions: Each of the following incomplete statements or questions is followed by five possible answers. For each item, select the answer which **best** completes the statement or answers the question, and put its **number** in the parentheses at the right.

1. An instrument used to measure pressure is a
   1-1 eudiometer.
   1-2 hydrometer.
   1-3 hygrometer.
   1-4 barometer.
   1-5 thermometer. . . . . .1(   )

9. All proteins contain the element
   9-1 tin.
   9-2 sulfur.
   9-3 phosphorus.
   9-4 manganese.
   9-5 nitrogen. . . . . .9(   )

Source: Alexander Calandra, *Cooperative Chemistry Test*, Form Q, Cooperative Test Service, New York, 1940.

The multiple-choice item, by far the most popular form in standardized testing, usually has three, four, or five alternative statements of which one correctly or best completes the preceding statement or answers the introductory question. This item form is highly flexible, for it can be used widely not only in subject-matter areas but also for measuring a variety of instructional outcomes. It is useful not only in

EXCERPT FROM GLENN-WELTON CHEMISTRY ACHIEVEMENT TEST

DIRECTIONS. Each of the following questions is followed by six alternative answers, of which only *one* is correct. In the parentheses after each question write the number of the *one* correct answer.

1. The white phosphorus match is not made now because it is too —
   1 expensive   2 hard to get   3 explosive   4 poisonous
   5 hard to light   6 unstable. . . . . (   )1

2. What is a solution called which conducts an electric current?
   1 an electrode   2 an ion   3 an electrolyte   4 a solvent
   5 electrolysis   6 a non-conductor. . . . . (   )2

Source: Earl R. Glenn and Louis E. Welton, *Glenn-Welton Chemistry Achievement Test*, Test 2, Form A, World Book Company, Yonkers, N. Y., 1938.

measuring factual knowledges but also in testing concepts, understandings, and applications of various types. Ingenuity is sometimes required on the part of the test constructor in finding sufficiently plausible incorrect answers. A modification often used is the multiple-response item, in which not only the alternative answers or choices but also the correct answers are multiple.

The matching exercise is in effect a series of multiple-choice items in combination, for each pairing of an item on one side of the exercise with an item on the other side presents multiple choices. The most typical matching exercises are of the balanced type, in which from 10 to 15 items such as facts, words, dates, or authors are matched with a like number of related items such as dates, definitions, events, or book titles. In the unbalanced set, which is ordinarily used with fewer than 10 matchings, one side of the exercise includes several plausible but incorrect items in order to reduce the chances of guessing correct answers. Although the matching exercise tends to be rather highly factual in nature and to test most easily the same *what, who, when, where, how many*, and *name* responses as does the simple recall, the matching test can be adapted to the measurement of less tangible instructional outcomes. It is important that consistency of categories and of grammatical form of statements be maintained in this type of exercise, if clues leading to correct answers and other forms of ambiguity are to be kept at a minimum.

Excerpt from Denny-Nelson American History Test

C. DIRECTIONS. The name of each man below is given a number. Write the correct number in the parentheses after the phrase that suggests a man's name.

Champlain (1)	36. Pioneered in Kentucky........................... ( )	
James Wolfe (2)	37. Captured Fort Ticonderoga......................... ( )	
Ethan Allen (3)	38. Helped to settle Jamestown....................... ( )	
John Winthrop (4)	39. Famous missionary to the Indians.................... ( )	
Ponce de Leon (5)	40. British Parliament member friendly to America.......... ( )	
Daniel Boone (6)	41. Governor of Massachusetts Bay colony................ ( )	
Vespucius (7)	42. Won battle resulting in fall of Quebec................. ( )	
William Pitt the Elder (8)	43. America was named after him....................... ( )	
Marquette (9)	44. Explored the St. Lawrence River country.............. ( )	
Captain John Smith (10)	45. Searched for the fountain of youth................... ( )	

Source: E. C. Denny and M. J. Nelson, *Denny-Nelson American History Test,* Form A, World Book Company, Yonkers, N. Y., 1928.

Suggestions for constructing objective items. No rule-of-thumb guides are possible for the construction of objective test items, but there are some guiding principles of value in avoiding the most glaring errors in item construction. Listed below are the suggestions made by Greene, Jorgensen, and Gerberich [16] for items of all basic types and for items of each of the basic types discussed above. The illustrations of poor and good items and the samples and explanations used in implementation of the suggestions are mainly original here. The illustrations and samples are intended to demonstrate points rather than to be in themselves good test items in the broad sense.

General Suggestions. Recommendations which apply in essentially the same manner to all basic objective item types are:

1. Rules governing good language expression should be observed.
   Poor: Sufficient data is available to justify the conclusion that . . .
   Good: Sufficient data are available to justify the conclusion that . . .

2. Difficult words should be avoided.
   Poor: Good harbors are often formed by diastrophism.
   Good: Good harbors are often formed by the gradual sinking of coast lines near the mouths of rivers.

3. Textbook wording should be avoided.
   Poor: In the derivation of grade norms for standardized tests, it is common but not universal practice to express the norms in terms of end-of-the-year achievement.
   Good: Grade norms for achievement tests are commonly stated in terms of end-of-the-year achievement.

4. Ambiguities should be eliminated.
   Poor: There are six days in a week.
   Good: A week consists of six days.

5. Items having obvious answers should not be used.
   Poor: A monthly magazine is published twelve times a year.
   Good: A weekly magazine is published fifty-five times a year.

[16] Harry A. Greene, Albert N. Jorgensen, and J. Raymond Gerberich, *Measurement and Evaluation in the Secondary School,* pp. 188–196, Longmans, Green & Co., Inc., New York, 1943.

6. Clues and suggestions should be avoided.
   Poor: A man who works in a bank is a: (*a*) Lawyer, (*b*) Banker, (*c*) Dentist, (*d*) Farmer, (*e*) Druggist. <u>(*b*)</u>
   Good: A man who accepts deposits of money on checking accounts is a: (*a*) Lawyer, (*b*) Banker, (*c*) Dentist, (*d*) Farmer, (*e*) Druggist. <u>(*b*)</u>

7. Items which can be answered by intelligence alone should not be included.
   Poor: In the autumn, deciduous trees shed their <u>(leaves)</u>
   Good: Trees which shed their leaves in the autumn are termed <u>(deciduous)</u>

8. Quantitative rather than qualitative words should be used.
   Poor: The Empire State Building is more pleasing architecturally than is the Chrysler Building. T (F)
   Good: The Empire State Building is taller than the Chrysler Building. (T) F

9. Catch words should not be employed.
   Poor: Runyan Kipling wrote *Just So Stories.* T (F)
   Good: Rudyard Kipling wrote *Just So Stories.* (T) F

10. Items should not be inter-related.
    Example: 1. Presidents John Adams and John Quincy Adams were father and son. (T) F
    Example: 2. No two Presidents of the United States have been blood relatives. T (F)

11. Response positions should preferably be aligned.
    Poor: Validity is a major criterion of a good examination. (T) F
    Good: Validity is a major criterion of a good examination. (T) F

Suggestions for Recall Items and Completion Exercises. As simple recall items and completion exercises are very similar in their major characteristics, recommendations applying to both of these recall types are:

1. Lines for responses should be of the same and of adequate length.
   Poor: Columbus discovered America in the year <u>(1492)</u>
   The Pacific Ocean was discovered by <u>(Balboa)</u>
   Good: Columbus discovered America in the year <u>(1492)</u>
   The Pacific Ocean was discovered by <u>(Balboa)</u>

2. Desired responses should be definite.
   Poor: Fruit may be kept for long periods of time by (refrigeration)
   Good: Fresh fruits may be kept from spoiling during
      long shipments by   (refrigeration)
3. Desired responses should be important.
   Poor: Portia is a character in a Shakespearean   (play)
   Good: The heroine of *The Merchant of Venice* is   (Portia)
4. Any correct answer should receive credit.
   Example: Fruit may be kept for long periods of time by   (grocers)
5. Spelling errors should probably not be penalized.
   Example: The "Nutmeg State" is   (Conneticut)
6. "A" or "an" should not immediately precede a blank.
   Poor: The unit of measurement of electrical resistance
      is an   (ohm)
   Good: The unit of measurement of electrical resistance
      is the   (ohm)
7. Positions for responses should ordinarily be at the ends of the sentences.
   Poor: There are (fourteen) lines in a sonnet.
   Good: The number of lines in a sonnet is   (fourteen)
8. Completion paragraphs should be unified wholes.
   Suggestion: Choose well unified paragraphs in which a logical sequence
      is narrated.
9. Completion paragraphs should not contain too many blanks.
   Poor: The principal _____ of the _____ War
      was _____.
   Good: The Battle of (Gettysburg) is usually considered to be the
      turning point of the Civil War.

Suggestions for Alternate-response Items. As some of the alternate-response item modifications are somewhat too complex and variable to permit specific suggestions, recommendations intended primarily for the true-false item form are:

1. Double negative statements should be avoided.
   Poor: Freezing weather is not entirely unknown in Florida. (T) F
   Good: Florida occasionally has freezing weather.   (T) F
2. Statements which are part true and part false should not be used.
   Poor: The Battle of Gettysburg, which is usually considered
      to be the turning point of the Civil War, was fought
      in 1862.   (T) (F)
   Good: The Battle of Gettysburg was fought in 1862.   T (F)

3. "Specific determiners" should be used sparingly and carefully.

Poor: Animals always have the power of locomotion.   T Ⓕ
Good: Some animals cannot move from place to place unless
carried by outside forces.   Ⓣ F

4. Answers should be required in highly objective form.
Suggestion: Have pupils encircle T or F, place "X" in column of
boxes under T or F, etc., rather than write "T" or "F,"
"True" or "False," etc.

5. Approximately an equal number of true and false statements should
be used.
Suggestion: Have not more than 60 per cent of either type.

6. Random occurrence of true and false statements should be employed.
Suggestion: Toss coin or use some other random method in arranging
items.

Suggestions for Multiple-choice Items. Recommendations applying
mainly to the basic multiple-choice item and only indirectly to such
modifications as the multiple-response item are:

1. As much of the statement as possible should occur in the introductory portion.

Poor: Columbus discovered America: (*a*) In the year 1487,
(*b*) In the year 1508, (*c*) In the year 1482, (*d*) In the
year 1492, (*e*) In the year 1516.   (d)
Good: Columbus discovered America in the year: (*a*) 1487,   ‾‾
(*b*) 1508, (*c*) 1482, (*d*) 1492, (*e*) 1516.   (d)
                                                             ‾‾
2. Alternative answers should be stated in correct grammatical
style.

Poor: Columbus: (1) Discovered America, (2) Circumnavigated the earth, (3) Discoverer of the Mississippi River,
(4) Finder of the Fountain of Youth, (4) Pacific Ocean.   (1)
Good: Columbus: (1) Discovered America, (2) Circumnavi-   ‾‾
gated the earth, (3) Discovered the Mississippi River,
(4) Found the Fountain of Youth, (5) Discovered the
Pacific Ocean.   (1)
                                                           ‾‾
3. Incorrect alternatives, or confusions, should be plausible.

Poor: The first President of the United States was: (*a*) Roose-
velt, (*b*) Hoover, (*c*) Washington, (*d*) Madison,
(*e*) Coolidge.   (c)
Good: The first President of the United States was: (*a*) Jef-   ‾‾
ferson, (*b*) Monroe, (*c*) Washington, (*d*) Madison,
(*e*) Hamilton.   (c)
                                                           ‾‾

4. "A" or "an" should not ordinarily be used to introduce the alternative answers.

Poor: "Him" is a: (1) Adverb, (2) Noun, (3) Adjective, (4) Pronoun, (5) Preposition.   (4)

Good: "Him" is a(n): (1) Adverb, (2) Noun, (3) Adjective, (4) Pronoun, (5) Preposition.   (4)

5. Items should ordinarily have four or five alternative answers.

Suggestion: Three alternatives may be enough for use with young children.

6. All items should ordinarily have the same number of alternative answers.

Explanation: Otherwise there is variation in the chance of guessing the correct answers.

7. Alternative answers should ordinarily occur at the end of the statement.

Poor: Of the criteria of a good examination, (1) Adequacy, (2) Objectivity, (3) Validity, (4) Scorability, (5) Administrability is the most important.   (3)

Good: The most important criterion of a good examination is: (1) Adequacy, (2) Objectivity, (3) Validity, (4) Scorability, (5) Administrability.   (3)

8. Answers should be required in a highly objective form.

Suggestion: Have pupils write numbers or letters of correct responses on indicated lines or in given parentheses.

9. Correct responses should be distributed with approximate equality among the possible answer positions.

Suggestion: Go a bit lighter on the extreme responses, a and e or 1 and 5, than on the centrally-located responses.

10. Random occurrence of correct responses should be employed.

Suggestion: Toss a die, disregarding the "6," or use some other random method of determining order.

Suggestions for Matching Exercises. Recommendations for constructing the balanced and unbalanced matching exercises are:

1. Only one correct matching for each item should be possible.

Poor: 1. Columbus   _____ Explorer
       2. De León   _____ Navigator
       3. Magellan   _____ Italian
       4. etc.   _____ etc.

Good: 1. Columbus   _____ Circumnavigated the earth
       2. De León   _____ Discovered America

THE METHODS WE USE   183

    3. Magellan   _____ Discovered Pacific Ocean
    4. etc.   _____ etc.

2. Consistency of grammatical form should be used.
   Poor: 1. Jackson   _____ Louisiana Purchase
        2. Lincoln   _____ Signed Emancipation Procla-
                                  mation
        3. Madison   _____ Statement of Monroe Doc-
                                  trine
        4. etc.   _____ etc.
   Good: 1. Jackson   _____ Effected Louisiana Purchase
        2. Lincoln   _____ Promulgated Monroe Doc-
                                  trine
        3. Madison   _____ Signed Emancipation Procla-
                                  mation
        4. etc.   _____ etc.

3. Consistency of classifications should be maintained.
   Poor: 1. Battle of Bunker
           Hill   _____ Andrew Jackson
        2. Spoils System   _____ 1775
        3. Forest conservation _____ Prohibition
        4. Thirteenth Amend-
           ment   _____ Slavery
        5. etc.   _____ etc.
   Good: 1. R. W. Emerson   _____ *Huckleberry Finn*
        2. Mark Twain   _____ *Leaves of Grass*
        3. Walt Whitman   _____ *Walden*
        4. etc.   _____ etc.

4. Matching sets should neither be too long nor too short.
   Suggestion: Use from 10 to 15 pairs in balanced matching; use un-
        balanced matching (some items on one side not to be
        used) if fewer than 10 items to be tested.

5. Items should be listed in random order in each list.
   Suggestion: Arrange alphabetically by initial letter of first words or
        chronologically by dates.

6. A set of matching items should always be complete on one page.
   Explanation: This avoids difficulty in referring from one page to
        another.

7. Answers should be required in a highly objective form.
   Suggestion: Have pupils write numbers from one column on lines
        or in parentheses provided with the other column.

Constructing an informal objective test. When an informal objective test is desired for testing over a fairly wide range, as for use in one period or as a final examination, the scope and coverage of the test are desirably determined before test items are actually constructed. Consideration is appropriately given in this planning both to the instructional objectives and the content of the course and to a proper parallelism of course and test content. It is helpful to prepare a brief outline of the course and of pupil activities in the course as a further guide in test construction.

Objective items of more than one type are desirably used in a comprehensive informal objective test, for three major reasons: (*a*) Subject matter is sometimes a limiting factor in the selection of item types, for a certain concept may more easily be put into one item form than into any other. (*b*) The degree of factual knowledge expected in the pupils is important to decide as a basis for selection of the appropriate item form for a particular concept, for the tendency of recall forms to be more factual than recognition forms restricts the usefulness of the former. (*c*) It is probable that predispositions of different pupils toward or against certain item types are such that a test consisting of several item forms is preferable to a test consisting solely of one item type.

It is usually advantageous in item construction to start with ideas which fall into such consistent patterns that matching exercises may appropriately be used. Multiple-choice items should ordinarily receive consideration before alternate-response or recall item forms, because of the requirement for several plausible but incorrect alternative answers. It is not recommended that all items of each type be constructed entirely apart from items of other types, but rather that consideration of the proper item form for each group of related concepts and each distinct concept occur in this order. Good practice is to write each item on a filing card when it is constructed, so that it may be sorted with others of the same type in final preparation of the test and so that it may be filed for later use in other examinations as desired.

After all items have been constructed, they should be sorted by types and carefully evaluated in relationship to others of the same form. Items should desirably range from very easy to very difficult, with an average difficulty of approximately 50 per cent.[17] Test length should be such

<hr>

[17] Herbert E. Hawkes, E. F. Lindquist, and C. R. Mann (Eds.), *The Construction and Use of Achievement Examinations*, pp. 32–33, Houghton Mifflin Company, Boston, 1936.

that all or very nearly all of the pupils can complete it during the testing period. Although a general indication of time requirements [18] suggests that two simple recall, three multiple-choice, or four true-false items may be considered to require 1 minute of testing time, such factors as pupil maturity, test difficulty, and nature of test content are important factors in the determination of test length. If items are thought provoking rather than highly factual in nature, the number pupils can do in 1 minute will probably be smaller than these estimates.

The final test items should be arranged in as many parts as there are separate item forms. The items in each part may be arranged in any desired order, although an arrangement based on the sequence of course content may be preferable to any other for informal objective tests. General instructions to the pupils should appear at the beginning of the test and at the beginning of each test part to indicate how they are to take the test and mark their answers, whether or not they should guess, and, preferably, how the part scores will be obtained. Sample items should be given if pupils are unfamiliar with objective tests. The test should be reproduced in desired quantity by mimeograph or some similar process if possible, although some simple item forms can be given orally if necessary and any item forms can be reproduced on blackboards if space and time permit.

Scoring an informal objective test. Although scoring methods may vary within certain limits, results of research studies have demonstrated the scope within which scoring methods should fall. In general, a simple recall item and a completion exercise blank are assigned one point of credit for a correct answer, and there is no subtraction for wrong answers or omissions. Pupils are usually instructed not to guess on alternate-response items, and the score is obtained by disregarding omissions and subtracting the number of wrong answers from the number of right answers. Pupils are typically instructed to answer all items in a multiple-choice test, and the score is usually obtained by use of the formula: Score $= R - \dfrac{W}{N-1}$, where R and W mean right and wrong answers respectively and N refers to the number of possible answers to each item. Thus, scores for tests having three, four, and five possible answers would be $R - \frac{1}{2}W$, $R - \frac{1}{3}W$, and $R - \frac{1}{4}W$ respectively. As the guessing possibility is slight in the five-response form,

[18] Greene, Jorgensen, and Gerberich, *op. cit.*, p. 163.

scores for it are often merely the number of correct answers. Matching exercises are usually scored by assigning one point of credit to each correct answer. A practice not uncommon of penalizing the pupil for omissions is not recommended in scoring any of these item types, for the pupil is adequately penalized by the fact that his possible score is automatically reduced by the number of items he fails to answer.

OTHER TYPES OF WRITTEN WORK

Teachers often need to evaluate and assign marks to such non-test types of written work as themes, notebooks, laboratory reports, and term papers. There exists for such written work, of course, the possibility that the work was not actually done by the pupil who hands it in. This possibility is worthy of consideration in setting up procedures for the preparation of such written work by the pupils and in the marking emphasis to be assigned.

In general, suggestions for the evaluation of essay test results apply to written work of these types, although the fact that such materials prepared by different pupils are usually on different topics or subjects raises a type of problem not operative in the scoring of essay test results. The suggestion of Sims [19] reported in a preceding section of this chapter that papers be sorted into piles representing five different degrees of merit seems to be practicable here. As is true of essay test scoring, attention should here be directed to the intrinsic aspects of merit rather than to such relatively detailed and extrinsic concerns as handwriting, spelling, neatness, and length.

TEACHERS' MARKS

Marking practices involve at least two phases: (a) the assignment of scores or marks on tests and other types of appraisals; (b) the assignment of final marks for 6-week periods or for semesters of study. The two studies discussed briefly below deal with these aspects of marking.

Lee obtained responses from 1,284 teachers to a question concerning their methods of marking self-made tests.[20] Of these teachers, 36.4 per

[19] Verner M. Sims, "The Objectivity, Reliability, and Validity of an Essay Examination Graded by Rating," *Journal of Educational Research*, 24:216–223, October, 1931.
[20] J. Murray Lee, *A Guide to Measurement in Secondary Schools*, pp. 260–262, D. Appleton-Century Company, Inc., New York, 1936.

cent used the percentage system, 22.5 per cent used a point-scale system based on the inherent quality of the examination papers, 25.5 per cent based letter marks on relative qualities of the examination papers, 8.8 per cent used scores only, and 6.0 per cent used ranks in the class. A negligibly small remainder gave still other responses. The first two groups, totaling 58.9 per cent, used systems of the type discussed here as most frequent accompaniments of the daily-assignment method of instruction. The third group, totaling 25.5 per cent, used a procedure typical in the subject-matter unit method of instruction, whereas the last two groups, totaling 14.8 per cent, employed procedures associated either with the subject-matter unit method or the experience unit method.

Odell surveyed the marking systems used in 281 Illinois high schools in 1925. His findings [21] were that 73.3 per cent assigned marks in percentage terms and that the remaining 26.7 per cent used point systems ranging from the most typical 5-point scale to a 4-point scale at one extreme and to an 8-point scale at the other extreme. Typical indecision concerning the meaning of a percentage mark was evidenced by the variation in the passing mark from 70 to 80, with 75 most common, and in the level below which pupils were passed conditionally from 60 to 74. Of the 75 schools which used a point scale, 31 gave plus and minus qualifications to letter marks, so that the total range of categories in these 31 schools was from 12 to 21. About 60 per cent of the schools using point scales defined the meaning of the letter symbols in percentages.

Although no recent studies comparable to the two discussed above have apparently been made, evidence presented in Chap. 11 concerning a developing use of point-scale systems shows that the methods outlined here are less typical today than they were in 1925 or 1936. However, it is certain that some schools today adhere to the point scale with more than 10 categories and even to the percentage system.

Brief mention of terminology appropriate in the marking of examinations, written work of other types, and final achievement for 6-week marking periods or semesters will be made here, as a key to the terms used in this section and corresponding sections of Chaps. 11 and 14. The practice of referring to the percentage of correct answers a pupil

[21] C. W. Odell, "High School Marking Systems," *School Review*, 33:346–354, May, 1925.

attains on a test as a grade is not uncommon. More correctly, however, the percentage is referred to as a score. A numerical representation of success on a test not scored on a percentage basis is also sometimes referred to as a grade. Again, however, the result is more properly called a score. Still further, a letter representation of merit is sometimes designated as a grade. More properly, it is called a mark. Modern practice is to designate numerical representations, whether percentages or not, as scores and to designate as marks the letter evaluations assigned to laboratory reports, term papers, and other written products, as well as to the final appraisals of pupil success for a period or semester. Percentages used as final appraisals are also correctly called marks.

Percentage marking system. Theoretically, a percentage mark of 100 represents complete mastery of all the instructional outcomes sought in a course, and the passing mark represents the lower limit of minimum success in the course. The concept of perfect attainment in a school course for a semester or even for 6 weeks is wholly untenable, unless education is to be reduced to rule-of-thumb procedures. Furthermore, there is no magic in a passing mark, whether it be 60, 65, or 70. Moreover, the degree of discrimination required in a percentage system of marking is far beyond that possessed by human beings. Inadequacies of the percentage marking system have been pointed out by educators on too many occasions to permit of serious consideration to this largely outmoded plan.

As percentage marks in their traditional form are probably used in very few schools today, teachers' problems are concerned more with other marking bases than with the percentage system. If percentage comparability to letter marks is specified in the marking system used, and if percentages must be reported for use in permanent records, even though letter marks are used for pupil reports, it is believed that letter marks should first be obtained and that, if necessary, they then be converted into the required percentages.

Point-scale marking systems. Point scales involving the use of A, B, C, D, and F or five other essentially similar symbols are more widely used in secondary schools today than are any other systems. Some schools have reduced to a 3-point scale of H, S, and F, meaning honors, satisfactory, and fail. A still smaller number of schools have adopted a 2-point scale similar to the 3-point scale except for the omission of honors marks.

In the transition from the traditional percentage marking system to a statistically and psychologically sounder system, the 5-point scale is doubtless merely an intermediate phase. The 5-point system is certainly more widely used today than is the older percentage system, but several unfortunate influences of the percentage basis still encumber many letter-mark systems. The first is the tendency still evident in the practices of some schools to identify each letter mark in terms of percentages arbitrarily decided upon as corresponding. The second is the use of letters in reporting marks to the parents of pupils but the use of percentages in the records of some schools. The third is the extension of the 5-point scale to as many as 10 or even more categories in some marking practices by the use of plus, minus, or both plus and minus signs.

Obtaining composite measures of achievement. The problems involved in obtaining numerical representations of pupil achievement over a 6-week period or semester to be used in the assignment of final marks are not simple. It is the purpose here to outline methods whereby such composite measures can be obtained for use in assigning percentage marks or letter marks.

If percentage marks are customarily assigned to examination results, to written work of other types, and even to oral recitations, the various percentages for each pupil can be averaged to obtain his final percentage mark. However, the use of a weighted average, by which important measures receive more weight than do unimportant measures, is preferable. In view of the unreliability and other deficiencies of percentage marks, however, it is believed that a point system such as that outlined immediately below is preferable for obtaining composite scores which can, if necessary, be converted by arbitrary methods into final percentage marks.

Wittler [22] suggested a marking procedure which has merit in combining results from a variety of measuring devices and situations into a cumulative numerical index. The accompanying illustration from Wittler shows results of his plan. His procedure involves the assignment of scores to each paper, test, and type of evaluation on a scale having only a few degrees of differentiation. If the performance to be evaluated makes reasonable only three degrees of merit, a 3-point scale

[22] Milton Wittler, "A Painless Plan for Assigning School Marks," *Educational Method*, 11:213–217, January, 1932.

is used. A 5-point scale may be appropriate where more discriminative judgments are possible. A summation of the points assigned to each pupil for each of the several types of appraisals used is the next step. Results of these summations may then be weighted according to their importance in obtaining the cumulative or composite score.

A METHOD OF DETERMINING COMPOSITE MARKS

Students	Assignments 1 2 3 4 5 6 7	Total 8	Quizzes 9 10 11	Total 12	Grand total 13 (8 + 12)
R. V.	3 √ √ 4 4 4 √	15	5 4 4	13	28
R. S.	3 √ 3 √	6	2 3 5	10	16
S. B.	3 √ √ 5 4 4 √	16	5 3 4	12	28
S. S.	3 √ √ 5 5 5 √	18	3 5 5	13	31
S. L.	2 √ √ 3	5	3	3	inc.

The scores resulting from the use of such a weighting system may then be arranged in descending order and such letter marks assigned on the basis of these composite scores as the teacher deems appropriate and as conform to the marking system of the school.

Methods such as those outlined above for the assignment of letter marks, or, if necessary, percentage marks by the teacher to represent various levels of pupil success are those deemed most satisfactory for use with the daily-assignment method of instruction.

SUMMARY

The measurement of pupil achievement is dependent for its methods upon the instructional outcomes the school seeks to develop in its pupils. The outcomes sought under the daily-assignment method of instruction are listed in Chap. 6 as knowledges, interests, attitudes, and skills. Therefore, it is with these types of behavior that the teacher is concerned in testing. Major emphasis unquestionably is placed upon the two most tangible types of outcomes—knowledges and skills. Hence, interests and attitudes are dealt with in Chap. 11, which is devoted to the subject-matter unit method of instruction, rather than in this chapter.

Ruch listed steps in construction of informal objective tests which well characterize the approach to testing in harmony with the daily-assignment method of instruction. Basic steps are the preparation of a topical outline of content to be covered in the test and the selection for each topic of the most important facts. The remaining steps are concerned with the construction of the objective test items, their arrangement in a test, and determination of the degree of reliability obtained for the test as a whole. The steps outlined by Ruch may be applied with only minor qualifications to other types of tests appropriate under the daily-assignment method of instruction.

The oral examination, the essay or traditional examination, short written quizzes, other written work, and the informal objective test are the instruments and techniques of most pertinence. Of these, the oral examination is highly questionable as a testing device except for a few very specialized uses. The essay test, short written quizzes, and other written work are typically marked quite unreliably, but their reliability may be increased markedly by the use of considerable care in the construction of questions, in their administration with more than usual concern for the purpose involved, and in the marking of pupil responses in a consistent and objectified manner. Basic informal objective item types fall under two major headings—recall and recognition. Suggestions for construction and scoring of the two recall types, simple recall and completion, and the three recognition types, alternate-response, multiple-choice, and matching, should aid the teacher in the effective construction and use of these basic objective item forms.

Teachers' marking practices under the daily-assignment method of instruction vary from the traditional percentage system to point scales having as few as three or even only two distinct marks. Most typical, probably, is a 5-point scale of A, B, C, D, and F or equivalent marks, although the indefensible percentage system is often perpetuated by statements of equivalence between percentages and letter marks. Suggestions made for obtaining composite achievement measures should aid the teacher in the assignment of final course marks for his pupils.

SELECTED REFERENCES

BRUECKNER, LEO J., and MELBY, ERNEST O.: *Diagnostic and Remedial Teaching*, Chap. 6, Houghton Mifflin Company, Boston, 1931.
CALDWELL, OTIS W., and COURTIS, STUART A.: *Then and Now in Education: 1845–1923*, Chaps. 4–6, World Book Company, Yonkers, New York, 1923.
GREENE, EDWARD B.: *Measurements of Human Behavior*, Chap. 6, The Odyssey Press Inc., New York, 1941.

GREENE, HARRY A., JORGENSEN, ALBERT N., and GERBERICH, J. RAYMOND: *Measurement and Evaluation in the Secondary School*, Chaps. 7–8, Longmans, Green & Co., Inc., New York, 1943.

LANG, ALBERT R.: *Modern Methods in Written Examinations*, Chaps. 4–9, Houghton Mifflin Company, Boston, 1930.

LEE, J. MURRAY: *A Guide to Measurement in Secondary Schools*, Chaps. 10–11, D. Appleton-Century Company, Inc., New York, 1936.

LINCOLN, EDWARD A., and WORKMAN, LINWOOD L.: *Testing and the Use of Test Results*, Chap. 11, The Macmillan Company, New York, 1935.

ODELL, C. W.: *Educational Measurement in High School*, Chap. 20, Century Company, New York, 1930.

———: *Traditional Examinations and New-type Tests*, Chaps. 7–16, Century Company, New York, 1928.

ORLEANS, JACOB S., and SEALY, GLENN A.: *Objective Tests*, Chaps. 2–5, 12–13, World Book Company, Yonkers, New York, 1928.

REMMERS, H. H., and GAGE, N. L.: *Educational Measurement and Evaluation*, Chaps 8–9, 12, Harper & Brothers, New York, 1943.

RINSLAND, HENRY D.: *Constructing Tests and Grading in Elementary and High School Subjects*, Chaps. 2–7, Prentice-Hall, Inc., New York, 1937.

ROSS, C. C.: *Measurement in Today's Schools*, 2d ed., Chaps. 4–6, Prentice-Hall, Inc., New York, 1947.

RUCH, G. M.: *The Objective or New-type Examination*, Chaps. 3–4, 7–10, Scott, Foresman & Company, Chicago, 1929.

RUSSELL, CHARLES: *Classroom Tests*, Chaps. 2–8, Ginn & Company, Boston, 1926.

SYMONDS, PERCIVAL M.: *Measurement in Secondary Education*, Chaps. 3, 25, The Macmillan Company, New York, 1927.

TIEGS, ERNEST W.: *Tests and Measurements for Teachers*, Chaps. 2–4, Houghton Mifflin Company, Boston, 1931.

DIVISION B

METHOD BASED ON THE SUBJECT–MATTER UNIT

Chapter 9. THE ORIGIN AND THEORY OF THE SUBJECT–MATTER UNIT METHOD

The pattern of procedures that comes into play when teachers organize their work on a day-to-day basis was described in Chaps. 6 and 7. It was shown that daily assignments are used when it is assumed that the school possesses a specific, well-defined body of subject matter —the mastery of which is more important for the pupils than any other activity in which they might engage at that stage of their development. What the school needs, it is felt, is a mass production method that will enable the teacher to expose the greatest number of pupils to the largest quantity of the designated materials in the time available for instruction. For many teachers throughout the history of education, the pattern of procedures associated with the daily assignment has met these specifications.

The assumptions underlying the daily-assignment method were not seriously challenged by educational theorists until the beginning of the twentieth century. Even today when some laymen and teachers speak of providing a better education for the youth of America, they have in mind merely the extension by 1 or 2 years of the total time pupils now spend in school. They assume that the education now provided is entirely satisfactory except that there is not enough of it. Not everyone is willing to give the prevailing educational practices this unqualified endorsement, however, for there are now some who believe that improvement can be secured only by offering a different kind of instruction.

THE EVOLUTION OF METHOD BASED ON LARGER UNITS OF SUBJECT MATTER

The critics of the daily-assignment method point out that the pupil who has from four to six assignments to complete each day seldom has much incentive left to explore interests or problems that lie outside of the prescribed limits. The result is a pernicious form of textbook learning without reference to the world of everyday concerns or the acquisition of necessary social skills and understandings. Herbart, whose description of the steps of learning did so much to formalize recitation teaching, strongly criticized the kind of teaching which so many of his followers have since practiced in his name. He is quoted as saying:

I cannot refrain from wondering what sort of a process is being worked out in the heads of schoolboys who, in a single forenoon, are driven through a series of heterogeneous lessons, each one of which on the following day, at the regular tap of the bell, is repeated and continued. Is it expected that these boys will bring into relation with one another and with the thoughts of the playground the different threads of thought there spun? There are educators and teachers who, with marvellous confidence, presuppose just this, and in consequence trouble themselves no further.[1]

In the light of the above statement, it is difficult to understand why so much of the teaching that has been modeled after the doctrines of Herbart became little more than the daily repetition of a formal pattern of procedure. One may surmise, however, that the tremendous demand for public education experienced at the turn of the century forced upon educators certain makeshift arrangements. To staff the rapidly expanding schools, particularly on the elementary level, many young men and women who had but recently ended their own meager schooling were employed as teachers. There was no time available to acquaint these young people with accepted pedagogical theory and practice in an adequate manner. Professional training was provided in 6-week terms offered during the summer months or at some other time during the year that was convenient to those who were about to become teachers. When the supply of teachers began to overtake the demand, the length of the training program was increased, first to 1 year, then to 2 years, and more recently to the 3 or 4 years of study offered by the modern normal schools and teachers colleges. It is probable, however, that in the early days there was not time to develop the understandings now afforded in these more adequate programs. In fact, the prospective teacher at the beginning of the present century could be expected, in

[1] As quoted by Charles A. McMurry, *The Elements of General Method,* pp. 163–164, The Macmillan Company, New York, 1907.

a 6-week term, to acquire little more than a pattern of procedures to be followed in each recitation. The steps of learning advocated by Herbart met this need for a pattern very nicely. Hence, thousands of teachers have followed what they believed to be the Herbartian theory of education not knowing that Herbart denounced the very formal procedures they developed by accepting only part of his educational views.

Contributions to the subject-matter unit from Herbart. There is, then, a second aspect of the educational doctrines of Herbart that has special implications for teaching. This aspect has to do with the arrangement of subject matter into related units in order that ideas, particularly ethical principles, might appear uppermost in the consciousness of the pupils. Herbart believed that the masses of sensory experiences, whether gained while at play or in the classroom, provide the basis for ideas which give direction to the future behavior of the individual. An idea, according to Herbart, is a generalization drawn from a number of related sensory experiences. The primary function of the school is to see that each pupil acquires a suitable collection of such ideas so that his subsequent behavior will be virtuous. Herbart felt that ideas of virtue would result from a broad background of knowledge—through building up the "many-sidedness of interest," not only in what is individual and subjective, but also in what is social and objective. That is, the pupil becomes virtuous, not merely through acquiring ideas of piety, but by acquiring in addition ethical ideas to govern his relations with others in the affairs of everyday life and in the manipulation of materials and the application of mechanical processes.[2] Charles A. McMurry, one of the men who helped introduce the Herbartian doctrines in America, stressed the importance of this aim. He wrote that, ". . . the moral, character-building aim . . . should be like a lodestone attracting and subordinating all other purposes to itself. It should dominate in the choice, arrangement, and method of study."[3]

The Theory of Correlation. It was thought that the organization of knowledge and experience around the major ethical ideas would make

[2] John Frederick Herbart, *Outlines of Educational Doctrine*, trans. by Alexis F. Lange and annotated by Charles DeGarmo, p. 44, The Macmillan Company, New York, 1904.

[3] McMurry, *op. cit.*, p. 7.

these ideas stand out as "centers of influence." This assumption points the way to the Herbartian doctrine of *correlation*. That is, the ideas of virtue that are to give direction to individual conduct are to be centers or nuclei around which all subject matter and instructional activity are to be organized. One may assume that these ethical ideas are the generalizations, or moral principles, which good teachers at all times have attempted to impart to their pupils. The difference is that Herbart would develop the ideas inductively by first giving the pupil the knowledge and experience out of which the ideas grow whereas the others were inclined to present them as generalizations already made. This throws some light on the arguments waged in educational circles over the relative merits of the "inductive" and the "deductive" methods of teaching.

Correlation, then, calls for the presentation of the items of subject matter and other learning experiences in a relationship that will lead logically to the ethical idea or ideas for which the teaching is undertaken. It follows that if ethical ideas are to be the centers of instruction, the organization of subject matter will follow of necessity a pattern that differs somewhat from the logical sequences used in the daily-assignment method. Three types of organization were suggested.

Correlation within Subjects. The first type provides for the organization of related items of subject matter within a given subject. Here Herbart rejected the prevailing practice of treating each item of subject matter as though it were of equal importance with every other item, thereby denying the pupil an over-all view. Instead, the field of knowledge should:

. . . resemble a mountainous district rather than a plain. To get the broadest views one must climb the highest ridges and summits. The knowledge embraced in any one branch of study is not to be considered as a miscellaneous accumulation of facts, nor even as a well-ordered but monotonous series of facts, to be simply memorized or stored away; but it is a field of conquest which can be best brought under control by taking possession of its strong, strategic positions.[4]

The implication here is that once a strong point has been established the surrounding details may be filled in as needed. This point of view

[4] Charles A. McMurry and Frank M. McMurry, *The Method of the Recitation*, p. 246, The Macmillan Company, New York, 1909. Italics in the original.

is supported in the opening pages of the book from which the above quotation was taken:

The mastery of the general truths of a study must remain the direct purpose of instruction in each branch of knowledge. These truths are what are known in psychology as general notions or concepts. They are the centers around which the knowledge of any subject is grouped and classified. It is the mastery of these rules and principles, and the ability to apply them, that are constantly aimed at in all the best school work.[5]

McMurry suggested several topics of this general nature around which the details of information in a given subject might be organized. A topic in geography, for example, might be "The Hudson River" or "The Falls of Minneapolis." In botany, a study built around the topic of "The Apple Tree" would relate much material into a unified system which might otherwise lose significance if treated in isolation.

The treatment of the apple tree in this manner would involve the time of several lessons, running through several weeks, with observations, excursions, etc. It would reach deep into the subject of plant life and growth, and turn up new soil in every lesson.[6]

The organization of instruction on the basis of units of work in history, algebra, chemistry, and in other subjects probably developed from this emphasis on correlation.

Correlation between Subjects. In the second type of correlation, an effort is made to bring related materials from two or more subject-matter fields to bear upon the development of a given idea.

The fundamental principle here is that what is learned and drilled upon in one study is learned for the purpose of applying it in all other recitations and studies. If this is not true, the thing learned is not worth learning. Knowledge is for use, and it is hypocrisy and inconsistency to emphasize a thing as important in one study and then neglect it in all others.[7]

To facilitate this type of correlation, it was urged that curriculum makers plan to have the work for a given grade, particularly in literature, history, and geography, deal with the same general topic at a

[5] *Ibid.*, pp. 10–11.
[6] Charles A. McMurry, *The Elements of General Method*, p. 172.
[7] *Ibid.*, p. 7.

given time. With proper planning, a class might study the literature of Colonial America at the time they are learning about the historical and the geographical aspects of the Atlantic coastal regions. Thus, whatever ideas or generalizations are developed in one subject could be related to the knowledge presented in each of the other two subjects.

An interesting outgrowth of this type of correlation was the culture-epoch movement. The advocates of that basis for organizing the curriculum believed that as individuals grow they relive the history of the race. The subject matter presented by the school should therefore reproduce in chronological order the major cultural stages through which the human race has passed in its long history. According to this view, very young children should be introduced first to the culture of primitive societies, learning their social forms and imitating their institutions, play, and manner of living. This should be followed by a similar introduction to nomadism, the city state, the Roman Empire, medieval feudalism, and so forth. The particular epoch under consideration would thus provide the subject matter for instruction in studies such as reading, language and literature, history, geography, music, and drawing. In other words, the culture epoch would provide the basis for inter-subject correlation. "Cooperative" units and studies, "integrated" studies, and "fused" courses represent more recent attempts to provide inter-subject correlation.

Correlation between School and Nonschool Experiences. A third type of correlation was proposed to develop relationships between things studied in the classroom and the experiences of everyday living. It was argued that only as these relationships are developed and the ideas of morality and conduct are given practical application can the pupil be expected to learn to live virtuously outside of the classroom. Furthermore, the practical applications will also help the pupil to understand and to grasp the subject matter by means of which the school attempts to develop the general truths and ethical ideas.

The prime mistake in nearly all teaching and in the textbook method is in supposing that the great truths are accessible in some other way than through the concrete materials that lie properly at the entrance. The textbooks are full of the abstractions and general formulae of the sciences; but they can, in the very nature of the case, deal only in a meagre way with the individual objects and facts upon which knowledge in different subjects is based. This necessary defect in a textbook method must be made good by excursions, by personal observation, by a constant reference of lessons to daily experience outside of school, by more direct study of our surroundings, by the teacher perfecting himself in this kind of knowledge and in its skillful use.[8]

And in a slightly different context, it is stated that:

interest in every study is awakened and constantly re-enforced by an appeal, not to books, but to life. . . . This is not a question of interest merely, but of understanding, of capacity to get at the meaning of an idea. Concepts are not the raw materials with which the mind works, but they are elaborated out of the raw products furnished by the senses and other forms of intuition.[9]

On the strength of the views stated above, the educators who advocated correlation condemned unmercifully the prevailing practice of teaching subject matter in isolation. These educators pointed to the fact that it is only in the schoolroom and in the scientific texts that one finds items of potentially useful information presented without reference to the practical situations where that information can make a contribution. It was argued that if children learn only to recognize things in their scientific form and isolation in the schoolroom, how shall they be able to disentangle the actual relations of life? Therefore, why should the school present as isolated bits of information "those things which in the common experiences of men are bound together by many important and vital links of connection"? [10]

The Effect upon the Curriculum. The influence of the doctrine of correlation, with its emphasis on the development of concepts or ideas and upon relating the classroom activities to life out of school, led to the preparation of new curricula and courses of study. A few major ideas or principles, selected because they were judged capable of giving suitable guidance to the pupil's future conduct, came to be the focal points around which lesser items of subject matter were clustered. Classroom activities became organized attacks upon whole systems of related materials and thereby began to replace the piecemeal mastery of single items of knowledge. These newer approaches made it necessary for the time devoted to a single assignment to be extended beyond the limits of the daily recitation. A week or even a month might

[8] McMurry, *The Method of the Recitation*, p. 238.
[9] *Ibid.*, pp. 236–237.
[10] *Ibid.*, p. 192.

now be required to cover adequately one of these larger units of subject matter. This development has been identified as one of the first, if not the first, of the many "unit" plans that have been proposed since that time.[11]

The phrasing of the central idea around which instruction was to be organized soon became a matter of importance to the teacher. A challenging statement of the unit topic could arouse pupil interest or serve as a "lodestone" to direct the study activities of the individual pupils. Hence, the central idea of the unit frequently was given the form of a question to be answered or a problem to be solved. When the central idea was stated in the form of a question or problem which could be answered or solved on a mental plane, the instructional procedure came to be known as the "problem" method. When it involved the solution of a problem or the consummation of a purpose in its natural setting, particularly if it dealt with the actual construction of something, such as building a table or making a dress, the procedure came to be labeled a "project."[12] If the pupils worked under the direction of a teacher who helped them, not only to find the answer or solution they had been assigned, but also how to go about finding the answer, the procedure was sometimes called "supervised study." When the work was done in the classroom during time usually set aside for recitations, the procedure was labeled the "laboratory" method.[13]

This description of the several types of procedures that have grown out of the Herbartian doctrine of correlation is, obviously, oversimplified. The advocates of any one type may claim with some justification that the description given here can be misleading. There seems to be no basis for disagreement, however, with the conclusion that the Herbartians insisted that every lesson must have a purpose or objective that is clearly recognized by both the teacher and the pupils. In time, these objectives were identified as the major ethical ideas, topics, and

[11] Jean M. Alexander, "Influence of Pedagogical Scholarship on Methods: from Herbart to Morrison," *Historical Approach to Methods of Teaching the Social Studies*, p. 22, Fifth Yearbook of the National Council for the Social Studies, McKinley Publishing Company, Philadelphia, 1935.

[12] Martin J. Stormizand, *Progressive Methods of Teaching*, p. 144, Houghton Mifflin Company, Boston, 1924.

[13] For a more detailed description of these methods, see Walter S. Monroe and Arlyn Marks, "General Methods of Teaching," *Educational Administration and Supervision*, XXIV:497–512, October, 1938.

principles around which lesser information was to be organized. To deal with these larger units of subject matter, it became increasingly apparent that a longer time span was needed than that provided for the conventional daily assignment. Thus, assignments were introduced that were intended to engage the class for a week, a month, or even for a longer period of time. It is these longer assignments that have come to characterize unit teaching in the minds of laymen and frequently of inexperienced teachers as well.

Contribution from the scientific study of human personality. As stated in Chap. 4, the theory that all secondary-school pupils would benefit from the same studies, pursued in the same way, prevailed until the beginning of the twentieth century. The Committee of Ten was quoted as supporting this view in a report published in 1893. At approximately the same time, however, scientifically controlled inquiries were being made into the nature of human personality and the reasons for the differences in behavior that had been observed. The names of Wundt, Galton, and Cattell are prominent among those who were engaged in these studies. The work of Binet, who believed he could find a basis for distinguishing between children who can learn and those who cannot, was described briefly in Chap. 3. It will be recalled that he proceeded on the assumption that there is a sharp distinction between the feeble-minded and the normal and that this distinction is present from infancy. He was spurred on by the thought that substantial savings might be realized if the two groups could be separated at an early age and if education were offered to the normal group only. A test was devised for this purpose which came to be used widely in America in the revised form published in 1916 by L. M. Terman and his associates. Ever since that time, this test, including the 1937 revision, has served as the standard instrument for studying what is believed to be the natural ability or native capacity of the individual.[14]

Studies of this nature led to the conclusion that some differences in individual behavior are due to differences in ability to learn. The data produced have given rise to grave doubts about the wisdom of treating all pupils in a given class in the same way regardless of their "probable destination" or the point at which their informal school-

---

[14] Paul A. Witty, "Intelligence and Aptitude: Their Nature, Development, and Measurement," *Elementary Educational Psychology*, C. E. Skinner (Ed.), pp. 94–96, Prentice-Hall, Inc., New York, 1945.

ing is to be terminated. Data showing the wide range of abilities represented in a typical high-school population were presented in Chap. 3. They demonstrated the existence of differences among pupils with respect to the kind of learning in which they can engage with profit, as well as differences with respect to other traits such as interests, purposes, and the general level of physical, mental, social, and emotional development which exist in typical classroom situations. In the light of these data, the practice so strongly recommended by the Committee of Ten that all pupils in a given class should be treated alike, cannot be justified except in cases where it is demonstrated that the supposed homogeneity does exist. It is now known that such cases are the exception rather than the rule, and educators have been stimulated by that knowledge to seek classroom procedures that will make possible the adjustment of study assignments to fit the personal requirements of each pupil.

Some Early Attempts to Individualize Assignments. One of the first educators to make a practical attempt to adjust instruction to the capacity of the pupil was Preston W. Search, superintendent of schools of Pueblo, Colorado, from 1888 to 1894. His solution consisted of abolishing nearly all recitations and homework and of supervising the study of pupils in school. Each pupil worked at his desk and advanced through his textbooks at his own rate. In this plan, the teacher served as a guide or helper. He made individual assignments tailored to the ability of the pupil, offered help as needed, and later checked upon the pupil's progress with the assignment.[15] In this manner, "each pupil found it necessary to master each line of Latin," but each pupil progressed at his own rate, "the fastest pupils completing 140 chapters while the slowest completed only 40 chapters."

In 1913, Professor Frederic L. Burk, president of the San Francisco State Teachers College, introduced a plan on the elementary-school level that abolished class recitations and group assignments, and provided each pupil with self-teaching instructional materials. The work in arithmetic, for example, was broken up into topics, or units. Each unit was so written that the pupil was given the directions needed to do the

[15] Preston W. Search, *An Ideal School*, D. Appleton-Century Company, Inc., New York, 1901. For a brief account, see C. S. Parker, *Methods of Teaching in High School*, pp. 366–379, Ginn & Company, Boston, 1920.

exercises on his own. When he had completed the work, a test covering that unit was provided. If the pupil passed the test satisfactorily, he was given the booklet covering the next unit. The well-known Winnetka Plan developed by Carleton Washburne, one of Burk's students, is a refinement of the system originated by Burk.

A similar procedure was developed by Miss Helen Parkhurst at Dalton, Massachusetts. In 1920, she was given an opportunity to put into practice in the Dalton High School the theories she had been developing for a number of years. Her system of instruction is now known as the Dalton Laboratory Plan and is used in the private schools she operates, as well as in a number of other schools. As in Burk's plan, the conventional subjects are broken up into units or "contracts," and each pupil is expected to work his way through the several series of contracts at his own rate. There are no recitations of the familiar type, but each classroom is furnished with books and other study materials related to a given subject. Thus, one room may be a mathematics "laboratory," while another is furnished as a social science laboratory. Each laboratory is supervised by a subject specialist. A pupil may go from laboratory to laboratory, use the study materials found there, and consult the specialist in charge as he needs in order to fulfill his contracts.

A distinctive feature of the Dalton Plan is the responsibility that is placed upon the pupil for planning his work. Not only must the pupil map out the work that he expects to complete in a given period of time, frequently a month, but he must also plan each morning the time budget for that day. This budgeting of time and work is, of course, carefully supervised by the staff, and the progress of each pupil in meeting his commitments is carefully noted by means of a well-developed checking procedure.[16]

The accounts given here of the Burk and Dalton Plans are not complete descriptions. They touch only upon those parts of the plan that were designed to make it possible for each pupil to secure a mastery of subject matter at his own rate. While these devices to individualize instruction are of particular interest here, it is desirable to note that both plans also have another aspect—that of group activity—by means of

[16] For a brief but good account of the Dalton Laboratory Plan, see Adolph E. Meyer, *The Development of Education in the Twentieth Century*, pp. 166–179, Prentice-Hall, Inc., New York, 1939.

which the pupil is to develop the social skills, appreciations, and attitudes that make for a well-rounded personality and a competent citizen.

The Burk, Winnetka, and Dalton Plans represent efforts to break out of the rigid framework that was forcing schools to treat all pupils as though they had the same abilities, interests, and needs. Each plan was designed to provide freedom for the pupil to progress at his own rate and, to a limited degree, to emphasize studies within his area of interests and aptitudes, even at the expense of other studies. The success of these efforts to individualize instruction stimulated the development of other innovations, most of which made use of the technique of breaking up courses of study into smaller teaching units. To many educators, these newer "units of subject matter" promised the flexibility needed to adjust the work of a given pupil to his own ability and needs without making it necessary for him to lose sight of the major topic or idea which was being pursued by the class as a whole.

The sociological influence on the development of subject-matter units. A third influence that helped give direction to the development of the subject-matter unit came from the educational theories of John Dewey. Dewey, who was born in Vermont in 1859, was influenced in his student days by the psychological theories of Herbart. This fact is reflected in his early writings on the subject of psychology.[17] Although he soon found the Herbartian psychology to be inadequate, Dewey shared Herbart's interest in education as a means of preparing individuals to live in a constantly changing social environment. At that time, the need for this type of education was only beginning to be recognized, although the need was becoming acute as a result of the accelerated rate of change brought about by industrial developments and the growing emphasis on the growth of the individual. Dewey's concern was not merely to help the individual to adjust to a given social and physical environment, but rather to help him give direction to the stream of environmental changes into which real life, as contrasted with the artificial life of the traditional classroom, plunges him. Dewey believed that the habits, skills, and facts which have been found useful by a previous generation, and which constitute the subject matter of the traditional school, are not likely to be of equal value to the present generation of pupils. Their needs in some instances may call for new

[17] See John Dewey, *Psychology*, Harper & Brothers, New York, 1887.

institutions, customs, and regulations. The emphasis in education, therefore, should be on developing the ability to create better forms of living rather than upon memorizing and practicing old habits and skills
without placing these under critical examination.

The School as a Simplified Society. To develop creative ability, that
is, to develop control in a dynamic world, pupils need a social environment within which their ability to shape the kind of world they want
and need has an opportunity to grow. According to Dewey, the school
should provide that kind of environment. It should be flexible, of the
pupils' own shaping, and developed by the pupils in response to the
interests and concerns that are of importance to them. As time goes on
and the pupils mature, their interests and concerns will change accordingly. Hence, there will arise from time to time a need for new social
arrangements. By their own decisions, the pupils will be put to the
task of devising arrangements that are more satisfying than the ones
they have outgrown. This form of self-direction is identical with that
which is called for in a mature, democratic society. Intelligence comes
into play when the participants select their arrangements on the basis of
the results that are expected, and when they are willing to retain or
discard arrangements on the basis of the results they produce. Intelligence, according to this view, is not some capacity or ability acquired
by inheritance, and which remains unchanged throughout the life of
the individual, but is developed through practice. In line with this view,
high-school pupils normally would not be expected to deal intelligently
with the financial problems of a large business venture. The data and the
consequences of any decisions they might hazard are too far removed
from the personal experiences of the pupils to serve them as reliable
guides. However, pupils can and do judge various regulations affecting the management of their school cafeteria. Such judgments frequently are quite intelligent because they are based on the effects these
regulations have upon the pupils themselves. Their personal experiences
enable them to see the connection between a regulation and its consequences. Thus, they can suggest modifications or substitutions with
reasonable assurance that the new regulations will be more satisfactory than the old ones. As time goes on and their experience increases,
these same pupils ultimately may become equally intelligent about
matters of corporate finance, but this should not be interpreted to mean
that the school should look upon the study of the financial structure

of corporations as having greater value for the pupils than the study of the management of the school cafeteria.

Education as Experience. According to Dewey, the best form of education is not a preparation for life—a process during which the pupil is stuffed with facts and information which might or might not come in handy at a later date—but is living at its best today. This is a rejection of the Herbartian emphasis on the systematic mastery of the subject matter of the natural and social sciences. In place of the teacher-directed, methodical march through the logically arranged subjects, Dewey called upon the school to foster the active participation of pupils in fashioning their common life. Learning activities, hence, become real-life activities, and the school environment becomes a social community fashioned along democratic lines.

In 1896, Dewey put his educational theories to the test in the Laboratory School at the University of Chicago. This experiment gained wide recognition and stimulated other experimental projects. In addition, Dewey's books, notably, *School and Society* and *Democracy and Education*, in which he expressed his educational theories, helped to establish social competence as one of the major objectives of democratic education.

THE SUBJECT–MATTER UNIT METHOD TODAY

The three objectives of subject-matter unit teaching. Twenty years ago, a teacher who conscientiously sought to comply with the leading educational theories of that day was faced with a difficult problem. Schools by tradition were concerned primarily with the task of conducting pupils through the conventional subjects. The Herbartian doctrines of correlation did not quarrel with that purpose, but urged that the subject matter be presented in larger bodies of related materials. The psychologists, on the other hand, presented persuasive evidence to demonstrate the need for the individualization of instruction. They no longer considered it democratic to expect all pupils to profit equally from identical assignments uniformly administered. Finally, the educational philosophers and sociologists thought it necessary to provide experience in the various forms of social activities. These three objectives, providing for the mastery of subject matter, adjusting learning activities to the ability and needs of the individual pupil, and providing experiences that will develop competence as a member of a democratic social group, could not be achieved in the traditional pattern of instruction based upon the assignment of study tasks in daily installments. New procedures were called for, and in the hands of those who wished to achieve all three objectives simultaneously, a new pattern of procedures —the subject-matter unit method—emerged.

Early attempts to coordinate the three objectives. The Extracurriculum. The modern forms of the subject-matter unit method did not emerge full blown. For a time, schools attempted to keep the subject-matter mastery and the socializing aspects of teaching in separate categories. A program of extracurricular activities was provided to take care of the latter, while the regular classroom activities provided for the former. In most instances there was no effective plan formulated to coordinate the curricular and the extracurricular activities. Teachers were employed on the basis of their ability to teach subject matter. Their extracurricular assignments were regarded by the teachers and the community alike as something that had been added to an already full load, or as "sugar coating" to make schooling tolerable to pupils who might otherwise flatly refuse to endure the regular program of instruction. This was true particularly in the many schools that provided a program of athletics primarily to keep in school boys who would drop out otherwise. Extracurricular activities carried on in this halfhearted manner were doomed to fail. They satisfied neither the needs of the pupils nor the purposes of the educators who argued for experience in genuine democratic living.

The Cocurricula. The Winnetka Plan, previously mentioned in connection with Burk and the Dalton Plan, offered a unique procedure for achieving the three educational objectives simultaneously. It was reasoned that there are two types of subjects that make up the conventional curriculum. The first type includes subjects like mathematics, reading, grammar, and chemistry which represent specific facts, skills, or processes that are the necessary tools for carrying on the activities of modern life, and particularly the more advanced studies in school and college. These studies represent the subject matter that each pupil must master. By breaking up this subject matter into related "units" and allowing each pupil to progress through the sequence of units at his own rate—a procedure that was described in some detail earlier in this chapter—the advocates of the Winnetka Plan felt they could achieve two of the three objectives of the subject-matter unit method. That is, the mastery of the essential subject matter would be achieved by each pupil, and the rate of progress as well as the kind and amount of mastery would be adjusted to individual ability and needs. Roughly, one-half of the school's day is set aside for instruction in these tool subjects.

The remainder of the pupil's time, under the Winnetka Plan, is set aside for the second type of subjects. This type includes literature, the social sciences, the conventional extracurricular activities, and "cultural" studies. All of these help to acquaint the pupil with his social heritage and thereby help him become an intelligent citizen. It is obvious that the pupils need not develop identical literary interests or social skills, because good citizens vary greatly with respect to these. It was recommended, therefore, that the learning activities in this cultural group of studies and activities should be carried on in an informal social atmosphere and to a large measure should be directed by the pupils themselves. Thus, a literature class studying types of recreational reading might break up into committees with each committee assuming responsibility for studying and reporting upon only one type of recreational reading materials. Planning the class activities and making individual assignments, carrying out the assigned responsibilities, working with others, and fulfilling responsibility delegated by the group thus would provide many opportunities for acquiring socializing experiences.

Thus it was planned that the third objective, that of providing experiences in group living, should be achieved in a recognized and regular part of the curriculum. The socializing activities were not to be "educational orphans," as in the extracurriculum, but an integral part of the regular school program. Teachers were employed on the basis of their own social competence as well as on their subject-matter achievements. Their pay and teaching load recognized instruction in these cultural areas as on a par with instruction in the tool subjects. The success of the plan in Winnetka, Illinois, where it was developed, did much to awaken the concern of teachers and administrators throughout the nation for a broader and better balanced program of instruction.

The Learning Unit. The Morrison Plan represents a further effort to develop an integrated procedure to achieve the three educational objectives of subject-matter unit teaching. This plan was developed by Henry C. Morrison, who served as a superintendent of schools and the commissioner of education in New Hampshire, and later as professor of education at the University of Chicago. As in the other plans that have been described, Morrison made the mastery of subject matter the primary objective of instruction. His plan called for the organization of the things to be learned—the facts, skills, operations, appreciations, and understandings that have their origin and existence apart from the learner—into integrated wholes or "learning units." He defined a learning unit as ". . . a comprehensive and significant aspect of the environment, of an organized science, of an art, or of conduct, which being learned results in an adaptation in personality." [18] The teacher's first responsibility, according to Morrison, is to determine the several learning units that constitute the course of study in a given subject. A typical unit in a course in elementary science would be organized around a topic, such as, "The Earth in Which You Live," or "Our Water Supply." In a course in elementary mathematics, a unit might be built around topics like "The Concept of Line Segments" or "Indirect Measurement." History courses readily lend themselves to this type of unit organization, with topics such as "Primitive Man," "The French Revolution," and "The Rise of Modern Democracy" virtually suggesting themselves to the searching teacher.

Having selected the learning unit and decided upon the nature and amount of materials that should be included, the teacher was directed to follow a specific teaching procedure. This pattern of instruction, called "the mastery formula," provided for a series of teaching steps as follows: ". . . pre-test, teach, test the result, adapt procedure, teach and test again to the point of actual learning." [19] By means of the pre-test, the pupil as well as the teacher could find out exactly what aspects of the unit had already been mastered. In this way the teaching step could be planned to stress the aspects of the unit that remained to be learned. Since pupils do not enter upon a unit with identical knowledge, each pupil would have his own body of materials to be mastered. Furthermore, the testing step that follows the teaching step would reveal differences in the rate of pupil progress so that the adaptation of procedures for further teaching would be determined by the needs of the particular pupils who had not yet mastered the unit.

It was assumed that the "test—adapt procedures—teach—test" steps would be repeated until the slowest member of the class had mastered

[18] Henry C. Morrison, *The Practice of Teaching in the Secondary School*, rev. ed., p. 24, University of Chicago Press, Chicago. 1931.
[19] *Ibid.*, p. 81.

the basic materials contained in the unit. In the meantime, the more able pupils would have achieved suitable mastery and would have been assigned to related materials of a supplementary or enrichment nature.

The Morrison Plan provided for the individualization of instruction as well as the mastery of subject matter by means of the mastery formula. The socializing objective was provided for through a variety of devices used in the teaching and reteaching steps. It was expected that the teacher would employ a variety of student activities such as student-led discussions, committee assignments, field trips, and the planning and use of study materials not usually located in the classroom. Also, the pupil was expected "to re-act as effectively as may be to the content of his learning." In this culminating stage, after each pupil had assimilated the materials of the unit in his own way and at his own rate, the class would again be brought together to organize the materials into a coherent whole and to appraise it in terms of the new attitudes or meanings the materials studied now made necessary. This is a form of group thinking and group participation—an essential part of the democratic process—seldom provided for in the teaching patterns previously described.

Compared with other "plans," the Morrison Plan was well received by secondary-school teachers. In 1932, there were 737 secondary schools that reported the use of the Morrison Plan or some modification of it. This was approximately 9 per cent of the secondary schools surveyed.[20]

A modern form of the subject-matter unit method. After carefully studying these and other unit plans, some of which are being used successfully by secondary-school teachers today, Umstattd has integrated the desirable features of each into a single pattern of procedures which may be said to describe subject-matter unit teaching at a high level of development.[21] The Umstattd pattern has four major divisions, with wide variations in the specific activities that may be included under each. The four divisions or parts are listed and briefly described in the section that follows.

[20] Roy D. Billett, "Provision for Individual Difference, Marking, and Promotion," National Survey of Secondary Education, Monograph 13, Office of Education, Bulletin 17, p. 9, U.S. Government Printing Office, Washington, D.C., 1933.

[21] J. G. Umstattd, Secondary School Teaching, rev. ed., Chap. IX, Ginn & Company, Boston, 1944.

The Introduction and Attack. The first of these divisions is the "Introduction and Attack." In this phase of the unit, the class as a whole is introduced to the major or "unit idea" around which the unit is to be organized and the study plan formulated. Some teachers prefer to do all the initial planning and to use this phase merely to motivate the pupils and to make the assignments. Others may outline the topic, offering as suggestions some interesting aspects that might be explored, but leaving to the class the task of developing their own detailed plan of attack. The purpose of the introduction and attack phase obviously is to acquaint each pupil with what is to be done and to make available a plan for doing that which is to be done. One class period or five may be needed to accomplish this purpose, depending upon the nature of the unit and the method of approach the teacher wishes to use.

The Study-work Period. The second phase is the "Study-work" period. In this division may be included any activity in which pupils are to engage to achieve the ends set up in the "Introduction and Attack." Frequently as much as 60 per cent of the time scheduled for a given unit is spent in this phase. Some teachers may elect to spend part or all of this time in class meetings and to supervise the work activities very closely. Others prefer to have no class meetings but to have the pupils use the time of the scheduled class periods for self-directed meetings, committee meetings, field trips, interviews with specialists, or any other appropriate activity that will serve to give the pupil a mastery of the central unit idea.

The Integration and Application Phase. "Integration and Application" is the name given to the third group of unit activities. During this part of the unit, individuals and groups of individuals bring before the class as a whole the results of the work-study activities in which they engaged during the preceding phase. An effort is made to relate all of the individual reports to the major unit topic and to organize all the information thus provided into a coherent and meaningful whole. This organization of information and experience may take the form of an outline, a comprehensive report, or even a motion-picture script or a radio program. There is ample opportunity here for the teacher who so desires, to conduct the integrating activities in the form of a socialized recitation.

The Appraisal of Outcomes. Finally, there is a need to appraise the progress that has been made by the pupils as a result of their efforts.

Some form of evaluation activity should be provided. This phase of the unit is named, appropriately enough, the "Appraisal of Outcomes."

Within these four divisions of the subject-matter unit method, there is ample room for teachers to include whatever procedures and activities seem most appropriate for a given class, or to achieve special desired individual or group outcomes. Teachers are free to make adjustments and adaptations to fit their own requirements and ideas. In fact, two teachers may employ vastly different techniques and still have their procedures properly classified as belonging within the pattern of the subject-matter unit method. That is, the procedures have in common the following characteristics:

1. The subject matter of the unit acquired its status as a unit "independent of the learner or of any group of learners." [22]

2. The scope of the unit is usually so large that it cannot be mastered within the time limits customarily allotted to a daily assignment, including the class period traditionally set aside for the recitation.

3. The unit topic is so broad and the time schedule is so flexible that pupils may be given individual assignments in keeping with their ability or special interests.

4. The flexibility of the unit pattern makes it possible for teachers to introduce planning, work, or discussion activities similar to those in which adult members of a democratic community engage.

In this manner three major objectives of modern educators, namely, the mastery of essential subject matter, the individualization of instruction, and the participation by pupils in desirable social activities, are provided for simultaneously in the pattern of the subject-matter unit.

SUMMARY

The daily-assignment method was described in Chaps. 6 and 7 as a way in which some teachers seek to transmit a specific body of subject matter. For these teachers, the pupil's mastery of that subject matter is the primary objective of the educative process. In this chapter it was shown that the early advocates of the subject-matter unit method had no quarrel either with the objective or with the particular body of knowledge, skills, and understandings thought to be important. However,

[22] Hollis L. Caswell and Doak S. Campbell, *Curriculum Development*, p. 403, American Book Company, New York, 1935.

they did call for the presentation of subject matter in large, related units instead of item by item as in the daily-assignment method. The basis for this newer organization of curricular materials was provided by the Herbartian doctrine of correlation.

The unit organization of subject matter soon was adopted by those educators who were seeking ways to adapt instruction to the ability of the individual pupil. Out of this movement emerged the Burk, Winnetka, and Dalton Plans. Somewhat later the educational theories of John Dewey encouraged teachers to look upon the development of social competence as a desirable educational outcome. Greater flexibility in instructional procedures was called for to accommodate the variety of activities that were to provide pupils the necessary social experiences. The unit organization again seemed to meet this need, and was seized upon as a framework within which pupils might engage in a variety of activities while pursuing a common purpose.

The modern subject-matter unit, therefore, is a method of teaching that is employed to achieve three educational outcomes. They are: (a) the mastery of a designated body of subject matter, (b) the individualization of instruction, and (c) the development of social skills and understandings by means of participation in selected activities. These objectives may be sought separately or simultaneously. One modern pattern of the subject-matter unit method has four divisions or stages, namely, (a) introduction and attack, (b) study-work, (c) integration and application, and (d) appraisal of outcomes. The scope of a single unit usually is of such a size that it will occupy the time of the class for several weeks. Occasionally the length of the class period to which the unit is assigned may be extended or even doubled. In all cases, the principle of orientation that provides unity to the activities engaged in is derived from a body of subject matter that has been prescribed for the pupils.

SELECTED REFERENCES

ALEXANDER, JEAN M.: "Influence of Pedagogical Scholarship on Methods: From Herbart to Morrison," *Historical Approach to Methods of Teaching the Social Studies*, Fifth Yearbook, The National Council for the Social Studies, McKinley Publishing Company, Philadelphia, 1935.

BILLETT, ROY D.: "Provision for Individual Differences, Marking, and Promotion," *National Survey of Secondary Education*, Monograph 13, Office of Education, Bulletin 17, U.S. Government Printing Office, Washington, D.C., 1933.

———: *Fundamentals of Secondary School Teaching*, Part III, Houghton Mifflin Company, Boston, 1940.

CASWELL, HOLLIS L., and CAMPBELL, DOAK S.: *Curriculum Development*, Chap. XV, American Book Company, New York, 1935.

GOETTING, M. L.: *Teaching in the Secondary School*, Parts III and V, Prentice-Hall, Inc., New York, 1942.

HERBART, JOHN FREDERICK: *Outlines of Educational Doctrine*, trans. by Alexis F Lange and annotated by Charles DeGarmo, The Macmillan Company, New York, 1904.

KILPATRICK, WILLIAM H.: "The Project Method," *Teachers College Record*, XIX (4):319–335, September, 1918.

McMURRY, CHARLES A., and McMURRY, FRANK M.: *The Method of the Recitation*, The Macmillan Company, New York, 1909.

McMURRY, CHARLES A.: *The Elements of General Method*, The Macmillan Company, New York, 1907.

MEYER, ADOLPH E.: *The Development of Education in the Twentieth Century*, pp. 166–191, Prentice-Hall, Inc., New York, 1939.

MONROE, WALTER S., and MARKS, ARLYN: "General Methods of Teaching," *Educational Administration and Supervision*, XXIV:497–512, October, 1938.

MORRISON, HENRY C.: *The Practice of Teaching in the Secondary School*, rev. ed., University of Chicago Press, Chicago, 1931.

SCHORLING, RALEIGH: *Student Teaching*, Chap. VI, McGraw-Hill Book Company, Inc., New York, 1940.

SEARCH, PRESTON W.: *An Ideal School*, D. Appleton-Century Company, Inc., New York, 1901.

STORMIZAND, MARTIN J.: *Progressive Methods of Teaching*, Chaps. V and XIII, Houghton Mifflin Company, Boston, 1924.

UMSTATTD, J. G.: *Secondary School Teaching*, Chaps. VI, VII, and IX, Ginn & Company, Boston, 1944.

Chapter 10. THE SUBJECT–MATTER UNIT
METHOD IN ACTION

In the preceding chapter it was shown how the traditional method of teaching, which was based on the daily assignment of subject matter to be learned or exercises to be covered, came to be replaced in many classrooms by a newer type of teaching. The change was brought about by a variety of factors. Chief among these were the psychological studies which show that subject-matter mastery takes place more readily when there is a logical connection or relationship between the several items to be learned, and when they are presented with due consideration to the maturation and ability of the learner. Other studies have produced evidence to show that there is great diversity in the chronological ages at which individuals reach a given maturational level, as well as in the abilities, interests, and needs presented by an unselected group of individuals at such a level. It follows that equality of educational opportunity, a major consideration in a democratic society, cannot be realized with a method that expects pupils to progress at a uniform rate through assignments that require identical learning from all. Unit teaching appeared in response to the demand for a more flexible method.

The search for a more realistic teaching method also received direction from a group of educators who believe that children should be given an opportunity to practice the social processes which they will be expected to use when they leave school. Daily assignments, which so frequently have encouraged memorization at the expense of other forms of learning, were not judged to be well suited for this kind of practice. What is needed, it was felt, is a method that will make it possible for pupils to engage in a variety of activities that require cooperative planning and effort.

THE OBJECTIVES OF THE SUBJECT–MATTER UNIT METHOD

From this brief statement concerning its origin, it should be clear that the outcomes sought through subject-matter unit teaching are threefold. First, it is expected that pupils will master a particular body of subject matter that has been prescribed for them. On this point there is no quarrel with the daily-assignment method. Second, it is insisted that there shall be equal opportunity for each pupil to emphasize or stress that aspect of the prescribed subject matter which has greatest value for him at his particular maturational level, that is, there shall be differentiated assignments within the unit based upon the abilities, needs, and interests of the individual pupils. Finally, the social needs of all the pupils shall be served by providing them opportunities to engage in activities that call for group participation.

Some characteristics of the subject-matter unit method. Any teaching method that can accommodate these three purposes must of necessity be so adaptable that many variations of the basic pattern will be found. Studies made in the field of unit teaching have verified this assumption.[1] There are, however, certain characteristics which are common to the several variations.

The subject-matter unit is essentially a large body of subject matter —knowledge, facts, and skills—the constituent parts of which have a logical relationship to some central topic or problem. It is this relationship to a common point of reference that provides the element of unity. The fact that the teacher, rather than the pupils, selects the point of reference around which the unit is to be developed distinguishes this type of unit from the experience unit which will be considered later.

The body of subject matter which constitutes the unit is assigned to be studied as a whole, even though it cannot be covered in the time formerly set aside for one lesson. As a consequence the time set aside for a single unit may extend over several days or weeks.

To accommodate differences in ability, need, and interest, as well as to provide opportunities for developing social skills, units may include a variety of pupil activities. Individual assignments may be given to fit the requirements of the particular pupil for whom they are

[1] Roy D. Billett, "Provisions for Individual Differences, Marking, and Promotion," *National Survey of Secondary Education*, Monograph 13, Office of Education, Bulletin 17, U.S. Government Printing Office, Washington, D.C., 1933.

intended. Thus, the slow reader may be directed to materials that are written on a level he can grasp. The artistic pupil may be encouraged to prepare a mural which will portray in graphic form the major ideas covered in the unit. Committees may be appointed to investigate this special topic or to carry out that particular project. There may be planning activities, research activities, and construction activities. Some of these may be carried out by individuals, others by small groups, and still others by the class as a whole.

Many of the activities now included in units cannot well be carried on in 45-minute installments, the time allotted by the conventional class period. In some schools, therefore, the class periods set aside for unit teaching have been lengthened, or two or more periods have been combined.

There are several unit patterns in use today, each of which has its own merits. One pattern that seems to be well recommended calls for the development of the unit in four distinctive stages, each stage having its own type of activities. These stages are:

1. The introduction and attack stage
2. The study-work stage
3. The integration and application stage
4. The appraisal of outcomes stage

The success of teaching by the subject-matter unit method is measured primarily by the amount of the prescribed subject matter that has been mastered by the pupils. Mastery is indicated by the number of facts that have been learned, the skill or skills that have been developed, and the ideas, understandings, and appreciations that have been acquired as a result of the activities in which the pupils have engaged.

PLANNING THE UNIT

Selecting the unit. As stated above, the teacher is responsible for selecting and planning the subject-matter unit. Although pupils may sometimes be given an opportunity to participate in the planning of certain details or in setting up specific objectives, the scope of the unit as well as the major learning outcomes are determined for them, that is, pupil planning is effectively contained within limits previously set up by the teacher.

Teacher planning begins with the course outline. Since the attack will be made upon large units of related materials, the work to be covered during the term or year must be broken down into appropriate subdivisions. In recent years some curriculum makers and textbook writers have recognized the trend toward unit teaching and have organized the materials as a series of units, that is, the major topics have been suggested and the lesser materials have been related to them in a manner that facilitates the development of units of work. The New Hampshire course of study for modern European history, grades 10 or 11, is an example. In this outline the work for the year has been divided into 11 units and the major problems in each unit have been designated. Unit I is entitled, "How the French Made a Revolution and Established a Republic Which Did Not Last." The major questions or problems to be touched upon are:

1. What were the economic, social and political conditions in France and the rest of Europe during the eighteenth century?
2. How and why did the people get control of the French Government and abolish the customs of previous years?
3. What conditions made it possible for Napoleon to become emperor?
4. How did Napoleon enforce and spread the ideas of the French Revolution?
5. What were the causes of Napoleon's downfall? [2]

The other unit topics are:

How the Industrial Revolution Created Problems for the Nations of the World.
How the Reactionary Powers Tried to Crush Democracy (1815–1848).
How Great Britain Decided the Important Issues of the Century before the World War.
How Italy and Germany Achieved National Unity.
How Russia Remained Autocratic until 1917.
How France, Germany, and Italy Developed between 1871 and 1914.
How Imperialism Was Extended to Other Countries.
How the World War Was Fought and Settled.
How the Balkan States Won Their Freedom from Turkey.
How the European Countries Tried to Solve Their Problems. [3]

[2] "Social Studies," *Program of Studies Recommended for the Public Schools of New Hampshire, Grades VII to XII*, Part V, State Board of Education, Concord, N.H., 1940.
[3] *Ibid.*, pp. 203–206.

There are situations, however, in which the teacher will find it necessary or desirable to prepare his own list of unit topics. Under such
circumstances the teacher must decide which particular facts or experiences called for in the course outline may be grouped together around
some central idea or principle. A great deal of freedom may be experienced in this matter. Thus in the course in English composition outlined in Chap. 7, units might be formed around the idea of "the
sentence," "the paragraph," or each of the seven other topics that are
listed. On the other hand, the problems of proper word usage are common to all forms of composition. Therefore, another teacher might
develop units around such topics as, "Meeting New Words and Learning How to Use Them." Again, nearly all of the topics listed might be
included in either one of two large units respectively entitled, "Learning
to Study Effectively," and "Learning to Prepare Items for the School
Paper."

It is considered good practice when formulating unit topics to prepare the entire series of topics to be covered in the term or year. This
is important in order that adequate provision will be made for each
item specified in the course of study. It is also desirable to prepare a
tentative time schedule at this point in order that each unit may receive attention in proportion to its importance. Obviously, the amount
of time spent on each of the several units will need to be varied in
keeping with the nature of the subject matter and the needs of the
class. It is improbable that many units can be developed adequately in
less than 2 weeks. Some persons of wide experience recommend a minimum of 3 or 4 weeks.[4] If this is a valid generalization, then the number of units that should be undertaken in a 1-year course will not
exceed 12.

Developing the unit plan. Setting Up the Teacher's Objectives. After
the topic or central idea has been selected around which a unit is to be
built, it is necessary to define the specific goals that are to be reached
within that unit, that is, a list should be made of the specific concepts,
facts, and skills that are to be mastered by the pupils while they are
working on the unit. The list may be a series of statements or questions,
each of which represents a specific objective. The five questions in
Unit I of the course in modern European history, which were given in

[4] Raleigh Shorling, *Student Teaching*, p. 95, McGraw-Hill Book Company, Inc.,
New York, 1940.

the preceding section, represent such a list. It is this list of objectives that determines the scope of the unit. Some teachers prefer to define the scope of the unit by preparing the test they expect to use when the unit has been completed. Whether it is a list of objectives or an examination, the teacher should use this statement of desired outcomes as a guide in the selection of pupil activities and study materials. Only when the scope of the unit has been clearly defined can learning activities be planned that effectively lead the pupils toward the desired goals. Such planning also helps avoid needless repetition of subject matter and may enable the teacher to emphasize aspects that have special significance for the pupils because of their geographical location or cultural backgrounds.

The following are sample statements of objectives taken from two unit plans which have come to the author's attention in recent weeks:

A. From a unit on American history.
   1. To arouse in the student an interest in history, particularly that phase of early American history which contributed to the formation of the United States as a world power.
   2. To aid the student to gain an understanding and appreciation of the colonial movement and its significance in the development of American democracy.
   3. To examine the causes and effects of the original colonization of America, particularly by the English settlers, and its later influence on the development of the United States form of democratic government.
B. From a unit in chemistry.
   1. The pupil learns to understand the reasons manufacturers often adulterate food, such as:
      a. To lower the manufacturing cost.
      b. To make the product more appealing.
   2. The pupil learns to understand the theory and calculation necessary to prepare "normal" and "molar" solutions.
   3. The pupil learns to weigh and measure chemicals accurately.
   4. The pupil learns to keep an accurate record of all data collected.

A distinction should be made between these objectives, which are formulated to guide the teacher in planning and teaching the unit, and the objectives' goals, or purposes, which may be formulated later to guide the pupil in his work.

Listing Possible Learning Activities. The statement of objectives should not be mere window dressing. Each item must be functional and possible of attainment if it is to have any worth-while effect. An objective should not be included unless there is some assurance that it can be reached within the limits imposed by the resources of the school and community, as well as by the abilities and needs of the pupils. As each objective is added, the teacher should consider by what means it will be attained. Thus, if the ability to use the library is one of the outcomes sought, an activity must be indicated that will require the pupils to use the library while working on their unit assignments. In this manner a list of activities, materials, and equipment will be developed at the same time that the scope of the unit is being defined.

The number and variety of pupil activities that may be used in unit teaching have been expanded far beyond the half dozen or so found in the typical classroom at the beginning of the century. As early as 1929, one author listed 52 study activities classified as:

A. Visual Activities
B. Listening Activities
C. Oral Activities
D. Writing Activities
E. Drawing Activities
F. General Activities [5]

The list of possibilities has been expanded considerably since that time.

From the list of possibilities the teacher should select those activities which have special value for the pupils who make up the class. Local resources or current interests may afford reasons for selecting one type of activity rather than another. The needs or interests of individual pupils may also provide leads as to what might be included. Helpful suggestions along these lines may be obtained by preparing a list of needs and interests from whatever data are available either in the form of pupil records, or reports of surveys of the community. In some circumstances, pupils might even conduct a survey as part of a unit.

Activities should also be selected in the light of the abilities of the pupils. Reading materials in particular should vary in difficulty so that

[5] Howard E. Wilson, "Things to Do in the Social Science Classroom," *Historical Outlook*, 20:218–224, May, 1929.

each pupil may find some references suited to his ability. Cooperative activities and self-directed activities should not be assigned unless the pupils have had previous satisfactory experience with them or can be given the necessary supervision. As an example, library assignments should not be made unless pupils know how to use the library or can be given instruction in using the library as part of the unit.

Since subject-matter mastery is the primary objective, many of the pupil activities will be of an "information-getting" nature. Books, magazines, newspapers, films, recordings, maps, pictures, slides, and other informational materials must be made available. Again it is the responsibility of the teacher to know what is available, what is appropriate, and to prepare a list of the materials which the class will be expected to use. It is also up to the teacher to see that these materials are kept in a place where the class will have access to them. The selection of learning materials may be made in certain instances with a view to developing the pupil's ability to find and use reference sources. In such cases, the development of research skill becomes a unit objective and calls for an appropriate developmental activity.

It is worth repeating that no objective should be set up for the unit unless a suitable activity can be provided by which that objective may be reached. In other words, each objective should call for a specific activity by which it can be achieved. It is up to the teacher to check the activities and the objectives against each other until a realistic list of objectives has been formulated and suitable developmental activities have been provided.

Selecting the Culminating Activity. By this stage in the planning the teacher should not be at a loss for ideas as to what needs to be done. The objectives to be reached, the study materials to be drawn upon, the pupil activities to be engaged in, and the resources of the school and community to be utilized will have been determined. There is the probability, however, that the pupils, each of whom will be working on the unit assignment in his own way and frequently with different purposes in view, may lose sight of the over-all objectives for which the unit study was initiated. There is a further need, therefore, for pulling together the information and experiences acquired by the pupils on an individual basis into an organized form that will be useful to them in group situations as well. The next stage in planning, therefore, involves the selection of an integrating or culminating activity.

The primary purpose of the culminating activity, of course, is to help the pupils see the logical relationships that exist among the discrete parts of subject matter that are contained in the unit. It will be recalled that the need for such integration is one of the major reasons for teaching by the unit method. When pupils work on individual assignments, such integration will be secured only to a limited degree unless well-selected culminating activities are provided. Furthermore, the review of subject matter which a good culminating activity makes necessary may also aid retention.

There are several kinds of culminating activities that have been found satisfactory. Some teachers prefer to have each pupil make a summary of the unit in outline form. In other instances a summarizing outline is prepared cooperatively by the entire class. Panel discussions and debates, in which members of the class examine the issues of which their study has made them aware, are sometimes used with good results. Projects such as pageants, dramatizations, the production of motion-picture or radio scripts, and exhibits are also effective. These latter forms are used less frequently than others because they require more time and effort than teachers generally care to devote to a single unit of work, or to the culminating stages of a unit. However, when other values are sought, such as practice in cooperative planning and participation in achieving group purposes, projects of this nature obviously merit more favorable consideration than they have received to date.

Preparing the Guide Sheet. The final phase of teacher planning consists of the preparation of the guide sheet. The general plan of procedure developed by the teacher while setting up the objectives, listing the desirable learning activities, and selecting the culminating activity now must be cast into a form that can be placed in the hands of the pupils.

Some teachers who are just beginning the transition from daily assignments to units of work prefer to tell the pupils what is expected of them each day. For these teachers, units consist merely of a series of daily assignments which have a common relationship to some major topic or problem. In such cases the guide sheet may be dispensed with, or used merely to provide an overview of the entire unit and to show the relationship of each lesson to the unit topic. Such a guide sheet might consist of the following parts:

A. The Unit Topic

B. The Overview with a List of Objectives

C. The List of General Reading Materials

D. The List of Daily Assignments

E. The Culminating Activity

In other cases, the individual members of the class will be expected to direct their own activities from day to day as the unit progresses into the study-work stage. It is evident that, in such instances, the instructions given at the beginning of the unit must be specific and detailed. Instructions given orally will be inadequate in most cases. Since teachers now generally have some simple duplicating service at their disposal, it is much better to prepare these instructions in the form of a guide sheet, a copy of which can be given to each member of the class.

A guide sheet suitable for a subject-matter unit which is not divided into daily lessons will generally include the following features:

1. A complete or partial list of purposes or goals toward which the pupils shall consciously strive.

2. A list of required reading and other source materials.

3. A list of exercise materials in the form of questions or problems.

4. A list of supplementary or optional reading, exercise materials, and projects which is intended to adapt the unit to the individual interests and needs of the pupils.

5. Detailed directions for the culminating activity if it is to be planned by the teacher instead of the class.

A list of pupil purposes or goals is included in order that independent study and research activity may have direction. These purposes, to be effective, must have meaning for the pupils and be related to their own background of experience. Individual pupils have been known to work with enthusiasm on the improvement of their language skills when these were shown to be directly related to the acquisition of proficiency in radio communication. Similarly, an interest in aviation has made the study of mathematics palatable for many young men who had been unresponsive to other forms of motivation.

If all members of the class are to achieve the minimum objectives of the unit, the list of required reading and other study materials must be extensive enough to include an adequate treatment of each item that is to be mastered. When possible, adequate directions should be given to enable the pupils to locate the desired materials without further assistance. Arranging the list of materials in an approved bibliographical form, with page or chapter references indicated, may be sufficient.[6] It may also help if each item is marked to indicate that the materials listed can be found in the classroom, school library, or in some other location. Furthermore, the list of basic study materials should include items that present a minimum of difficulty to those who have reading or other study handicaps. To provide for all of these contingencies, the teacher must be thoroughly acquainted with the study materials that are available or that can readily be secured. The list of required reading must not be too long. No more materials should be listed as required reading than can be covered by the slower readers in the class. High-school pupils almost invariably react to an impossible assignment by refusing to do any part of it.

A list of questions and problems is generally included in the guide sheet to point out the subject matter that is of special importance. As in a good test, the list should be a fair sampling of all the important points that are to be mastered. Items that are incorrectly stated or to which a satisfactory answer cannot be found within the limits of the unit may become the source of considerable embarrassment to the teacher. It is a good policy, even for experienced teachers, to answer each question and to work each problem before the guide sheet is placed in the hands of the pupils.

Some teachers who claim to use the unit method make no effort to adapt the work to individual differences in ability, needs, or interests. Others have found that the work can be varied quite easily by the simple expedient of including a list of optional or supplementary study ma-

[6] One approved form calls for the alphabetical arrangement of the items by the last names of the authors. The author's name is followed by the title of the book or article, the publisher from whom it may be secured, the date of publication, and the pages or chapters to which the reader is directed. This form is illustrated as follows:

1. Magruder, Frank Abbott, *American Government*, Allyn & Bacon, Boston, 1941, Chap. XXXVI.
2. Wallis, Grace Allen, and Wilson, D. Wallis, *Our Social World*, McGraw-Hill Book Company, Inc., New York, 1933, pp. 164–186.

For the purposes of the guide sheet, the form may be abbreviated to include merely the last name of the author, the title of the source, and the page references, as follows:

1. Magruder, *American Government*, Chapter XXXVI.
2. Wallis, *Our Social World*, pp. 164–186.

terials, exercises, and projects. It is the practice in some schools to indicate which items require work of a level sufficiently above the average to warrant a mark of B or A. Pupils who fulfill the minimum requirements before the unit is completed may then try for a higher grade. There are other teachers who believe that enrichment is desirable on all levels of ability and that the slow to learn not only need more drill on fundamentals, but also are especially responsive to materials that are directly related to their interests. Teachers who subscribe to this point of view generally attempt to include optional activities representing a range of difficulty and interests sufficiently wide so that each member of the class can find something he can do reasonably well and with enthusiasm. In such cases, the choice of optional work is left strictly with the pupil.

Guide sheets should also include instructions for the culminating activity. If each member of the class is to be required to prepare a summary or outline of the unit, the necessary directions should be stated clearly and in detail. Unless the pupils are known to have had previous successful experience with this type of work, a suitable form should be described and illustrated. The same principle applies when individual projects are used, even though the specific nature of the project may vary from pupil to pupil. On the other hand, debates, panel discussions, dramatizations, and exhibits are group activities and require detailed group planning as part of the project. Therefore, only general instructions for these activities need be included in the guide sheet.

Finally, the guide sheet should be logically arranged and neat in appearance in order that it may be followed with ease. It should not be necessary to add that copies must also be legible, but many have been seen in the hands of students which were so blurred in places that the meaning was obscured.

The particular form of guide sheet used will vary from unit to unit as well as from teacher to teacher. The following very much abbreviated form, however, will illustrate the kind of information and material that should be included.

Unit II

The Birth of the American Nation

A. For the next five weeks we will try to find out how the American colonists organized themselves into an independent and free nation.

This study should be particularly interesting because it will show how our freedoms became part of our governmental structure. The nation that our forebears founded is different in many ways from the nations from which the colonists came. We will want to find out:

1. From where the colonists came.
2. Why they left their homes.
3. How the life they lived here differed from the life they had fled.
4. How they went about setting up a new government.

B. Everyone will find some help from reading the following materials:
1. Freeland and Adams, *America and the New Frontier*, pp. 300–328.
2. Hamm, *From Colony to World Power*, pp. 3–151.

C. By answering these questions and doing these things you should become familiar with the most important parts of the unit.
1. Draw an outline map of the thirteen original colonies and show from which countries the settlers in each colony came.
2. Who coined the money used by the colonists?
3. What frequently happened to people who could not pay their debts?

D. You should choose one of the following activities as your special project. Please let me know before the end of this week which one you have selected, or talk with me about some other project you would like to undertake.
1. Make an oral report to the class on any items such as books, clothing, pictures, maps, tools, and furniture you have seen in your home or in the community that may have been used by people living in the colonial period.
2. Sketch a map of our state as it existed at the time of the Revolutionary War.

E. You may find special help or additional interesting materials on the unit as a whole or on your project in particular in the following places or sources:
1. By visiting the ——— museum.
2. By reading the following library books:
   a. Forbes, *Johnny Tremain*.
   b. Outhwaite, *Unrolling the Map*.
   c. Wilder, *Little House in the Woods*.

F. Near the end of the five weeks we have set aside for this unit, we will develop a summary of the important things we have learned. Therefore, you need to make a list of the important and the especially interesting things you find so these may be shared with the class.

TEACHING THE UNIT

Up to this point, the present chapter has dealt with the activities of the teacher while he is engaged in preparing the unit plan. If the planning has been done carefully, the unit is ready to be presented to the class. The attention of the teacher must now shift from the organization of subject matter and learning materials, to the direction of the learning activities of the pupils. This is a major transition, for the teacher must now deal with dynamic, purposing, human personalities instead of with inanimate facts and ideas which can be pushed this way and that without arousing opposition.

In directing a class through a subject-matter unit, the activities of the teacher fall roughly into four categories. These categories parallel the four stages in the development of the unit and will be discussed separately.

The introduction and attack stage. The first problem encountered in teaching a unit is to present it to the pupils in a way that will induce them to accept their assignments in a cooperative spirit. This problem consists of two parts, namely, the motivation and the assignment.

The Problem of Motivation. Pupils have been satisfactorily motivated as soon as they see within the scope of the unit certain desirable goals which include the minimum objectives the teacher has set up for them. This problem of inducing pupils to accept as their own the purposes of the teacher is likely to be a severe test of the teacher's ability to stimulate desirable learning activity. In a later chapter, it will be shown that some teachers object to this form of salesmanship and insist that all learning should start with a need or interest that has developed from the experiences of the individual members of the class. However, the subject-matter unit method is based on the assumption that the teacher knows with certainty that which the pupils need to learn, and the motivation is designed to make the learning process as interesting and challenging as possible.

The particular form of motivation that is used in a given situation will depend upon the degree of familiarity the class may have with the materials to be studied. Now and then a unit may need to be undertaken that involves subject matter foreign to the experiences of the pupils. For example, a class in a city high school may need to learn about farm life in the agricultural Middle West. Goals involving a mastery of the principles of crop rotation, the annual cycle of planting, cultivating, and harvesting, and the unique circumstances that condition the social life of rural people can scarcely become strong, directing factors unless some initial acquaintance with these items can be provided. What is needed is an introductory survey of the subject matter to be mastered in the later stages of the unit. A series of pictures, motion and still, depicting the activities and life on the farm may be helpful. Exhibits of grain and other farm produce, a scale model of a typical farm, or a demonstration of the different ways by which plants are propagated might also serve to open up problems for further study. Some direct experience may be provided by a field trip to a near-by farm, even though it may not be representative of the farms in the area that is to be studied. These activities should be supplemented with directed reading. When the class as a whole has acquired some knowledge of the subject to be studied, it is ready to give consideration to the list of purposes the teacher has set forth in the guide sheet with some hope that these will be meaningful. The list of purposes may then be discussed and accepted, or amended and extended until the members of the class feel that the list is satisfactory. It is obvious that this type of motivation requires considerable time and effort and is not likely to be completed in one or two class periods.

In another case, the class may be familiar, in a general way, with the subject to be studied. When a class in civics, for example, is ready to study how the community protects the health of its members, the pupils may know something about quarantine laws and the operation of the city water and sewage disposal systems. This knowledge alone is not likely to make them eager to extend their research activities into other areas worthy of investigation. A class of this nature will require a form of motivation that will reveal new aspects of an already familiar subject in such a manner as to create new interests. This may be achieved by means of a lecture by the teacher or a guest speaker, an appropriate audio or visual aid, or a special reading assignment. This form of motivation might be provided in one or two class periods.

There are some courses offered in secondary schools which are selected by pupils for very specific reasons. A course in solid geometry, credit for which must be presented for admission to engineering colleges, is an excellent example. The pupils in a course of this nature generally have a superior background of experience in the subject and require very little in the way of motivation other than to be shown areas of subject matter that remain to be mastered. A pre-test which touches upon the major problems to be covered in the new unit of work may serve to introduce the new areas in a satisfactory manner. The pre-test is usually administered in written form. It can, however, be given orally in the form of a class discussion. This procedure enables the skillful teacher to delve more deeply than does the written test into the knowledge the individual members of the class have of the subject, and to utilize unanticipated class resources if any are revealed. During the discussion, the teacher will try to lead the class to raise precisely those points that have been set forth as pupil goals in the guide sheet. As these are brought forth, they are written on the blackboard. The list on the board need not be identical with the list in the guide sheet, but when it is completed, the necessary additions and alterations should be made to bring the two lists into agreement. This type of motivation might be completed in one class period.

These three motivation procedures are similar in so far as they end in a discussion by the class of the pupil purposes or goals listed in the guide sheet. They differ chiefly in the amount of information that must be provided before the purposes can be considered intelligently. When adequate preparation has been made, the pupils are ready to participate in revising the list of pupil objectives to conform to their own interests. In fact, some teachers prefer to develop all or part of the pupil purposes by means of such class discussions. The inexperienced teacher, however, needs to prepare a list in advance to guide him in leading the class discussion and to insure against omitting some important points.

Making the Assignment. The final phase of the introductory step consists of the assignment. It is at this point that the guide sheets are distributed and the pupils are given an opportunity to amend the listed pupil goals to conform with those developed in the preceding class discussions, to examine the reading assignments and other suggested activities with a view to asking for explanations of any points which are not clearly understood, and to select from the suggested optional materials the items that are to be undertaken by individual pupils. The teacher should make a record of the work each pupil elects to do and hold him to the agreement. Freedom to choose does not imply liberty to abandon tasks half done without good reason.

The importance of the introductory step can be realized when it is recognized that during this stage of the unit each member of the class must be made to comprehend the significance of the work to be undertaken, provided with a sufficient background of understanding to make the study activities meaningful, and given a definite understanding of the work that he will be required to do over a period of time that may cover several weeks. The introductory step, therefore, should not be hurried. One, two, or even more class periods may be devoted exclusively to this phase of the unit. Ideally, it should not be concluded until each pupil knows what he is to do and why it is worth doing.

The study-work stage. Following a successful introductory period the class should move rather quickly into the study-work phase of the unit. The degree to which the transition is made quickly and purposefully depends upon the skill of the teacher in providing adequate motivation, the clarity of the assignment, and the experience and ability of the members of the class. If this is a pupil's first experience with the unit procedure, he may be at a loss to know how to use the array of research materials to which he has been referred. Individuals in the early stages of adolescence are particularly prone to meet unusual situations with their peculiar brand of swagger and flippancy, and if neglected are likely to develop discipline problems. For this reason, some teachers prefer to divide the unit of work into daily assignments, and indicate on the guide sheet just what is to be done each day. This procedure, no doubt, aids in preventing waste motion and loss of control, but it fails to help the student develop self-reliance and independence beyond a certain point. It is not recommended as a general practice except as a transitional step from the daily-assignment method to a more advanced unit method.

In most instances the study phase of the unit should continue over an extended period of time. The members of the class should spend this time reading, taking field trips, conducting experiments, listening to lectures and radio programs, seeing motion pictures, and gathering pertinent information from other available sources. Many teachers who have been accustomed to daily recitations find it difficult to devote regularly scheduled class time to study tasks rather than to the conventional teacher-centered recitation. It must be emphasized, however, that with relatively few exceptions the scheduled class periods are not to be used for recitation during the study-work stage, but for individual and group study and work. Thus, the classroom becomes a combination workroom and study hall. Ideally, reference books and other source materials should be located there. Tables should be provided on which the pupils will have room to spread out their collection of materials. The pupils should be free to visit the library, shops, and laboratories, if these activities contribute to the attainment of their purposes. There should be opportunities for committees to meet to plan and to carry out their joint assignments. In the background of the scene of all this activity is the teacher, constantly alert to the needs of any individual or group. He gauges the progress that each is making from information gathered in friendly conversation. He observes in which book and on what page a particular pupil is reading, or stops to discuss with a committee at work the exhibit they have agreed to prepare. When necessary, the teacher is ready to point out new vistas for further explorations, to provide remedial work or drill to overcome a special handicap, to call the class together to deal with a problem that had not been anticipated, or to plan in greater detail a part of the unit which now seems to require further attention. In all this, every precaution must be taken so that an excess of control does not cause pupil initiative and resourcefulness to wither from a lack of exercise.

The culminating stage. In the study-work stage each pupil makes his own individual attack upon the problem at hand. Although each is directed by the guide sheet, it is unlikely that any two individuals will read the same references in the identical sequence or give equal emphasis to the several aspects of the unit topic. The information gathered and the conclusions drawn will be distinctly individual. Useful as such results may be in satisfying individual purposes, the knowledge and skill acquired may not be in a form that can be used in cooperative endeavors or social situations. It is necessary, therefore, to organize the information that has been acquired into a logical system that has social recognition and usefulness. To illustrate, the boy who has received a chemistry kit for his birthday may acquire much interesting information about the physical properties of a variety of compounds and the nature of their behavior in the presence of other substances. These experiences alone do not make him a chemist, however; that is, they do not prepare him to gather meaning from technical writings and to converse intelligently about the science of chemistry with those who are also working in that field. Before he can do these things, the boy must first learn by what name chemists designate this substance and that reaction, as well as to understand the accepted principles that describe the manner in which substances react. In other words, he must learn to speak the language of chemists before he can become an intelligent and capable chemist.

So it is with high-school pupils in whatever area they may be working. The unit will have failed to fulfill its promises unless it provides the pupil with some summary statement or logical arrangement of the acquired information in a form that will point up the basic ideas the unit is intended to develop and will enable him to discuss those ideas with others. Indeed, it is this integrating activity which gives point to the organization of subject matter about a central idea, the basic idea behind the subject-matter unit method.

When the integrating activity is to be in the nature of a summary or outline, the teacher has full responsibility for determining its acceptability, which is to say, its conformity to a recognized pattern. In most instances, the teacher will have provided for this contingency by setting forth in the guide sheet the conditions that must be met. Oral directions may be needed to supplement these instructions and in many instances individual assistance will also be required.

However, teachers are learning to culminate units in ways that are more fruitful. In the form of dramatizations, radio and motion-picture scripts, exhibits, and other group projects, subject matter may also be organized into meaningful patterns. In addition, pupils gain skill in social participation and group planning by working together in projects of this nature. They learn to apply the principles developed in textbooks to real-life settings, and in doing this the principles are mastered to the point of permanent retention. This type of activity is particularly valuable in a long unit where ample time may be set aside for developing a group project. It is scarcely feasible in a unit that must be completed in the space of 2 weeks' time. The extent to which teachers utilize class or group projects as culminating activities depends upon the relative importance they attach to the mastery of the subject matter as contrasted with the development of social skills. Those who employ the subject-matter unit method in the stricter meaning of the term have generally been inclined to place the greater emphasis on the former.

The appraisal of outcomes stage. Inasmuch as the appraisal of the outcomes sought through the use of the subject-matter unit method will be discussed in the following chapter, little need be said about this subject here. The fact that subject-matter mastery is the primary objective indicates that appraisal will be predominantly of the measurement type. Teacher-made and standardized tests will be used to determine which knowledge, facts, and skills have been acquired, and to what degree. The significance attached to individual differences, however, may encourage the practice of reporting progress on the basis of individual growth rather than upon the basis of the class average. Also, there may be an attempt made to appraise progress in developing the ability to plan and work with others. Mere retention of isolated facts or the acquisition of specific skills is not enough. The correlation principle which figured so prominently in the development of the subject-matter unit method calls for the mastery of subject matter in its relation to practical problems and life situations. It is this connection between the school and the nonschool experiences which is sought in unit teaching. The appraisal activities should, therefore, direct some attention to the question of whether or not the instruction is properly directed to establish such relationships in the minds of the pupils.

SUMMARY

Subject-matter unit teaching is undertaken to accomplish a threefold purpose. By means of appropriate procedures, techniques, and devices, teachers employing this method strive for (a) the mastery of a prescribed body of subject matter, (b) with due regard for the pupils' differences in ability, needs, and interests, and (c) with some provision for the development of social competence through practice in planning and working with others. Subject-matter mastery and the accommodation of individual differences are achieved by assigning learning materials in large segments or bodies of related items. These units usually are so large and have so many aspects that it is impossible for any one pupil to master all the items that are included. Hence, the emphasis in teaching can be upon the mastery of the general principles around which the unit is built and individual assignments may stress those specific items or aspects of the unit that have greatest value for the particular pupils for whom they are intended. The development of social skills is accomplished by means of learning activities in which groups of students engage.

There are many variations of the unit pattern in use today. In general, however, units may be said to develop through four stages. They are:

(*a*) the introduction and attack stage, (*b*) the study-work stage, (*c*) the integration and culmination stage, and (*d*) the appraisal of outcomes stage. The nature of the subject-matter unit method places major responsibility on the teacher for selecting, planning, and developing the unit.

SELECTED REFERENCES

BILLETT, ROY O.: *Fundamentals of Secondary School Teaching*, Part III, Houghton Mifflin Company, Boston, 1940.

BURTON, WILLIAM H.: *The Guidance of Learning Activities*, Parts II and IV, D. Appleton-Century Company, Inc., New York, 1944.

BUTLER, FRANK A.: *The Improvement of Teaching in Secondary Schools*, University of Chicago Press, Chicago, 1946.

GOETTING, M. L.: *Teaching in the Secondary School*, Prentice-Hall, Inc., New York, 1942.

JACKSON, DOYLE D., and IRVIN, W. B.: *The Unit Method of Learning and Teaching*, John S. Swift Company, St. Louis, Mo., 1942.

JONES, ARTHUR J., GRIZZELL, E. D., and GRINSTEAD, WREN JONES: *Principles of Unit Construction*, McGraw-Hill Book Company, Inc., New York, 1939.

MORRISON, HENRY C.: *The Practice of Teaching in the Secondary School*, rev. ed., University of Chicago Press, Chicago, 1931.

PARKHURST, HELEN: *Education on the Dalton Plan*, E. P. Dutton & Co., Inc., New York, 1922.

RISK, THOMAS M.: *Principles and Practices of Teaching in Secondary Schools*, Chaps. XIV–XXI, American Book Company, New York, 1941.

SCHORLING, RALEIGH: *Student Teaching*, McGraw-Hill Book Company, Inc., New York, 1940.

STORMIZAND, MARTIN J.: *Progressive Methods of Teaching*, Chaps. V and VII, Houghton Mifflin Company, Boston, 1924.

STRICKLAND, RUTH G.: *How to Build a Unit of Work*, Bulletin 5, U.S. Office of Education, Government Printing Office, Washington, D.C., 1946.

UMSTATTD, J. G.: *Secondary School Teaching*, Ginn & Company, Boston, 1944.

WILSON, HOWARD E.: "Things to Do in the Social Science Classroom," *Historical Outlook*, 20:218–224, May, 1929.

Chapter 11. THE MEASUREMENT OF PUPIL PROGRESS
IN THE SUBJECT–MATTER UNIT METHOD

Brief attention seems appropriate here to the behaviors sought in pupils taught under the subject-matter unit method. The degree to which pupils attain desired educational outcomes can be determined only by observing and measuring pupil behavior. Furthermore, the selection of measuring techniques is dependent largely upon the behavioral outcomes sought and the relative emphasis attached to different outcomes in the instructional method under consideration.

The educational outcomes receiving attention in the subject-matter unit method were presented in Chap. 9. Those discussed were physical and social skills, habits, knowledges, ideas and concepts, understandings, interests, and attitudes, whereas appreciations and ability to apply subject-matter masteries to the needs of group living were at least implied. Measurement of instructional outcomes must depend in considerable degree upon these desired behavioral changes and the frame of reference within which they are organized.

When these outcomes are compared with the possible types of learned behavior discussed in Chap. 5, it seems apparent that skills, knowledges, concepts, understandings and certain tastes and preferences received direct consideration. However, appreciations and applications received only indirect attention, for subject-matter masteries were conceived to be effective in providing the pupil with the necessary equipment for group living. Psychological and philosophical bases for this emphasis are those generally accepted at the time the subject-matter unit method emerged as a new instructional procedure.

Measuring procedures characteristic of the subject-matter unit method. Of the various unit plans of instruction, the problem method, the project method, the Winnetka Plan, and the Morrison Plan directly and the

Dalton Plan less directly include provision for measurement of pupil behavior, as was brought out in Chap. 9. Umstaddt[1] coordinated major features of eight unit plans and evolved the four stages in the teaching process of introduction and attack, study and work, integration and application, and appraisal of outcome. Measurement is therefore a direct and major concern when instruction is organized under a subject-matter unit method.

Such factors in this instructional method as attention to individual differences among pupils and the consequent emphasis upon individualization or differentiation of instruction result in an approach to achievement measurement not only by means of teacher-made or classroom tests but also by standardized achievement tests. The approach to the construction of standardized achievement tests which emphasizes subject-matter mastery is well characterized by the revision given below of the steps outlined by Monroe, De Voss, and Kelly.[2]

1. Determination of the minimum essentials of a subject
2. Decision concerning type of test—rate test, power test, quality scale
3. Decision concerning type of test exercises
4. Construction of test exercises
5. Tryout of initial test exercises
6. Selection of final test exercises
7. Construction of directions for administering and scoring
8. Establishment of test norms
9. Critical evaluation of the test

The subject-matter orientation of this approach to standardized test construction is not only in harmony with the emphasis upon subject-matter mastery in the instructional method under consideration but is also the guiding principle in the construction of many recently published, standardized tests. Although some of the evaluative instruments published within the last decade or so are properly considered to be standardized, their distinctly different approach to selection of content and to types of norms provided justifies their designation as evaluative instruments rather than as standardized tests.

[1] J. G. Umstaddt, *Secondary School Teaching*, rev. ed., Chap. 9, Ginn & Company, Boston, 1944.
[2] Walter S. Monroe, James C. De Voss, and Frederick J. Kelly, *Educational Tests and Measurements*, rev. and enlarged ed., pp. 394–404, Houghton Mifflin Company, Boston, 1924.

The types of tests, techniques, and tools discussed in this chapter are those particularly adapted to the subject-matter unit method of instruction, although they should be considered in large measure to be additions to, and not substitutes for, the tests and techniques presented in Chap. 8 for the recitation method of instruction. Standardized tests and scales, modifications of the five basic informal objective test items, and product and procedures measurement techniques are keyed mainly to the tangible informational and skill outcomes. Personality scales of the attitudes and general interests types and such tools as the profile chart and class analysis chart are useful in measuring outcomes of a less tangible nature. Teachers' marks constitute the remaining technique presented here for use with the subject-matter instructional method.

STANDARDIZED TESTS AND SCALES

The informal objective test differs little in form from the standardized test, which was its progenitor, for the same types of test items and testing procedures are used in both. It is true that they often differ in quality, for not all informal objective tests are well constructed. Neither are all standardized tests well constructed, for that matter. The major difference between the two types of instruments doubtless lies in the greater degree of preliminary work involved in the construction of the standardized test and in the availability of norms for attaining comparability of results for the standardized test. The informal objective test is not ordinarily tried out before it is used for its designated purpose, although it is subject to continuous improvement by use of techniques similar to those employed in standardized test construction. Bases for attaining comparability of results from test to test must be established for the informal objective instruments, as there are no norms by means of which comparability is obtained directly.

Considered here are those paper-and-pencil tests and those scales which give rise to paper-and-pencil tests useful mainly in measuring or aiding in the attainment of subject-matter instructional outcomes. Prognostic and inventory tests are used primarily before or at a very early stage of instruction, whereas the quite similar diagnostic and analytic tests and the related instructional and practice tests have major functions during the teaching process. Survey tests and product scales have most significance when used at strategic points in the school year for measuring the progress of a class group through the school grades.

Standardized test titles are often inexact in designating the real nature of the tests and are sometimes misleading. This may be a result of an attempt on the part of test authors and publishers to be specific in designating the function of the test in many cases, but it also results from the fact that most standardized tests furnish scores useful in more than one way and the fact that a similar function may sometimes be performed by quite different types of tests. Consequently, the sections which follow will frequently include reference to and even illustrations from tests the titles of which seem remote from the type under major consideration.

Prognostic and inventory tests. Standardized tests of the prognostic and inventory types are distinguishable more by their functions and by the specificity of the scores they furnish than by their content. Prognostic tests are designed for the prognosis or prediction of success in specific courses or subject areas, whereas inventory tests are intended to survey the pupil's background preparation in a subject area in sufficient detail to discover subject aspects in which reteaching should be provided. Prognostic tests are of major value in pupil guidance and in such a primarily administrative function as sectioning of classes, whereas inventory tests are more often used to provide the teacher with background information concerning pupil achievement levels in a school subject or field of study for use in his classroom teaching.

Prognostic Tests. Prediction of individual pupil success in a school subject or area is the major function of prognostic tests. In this respect, the prognostic test and the aptitude test are similar. However, the aptitude test, discussed in some detail in Chap. 16, attempts to measure the potentialities or aptitudes of pupils in large degree apart from what they have learned, whereas the prognostic test attempts rather to measure the instructional outcomes previously attained by the pupils in foundation subjects and their significance for success in the new subject or area.

Prognostic tests are most often found in school subjects for which certain well-defined basic abilities are prerequisite to success. Tests so designated are most common in the secondary-school areas of foreign languages and mathematics, although a similar predictive function is performed in other subject areas by aptitude tests. Prognostic tests are of two general types—those which measure pupil ability to acquire skills and information in the new field of study, and those which measure his degree of mastery in underlying skills upon which success in the new subject depends. The first type is similar to the aptitude test, or is intermediate between the aptitude and the achievement test in nature, but the second type definitely falls under the achievement test heading.

Inventory Tests. Inventory tests are designed to obtain a preview of the pupils' backgrounds in content or skills prerequisite to a field of study about to be undertaken. Their purpose is to afford the teacher insight into such gaps as may exist in the preparation of individual pupils so that work not unlike that involved in remediation can be supplied as needed. Survey tests, often given near the end of a school year, may sometimes serve the inventory purpose for the teacher who has the pupils in a related, higher level course the following year. Prognostic tests may also provide information of an inventory nature, although their primary purpose is prediction of success in a school subject or area.

It is not uncommon to find that many pupils come to high school with what teachers and administrators believe to be inadequate preparation in such basic skills as computing, reading, writing, and speaking. In the attempt to make certain that such skills are not permanently neglected for such pupils, standardized tests in arithmetic, reading, and English mechanics really designed for use at the intermediate and junior high-school grade levels are sometimes used with secondary-school pupils. Pupils who score below the level deemed necessary for a citizen of a democratic society are then frequently given instruction of a broadly remedial or refresher type in the skill areas where their deficiencies appear.

Tests useful for this inventory purpose are very numerous, although they are seldom called inventory tests. They often afford measures in the different aspects of the school subject, such as the fundamental processes of addition, subtraction, multiplication, and division in arithmetic; word meaning, sentence meaning, paragraph meaning, and speed in reading; and spelling, punctuation, capitalization, and grammatical usage in English mechanics. Such tests have an inventory rather than a narrowly diagnostic purpose, and their use leads to the provision of re-teaching for the deficient pupils. Blair [3] gives an extensive treatment to

[3] Glenn M. Blair, *Diagnostic and Remedial Teaching in Secondary Schools,* Chaps. 2, 8–11, The Macmillan Company, New York, 1946.

this inventory use of tests in the areas of reading, arithmetic, spelling, handwriting, and English expression.

Diagnostic and analytic tests. Instruments and procedures for the diagnosis or analysis of pupil performance have the same general aim—determination of pupil deficiencies as a basis for the provision of remediation. The purpose in each instance is similar to that of the physician who attempts to diagnose a patient's ailment. His ultimate, and indeed his only worth-while, purpose is to go beyond the symptoms to the point where causes can be identified, for it is only through the identification of causes that the most effective remedial treatment of the patient can be prescribed. Similarly, the teacher must go beyond symptoms to the diagnosis or analysis of pupil performance until the causes become apparent. Remediation applied to symptoms is almost certain to be ineffective, but remediation based on a knowledge of causes stands an excellent chance of being effective.

Diagnostic Tests. Diagnostic tests, in the narrow sense of the term, are found mainly in subjects where a definite pyramiding or hierarchical arrangement of skills or content exists. The mathematical subjects best illustrate this organization of subject matter. It is in such skill subjects primarily that a definite sequence must almost inevitably occur in learning. For example, a skill prerequisite to the solution of quadratic equations in algebra is that involved in the solution of linear equations, so a pupil cannot be expected to perform the higher level skill satisfactorily unless he has adequate competency in the prerequisite skill. Similarly, understanding of certain geometrical theorems concerned with lines is prerequisite to a group of theorems which deals with triangles. Diagnosis in this sense is also possible for handwriting skills.

Analytic Tests. Analytic tests are found in subject areas where no such definite hierarchies or psychological organizations of content or skills apparently exist. In reading, for example, pupils can comprehend such large thought units as paragraphs at a given level of difficulty before they necessarily possess word comprehensions at a higher difficulty level, although paragraphs and words doubtless cannot be scaled in definite and precise steps of difficulty. Furthermore, pupils may gain adequate comprehension of paragraphs in which one or more words unknown to them occur by gaining meanings from the context. No such exact organization of reading skills has yet been evolved, nor perhaps can ever be evolved, as has been generally accepted for mathematical skills. The best that is to be expected today in reading is that a similar rough sequence of learning experiences may receive general acceptance by teachers of reading. In the social studies, to mention a second area where analysis rather than diagnosis applies, it is difficult to conceive any consistent organization or pyramiding of learnings in one exact and immutable sequence.

Tests referred to here as analytic in function may be thought of as diagnostic in the broad sense of diagnosis. Diagnostic and analytic tests may be considered as narrowly diagnostic and broadly diagnostic, to make the distinction in a second way not uncommonly used. Test titles do not differentiate between the two levels of diagnosis, for both types are designated as diagnostic in common practice. Analytic tests, relatively newer in test titles, are diagnostic in the broad sense only. Such other instruments as survey tests, inventory tests, and even instructional tests are often diagnostic in the broad meaning of the term.

Not all diagnostic and analytic devices are properly classified as tests. Some of the product and procedure measures discussed in a following section of this chapter are designed for diagnostic and analytic functions. Among them are certain quality scales and such other devices as check lists, profile charts, and class analysis charts.

Instructional and practice tests. Partially standardized test material more often designed to serve instructional than measurement functions are available in many fields of subject matter. Although such materials exist in greater quantity at the elementary-school level than for the secondary-school subjects, they are found for at least the major high-school subjects in one or another of several forms. Variously known as instructional tests, drill tests, practice tests, workbooks, and practice exercises, these materials are available in different formats and from various sources. Some are available as independent series of tests and others in the form of workbooks or practice exercises designed to accompany particular textbooks. Lincoln and Workman[4] present a general discussion of such materials, and Blair[5] deals with their values and uses more extensively in connection with diagnostic and remedial procedures in major secondary-school subjects.

Justification for brief consideration of these semistandardized in-

[4] Edward A. Lincoln and Linwood L. Workman, *Testing and the Use of Test Results,* Chap. 10, The Macmillan Company, New York, 1935.
[5] Blair, *op. cit.,* Chaps. 7–11.

structional tests here is found in the fact that they provide exercise materials not incomparable to the informal objective test exercises the teacher might construct and that they usually provide a basis for self-evaluation by the pupil. The exercises are often so set up that the raw score or a score derived from it has a defined meaning on a point scale of some type. A profile chart is often provided, on which the pupil graphically represents his progress from unit to unit of the material. The scores are usually established in such manner that the pupil profile line will have a pronounced upward trend over a period of time as evidence to him of progress made.

Survey tests. Tests of the survey type are by far the most numerous, the best known, and the most widely used of all standardized instruments. The reason doubtless lies in the fact that survey tests serve general rather than specific measurement functions. Such tests are ordinarily accompanied by age norms, grade norms, or percentile norms by means of which comparability of results is established. Survey tests are available in practically all subject-matter areas at the secondary-school level, although they are less numerous in such performance areas as the fine arts, manual arts, home economics, physical education, and business education than in the academic subject areas.

Survey tests may be divided into three types in terms of their scope or coverage. Most broad are the test batteries, more common at the elementary-school than at the secondary-school level, which include separate parts, or even booklets, and provide separate scores for such major subject areas as English, social studies, science, and mathematics. Intermediate in breadth are the tests in separate subject areas such as the above and in the somewhat more specific areas of literature, reading, English usage, foreign languages, and health. Most specific are the tests designed for use in certain courses, such as algebra, plane geometry, solid geometry, and trigonometry in mathematics; ancient, medieval, modern, and world history in that social study area; general science, biology, physics, and chemistry in the science field; and similarly specific tests in other subject areas.

The distinction among these three types of survey tests is not clear-cut, for tests in major subject areas are sometimes combined into a battery covering the fields in which practically all high-school pupils take courses. Furthermore, tests in areas and in specific subjects are distinguishable more by the specificity of the subject than by any other means. For example, tests in French often provide for pupils at all points in a 2-year study of that subject, whereas tests in plane geometry are based on a quite definite 1-year course.

Norms for these various types of survey tests commonly follow certain general patterns. The batteries of tests and the tests in separate major areas of study most often provide grade norms at the high-school level. A pupil commonly grows in such abilities as are involved in reading, English expression, social studies, science, and mathematics regardless of the particular courses he takes, for he is certain to take courses, or at least to have experiences, in most if not in all of these major areas. In foreign languages, taken variously by different pupils and not at all by some pupils, norms of the percentile type are commonly provided in terms of the number of semesters or years the subject has been studied. Still different are the specific courses, taken largely as electives by some pupils but by other pupils not at all, and occurring in no absolute sequence, for which percentile norms applicable to the particular course are commonly provided.

Standardized survey tests are sometimes mistakenly used as a major or even a sole basis for determining final course marks and consequently for determining whether pupils pass or fail. Such a use is unjustifiable, for standardized tests can measure achievement only in the core materials thought to be common to a subject or subject area in all schools, and are not intended to provide for the differences in objectives and content which properly characterize the same subject in different schools. Such factors as section of the country, size of the community, major employment possibilities in the community, type of school, and type of pupil enrolled are among the most important in determining instructional emphases. The standardized survey test should be used as a basis for marking only when its results are supplemented by adequate measurements of the other and more specific or locally important outcomes. Teacher-made tests and techniques provide the best means for accomplishing this purpose, inasmuch as the teacher better than any other person knows the content of, and the activities provided in, the course he has taught.

The other uses of standardized survey test results are numerous. Results from such tests afford a means of comparing pupil performances with those of comparable pupils in other schools. Indirectly this makes possible an evaluation of the program of the school. Even more important, such results afford a basis for a broad diagnosis or analysis of individual pupil achievement useful in individualized educational and vocational guidance. The fact that survey tests often provide scores in such separate areas as vocabulary or word meaning, sentence meaning, paragraph comprehension, speed, and level of comprehension in reading; spelling, usage, sentence structure, effectiveness of expression, and, even more specifically, punctuation and capitalization in written English; and reading, vocabulary, grammar, and knowledge of the civilization in foreign languages indicates the broadly diagnostic or analytic values found in resulting scores.

Product scales. Only in the field of spelling are product scales provided for a type of testing widely important at the secondary-school level. A product scale in spelling lists words in groups of equivalent difficulty, as shown by the percentages of pupils at various grade levels found to spell them correctly or to misspell them. A teacher who wishes to construct a spelling test at a given level of difficulty and with a predetermined range of word difficulty may do so by choosing words appropriately from the different groups shown in such a product scale. The scale itself does not go into the hands of the pupils; rather, it is a test construction instrument used solely by the teacher in constructing what might be called a semistandardized spelling test.

INFORMAL OBJECTIVE TESTS

The five basic types of objective item forms discussed in considerable detail in Chap. 8 represent only a small fraction of the item varieties which have been evolved, although most of the other forms are based on, and are modifications of, the five basic item forms. A few of the additional item types appropriate to the subject-matter unit method of

EXCERPT FROM NELSON'S HIGH SCHOOL ENGLISH TEST

DIRECTIONS: Mark "X" in the square numbered the same, as the word or group of words that you think would represent the better literary form if it were inserted in the blank.

1. Amy ...... her dinner with her. 1 brung 2 brought................... 1   1 ☐ ☐

2. "They have ...... all my ice-cream," cried Tommy. 1 ate 2 eaten....... 2   2 ☐ ☐

3. He ...... feel well this morning. 1 don't 2 doesn't.................. 3   3 ☐ ☐

4. Did you notice how many books there ......? 1 was 2 were............ 4   4 ☐ ☐

Source: M. J. Nelson, *Nelson's High School English Test*, Form A, Houghton Mifflin Company, Boston, 1931.

EXCERPT FROM COOPERATIVE TEST OF SECONDARY SCHOOL MATHEMATICS

(Items 59 through 65 refer to the diagram below.)

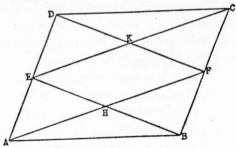

$ABCD$ is a parallelogram. $DF \perp BC$, $BE \perp AD$, EKC and AHF are straight lines.

Some of the statements in the list below (items 59 through 65) are necessarily true; the rest are false or not necessarily true.   Mark each item as follows:

1   if the statement is necessarily true.
2.   if the statement is false or not necessarily true.

59. $DF \parallel EB$ . . . . ( )

60. $AE = ED$ . . . . ( )

61. $\angle ADC + \angle ABC = 180°$ . . . . ( )

62. $AE = FC$ . . . . ( )

63. $\angle CEB = \angle DFA$ . . . . ( )

64. $EK = KF = HF = EH$ . . . . ( )

65. $\angle EDK = \angle FCK$ . . . . ( )

Source: Margaret P. Martin, *et al., Cooperative Test in Secondary School Mathematics*, Form S, Cooperative Test Service, New York, 1942.

instruction are illustrated and discussed here briefly. Many other forms involve such minor modifications or are so complex as not to warrant treatment. No attempt is made to suggest methods of construction, for the recommendations given in Chap. 8 apply with minor modifications.

Alternate-response item modifications. Several rather simple adaptations of the basic alternate-response item forms are highly useful. Among these are the type in which the pupil is asked to select the proper word

EXCERPT FROM COOPERATIVE PLANE GEOMETRY TEST

Directions: Some of the statements below are always true, some are always false, and others are sometimes true and sometimes false, depending on the particular situation.   Read each statement and mark it in the parentheses at the right as follows:

Put in the parentheses a plus sign (+) if you think the statement is always true.
Put in the parentheses a zero (0) if you think the statement is always false.
Put in the parentheses the letter (S) if you think the statement is sometimes true and sometimes false.

1. A circle can be inscribed in a regular
    polygon. . . . . .1(   )

2. Two triangles which are similar to the
    same triangle are similar to each other. 2(   )

17. The ratio of two corresponding me-
     dians of two similar triangles is the
     same as the ratio of the sides to which
     they are drawn. . . . . .17(   )

Source: Margaret P. Martin, *Cooperative Plane Geometry Test*, Form T, Cooperative Test Service, New York, 1943.

to complete a sentence grammatically in English or in a foreign language, the type in which true-false statements occur in groups based upon a chart or other data provided, and the type in which provision is made for one degree, or even as many as three degrees, of certainty between the extremes of true and false. The accompanying illustrations provide samples of these item forms.

EXCERPT FROM IOWA SILENT READING TESTS

DIRECTIONS. Read each paragraph carefully, and then study the questions *A*, *B*, and *C* at the right. Select the correct answer. Notice the number of this answer. In the margin at the right, fill in the answer space under this number.

1. In some parts of the world metal pins have been in use for ages. In certain Egyptian tombs pins of bronze and copper have been found. Pins like our hatpins, and others like the safety pins of today, were used by people in very ancient times. The first pins made in our country were nothing but bits of wire. The wire was rolled up at one end to form a head, while the other end was sharpened.

1

A. Choose the best title for the paragraph.
  1 Bronze and Copper Pins   2 Early Metal Pins
  3 The Use of Hatpins. .A

B. Over how long a period have pins been made and used?
  1 since modern times   2 since very ancient times
  3 since the founding of this country. . . . . .B

C. The pins found in Egyptian tombs were made of —
  1 bronze and copper   2 copper wire
  3 iron wire. C

Source: H. A. Greene, A. N. Jorgensen, and V. H. Kelley, *Iowa Silent Reading Tests*, new ed., Advanced, Form AM, World Book Company, Yonkers, N. Y., 1939.

Multiple-choice item modifications. Two forms of multiple-choice item modifications illustrated herewith are quite widely used. The first shows how discriminative reading ability may be measured by basing typical multiple-choice items in groups on accompanying passages. The sec-

EXCERPT FROM INFORMATION TESTS IN AMERICAN HISTORY

Place a check mark (✓) after all correct responses.

1. The following were Northern Generals during the Civil War:

U. S. Grant............................... —
McClellan .... —
Bishop Polk .... —
Albert Sidney Johnston.................. —
Meade .... —

Source: A. S. Barr and C. J. Daggett, *Information Tests in American History,* Form A, Educational Test Bureau, Minneapolis, Minn., 1932.

ond, a multiple-response form, differs from the basic multiple-choice form by providing correct answers as well as alternative answers in numbers greater than one.

Matching exercise modifications. Unbalanced matching sets, multiple-matching sets, and identification exercises represent three common variations in the matching exercise. The unbalanced matching may provide

EXCERPT FROM COOPERATIVE GENERAL SCIENCE TEST

Directions (Items 1 through 12): For each group of items below, place in the parentheses after each word or phrase in the right-hand list the **number** of the word or phrase in the left-hand list with which it is **most directly associated**.

1 Heart	1. Circulatory system . . . .1( )	1 Mendel	7. Laws of biological inheritance . 7( )
2 Kidney		2 Pasteur	
3 Lung	2. Excretory system . . . . .2( )	3 Hooke	8. Germ theory of disease . . . 8( )
4 Stomach		4 Burbank	
5 Spinal cord	3. Nervous system . . . . .3( )	5 Carrel	9. Plant breeding . . . . . . .9( )

Source: O. E. Underhill and S. R. Powers, *Cooperative General Science Test,* Form Q, Cooperative Test Service, New York, 1940.

for the pairing of 3 statements with the 3 corresponding statements from 5 given on the other side of the exercise, as in the first accompanying illustration, or may avoid guessing in even longer exercises by providing 5 and 8 or 10 statements for appropriate matching of 5 concepts. Two forms of multiple-matching exercises are quite common, as illustrated herewith. In the first, each statement on the short

EXCERPT FROM SONES-HARRY HIGH SCHOOL ACHIEVEMENT TEST

DIRECTIONS. In the parentheses after each literary product in Column 2 write the number of the form in Column 1 that tells what type it is.

COLUMN 1 (LITERARY FORMS)		COLUMN 2 (LITERARY PRODUCTS)	
1. ballad	6. essay	46. The Gold Bug..............(	) 46
2. biographical novel	7. historical novel	47. Ivanhoe...................(	) 47
3. comedy	8. short story	48. The Iliad.................(	) 48
4. elegy	9. sonnet	49. To Solitude (Keats)........(	) 49
5. epic poetry	10. tragedy	50. Sesame and Lilies...........(	) 50

Source: W. W. D. Sones and David P. Harry, Jr., *Sones-Harry High School Achievement Test*, Form A, World Book Company, Yonkers, N.Y., 1929.

side of the exercise is needed from one to several times for filling all the blanks on the long side of the set. In the second, the matching extends

EXCERPTS FROM ELY-KING TESTS IN AMERICAN HISTORY

I. State how each of the following is especially noted by placing "a" before the names of writers, "b" before the names of statesmen, "c" before inventors, "d" before pioneers, "e" before educational leaders, and "f" before military leaders:

1. ( ) Clay			7. ( ) Webster	
2. ( ) Whittier			8. ( ) Scott	
3. ( ) Whitney			9. ( ) Mann	
4. ( ) Houston			10. ( ) Calhoun	
5. ( ) Austin			11. ( ) Hawthorne	
6. ( ) Mary Lyon			12. ( ) Fulton	

Source: Lena A. Ely and Edith King, *Ely-King Tests in American History*, Test IV, Southern California School Book Depository, Ltd., Hollywood, Calif., 1927.

to three related lists organized on a balanced or an unbalanced basis. The third common adaptation is that known as an identification exercise, in which parts of a map, chart, or other graphical representation are matched with names of states, as in the accompanying illustration, or with terminology of the science or other subject area from which the chart is taken.

EXCERPT FROM SONES-HARRY HIGH SCHOOL ACHIEVEMENT TEST

DIRECTIONS. In the first parentheses after the name of each book in Column 3 write the number of its author from Column 1. In the second parentheses after each book in Column 3 write the number of its author's nationality from Column 2.

COLUMN 1 (AUTHORS)	COLUMN 2 (NATIONALITIES)	COLUMN 3 (BOOKS)		
1. Cervantes	1. American	59–60. The Odyssey......Author (	) 59	
2. Dante	2. English	Nationality (	) 60	
3. David	3. French			
4. Emerson	4. German	61–62. The Psalms........Author (	) 61	
5. Goethe	5. Greek	Nationality (	) 62	
6. Homer	6. Hebrew	63–64. Faust............Author (	) 63	
7. Hugo	7. Italian	Nationality (	) 64	
8. Ibsen	8. Norwegian	65–66. Paradise Lost ......Author (	) 65	
9. Milton	9. Russian	Nationality (	) 66	
10. Tolstoi	10. Spanish			
		67–68. The Wild Duck ....Author (	) 67	
		Nationality (	) 68	

Source: W. W. D. Sones and David P. Harry, Jr., *Sones-Harry High School Achievement Test*, Form A, World Book Company, Yonkers, N.Y., 1929.

EXCERPT FROM COOPERATIVE AMERICAN HISTORY TEST

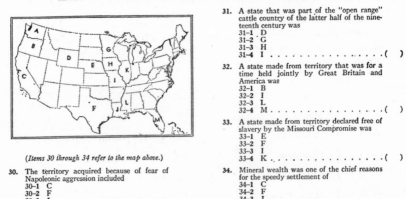

(*Items 30 through 34 refer to the map above.*)

31. A state that was part of the "open range" cattle country of the latter half of the nineteenth century was
31-1 D
31-2 G
31-3 H
31-4 I ....( )

32. A state made from territory that was for a time held jointly by Great Britain and America was
32-1 B
32-2 I
32-3 L
32-4 M ....( )

33. A state made from territory declared free of slavery by the Missouri Compromise was
33-1 E
33-2 F
33-3 I
33-4 K ....( )

30. The territory acquired because of fear of Napoleonic aggression included
30-1 C
30-2 F
30-3 J
30-4 M ....( )

34. Mineral wealth was one of the chief reasons for the speedy settlement of
34-1 F
34-2 F
34-3 J
34-4 M ....( )

Source: Mary Willis, *Cooperative American History Test*, Form T, Cooperative Test Service, New York, 1943.

PRODUCT AND PROCEDURE MEASURES

Tests of the paper-and-pencil variety are useful in measuring many types of instructional outcomes, but there remain many outcomes not possible of measurement by such means. Among such are the many skills involved in such subjects or areas as manual arts, home economics, fine arts, business education, laboratory science, and even handwriting. It is possible to test knowledges pertaining to such skills by paper-and-pencil tests, but the ability to perform the skill must be measured more directly. It is possible, for example, to determine whether a boy in manual training knows how to plane up a board by a verbal test, but measurement of his ability to perform that task must be by more direct means.

Two methods of measurement are available for use with these skill outcomes. Product measurement is based on an appraisal of the completed task, whereas procedure measurement requires observation and appraisal of the various processes involved in completing the product.

Product measures. Measurement of pupil achievement indirectly in terms of the characteristics found in the products they produce may be accomplished by using such paper-and-pencil, but non-test, devices as quality scales, rating scales, and score cards, and also by using various non-test techniques involving paper and pencil only incidentally. The quality scales, rating scales, and score cards usually result in the assignment of numerical representations to qualitative performances, while the other techniques more often result in the assignment of numerical representations to quantitative performances.

Product measures of the qualitative and quantitative types must often be interpreted together to obtain a complete appraisal of pupil performance. In handwriting, for example, both quality of the product and speed in its attainment are important. Similarly, reading speed and comprehension are factors in reading proficiency, and typewriting measurement involves both speed and accuracy. It is true, however, that time requirements are of no major significance in some productions, such as the writing of an essay or the painting of a picture. Similarly, quality of performance is less directly important in some measures, such as points scored in a basketball game, than is the quantity produced.

Quality Scales. The quality scales most widely used today are designed for measurement of handwriting ability, although the less widely used scales for the measurement of composition ability are similar in nature. It is interesting to note that handwriting quality scales were among the first standardized measuring instruments developed.

Standardized handwriting scales consist of samples so distributed along a numerical scale that equal numerical differences represent equal differences in quality of handwriting. Samples of pupil handwriting for evaluation by means of the scale may be obtained either from regular written work or from a special class activity in which each pupil writes a certain selection according to standardized directions. The pupil samples are then compared with the scale, and the numerical value of the scale sample most nearly like each pupil's writing is assigned. The accompanying illustration of two levels from the handwriting scale of the *Progressive Achievement Tests* shows the general nature of these quality scales.

SAMPLES FROM HANDWRITING SCALE OF PROGRESSIVE ACHIEVEMENT TESTS

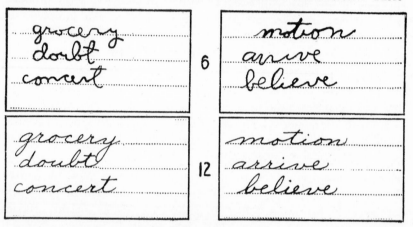

Source: *Manual of Directions, Progressive Achievement Tests,* Advanced Battery, p. 6, California Test Bureau, Los Angeles, 1943.

Rating Scales and Score Cards. Two similar instruments which provide for evaluation of pupil behavior by assigning numerical equivalents to descriptive statements are rating scales and score cards. Rating scales are available for measuring various types of instructional outcomes and also for use in personality measurement, whereas score cards are usually limited to appraisal of pupil behavior indirectly by means of the products the pupils produce. Rating scales typically deal with important characteristics of pupil behavior, but score cards are concerned with characteristics of the work produced by pupils.

The accompanying excerpt from the *Haggerty-Olson-Wickman Behavior Rating Schedule* illustrates the graphic feature often found in rating scales. Descriptive statements representing scaled degrees of quality or merit appear at equal intervals along a line usually divided into 5 or 10 segments, and the rater indicates his evaluation of pupil behavior by placing a check mark at the appropriate place on each line. Such rating scales are more applicable to the evaluation of work habits and study skills than to the informational types of instructional outcomes and to the broader behavioral characteristics usually considered under the heading of personality.

EXCERPT FROM HAGGERTY-OLSON-WICKMAN BEHAVIOR RATING SCHEDULES

15. Is he quiet or talkative?   *Score*

| Speaks very rarely (3) | Usually quiet (1) | Upholds his end of talk (2) | Talks more than his share (4) | Jabbers (5) | ____ |

16. Is his behavior (honesty, morals, etc.) generally acceptable to ordinary social standards?

| Unacceptable, Extreme violations (5) | Occasional violations (4) | Ordinarily acceptable (3) | Always acceptable (1) | Bends backward, Very rigid standards (2) | ____ |

17. What are his social habits?

| Lives almost entirely to himself (4) | Follows few social activities (3) | Pursues usual social activities and customs (1) | Actively seeks social pleasures (2) | Prefers social activities to all else (5) | ____ |

Source: M. E. Haggerty, W. C. Olson, and E. K. Wickman, *Haggerty-Olson-Wickman Behavior Rating Schedules,* Schedule B, World Book Company, Yonkers, N.Y., 1930.

Standardized score cards have been provided in the field of home economics more than in any other subject area. They are designed for the evaluation of foods, clothing, personal appearance, and other products and characteristics. Some are available for use with commercial products, and hence are valuable in consumers' education. Others are intended for use in evaluating pupil-made products, and hence measure complex skills or sets of related skills. The food score card for meat roast, reproduced in the illustration on page 254, is representative of this type of instrument.

Other Techniques. Product measurement is often applied in situations where the quantity of something produced in a given time or the time required to perform a given task is the result desired. Speed of reading tests are product measures of this type. So also are measures of proficiency in athletics and physical education, such as the time required for a boy to run 100 yards or the number of points he scores in a basketball game. Similarly, the number of letters produced per

Food Score Card for Meat Roast and Gravy

MEAT ROAST   31

	1	2	3	Score
Appearance	1. Shriveled		Plump and slightly moist	1.
Color	2. Pale or burned		Well browned	2.
Moisture Content	3. Dry		Juicy	3.
Tenderness	4. Tough		Easily cut or pierced with fork	4.
Taste and Flavor	5. Flat or too highly seasoned		Well seasoned	5. _____
	6. Raw, tasteless, or burned		Flavor developed	6.

GRAVY   SCORE _____

	1	2	3	Score
Color	1. Insipid		Light or dark brown; appetizing	1.
Consistency	2. Watery or too thick		Slightly thicker than whipping cream	2.
Texture	3. Lumpy		Smooth	3.
Taste and Flavor	4. Greasy		Not greasy	4. _____
	5. Flat or overseasoned		Well seasoned	5. _____
	6. Raw or scorched		Flavor developed	6.

SCORE _____

Source: Clara M. Brown, *Food Score Cards: Meat Roast and Gravy*, No. 31, University of Minnesota Press, Minneapolis, Minn., 1940.

minute in handwriting and the number of words produced per minute in typewriting are quantified product measures.

Procedure measures. Despite the fact that there are times when quantity of production is of paramount importance and quality of performance is a secondary concern, the quality of performance often determines in considerable degree the quantity produced. A typist who uses the "hunt-and-peck" system may be rapid and accurate, but she would doubtless be more rapid and accurate if she had acquired the touch system of typewriting. The fastest runners and hurdlers, the highest scoring basketball players, the best mechanics, the best typists, and in fact the persons high in their level of achievement in any type of skill performance attain quality in the finished product and speed in its attainment largely by virtue of the techniques or procedures they employ. Although individual differences in pupils in part determine what may be the best method for each to use, some methods can be demonstrated as superior to others in terms of such a purely physical factor as mechanical advantage. Hence, development of appropriate techniques in the pupil is important in teaching, and procedure measurement is an important aspect of teaching which has such a purpose.

Check Lists. The check list is the most common device for procedure measurement in laboratory science and other types of manual skills. Check lists may well be used to appraise procedures for pupils whose proficiency is shown by product measurement to be defective or incomplete. As the check list must ordinarily be used with individual pupils under direct observation of the teacher, such a device is time consuming. Its use should probably be limited, therefore, to exceedingly important skills and to the supplementation of product measurement.

Both product and procedure measurement, the latter by use of a check list, are illustrated by a method devised at Ohio State University for measuring ability to use a microscope.[6] By presenting a problem to a class in which each member was equipped with a microscope and a prepared slide, allowing adequate time for completion of the problem, and observing each student's setting of his microscope, it was possible by this simple product evaluation to distinguish those who could from those who could not use the microscope properly. Those who did not attain the desired product, which was a microscope so adjusted that the desired image showed clearly, were subjected to the procedure measurement.

The check list pictured in the accompanying illustration was used by the instructor with each such student individually as he attempted to prepare a slide from yeast culture and locate a yeast cell under the microscope. As the student manipulated the apparatus, the instructor recorded the sequence and nature of his actions. From the resulting record, the instructor was able to obtain not only a measure of how well the student could perform this laboratory skill but also diagnostic information valuable in later remediation of his defects. (See page 256.)

This device is widely applicable to laboratory skills in science and to many skills in manual arts and home economics, especially those in which definite sequences or steps of procedure are necessary or preferable.

Other Techniques. Pupil procedures in skill performances are often evaluated by teachers through direct observation of the process under

[6] Ralph W. Tyler, "A Test of Skill in Using a Microscope," *Educational Research Bulletin*, 9:493–496, Nov. 19, 1930.

CHECK LIST OF STUDENT REACTIONS IN FINDING AN OBJECT UNDER THE MICROSCOPE

STUDENT'S ACTIONS	Sequence of Actions	STUDENT'S ACTIONS (Continued)	Sequence of Actions
a. Takes slide	1	ag. With eye away from eyepiece turns down fine adjustment a great distance	15
b. Wipes slide with lens paper	2	ah. Turns up fine adjustment screw a great distance	
c. Wipes slide with cloth		ai. Turns fine adjustment screw a few turns	
d. Wipes slide with finger		aj. Removes slide from stage	16
e. Moves bottle of culture along the table	3	ak. Wipes objective with lens paper	
f. Places drop or two of culture on slide		al. Wipes objective with cloth	
g. Adds more culture		am. Wipes objective with finger	17
h. Adds few drops of water	4	an. Wipes eyepiece with lens paper	
i. Hunts for cover glasses	5	ao. Wipes eyepiece with cloth	
j. Wipes cover glass with lens paper		ap. Wipes eyepiece with finger	18
k. Wipes cover with cloth		aq. Makes another mount	
l. Wipes cover with finger		ar. Takes another microscope	
m. Adjusts cover with finger		as. Finds object	
n. Wipes off surplus fluid	6	at. Pauses for an interval	
o. Places slide on stage		au. Asks, "What do you want me to do?"	
p. Looks through eyepiece with right eye	7	av. Asks whether to use high power	
q. Looks through eyepiece with left eye	9	aw. Says, "I'm satisfied"	
r. Turns to objective of lowest power	21	ax. Says that the mount is all right for his eye	19,24
s. Turns to low-power objective		ay. Says he cannot do it	
t. Turns to high-power objective	8	az. Told to start new mount	20
u. Holds one eye closed		aaa. Directed to find object under low power	
v. Looks for light		aab. Directed to find object under high power	
w. Adjusts concave mirror		NOTICEABLE CHARACTERISTICS OF STUDENT'S BEHAVIOR	
x. Adjusts plane mirror			
y. Adjusts diaphragm	10	a. Awkward in movements	
z. Does not touch diaphragm		b. Obviously dexterous in movements	✓
aa. With eye at eyepiece turns down coarse adjustment	11	c. Slow and deliberate	✓
ab. Breaks cover glass	12	d. Very rapid	
ac. Breaks slide		e. Fingers tremble	
ad. With eye away from eyepiece turns down coarse adjustment		f. Obviously perturbed	
ae. Turns up coarse adjustment a great distance	13,22	g. Obviously angry	
af. With eye at eyepiece turns down fine adjustment a great distance	14,23	h. Does not take work seriously	
		i. Unable to work without specific directions	✓
		j. Obviously satisfied with his unsuccessful efforts	✓

SKILLS IN WHICH STUDENT NEEDS FURTHER TRAINING	Sequence of Actions	CHARACTERIZATION OF THE STUDENT'S MOUNT	Sequence of Actions
a. In cleaning objective	✓	a. Poor light	✓
b. In cleaning eyepiece	✓	b. Poor focus	
c. In focusing low power	✓	c. Excellent mount	
d. In focusing high power	✓	d. Good mount	
e. In adjusting mirror	✓	e. Fair mount	
f. In using diaphragm	✓	f. Poor mount	
g. In keeping both eyes open	✓	g. Very poor mount	
h. In protecting slide and objective from breaking by careless focusing	✓	h. Nothing in view but a thread in his eyepiece	
		i. Something on objective	
		j. Smeared lens	
		k. Unable to find object	✓

Source: Ralph W. Tyler, "A Test of Skill in Using a Microscope," *Educational Research Bulletin*, 9:493–496, Nov. 19, 1930.

way. A teacher of any skill subject well versed in his field is able to distinguish poor from good techniques when he observes them and to aid pupils in the attainment of better techniques and procedures. In doing so, improvement of the product, both in terms of its quality and speed in its attainment, is usually the goal.

PERSONALITY SCALES

Two types of instruments often classified as personality scales appear to be useful in the measurement of outcomes from the subject-matter unit method. These are the attitude scale and the interests inventory of the general or nonvocational type. Both are of the type known as personal reports, for it is the pupil who personally indicates his attitudes or his interests in the manner prescribed.

Attitudes scales and general interests inventories both reveal information which represents pupil attainments. Both, however, measure outcomes for which it is often difficult to establish sound criteria of worth. Attitudes appear in some controversial areas where no complete agreement exists nor may be expected to develop. Interests are often highly individualized and so related to such other factors as aptitudes and environmental influences that no pattern of interests desirable in all pupils is conceivable. Hence, results from attitudes and interests measurement should most often be used in obtaining insight into pupil characteristics. There are some areas, of course, in which relative agreement exists, as in attitudes appropriate in a good citizen and interests in desirable forms of cultural experiences, but desirable pupil outcomes cannot be set up too exactly even in such areas. Persons differing widely in their attitudes and interests may be equally good citizens.

Attitudes scales. Attitudes of varied types are instructional objectives in the school subjects. Representative are attitudes of good citizenship and cooperation in the social studies and scientific attitudes in the sciences. Attitudes may be either quite general or rather highly specific. For example, a person who has a fundamentally liberal attitude on social and economic issues may behave in a very conservative manner in a situation where his security is threatened. An attitude on such a broad issue as war is much more general than an attitude toward a particular person.

Standardized scales for the measurement of attitudes are widely available. The two most widely known and probably most widely used series of such scales are the *Thurstone Scales for the Measurement of Social Attitudes* and the *Generalized Attitudes Scales* devised by Remmers and his colleagues. The *Pressey Interest-Attitude Tests*, illustrated herewith, measure both of these closely related evidences of personality types. The first part of the illustration is representative of the check list method of attitudes measurement.

General interests inventories. Pupil interests may be measured in a variety of general, as contrasted with vocational, areas of behavior.

Among the areas where pupil interests are of direct concern to the teacher are types of persons, recreations, school subjects, motion pictures, and radio; and book, magazine, and newspaper reading. Interests in these areas are possible of measurement informally by means of questioning individual pupils or class groups, asking pupils to write lists of

EXCERPTS FROM PRESSEY INTEREST-ATTITUDE TESTS

Directions: Below is a list of things which some people think are wrong—that some people think a person ought not to do or is to be blamed for. Place a cross (X) on the dotted line in front of everything YOU think is wrong. Place two crosses (XX) in front of everything which you think is VERY WRONG—that a person is very much to be blamed for. You may mark as many or as few words as you wish. But be sure to mark everything which you think is wrong—that a person is to be blamed for.

1...........accidents	31...........aristocrat	61...........being stubborn
2...........fighting	32...........day-dreaming	62...........broker
3.........ignorance	33...........freak	63...........dispute
4...........talking back	34...........kidding	64...........playing cards
5...........crying	35...........poker	65...........divorce

Directions: Below is a list of things that people often like or are interested in. Place a cross (X) on the dotted line in front of everything which YOU like or in which YOU are interested. Place two crosses (XX) in front of everything in which you are VERY MUCH interested . . . which you like VERY MUCH. You may mark as many or as few words as you wish. But be sure to mark everything which you like or in which you are interested.

1...........artist	31...........card parties	61........._____dress
2...........drawing	32...........dancing	62...........reading
3...........cartoonist	33...........doctors	63...........children
4...........movie star	34...........fashions	64...........professors
5...........engineers	35...........leaders	65...........science

Source: S. L. Pressey and L. C. Pressey, *Pressey Interest-Attitude Tests*, The Psychological Corporation, New York, 1933.

their interests, or preparing an informal interests check list and administering it to pupils. Such techniques should ordinarily be delimited to one type of interests at a time if reasonably specific responses are desired.

Standardized inventories are available for measuring interests in some of the activities listed above. One of these is the *Pressey Interest-Attitude Tests*, which, as was mentioned above, also measure attitudes. In the accompanying illustration from those tests, the second part shows a typical approach to measurement of interests in types of persons and activities.

OTHER MEASUREMENT TOOLS

Materials accompanying many standardized achievement tests often serve a measurement function indirectly through the manner in which they provide for the summarization and integration of test results for individual pupils or class groups. Although such summarizations as class record forms supply are useful, lists of pupil names and corresponding scores provide at best only a summarization of results from testing. Several other devices, of which the profile chart and class analysis chart seem most pertinent here, easily make possible a graphically descriptive and analytical representation of an individual pupil or class performance.

Profile Charts. A measurement tool having considerable analytic value is the profile chart, on which are shown pupil results in comparable form and in relation to meaningful derived scores for the various parts of a test or various tests of a battery. Such profile charts commonly appear on the cover of the test booklet, on a separate answer sheet, or as a separate sheet for comprehensive achievement tests and for some personality instruments. The accompanying illustration of the profile chart

SAMPLE PUPIL PROFILE FOR IOWA TESTS OF EDUCATIONAL DEVELOPMENT

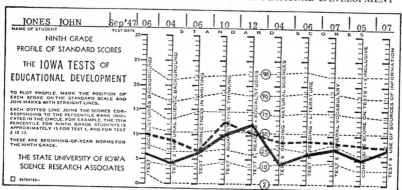

Source: *How to Use the Test Results: The Iowa Tests of Educational Development*, p. 6, Science Research Associates, Chicago, 1947.

provided with the *Iowa Tests of Educational Development* shows how the profile for an individual pupil supplies information of a broad diagnostic or analytic type.

Class Analysis Charts. Although forms designed for use in class

SAMPLE CLASS ANALYSIS CHART FOR

The data for Columns 1 to 16 are obtained from the Metropolitan Achievement Tests.

Grade Equiv.	1. Reading	2. Vocabulary	Ave. Reading	3. Arith. Fund.	4. Arith. Prob.	Ave. Arith.	5. English	6. Literature	7. History
above 9.0	5,10,13	5,10,13	5,10,13		10	10	10,13	3,5,10,12,13,18	3,5,10,12,13
9.0		11,19							
8.9									
8.8			19				1		
8.7	19								
8.6							3,11,19		
8.5									
8.4							12		
8.3									
8.2	1,12						14,21	19	
8.1									14
8.0		3	1,11,12						
7.9									
7.8									
7.7		1,12,18,21							
7.6				10				1	
7.5							17,18		11,19
7.4			21						
7.3								21	
7.2							7,9,20		
7.1	14,21								
7.0	11						5,8	14	
6.9		7	18		3,13				1,16,17
6.8	7		7			3,13	11,17		
6.7			14		3,13	16		4	4
6.6									
6.5		17	3	12					
6.4									
6.3		14	1		5,18,19				7,21
6.2		16	17	19	22	5,18,19,12			
6.1	18			21			4,22	2,7,8,9,20	
6.0	22	4,22	22	5,11,18	17,20	1,17,20			
5.9	17	20	16	17,20		11	2		9
5.8			4,20		1,11,12,16	16,21	16	16	
5.7	8,9,20	9	9	14,16					2,15
5.6	4,16	8	8	2		14			
5.5				7	9,14,15,21	22			
5.4		2	2	8,9		9			8,18
5.3	2,6			6			6,7,8		
5.2									
5.1		6			6		15	22	
5.0	3						15		
4.9		6			7,8				
4.8				22		2			
4.7				4				15	
4.6							4	15	6
4.5			15						
4.4				4					
4.3									
4.2		15							22
4.1			15						
4.0					2				
3.9	15								
3.8									
3.7									
3.6									
below 3.6									6,20
No. pupils	22	22	22	22	22	22	22	22	22
Median	6.1	6.7	6.6	5.9	5.8	5.8	7.4	6.8	6.8

Source: Gertrude H. Hildreth, *Metropolitan Achievement Tests: Manual for*

analysis more often accompany elementary-school than secondary-school test batteries, they are provided with several test batteries overlapping the two levels at the junior high-school grades. Such charts commonly provide for representation of individual pupil status and median class achievement levels in relation to age norms, grade norms,

METROPOLITAN ACHIEVEMENT TESTS

The data for Columns B and E should be obtained from an intelligence test.

11	12	13	14	15	16	A	B	C	D	E
8. Geography	Ave. Social Studies	9. Science	10. Spelling	Ave. Ach'v'm't	Age Equiv.	IQ Scale	IQ	Age Scale	Chronological Age	Mental Age
3,5,10,12,13	3,5,10,12,13	3,5,10,12,13	10	10,13	above 16-0	above 130	10	above 16-0		10
					16-0	130		16-0		
			5		15-10	129		15-10		
					15-8	128		15-8		
					15-6	127		15-6		
			16	3	15-4	126		15-4		
					15-2	125		15-2		
					15-0	124		15-0		
			17	12	14-10	123	5,12	14-10		
					14-8	122		14-8		
					14-6	121		14-6	22	5
19					14-4	120		14-4		
		11	13,20		14-2	119		14-2		
	19				14-0	118		14-0		
		19	18		13-10	117		13-10		19
				19	13-8	116		13-8		
					13-6	115	13	13-6		12
					13-4	114		13-4		
	14		12		13-2	113	19	13-2		
		21	3		13-0	112		13-0	4	13
			7		12-10	111		12-10		3
					12-8	110	3	12-8		
			14,21		12-6	109		12-6		
	11		5	14,18,21	12-4	108		12-4		
	1		4,11		12-2	107		12-2		
14		7,14	6,19		12-0	106		12-0	8,16,19,20	1
					11-10	105	1	11-10	17	
		1,17	17		11-8	104	11,18	11-8	21	
1	7		8,9		11-6	103		11-6	3,9	11,21
7	16	16	16		11-4	102		11-4	1,2	18
					11-2	101		11-2	5,15	
11,18,22		4,9			11-0	100		11-0	11,13	
	4,21				10-10	99	21	10-10	7,10,12,14,18	8
8			9		10-8	98	7	10-8	6	7
	18		8	9	10-6	97		10-6		4,14,17
	8	8	4,20	8	10-4	96		10-4		
	9,15		22		10-2	95	14	10-2		6,15,20
16,21	17		2,15	22	10-0	94	6	10-0		2
	2		2		9-10	93		9-10		9
4,15		2,6,22		2	9-8	92	8,15	9-8		
9	22		6		9-6	91		9-6		
2					9-4	90	17	9-4		22
		22			9-2	89	2	9-2		
20			15		9-0	88		9-0		
				6	8-10	87	9	8-10		16
					8-8	86	20	8-8		
					8-6	85		8-6		
		15			8-4	84		8-4		
6				15	8-2	83	4	8-2		
	20	20			8-0	82		8-0		
17	6				7-10	81		7-10		
					7-8	80		7-8		
					7-6	79		7-6		
					7-4	78		7-4		
					7-2	77		7-2		
					7-0	76		7-0		
					below 7-0	below 76	16,22	below 7-0		
22	22	22	22	22	No. pupils	No. pupils	22	No. pupils	22	22
5.9	6.0	6.3	6.8	6.6	Median	Median	96.5	Median	11-4	10-9

Interpreting, pp. 56–57, World Book Company, Yonkers, N. Y., 1948.

or both, or even in terms of percentile ranks. The accompanying sample from the *Metropolitan Achievement Tests* illustrates the appearance of a completed class analysis chart and indicates the graphic manner in which important information concerning individual pupil and class performance is displayed in relation to meaningful derived scores.

TEACHERS' MARKS

The two marking bases which seem to be most characteristic of the subject-matter unit method of instruction and most closely in harmony with the philosophy and method embodied in it are the point-scale and the trait rating methods. The first definitely and the second only somewhat less involve the marking of each pupil in terms of his status as compared with that of other members of his class. William R. Ross [7] found in 1939 that more than 80 per cent of secondary schools used a point system ranging from 2 to 10 categories and that 23 per cent of such schools employed ratings on character or personality traits as a supplementary device. It seems likely, therefore, that the patterns of marking which we have discussed here are most typical in present practice.

The point-scale marking procedures discussed in Chap. 8 are based on the grade-standard theory, whereas those discussed in this section are based on the normative or class-average theory. These theories and the theory based on accomplishment in relation to potentialities for accomplishment were discussed in Chap. 5. Although the resulting letter marks are stated in the same terms in the grade-standard and normative treatments, the methods involved in obtaining the marks are distinctly different. It is probable that the tendency in schools using the subject-matter unit method is to use fewer categories, say two, three, or five, than is true of schools using the recitation method, where five or more categories appear to be typical.

Normal curve marking systems. A marking system based on the normal curve is used in some manner in most schools which prefer to mark pupils on a point scale in terms of their relative achievement levels. Although the assignment of certain percentages of each letter mark can obviously be determined only by arbitrary means, as there are no standards which can conceivably be applied, the usual practice is to assign more marks toward the middle of the distribution and decreasing numbers of marks as the deviations from the average become greater in either direction. This is in harmony with the characteristics of the normal curve discussed briefly in Chap. 16.

Various proposals have been offered for percentages of each letter

---

[7] William L. Wrinkle, *Improving Marking and Reporting Practices*, pp. 50–52, Rinehart & Company, Inc., New York, 1947.

mark on a 5-point scale, but Symonds offers such patterns [8] for scales having anywhere from three to seven distinct marks. The first of the two methods suggested below for assigning marks can easily be adapted to any number of points from three to seven, but the second method, illustrated in terms of the most popular 5-point scale, is less readily adapted to scales having other numbers of points.

PERCENTAGE DISTRIBUTIONS FOR MARKING SYSTEMS
BASED ON DIFFERENT NUMBERS OF POINTS

3 points	4 points	5 points	6 points	7 points
20	11	7	5	4
60	39	24	15	10
20	39	38	30	22
	11	24	30	28
		7	15	22
			5	10
				4

Neither of the two methods briefly outlined here should be used with absolute rigidity. There are too many instances in which two or more pupils have identical composite scores or too closely similar scores to warrant assignment of different final marks and in which there is too great variation in the caliber of pupils taking the same course from year to year. It may sometimes be justifiable to assign a greater or smaller percentage of one or more letter marks than is called for in the plan or even to assign no F or no A marks for a class definitely above average or below average.

Linear Marking. The simplest and perhaps most widely used system of marking by which specified percentages of each letter mark are awarded may be termed linear. It merely involves the arrangement of composite achievement measures, obtained by a method such as that outlined in Chap. 8, in descending order and counting downward from the highest to the lowest scores in terms of the desired percentage of each letter mark. If, for example, there are 32 pupils in a class and an A, B, C, D, F system based on Symonds' 5-point pattern is in use, the

[8] Percival M. Symonds, *Measurement in Secondary Education*, p. 512, The Macmillan Company, New York, 1927.

numbers of pupils receiving each mark are: A, 2 (7 per cent = 2.24); B, 8 (24 per cent = 7.68); C, 12 (38 per cent = 12.16); D, 8 (24 per cent = 7.68); and F, 2 (7 per cent = 2.24).

Russell developed a *Classroom Scaler and Grader*[9] useful in assigning marks on a 5-point normal curve scale. Various cards providing for different percentages of A, B, C, D, and F marks, chosen by the user as desired, may be slipped into a frame. After the pupils have been ranked from highest to lowest in achievement on a test or on a semester's work, the mark corresponding to each rank can be obtained by a simple manipulation of the instrument. Provision is made for classes ranging in size from 16 to 60.

Deviation Marking. A marking system which takes into account the range or variability of achievement existing in a class group is proposed by Lindquist.[10] The first requirement is to obtain two measures —the arithmetic mean (A.M.) and the mean deviation (M.D.). The arithmetic mean is the sum of the scores divided by the number of pupils. The mean deviation is obtained by determining the amount by which each pupil score deviates from the arithmetic mean, adding these deviations, and dividing by the number of pupils. The second requirement is to use these two measures in establishing points separating adjacent marks on the 5-point scale from A to F. Pupils whose scores are

More than two M.D. above the A.M. should receive A.
Between two-thirds and two M.D. above the A.M. should receive B.
Between two-thirds M.D. below the A.M. and two-thirds M.D. above the A.M. should receive C.
Between two-thirds and two M.D. below the A.M. should receive D.
More than two M.D. below the A.M. should receive F.

Trait Ratings. Provision for the reporting of teacher evaluations of pupil character and personality traits is not uncommon on report cards in supplementation of the marks regularly reported in school subjects. Pupil traits are probably more often rated by the use of such symbols as E (excellent), S (satisfactory), I (improving), and U (unsatisfactory) than by the use of A, B, C, D, and F marks. This represents a desirable

[9] Charles Russell, *Classroom Scaler and Grader*, Ginn & Company, Boston, 1931.
[10] Herbert E. Hawkes, E. F. Lindquist, and C. R. Mann (Eds.), *The Construction and Use of Achievement Examinations*, pp. 118–125, Houghton Mifflin Company, Boston, 1936.

deviation in selection of symbols, for the A, B, C, D, F symbols seem too definitely subject centered for application to character traits.

Character and personality traits are very difficult to classify in such manner that the desirable areas are adequately covered without overlapping and so that the traits chosen are clearly defined in the thinking of teachers. Traits of reliability, dependability, and responsibility, sometimes listed on the same card, appear to overlap seriously. Such traits as neatness, promptness, cooperativeness, accuracy, and many others are variously used by different schools. A not uncommon result is that the traits listed are stated so tersely, often as single words, that their meanings are obscure and subject to very different interpretations by different teachers.

Obtaining composite measures of achievement. A third method of obtaining composite measures, to add to those presented in Chap. 8, is based on the assumption that A, B, C, D, and F marks or their equivalents are used in interpreting results for all types of tests, other written work, and even appraisals of other types. On tests, where results are often distributed widely enough in terms of scores to permit, plus and minus symbols may be used to indicate high and low marks of each letter category. On term papers, however, where scoring objectivity is not high, only the five major categories may appropriately be used. A table of the type shown below is advantageously prepared, and the number of columns of weightings can be determined by the degrees of emphasis desired for various types of marks.

To illustrate the use of this method, it may be assumed that the marking bases and their relative weights in a particular course are as follows: final examination—5; two less comprehensive examinations—2 each; a summation of several short, written quizzes—1; a term paper —3; and a summation of several other less comprehensive written reports—1. It may also be assumed that plus and minus signs have been used in assigning marks to the examinations, but that the letter marks of A, B, C, D, and F only have been used for the term papers, the summation of quizzes, and written reports. The marks and corresponding point weightings obtained from the table might be as follows for a particular pupil: final examination B— (45); two less comprehensive examinations C+ and B— (16 and 18); summation of written quizzes B (10); term paper C (21); and summation of other written papers D (4). The pupil's composite score would then be 114. When this and comparable scores for other pupils are arranged in descending order, it should not be difficult for the teacher to convert these composite scores into letter marks by the same general type of procedure as is used in assigning letter marks to the various tests and other measures.

TABLE 2. TABLE FOR OBTAINING WEIGHTED COMPOSITE SCORES

Mark	Weighting			
	One	Two	Three	Five
A +	14	28	42	70
A	13	26	39	65
A −	12	24	36	60
B +	11	22	33	55
B	10	20	30	50
B −	9	18	27	45
C +	8	16	24	40
C	7	14	21	35
C −	6	12	18	30
D +	5	10	15	25
D	4	8	12	20
D −	3	6	9	15
F +	2	4	6	10
F	1	2	3	5
F −	0	0	0	0

SUMMARY

The types of behavioral outcomes sought in the subject-matter unit method of instruction must receive basic consideration in the selection of appropriate measurement techniques. Physical and social skills, habits, knowledges, ideas and concepts, understandings, interests, and attitudes were listed as important outcomes in Chap. 9, whereas appreciations and ability to apply subject-matter masteries to the needs of group living were mentioned as supplementary outcomes. Appreciations and abilities to apply subject-matter masteries are dealt with in Chap. 14, and understandings, which receive indirect attention here, are considered more definitely in Chap. 14.

Measurement procedures characteristic of this instructional method were outlined by Monroe, De Voss, and Kelly primarily for standardized tests. Initial steps are determination of the minimum essentials of the subject and selection of the appropriate type of test and of test exercise. Additional steps are concerned with the construction and validation of the test. These procedures may be applied to some of the nontest techniques as well as to the tests appropriate for the subject-matter unit method of instruction.

Standardized or semistandardized instruments of greatest significance here are prognostic and inventory tests, diagnostic and analytic tests, instructional and practice tests, survey tests, and product scales. Certain simple modifications of the basic informal objective item types are also directly in line with the subject-matter unit method of instruction. Product and procedures measurement, represented primarily by standardized quality scales and by rating scales, score cards, and check lists, are of major significance in the measurement of skill outcomes.

Less tangible outcomes of the attitudes and general interests types are measured most effectively by the use of standardized scales or teacher-constructed questionnaires. The profile chart and the class analysis chart are designed for presenting overviews of pupil and class performance on standardized achievement tests.

Marking practices of teachers working under this instructional method appropriately include either a linear or a deviation method of applying the normal curve concept to a point-scale system. A 5-point A, B, C, D, and F scale is probably most typical, but many schools have reduced to a 3-point or even a 2-point marking base. Trait ratings are also employed in some schools under the subject-matter unit method. A procedure useful in obtaining composite measures of subject-matter masteries for pupils should aid the teacher in assigning final course marks.

SELECTED REFERENCES

BLAIR, GLENN M.: *Diagnostic and Remedial Teaching in the Secondary School*, The Macmillan Company, New York, 1946.

BRUECKNER, LEO J., and MELBY, ERNEST O.: *Diagnostic and Remedial Teaching*, Chaps. 3, 5, 7–14, Houghton Mifflin Company, Boston, 1931.

BRUECKNER, LEO J. (Chairman): *Educational Diagnosis*, Chaps. 6–8, 11–16, Thirty-fourth Yearbook of the National Society for the Study of Education, Public School Publishing Company, Bloomington, Ill., 1935.

GREENE, EDWARD B.: *Measurements of Human Behavior*, Chaps. 9, 12, 16, The Odyssey Press Inc., New York, 1941.

GREENE, HARRY A., JORGENSEN, ALBERT N., and GERBERICH, J. RAYMOND: *Measurement and Evaluation in the Secondary School*, Chaps. 5–6, 13–24, Longmans, Green & Co., Inc., New York, 1943.

LEE, J. MURRAY: *A Guide to Measurement in Secondary Schools*, Chaps. 2, 8–9, D. Appleton-Century Company, Inc., New York, 1936.

LINCOLN, EDWARD A., and WORKMAN, LINWOOD L.: *Testing and the Use of Test Results*, Chaps. 2–3, 8–10, The Macmillan Company, New York, 1935.

ODELL, C. W.: *Educational Measurement in High School*, Chaps. 4–14, Century Company, New York, 1930.

ORLEANS, JACOB S.: *Measurement in Education*, Chap. 6, Thomas Nelson & Sons, New York, 1937.

REMMERS, H. H., and GAGE, N. L.: *Educational Measurement and Evaluation*, Chaps. 10–11, 17, Harper & Brothers, New York, 1943.

ROSS, C. C.: *Measurement in Today's Schools*, 2d ed., Chaps. 12–13, Prentice-Hall, Inc., New York, 1947.

RUCH, G. M., and STODDARD, GEORGE D.: *Tests and Measurements in High School Instruction*, Chaps. 5–11, 13, 17–20, World Book Company, Yonkers, New York, 1927.

RUSSELL, CHARLES: *Standard Tests*, Chaps. 5, 9, 14–16, Ginn & Company, Boston, 1930.

SYMONDS, PERCIVAL M.: *Diagnosing Personality and Conduct*, Chaps. 3, 6, 9, D. Appleton-Century Company, Inc., New York, 1931.

——: *Measurement in Secondary Education*, Chaps. 5–11, The Macmillan Company, New York, 1927.

THURSTONE, L. L., and CHAVE, E. J.: *The Measurement of Attitude*, University of Chicago Press, Chicago, 1929.

TIEGS, ERNEST W.: *Tests and Measurements for Teachers*, Chaps. 5–6, Houghton Mifflin Company, Boston, 1931.

——: *Tests and Measurements in the Improvement of Learning*, Chaps. 3–4, 9–10, Houghton Mifflin Company, Boston, 1939.

WILSON, GUY M., and HOKE, KREMER J.: *How to Measure*, rev. and enlarged ed., Chaps. 18–22, 26, The Macmillan Company, New York, 1928.

WRINKLE, WILLIAM L.: *Improving Marking and Reporting Practices*, Chap. 5, Rinehart & Company, Inc., New York, 1947.

DIVISION C

METHOD BASED ON THE EXPERIENCE UNIT

Chapter 12. THE ORIGIN AND THEORY OF THE EXPERIENCE UNIT METHOD

The experience unit as a method of teaching on the secondary-school level is a comparatively recent development. Even now its use is not widespread, and much of the pioneer work that led to its introduction was conducted by elementary-school teachers and supervisors. Like many other innovations in education, this new form of instruction made rapid strides during a period of social and economic uncertainty. The experience emphasis gained important attention during the depression years which preceded the Second World War. At that time the economic and social life of the nation was marked by widespread unemployment and the failure of existing institutions and arrangements to provide adequately the wants of all the people. A search for more effective arrangements brought about new governmental services such as unemployment insurance, the minimum wage, old-age pensions, and the regulation of the sale of securities. The lack of employment opportunities forced many boys and girls either to spend their days in idleness or to continue in secondary school beyond the age they normally would leave to go to work. It is not surprising, therefore, that the spirit of dissatisfaction with existing conditions which encouraged the search for better arrangements in the social and economic realms, also made its way into the schools.

It would be a mistake to assume, however, that the experience unit is the product solely of the Great Depression. On the contrary, the appearance of this method of teaching during the present century was brought about by the convergence of several lines of thought and practice, some of which are almost as old as Western civilization itself. Several are the natural outgrowths of developments described in previous chapters. None had its origin exclusively within the twentieth century. Three of these major contributing factors will be described briefly in this chapter in order that the nature of the experience unit may be more easily understood.

THE MAJOR CONTRIBUTING INFLUENCES

The activity movement. Perhaps the most obvious point at which the experience unit differs from other teaching methods is found in the view that the learner must be actively engaged in the learning process. The leaders in the experience movement looked with disfavor on the prevailing forms of instruction in which the pupil is passive and is expected to receive whatever information, discipline, or behavior habits are thought by the school authorities to be the best for him. This arrangement, it was claimed, makes it entirely too easy for the school to impose whatever economic, social, or political views the school happens to favor.

The older view that the learner is the passive recipient of education was derived from psychological theories that held that learning is the business of the mind. From this it followed that if the body is engaged in activity of any kind, the activity will distract and hinder the mind in its work. Hence, pupils were expected to sit still, to listen attentively, and in general to maintain a school atmosphere so orderly and so quiet that if the proverbial pin were dropped, it might be heard by everyone within the classroom. The lock-step type of mass education developed by some of the followers of Herbart in America was particularly given to the notion that the pupil is merely a container into which the teacher must pour whatever knowledge is good for him. It was this same group of educators who believed that learning depends primarily upon the activities of the teacher rather than upon those of the pupil.

Activity for Physical Development. Historians point out, however, that some forms of physical activity have been encouraged by the schools at various times throughout the history of the Western world. It is a well-known fact that the Greek and Roman educators placed considerable emphasis upon participation in games and sports as part of the education of every young man. Their reason for this emphasis, however, was not that physical activity was thought capable of improving the participant's ability to reason or to change his forms of conduct to secure more satisfactory results, but rather to help him become a strong and capable defender of the state. It must be remembered that the sons of Greek and Roman citizens were destined to become not only the political and social leaders, but also the military leaders of their day. Thus, while a strong and disciplined body was not thought to be necessary for the exercise of wise political and social judgment, physical strength was necessary to carry out whatever policies might be agreed upon in the council chambers. In brief, the Greek and Roman attitude may be summarized in the statement, current even today, that the educated individual is one who has a "strong mind in a strong body."

Even this grudging concession to physical activity disappeared for a time following the fall of the Roman Empire. The early Christians renounced concern for material things and fixed their hope for a better world on the promise of a spiritual existence after death. For them, preparation for life in the hereafter became the all-absorbing purpose of this life, and anything that tended to divert the individual from this high purpose obviously was inspired by the devil. The wants and needs of the body, including the play of children, fell into the category of things to be avoided, and education became a matter of fostering the things of the spirit. It was not until the Humanist movement appeared in Italy roughly twelve hundred years after the birth of Christ that the schools of Western Europe again accepted responsibility for the physical well-being of the pupil. DeFeltra, one of the first of the humanists to introduce games and competitive sports into the program of school activities, admittedly was following the pattern of Roman secondary education described by Quintilian in the *Institutes of Oratory*.

Secondary education was introduced to America in the form of the Latin grammar school, a direct descendant of the type of school established by DeFeltra several centuries earlier. The Puritanical views of the early settlers, however, did not permit them to look kindly upon anything that might please or glorify the body. Education was for them a serious matter, closely related to their religious duties. Obviously the school was not a place in which to harbor foolish notions or laxity of discipline that would encourage the development of concern for the welfare of the body. Thus, it was not until a more worldly outlook on life became prevalent that the principle of "a sound mind in a sound body" gained widespread acceptance among American secondary schools.

Activity for the Stimulation of Mental Development. Meanwhile, the educational views of J. J. Rousseau were receiving wide attention in

Europe. This eighteenth-century intellectual had proposed the revolutionary theory that human nature is inherently good, but that individuals acquire their tendency toward evil from the corrupt social environment into which they are born. In the opening paragraph of his book, *Emile*, Rousseau set forth his theories as follows:

Everything is good as it comes from the hand of the Author of Nature; but everything degenerates in the hands of man. He forces one country to nourish the productions of another; one tree to bear the fruits of another. He mingles and confounds the climates, the elements, the seasons: he mutilates his dog, his horse, and his slave; he overturns everything, disfigures everything; he loves deformity, monsters; he will have nothing as Nature made it, not even man; like a saddle horse, man must be trained for man's service—he must be made over according to his fancy, like a tree in his garden.[1]

According to Rousseau, the instincts that would lead to right action in all things are implanted in the mind of man at birth. These instincts need only an opportunity to unfold and develop without restraint by or contact with the warping influences of man-made society. The unfoldment should occur during the years of childhood and youth in much the same manner that the genes implanted in a seed unfold into a perfect plant under suitable conditions. Rousseau recommended, therefore, that the child be placed in the care of a suitable tutor at an early age and transported to a rural environment where his contacts with organized society would be reduced to a minimum. On the other hand, the stimulation found in this unspoiled, natural environment would arouse the inborn instincts and cause them to unfold in much the same way that the rain, sun, and the chemicals in the soil call forth the potentialities implanted in the seed. It was to be the tutor's responsibility first, to protect the child from harm; and second, to arouse the child's curiosity about the objects and experiences encountered as the two of them proceeded to explore their environment. This curiosity was then to be used by the tutor to motivate the child to discover useful facts about his environment and to improvise suitable forms of adjustment with reference to it. If this system of education were to be employed, Rousseau claimed, the child would, upon reaching maturity, have de-

[1] J. J. Rousseau, *Emile*, trans. by William H. Payne, p. 4, D. Appleton-Century Company Inc., New York, 1893.

veloped natural habits of behavior in contrast to the artificial customs and practices perpetuated by the existing society. In addition, he would have developed the stability necessary to withstand the pressures exerted by society to induce him to conform.

Impractical as Rousseau's views on education may have been, they influenced profoundly the thinking of Pestalozzi, Herbart, and Froebel, the three European educators of the nineteenth century with whom modern education is said to begin. Froebel in particular incorporated in his educational theory that part of Rousseau's doctrine which held that the nature of the child is vastly different from that of the adult, and that each stage of maturity calls for a unique set of interests and forms of activity. Froebel's method was founded on the assumption that the child's potentialities unfold from within under appropriate external conditions. Obviously, the school should provide the necessary conditions, and Froebel's efforts to devise such a school led to the development of the kindergarten. He insisted that children will develop most favorably when they participate actively and pleasurably in activities motivated by their own interests, curiosity, and desires. One can recognize in this view the free play activities of the modern kindergarten. Froebel differed sharply with Rousseau, however, on the removal of the child from social contacts, for Froebel made active social participation one of the most important elements of his educational program.[2]

From this description it should be evident that Rousseau and Froebel were interested in physical activity on the part of the learner not merely to build for him a healthy body, but also to stimulate the unfoldment of desirable social and moral values. Since an active child receives more stimulation from his environment than does a passive child, the school should encourage the pupil to move about, to see, to touch, and to manipulate objects of all kinds. It should be made clear that Rousseau did not regard moral and social ideals as the product of such physical activity, for these ideals were thought to have been present in the mind from birth. Froebel, on the other hand, believed that the activities helped shape the ideals and therefore helped determine their nature. However, both agreed that such activities are important in helping the learner acquire the ideals that should give him direction on social and

[2] Samuel C. Parker, *A Textbook in the History of Modern Elementary Education*, p. 432, Ginn & Company, Boston, 1912.

moral issues. This view that physical activity is an important condition in setting up desirable learning situations, represents the second phase in the development of the activity movement.

Activity for the Development of Social and Moral Ideals. The third stage in the activity movement is marked by the introduction of the view that physical activity can determine, in part at least, the nature of that which the individual should think and believe. The basis for this theory was set down by a line of philosophers that includes among others Thomas Hobbes and John Locke. These men were influenced by the discoveries of individuals who had turned to scientific research as the method for discovering truth and whose discoveries were disproving many of the traditional beliefs and conclusions that had been supposed to be founded on absolute truth derived from a nonphysical source. In the light of the new scientific discoveries, Hobbes and Locke concluded that man can have no knowledge except that which has come to him through his physical senses, or is based on such sensory experiences. It follows from this theory that learning results from the activities of seeing, hearing, touching, tasting, and smelling, and upon the organization of these "sense ideas" into "ideas of reflection." In this type of learning, the pupil must reach out into his world to gain knowledge. The more actively he seeks, the more knowledge he will acquire; and the larger his supply of knowledge, the better his judgments will become. It follows logically that schools should provide many sensory experiences as well as practice in organizing this sensory knowledge into the "ideas of reflection" which are man's guiding principles and ideals. Pestalozzi, who was influenced by this theory, devised a type of instruction which is known as "sense" teaching. In Pestalozzi's schools the garden, the workshop, and the farm took their places beside the classroom as the stages on which teaching took place. In spite of his personal shortcomings, Pestalozzi proved to many influential Europeans the soundness of his philosophy and of his methods. Herbart, who followed Pestalozzi, laid particular stress upon the method by which moral ideals were thought to grow out of "ideas of sensation." It was he who developed the formal teaching steps that were adopted so widely in America as the method for giving pupils a mastery of subject matter, particularly facts and processes, in the shortest time possible. The nature of his teaching method was described in some detail in preceding chapters.

Although Pestalozzi and Herbart recognized the part played by sensory experiences in determining the nature of moral ideals, it remained for Froebel, the third member of this group of pioneers in modern education, to employ pupil activity as an integral part of the educative process. Reference has already been made to Froebel's belief that physical activity can stimulate the development of moral ideals. He went much farther, however, and claimed for such activity the ability to determine the nature of the ideals themselves. His careful selection of activities or "gifts" suitable for kindergarten pupils reflected his faith in these particular forms of activities for bringing about the emergence of the right ideals.

Froebel's kindergarten movement helped foster a new faith in the interdependence of manual activity and mental development. On the secondary-school level, this new line of thought took the form of the manual training movement. When it had first been introduced on economic grounds, manual training had not been accepted as a respectable branch of the educational program by the discipline-minded educators of the nineteenth century. However, the argument that manual activity has a direct bearing upon mental development ultimately helped transform the academic atmosphere from one of hostility to one of tolerant acceptance. Some of the numerous shop courses found in many modern secondary schools had their origin in this line of thought.

The psychological developments of the twentieth century gave further impetus to the activity movement. The first of these developments to gain general attention, namely, the behaviorist school of psychology, was based on the theory that all behavior, including "mental" activities such as thinking, remembering, and enjoying, can be accounted for in terms of body functions alone. To the behaviorist, learning is a purely physical process which can take place only when the learner is actively engaged. The process is one of finding satisfactory forms of adjustment to the physical and social environment through trial and error, a process that involves the establishing of a specific neural connection between a given sensory stimulus and a given form of response. To carry on the learning process, the learner must be actively responding to the given stimulus in a more or less random manner until he happens to hit upon a particular form of response that will terminate the stimulation. The resulting satisfaction to the learner, together with subsequent repetitions of the satisfaction-giving response, will cause that response to become habitual. The learner, however, must go through the trial-and-error stage, for the teacher cannot reach into his central nervous system and establish the desired neural connection for him directly. The teacher's responsibility is to control the learning situation so that, if possible, only one new stimulus is presented at a given time, and to control the trial-and-error process so that only the desired response will yield satisfaction to the learner.

The German school of Gestalt psychology and its American version, the organismic school, followed close on the heels of the behaviorists. Rejecting the behaviorist's theory of specific neural connections between stimulus and response, as well as his definition of the learning process, these newer schools of psychology hold that the individual undergoes changes as the result of his experiences so that he becomes, in effect, a new individual. His response to subsequent situations therefore is determined in part by the experiences he has already undergone, as well as by the nature of the new situations.[3] Much emphasis is given to the learner's purpose, for it is this purpose and not merely the sensory stimuli immediately present that will determine the nature of the response. The stress in teaching, therefore, should be on helping the learner develop desirable purposes, a process that requires the learner to define his purposes, to put them to use in the activities that are of concern to him, and to redefine them in the light of his experiences for use as guides to further learning. Since purposes grow out of experience, are tested in experience, and take on new meaning in the light of experience, learning must be an active, ongoing, experience-producing process. It is from this emphasis that learning has been defined as "doing," and teaching as the guiding of pupil experience.

From this brief description of the evolution of the activity movement in education, it should be evident that considerable support is being given by psychologists to the theory that the pupil learns only as he actively participates in the educative process. While teachers may help the process along in various ways, the dynamic force that makes learning possible must be provided by the pupil himself. This calls for an educational content that grows out of the problems, needs, and interests of the learner. Pupils must see the purpose of that which they are doing in school before they can enter actively into the learning process.

[3] John Dewey, *Experience and Education*, pp. 26–27, The Macmillan Company, New York, 1938.

School work that is assigned by the teacher for reasons that are not clearly recognized or accepted by the pupil deteriorates into mere busy work, whereas work undertaken by the pupil for reasons of his own provides an opportunity for the teacher to introduce new points of view, new modes of attack, and in general to help the pupil acquire a better understanding of himself and his physical and social environment as a basis for devising better forms of living.

The project method. From the description given in Chap. 9, it will be recalled that during the latter stages of their movement the Herbartians placed a great deal of emphasis on the principle of correlation. On the assumption that broader, more inclusive generalizations and ideas of conduct result when subject matter is presented in large units of related materials than when it is presented in fragmentary, daily assignments, they called upon the schools to provide the desired integration. Three types of correlation were recommended: First, correlation within single subjects; second, correlation between subjects; and third, correlation between school and out-of-school experiences. While each of these three types has left its imprint, the third type has influenced the development of the experience unit directly and to a marked degree.

The Project as the Illustration of Things Previously Taught. One of the first organized efforts to relate out-of-school activities to classroom instruction was sponsored by the Massachusetts Board of Education early in the twentieth century. In an effort to make the teaching of agriculture in the high schools of Massachusetts more effective, it was proposed that home projects should be carried on by the pupils to supplement the instruction offered in the schools. In 1908, a specially trained teacher was employed by the Smith Agricultural High School in Northampton to supervise well-selected projects to be carried out by the pupils during the summer months. These projects were to be selected for their value in illustrating the general principles of agriculture taught during the school year. This arrangement proved to be so successful that in a short time a number of states followed the example set by Massachusetts, and in 1917 the Smith-Hughes law was passed by Congress which made some federal funds available to any high-school district that wished to introduce a program of home projects and was willing to comply with the standards for such a program established under the law.

Thayer has written that it was the original purpose of these projects

FOUNDATIONS OF METHOD FOR SECONDARY SCHOOLS

merely to supplement the regular school work.[4] It was not expected
that this outside work would affect in any direct way the usual classroom procedures or subject-matter content. The projects were expected merely to illustrate principles, previously learned in the classroom, in what might now be called "real-life situations." Thus the
project was thought of not as the beginning, but rather as the culmination of the learning process.

It was recognized at an early date that these out-of-school projects
captured the interest of the pupils to a degree that the conventional
subject matter seldom achieved. This was so because the project involved a readily recognized goal which the pupil could accept because
of its direct and immediate personal value. But this pupil interest,
although considered to be good, particularly in reducing problems of
discipline to a minimum, was treated as an incidental by-product of
learning rather than as an end to be sought directly. It was not long,
however, until teachers of subjects other than agriculture noticed the
good influence these supplementary projects exerted upon the interest
and understanding of the pupils. For a time, therefore, other teachers,
among them teachers of Latin, sought to encourage the interest of
reluctant boys by assigning them projects to be carried on outside of
school such as the construction of a model of Caesar's bridge. Sometimes girls were encouraged by history teachers to dress dolls in the
costumes of whatever period happened to be the topic for study in class.
In general, teachers displayed unanticipated ingenuity in devising such
supplementary activity for their pupils. As might be expected, the
projects were usually carried on independently by individual students
in addition to the regularly required classroom work and were not
permitted to interfere with the conventional classroom procedures. At
this stage the project was regarded primarily as a motivating device,
although its correlation value may have been recognized by some.

The Project as Supplementary Instruction. In time, however, teachers
began to recognize that activities engaged in outside of the classroom
could do more than arouse pupil interest. It was discovered that such
activities helped pupils acquire a better understanding of the basic
principles that were being taught. This fact, plus the growing desire
to adapt instruction to the abilities and needs of the individual pupil,

[4] Vivian T. Thayer, *The Passing of the Recitation*, Chap. 16, D. C. Heath and
Company, Boston, 1928.

called for the organization of subject matter into units and the listing under each unit of a variety of activities each of which might throw special light on some particular aspect of the general topic under consideration. Thus, individual pupils were given an opportunity to carry on outside of the classroom some activity specifically suggested by the teacher to help them gain the desired mastery or understanding. In some cases, the term "project" came to be applied to these supplementary activities, and they included not only activities of a real-life nature but also purely academic activities such as research assignments and special reading to be done. At this stage of development, the term "project" was used more or less synonymously with the term "supplementary activities" described in the chapters on the subject-matter unit. The significant point to note is that at this, the second stage of its development, the project had become an integral part of the learning process.

The Project as the Center of Instruction. In the third stage, the project, which from the very beginning had been centered in the out-of-school life of the pupil, took on new educational significance. These "real-life" activities were no longer to be used merely to motivate or to supplement the work carried on in the classroom, but were to become in fact the center of the classroom activities themselves.

This shift reflects the fact that the emphasis in education has shifted in recent years from the position that school is the place where young people acquire the facts, habits, and skills they will need as adults, to the view that school is the place where pupils learn to live better the lives they must live while they are becoming adults. Whatever is to engage the attention of the pupil while he is in school must, therefore, be of concern to him and must be worth doing for reasons that are immediately and directly apparent to him. The distinctions that habitually have been drawn between the in-school and the out-of-school activities of pupils are no longer acceptable. Life for the pupils, as for everyone, is one continuous process. The problems pupils face because they are also participating members of a family, a social set, and a community cannot be placed in their lockers, together with their hats and coats, for the duration of the school day. Therefore, the boy who must earn some money, for whatever reasons, might well spend at least part of his school time planning his farm project and making preparation for initiating and conducting it. The city or village boy would do equally well to survey the employment opportunities within the community and to prepare himself in a systematic manner for the particular prospect that offers greatest promise in the light of his present needs and hopes for the future. In this light, building a model of a bridge or making period costumes for dolls might become the basis for studying engineering as a possible future occupation in the one case, and of costume designing in the other. Pupils engaged in these study activities certainly would acquire much information of general use and some that is of particular value to engineers and clothing designers. They might even discover that these vocational fields owe much to the past, and a few might elect to study Latin or history intensively and systematically as a means of becoming better engineers or designers.

Thayer has shown that, in this latest version, the project has become the central point around which much of the traditional subject matter is brought together. The project and its successful completion are recognized by all those who engage in it as the most important consideration in planning and conducting the instructional program. The transmission of a predetermined body of facts, skills, and general principles, which for so many years has been the primary objective of teaching, now has been reduced to a subordinate position. When the project becomes the primary concern, and the mastery of subject matter merely secondary, it follows that pupil interests and purposes become the major factors in determining not only that which is to engage the attention of the learner, but also the time when it is to be taken up. Thus, pupil interest which during the early stages of the project movement was an incidental by-product of learning has now been elevated to a position of first importance. In this third stage, the project is defined as a purposeful activity undertaken by the pupil because he has an immediate and recognized need for that activity.

The contribution of various other techniques and devices. The project is not the only innovation in the field of educational methods to influence the development of the experience unit. The socialized recitation, the problem method, supervised study, the laboratory method, and numerous other inventions have, each in its own way, exerted some influence. Just as the nature of the project changed with the development of educational theory, so also have these others acquired new forms or been absorbed within the framework of the broader, unit procedures. In general, all of them tended to develop in the direction of large assignments that included whatever school and nonschool activities were related, or reasonably might have been related, to an immediate and conscious pupil concern. Such pupil concerns or centers of interest emerged as the central core of an experience unit when educators recognized that the interests and concerns arose from the experiences of the pupils and could not be dealt with in a satisfactory manner except by engaging in other experience-producing activities. At this point the pupil came to be regarded not merely as an active, experience-getting being, but as a purposing, goal-seeking being as well.

The social objective in education. At the beginning of this chapter a reference was made to the influence exerted upon the development of the experience unit by those who wanted to use the schools to develop improved social arrangements. While this desire has motivated many educators at various periods in the history of education, it was brought to a high level of ferment by the maladjustments that followed The First World War, particularly during the years of the Great Depression.

There are two ways by which the schools may be used to build a new social order. In one case, those who have control over the schools may think they know with certainty the kind of institutions, regulations, and forms of action that would bring about the general state of happiness and well-being sought by everyone. Even though they may be only a small minority, those who hold this view may have the confident air and the singleness of purpose characteristic of the prophets of old who believed they had been singled out from among all the others to speak directly with God. Reformers of this type operate in the manner of a builder who has been given a detailed blueprint of the structure he must erect. No deviations from the specifications are to be permitted, and the schools, therefore, may become the agency by which each individual is told where he is to fit in the new structure and is prepared to take his designated place. The schools maintained by authoritarian governments are of this nature, whether those governments seek to perpetuate a class in power or to create a classless state. Whenever those in control of the school pretend to have a clearer knowledge of that which is best for the pupil than the pupil himself can ever have, then that school is being used to build the kind of social order desired by the persons in power.

The second way to use the school to build a better social order is based on the assumption that no individual, or even a given group or generation of individuals, is so wise and so good as to be able to determine for all others the forms and arrangements that are best for them at all times. This approach views social reform as a continuous process in which all individuals who will be affected by the decisions reached shall have a part in determining the action to be taken. It is not expected that a proposed line of action will affect each individual in the same way, yet the well-being and contentment of each individual becomes the test by which the desirability or the suitability of the action is measured. Individuals must, therefore, learn how to appraise social forms in terms of their own experiences, to pool their judgments with the judgments of others, and to work with others in planning changes and improvements that will bring about better living opportunities to a greater number. Those who follow this way of securing social reform look upon the schools as the agency which teaches individuals to evaluate their present status, to share their findings with others, and to cooperate in planning what they judge are the institutions and arrangements that will give them maximum opportunity for self-realization. In this approach, the school has no particular social order to impose. Instead, it operates on the general principle that each generation of pupils must be given the freedom and the help necessary to plan its own social order as it acquires an understanding and knowledge of the known possibilities.

Beyond all doubt, the leading exponent of this second approach to social reform through education is John Dewey. He became interested in the problems of society and education as a young man and developed many of his theories long before the period of educational reform that followed the First World War. In cooperation with friends, he founded an experimental school at the University of Chicago in 1896 to test and to demonstrate his theories. This school differed radically from the conventional schools of that day. The physical equipment was selected and arranged to provide maximum opportunity for pupils to engage actively in carrying out the plans they made as they lived and worked together. Movable tables and chairs were substituted for the conventional rows of immovable desks. Work benches, tools, and materials useful in making the things the pupils might want or need to carry out a plan were provided as standard equipment. The conventional subject-matter courses of study—grammar, history, mathematics, etc.—as definite bodies of knowledge to be covered in a systematic, step-by-step manner were discarded. In their place came the study of occupations with which the pupils had contact in the community. This study took the form of working with the tools and materials common to a given occupation, of tracing the historical evolution of the occupation, and of learning about its present status and significance in the world at large. With reference to this shift in the educational content of his school, Dewey wrote:

We must conceive of work in wood and metal, of weaving, sewing, and cooking, as methods of life not as distinct studies. We must conceive of them in their social significance, as types of processes by which society keeps itself going, as agencies for bringing home to the child some of the primal necessities of community life, and as ways in which these needs have been met by the growing insight and ingenuity of man: in short, as instrumentalities through which school itself shall be made a genuine form of active community life, instead of a place set apart in which to learn lessons.[5]

The kind of community life Dewey expected his school to foster is that which results when individuals are "held together because they are working along common lines, in a common spirit, and with reference to common aims." It is the kind of community relationship that springs up spontaneously on the playground, in games and sports, because there is something to do "requiring natural division of labor, selection of leaders and followers, mutual cooperation and emulation." That this type of community life is impossible in the subject-matter dominated school was asserted in the following excerpt from the same publication:

The mere absorption of facts and truths is so exclusively individual an affair that it tends very naturally to pass into selfishness. There is no obvious social motive for the acquirement of mere learning, there is no clear social gain in success thereat. Indeed, almost the only measure for success is a competitive one, in the bad sense of that term—a comparison of results in the recitation or the examination to see which child has succeeded in getting ahead of others in storing up, in accumulating the maximum of information. So thoroughly is this the prevalent atmosphere that for one child to help another in his task has become a school crime. Where the school work con-

[5] John Dewey, *School and Society*, p. 27, University of Chicago Press, Chicago, 1899.

sists in simply learning lessons, mutual assistance, instead of being the most natural form of cooperation and association, becomes a clandestine effort to relieve one's neighbor of his proper duties.[6]

Dewey hoped that in the kind of school he was trying to develop at Chicago, a natural, normal social environment would come about as a result of the pupils' seeking of a common goal. In this common, goal-seeking kind of school

helping others, instead of being a form of charity which impoverishes the recipient, is simply an aid in setting free the powers and furthering the impulses of the one helped. A spirit of free communication, of interchange of ideas, suggestions, results, both successes and failures of previous experiences, becomes the dominating note of the recitation.[7]

The success or failure of a given pupil is measured not in terms of the amount of subject matter he has absorbed, but in how effectively he has executed the job he set out to achieve, which as Dewey puts it, is "the genuine community standard of value."

The study of occupations, which engaged the attention of the pupils in the Chicago school to such a marked degree, was undertaken not for the purpose of providing the pupil with vocational knowledge and skill, although some such learning would be inevitable, but to provide the pupils with genuine motives. By engaging in the activities of the weaver or coppersmith and studying his way of life, Dewey reasoned that the pupils would acquire direct experiences that would bring them into direct contact with the stream of life in the world about them. In addition, they would learn to look upon the occupation in terms of "its historic values and scientific equivalences." It is in this manner that the pupils would become familiar with the vast body of scientific and social knowledge acquired by the human race in its long history, and would learn to draw upon that heritage, as it can be used to clarify and solve their own problems. Dewey illustrated this point by describing the study of weaving and spinning as part of the clothing-making occupation which had been undertaken by a group of pupils in his school. He concluded that one can concentrate "the history of all mankind into the evolution of the flax, cotton, and wool fibres in clothing." It was Dewey's contention that anyone who has successfully engaged

[6] *Ibid.*, p. 28.
[7] *Ibid.*, pp. 29–30.

in the type of learning he was attempting to define will become increasingly conscious of the purpose and principles which govern the activities in which he is engaged and in addition will acquire a better understanding of the what, why, and how of activities in which he might better engage.

Dewey's objective throughout was to develop through education the consciousness of purpose in individual matters and in social institutions, forms, and activities that is necessary if social reconstruction is to occur naturally and in an orderly manner. He emphasized again and again that the understandings and skills essential to the success of a democratic society can be developed only in a social setting, and that each individual member of that society must become aware of the common goals if his efforts are to be coordinated with those of the group. The only kind of social setting hospitable to the traits that make for effective membership in a democratic group is one that is planned, established, and modified as needed by the individual members themselves. It follows that the school must be an embryonic democratic society in which the pupils as citizens learn to conduct their affairs as members of a group. To this end those engaged in the learning situation must be free to study and experiment, to evaluate and reconstruct as their own experiences, suitably enriched by the experiences of the race, may suggest. It is in this manner that each generation of citizens is empowered to evaluate, plan, and reconstruct as needed the social order it inherits from its predecessors.

THE EXPERIENCE UNIT METHOD TODAY

The experience unit method has many variations. It is difficult to secure agreement among educators today on a definition of the experience unit method. The various routes by which individual teachers have come to recognize the importance of pupil experiences in education have caused each of them to emphasize the aspects that have loomed largest in the course of his own professional development. Some teachers have come by way of the socialized recitation, others by way of the laboratory method, the problem method, supervised study, or some other procedure. Some have been motivated by the desire to give each pupil the opportunity that is of greatest value to him at a particular stage in his development. Others have been led on by the psychological considerations summed up in the phrase "learning by doing." Still others have sought ways to provide the pupil experiences in democratic living which are to prepare him to participate intelligently and effectively with others in a cooperative search for a better world. And some teachers may have been searching merely for more effective ways to transmit the body of knowledge the human race has accumulated since the beginning of time. It is not to be expected that all of these, working independently for the most part, will have developed identical views or a single, uniform pattern of instructional procedures.

The problem of definition and description is further complicated by the fact that no two individuals or groups of individuals can have identical needs, interests, purposes, or sequences of experiences. For that reason, no two learning situations planned and conducted by two different groups to achieve ends that are respectively appropriate to each group, can be identical, even though they may deal with the same general problem or topic. Nor will any two teachers, each with his own unique background of experience, be likely to work out identical units, even though it were possible for them to work with the same group of pupils.

General characteristics of the experience unit method. There are, however, certain generalizations one may draw from the diverse practices employed by those who look upon learning primarily as an experiencing process. The *first* of these is found in the general practice of projecting a series of activities that have a significant connection or relationship. It is not enough for pupils to engage in an activity for the sake of the experience it will produce. All activities are experience producing but all experiences are not of equal educational worth. Were this not so, pupils might as well avoid school and engage in whatever form of activity impulse and curiosity, supplemented by the stimulations provided by the adult world, impel them to carry on. To be educative, experiences must be related to some end or goal, and each succeeding experience should give the learner increased control over his resources and other environmental circumstances as means for attaining desired goals. It is this connectedness of educative experiences and their reference to an end in view that give meaning and unity to this kind of education. Thus, an experience unit generally consists of a series of activities planned and carried through by the learner for the purpose of advancing himself toward a recognized purpose or objective.

A *second* characteristic is found in the source of the purpose or objective that gives unity to the series of activities. Experience units "seek their primary point of orientation in the experiences of the learner." [8] This is in sharp contrast to other kinds of units which, for the most part, derive their orientation in subject matter. It is this distinction which is expressed in the phrase, "child-centered *versus* subject-centered schools," which is encountered so frequently in educational circles today. It is the needs, purposes, and interests that grow out of the experiences of a given pupil or group of pupils that determine the learning activities to be undertaken by that pupil or group of pupils in an experience unit. Since experience is personal, it is not likely that any two individuals or groups of individuals will have identical needs, interests, or purposes, or that similar needs, interests, and purposes will appear for them in the same order. The experience unit must begin, therefore, with the identification of goals by the learner himself in cooperation with all the others who will engage in the learning situations with him.

A *third* point grows out of the psychological considerations mentioned at the end of the discussion of the activity movement. The learner must engage actively and purposefully in activities that he recognizes as steppingstones to ends he seeks. To this end the learner may engage in research activities. Frequently, this involves subject matter of the kind that dominates learning in the traditional school. In the experience unit, however, the learner is using conventional subject matter as a means to an end rather than as an end in itself. He draws upon the experiences of the race in relation to a present problem or goal, and in that manner the cultural heritage becomes a vital and direct part of his own experience to be used again and again as future need may dictate.

A *fourth* characteristic arises from the increasing demands placed upon the individual to engage in cooperative action and other forms of social participation if he is to find the personal satisfactions he seeks. The modern world has become increasingly more social in nature, so that the necessities of good living, such as food, shelter, fuel, transportation, and recreation, are seldom secured through strictly individual efforts. If these necessary social processes are to be carried on satisfactorily, or if the individual is to secure the personal satisfaction made

[8] Hollis L. Caswell and Doak S. Campbell, *Curriculum Development*, p. 403, American Book Company, New York, 1935.

possible through social action, he must acquire the understandings, attitudes, and skills that make for effective social relations. The psychological principle of learning by doing, which figures so prominently in the experience unit, demands that these be developed through participation in a social group. In the experience unit, opportunity for social participation grows naturally out of the projection of common purposes, cooperation in attaining them, and the sharing of experiences in a common enterprise. Teachers employing the experience unit method, therefore, seek to direct the learner into activities that will increase his control over his social environment. In short, one of the major reasons why the experience unit was invented was to provide the socializing experiences desired to prepare the pupil to become an effective citizen in a democratic society.

A *fifth* characteristic is to be found in the role played by the teacher. Instead of functioning as a taskmaster who prescribes the learning activities, and supervises and evaluates the pupil's efforts in carrying out his assignments, the teacher now functions as a guide who helps the pupil identify, work toward, and ultimately to reappraise his own objectives. In the experience unit, the teacher does not necessarily know all the answers sought by the learners, but as an experienced student and citizen he can help the learners direct their own search. The process can be compared with the functioning of an experienced woodsman who is employed by a group of inexperienced adventurers to lead them to a distant lake which none of them, not even the guide, has visited. The guide does not determine the ultimate objective, but his rich knowledge of woodcraft and the wealth of his experience is drawn upon by the group at every stage of the journey. Furthermore, he studies the individual members of the group and suggests daily objectives as well as divisions of responsibilities, with the abilities and limitations of the members in mind. Gradually the members of the group acquire experience and grow in strength and endurance. As they gain confidence in their judgment and resourcefulness, they can proceed more rapidly, traverse more difficult terrain, and even split up into separate groups for the purpose of making side trips unaccompanied by their guide. Ultimately they can strike out on their own safely and confidently to seek whatever destination they may choose. In the experience unit, the teacher strives to develop a similar power for independent action in individual and social matters.

Finally, the experience unit is characterized by a freedom that is unknown in the traditional school. This freedom is of three kinds. First,
there is the freedom from a rigid time schedule. Learning activities, if
they are to represent a natural relationship between the things done and
the ends sought, must be allowed to run their course in a natural manner. Such activities cannot be fitted neatly into a 45-minute class period every day. Second, there is freedom from subject-matter prescription. The interests, needs, and purposes of adolescent boys and girls
growing up in an active social world are not likely to be anticipated
precisely by adult curriculum makers. Third, there is freedom to study,
examine, discuss, draw conclusions about, and try the conclusions
reached regarding whatever problems or concerns that may arise from
the experiences of the learner.

Many teachers and parents are not accustomed to this kind of freedom, and some shrink from accepting the responsibilities it may en-
tail. Perhaps for this reason, more than any other, instruction based
upon the experience unit has not yet made its way into secondary
schools except in a relatively few instances.

SUMMARY

The contributions of three major influences in the development of
the experience unit method have been described in this chapter. These
influences are: (*a*) the recognition of the importance of direct experience in learning, (*b*) the recognition of the superiority of learning that
is consciously directed by the learner toward ends that have value for
him, and (*c*) the growing conviction that the type of social competence
that is needed in a free society is developed only through social living
that is directed toward the goal of improving the status of the individual, a process in which the individual must be free both to project
that which he considers to be good and to judge social arrangements
in the light of his own experiences. From these three origins, there is
now being developed a method of teaching which seeks to initiate the
educative process with the problems and concerns of the learner, and to
direct it in the light of the democratic social principle. It is a flexible
method which is adaptable to a variety of situations and to the use of
teachers with widely different notions of how it is to be applied. There
is agreement, however, that while the unit is selected and developed by
the pupils, the teacher is responsible for directing their efforts in such

a way that increased power to deal satisfactorily with future in-school and out-of-school situations will result from their experience in the unit.

SELECTED REFERENCES

ALBERTY, HAROLD B.: *Reorganizing the High-School Curriculum*, Chaps. V and VIII, The Macmillan Company, New York, 1947.

BODE, BOYD H.: *How We Learn*, particularly Chaps. XIII–XVII, D. C. Heath and Company, Boston, 1940.

————: *Progressive Education at the Crossroads*, Newson and Company, New York, 1938.

BURTON, WILLIAM H.: *The Guidance of Learning Activities*, Part II, D. Appleton-Century Company, New York, 1944.

CASWELL, HOLLIS L. (Ed.): *The American High School*, Eighth Yearbook of the John Dewey Society, Harper & Brothers, New York, 1946.

————, and CAMPBELL, DOAK S.: *Curriculum Development*, Chaps. VIII, IX, and XV, American Book Company, New York, 1935.

DEWEY, JOHN: *Democracy and Education*, The Macmillan Company, New York, 1916.

————: *Experience and Education*, The Macmillan Company, New York, 1938.

————: *School and Society*, University of Chicago Press, Chicago, 1899.

Educational Policies Commission: *Learning the Ways of Democracy*, National Education Association, Washington, D.C., 1940.

KILPATRICK, WILLIAM H.: *Foundations of Method*, The Macmillan Company, New York, 1925.

MEAD, CYRUS D., and ORTH, FRED W.: *The Transitional Public School*, The Macmillan Company, New York, 1937.

MELVIN, A. GORDON: *Methods for New Schools*, The John Day Company, New York, 1941.

————: *Teaching*, The John Day Company, New York, 1944.

MOSSMAN, LOIS COFFEY: *The Activity Movement*, The Macmillan Company, New York, 1938.

National Society for the Study of Education: *The Activity Movement*, Part II, Thirty-third Yearbook, Public School Publishing Company, Bloomington, Ill., 1934.

RUGG, HAROLD: *Foundations for American Education*, particularly Chaps. XVII, XVIII, and XIX, World Book Company, Yonkers, New York, 1947.

SAUCIER, W. A.: *Introduction to Modern Views of Education*, Ginn & Company, Boston, 1937.

SCHOENCHEN, GUSTAV G.: *The Activity School,* Longmans, Green & Co., Inc., New York, 1940.

THAYER, VIVIAN T.: *The Passing of the Recitation,* D. C. Heath and Company, Boston, 1928.

———, ZACHARY, CAROLYN B., and KOTINSKY, RUTH: *Reorganizing Secondary Education,* particularly Chap. XI, D. Appleton-Century Company, Inc., New York, 1939.

Chapter 13. THE EXPERIENCE UNIT

METHOD IN ACTION

Pupils have been expected for so long to have faith in the wisdom of their teachers and to accept their assigned school tasks without question that many people are disturbed when they hear about schools in which the pupils participate in the selection and direction of their own activities. Such people may have no difficulty in thinking of adults as self-directed and responsible beings, or in anticipating that pupils will be prepared to participate as citizens in a democratic society upon reaching maturity. They may not be particularly disturbed when such pupils are asked to shift for themselves in the playground, on the street, or at home. Nor are they surprised when these pupils use good judgment, make ingenious adaptations, or persevere in the face of discouraging obstacles while engaged in self-initiated activities, such as building a tree house or putting on a dance, undertaken to reach clearly recognized and desired ends. The fact remains, however, that they do not expect pupils to demonstrate any of the above attributes in school. Nor is the school expected to seek their development in a direct manner. In short, the capacity for self-direction and self-regulation so essential in a democracy is looked upon either as though it were inborn, or were to be acquired without conscious effort from the out-of-school experiences.

In the light of the threat of conflicting ideologies, increasing numbers of people are now asking if a democratic society can depend upon this casual type of learning for the preservation and transmission of the understandings, attitudes, and skills that make a free society possible. There is a growing conviction that it cannot and that a more direct form of education is needed. Acting upon this conviction, educators here and there have launched a search for ways in which to provide for pupils more direct experiences in democratic living while they are still in school. The experience unit method is one of these newer educational developments.

The objectives of the experience unit. It was shown in the first two chapters that democracy is a way of life that derives its distinctive character from a controlling principle that calls for safeguarding and extending the opportunities for individual development. It was also shown that the experiences of democratic peoples have led them to believe that the most satisfactory conditions for individual well-being result (*a*) when the opportunity for self-realization is made the right of each individual, (*b*) when the individuals having common concerns or purposes pool their efforts and resources to reach the desired ends, and (*c*) when problems, whether individual or group, are solved by a process described as the method of intelligence. The function of the democratic school was defined in terms of helping the individual to become intelligent about democracy as a guiding social principle, and of fostering the attitudes, understandings, and skills that make for satisfactory participation as a member of a democratic society.

In the preceding chapter the experience unit was presented as a teaching method by which it is hoped pupils can be acquainted with the meaning of the democratic social principles, and be given a better opportunity to develop the ability to live democratically than is provided by other methods. It is a unique method in the sense that it is based on the "experience" theory of learning. Thus, in an experience unit it is possible for the learner, under the direction of the teacher, to deal with his personal and social problems by using the democratic social principle as his guide. If the learning situation is democratically oriented, the learner will gain from his experiences (*a*) a better understanding of the meaning of democracy; (*b*) increased respect for human personality, including his own; (c) a stronger faith in the method of intelligence; and (*d*) increased control over his physical and social environment. In short, the learner should emerge from this type of learning experience better prepared to determine the kind of life he wants to live, and to take whatever action is best suited to achieve it.

Some characteristics of the experience unit method. As previously stated, the content of an experience unit is determined by the purposes, interests, and needs of the pupils rather than by prescription. It is this freedom from the restrictions traditionally imposed by textbooks, courses of study, and the educational system in general that makes it possible for the school to deal with the genuine concerns of the pupils.

When the educative process is based upon the concerns of the pupils, the activities engaged in are likely to have about them the quality of real, out-of-school life. Under the direction of the teacher, such concerns may be studied, discussed, and dealt with in an enlightened manner. Action can be taken, and the action may be judged in the light of its natural and direct consequences. These judgments then provide a better basis for deciding upon the next steps to be taken. It is this progressive redirection of action to achieve more completely the purpose or purposes sought and the subsequent redefinition of the purposes themselves that constitute the process which pupils are expected to practice in the experience unit method.

Freedom from subject-matter prescriptions is matched by a corresponding freedom from the traditional 45-minute class period. The time block set aside for the experience unit in the daily schedule generally is long enough to make it possible for pupils to engage with satisfaction in the activities they have planned or have under way. Thus, there is time to continue a planning conference until suitable agreements have been reached or it is recognized that additional information is necessary. There is a corresponding freedom from the notion that learning takes place only in the classroom. Thus, field trips, library research, and laboratory or workshop projects may be undertaken, and they may be pursued long enough so that pupils can make recognizable progress.

There is also freedom from the coercion of examinations and marks. As previously stated, the purpose of the unit arises from the experiences of the particular individuals who make up the group. It reflects the particular physical, social, political, and economic forces that happen to be pushing in on them at that time. Thus the teacher does not exercise exclusive control over the content of the unit, and pupil progress cannot be measured in terms of a particular, predetermined body of subject matter. Unlike traditional methods, the experience unit has no clearly defined body of facts, habits, and skills that must be mastered in a given sequence or at a given time. Rather, a pupil's progress is measured by the evidence of increased growth in his ability to identify purposes, to plan intelligently, to work with others, to respect and to understand himself and others, to evaluate outcomes in the light of the goals that are sought, to use the physical and social resources that are or can become available, and to look upon the world not only as it is but also as it might become.

Finally, the purpose or goal sought, which is used as the standard for judging the appropriateness of action taken, also is made the point of orientation around which the learning situation is developed. It is this purpose or "end-to-be-achieved" that gives the activities engaged in during the course of an experience unit their unitary character.

DEVELOPING AN EXPERIENCE UNIT

The initiating and planning stage. While no two experience units are likely to develop in an identical manner, there are certain general stages common to all. The first of these frequently is called *the initiating and planning stage.* It begins with the acceptance by the class of responsibility for the selection and development of the unit. This acceptance marks the beginning of a unifying force at work in the enterprise.[1] It signifies that the individual members of the group are now ready to embark upon a cooperative enterprise for ends that are to be mutually advantageous.

Classes that have had little or no background in this type of learning may need to examine the meaning of cooperation and of group planning. If so, the advantages and disadvantages of group action should be considered, and it may be desirable to inquire into the responsibilities that fall upon the individual when he accepts membership in a cooperating group. The place of individual interests and desires in a group enterprise should also be discussed in the light of the effect such interests and desires may have upon the common enterprise. Definite agreements should be reached which define the procedures the pupils wish to employ, and if such agreements are not possible or if the group is not willing to accept responsibility for the unit, it is doubtful that the group is ready to engage in a learning situation organized on the experience unit basis. In such cases, other types of instructional procedures which provide a greater measure of teacher planning are recommended and should be continued until such a time as the school has succeeded in developing in the pupils the necessary confidence and ability through carefully selected developmental experiences.

[1] H. B. Alberty and others, *Science: Master or Servant,* p. 102, a resource unit, College of Education, Ohio State University, Columbus, Ohio, 1947.

In other cases where pupils do accept responsibility for their activities and are willing to agree upon general procedures for working together, they are ready to set up purposes that can be made the basis of an experience unit. The purposes arise from interests and questions voiced by members of the class. These in turn are examined to see where they might lead. School, home, and community resources may be drawn upon during this examination to gain a clearer understanding of what is involved in the several leads that are brought before the class. As a result of such study, some of the possibilities are found to be more promising than others, and ultimately the group may take a vote to determine which particular purpose or group of purposes they think is best suited to serve as the central point around which their unit is to be developed.

Group planning of this nature may appear to be time consuming and slow when judged by traditional standards. But it is an important element in the democratic process, and time devoted to it will be very well spent. Participation in the formulation of the purposes which are to give direction to the unit will help clarify their meaning to each member of the group. Not only will these purposes give direction to the individual activities, but they will also become the standard to which all activities and processes admitted to the unit must conform. Finally, the skill developed through participation in a group planning activity will be used again and again throughout life, and from the school's point of view the development of this skill is of greater educational importance than the particular purpose that resulted from the planning.

As these exploratory activities are carried on, pupils will discover issues, problems, beliefs, attitudes, and practices that call for further investigation. One individual after another will find particular aspects of the unit that have special significance for him and will proceed to go to work on them.

The initiatory period ends for individuals and groups at various times during this study, but the class as a whole works into the developmental phase of the unit when the majority of the students are involved in some activity and when they are more or less grouped and ready to answer in the affirmative the following questions:

1. Will these activities satisfy our needs?
2. Will they be interesting to us and to others with whom we plan to share them?

3. Are they practical and can we do them in the way we planned them?

4. In what activities is the majority of the class most interested?

5. Are there activities that appeal to the individual interests of the pupils?

This is the part of the work which helps to protect the unity of the enterprise.[2]

The developmental stage. In the second or *developmental* stage, the members of the class concentrate their efforts on achieving the purposes that have been established. They engage in library research, field trips, interviews, laboratory experiments, workshop activities, committee meetings, group discussions, and the like. Continuous planning is required—both individual and group planning—to keep these data-seeking activities from "bogging down" or from going astray. As new evidence is found, some of the original purposes may need to be modified or activities already under way may need to be redirected. Hence, it is a good practice to have frequent group meetings during which members may help each other by redefining the objectives, exchanging information, and offering suggestions. All of these afford excellent opportunities for developing greater skill in democratic procedures.

It is in the developmental stage that the uninitiated, whether student, teacher, or observer, may lose sight of the objectives sought because of too close attention to the activities themselves. When this happens, confusion or the appearance of confusion is the result. Reorientation and redirection are secured by returning to the purposes developed in the initial stage of the unit. Since pupils are very likely to become lost in this manner, particularly when engaged in an extensive activity or unit, the teacher must be alert always to the need for further clarification of purposes and reorientation. When the purposes are kept before the group, that which appears to be confusion and undirected activity to the casual observer will be found to be nothing more than diversity of activity in which each pupil knows what he is doing and is engaging his energy in the most efficient manner possible for him at his level of maturity.

It should be stated again that the developmental stage includes more than activities conducted on an individual or small group basis. "There will be much class discussion and many reports of progress of individuals and groups. *The teacher will need to plan with the class for sufficient all-group activities to protect the unity of the enterprise.*"[3]

[2] *Ibid.*, p. 106. Italics in the original.   [3] *Ibid.*, p. 109. Italics in the original.

The culminating and evaluating stage. During the developmental stage, the pupils are likely to be working on individual projects or on larger projects with a small group of their classmates. Thus, there is a tendency for the class to break up into small fragments, each interested primarily in its own problem. If the unit were terminated at this stage, each member would gain from the study only that which has been secured through personal effort. The individual pupil would fail to gain a broad overview of the entire area covered by the class, and little or no progress would have been made toward developing the common understandings that make the communication and interchange of ideas possible. What is needed at this point is a class activity that will provide for the sharing of the information gathered through individual effort, and that will encourage the formulation of group attitudes, ideas, and appreciations. This bringing together or organization of the results of individual studies into a form that is usable by the entire group is called *the culminating and evaluating stage.*

Since the information gathered and the experiences gained in a given unit are unique and peculiar to that unit, there is no ready-made pattern available for reporting and organizing the findings. A special plan must be developed with each class for each unit. This affords additional opportunities to gain experience in group discussions, planning, and acting. Here are opportunities to work with a group that is larger than the one with which the pupil may have worked during the developmental stage. There are opportunities to develop skill in self-expression whether the medium is art, music, dramatics, speech, writing, or some other form. Ideas, values, and attitudes held by individual members of the class will be brought to light where they may be examined and discussed. Conclusions drawn will be open to challenge by the class. From this interchange of ideas broader attitudes, values, and appreciations to which many may subscribe will emerge.

In one sense this examination of ideas and conclusions is an evaluating procedure, but evaluation has a second aspect as well. As individuals report their findings and state the conclusions and interpretations drawn from them, omissions are noted by the members of the group. New information may be called for and new learning activities planned. From this second type of evaluation new purposes are formulated in the light of the experience the group has had, and plans are drawn for extending the present unit, or for moving on to a new unit.

By this time it should be apparent that the three types of activities—planning, developmental, and evaluating—are engaged in repeatedly throughout the course of a unit. There is no stage at which only one type is engaged in to the complete exclusion of the others. There is opportunity, however, for the teacher to focus the attention of the class from time to time on what are good planning procedures, or good working procedures, or good evaluating procedures. In this manner pupils may be led to examine their own habits and methods of work in a critical light and encouraged to develop better forms. It is in this manner that the ability to participate in a social group may be developed. It is also the manner in which pupils may be acquainted with the democratic principles of living and working together and encouraged to try them out as guides to better social arrangements.

SOME EXAMPLES OF EXPERIENCE UNIT PROCEDURES

Selecting a unit. Without a course of study to follow and without advance knowledge of the specific content to be dealt with or the direction to be taken, many prospective teachers are puzzled to know how an experience unit is selected and developed. The process of selection may be illustrated with a hypothetical case on the college level. Suppose that all seniors in a given college were offered the opportunity during the seventh semester of earning half the usual number of hours of credit by registering for a single course. Inasmuch as this course would be equal to one-half the student's load, half of his time should be available for this purpose, that is, the group to which the student is assigned would meet at a stated time every forenoon from Monday through Friday, and no other classes or activities would be scheduled for them at this time. Furthermore, each group would be free to work on any project or problem, or to investigate any aspect of the culture or environment which in the judgment of the group promises to yield the greatest satisfaction to its members. The materials studied would not be restricted by conventional subject-matter boundaries. The course would, however, be in charge of an informed and respected member of the faculty with the understanding that the class and instructor together may call upon the personnel of any department of the college for assistance or to render special services, and to utilize other resources of the college needed in planning and carrying on the work of the group. Any group willing to accept responsibility for selecting and planning its own project on this basis would be ready to initiate an experience unit. What problem might such a group of students care to investigate or explore?

The opportunities described in this hypothetical case are so unusual that, in most instances, college students who are asked to list problems they would care to investigate under these circumstances, cannot immediately offer any constructive suggestions. After giving the matter considerable thought, the members of one college class finally suggested the following topics:

1. What are the characteristics of the literature of a society that is undergoing a revolution?
2. How can the nations of the world find security without sacrificing sovereignty?
3. To what degree is the contemporary social scene revolutionary in nature?
4. What scientific principles are utilized in music?
5. How will changing social conditions affect the status of women over the next 50 years?
6. Why is socialized medicine opposed?

After further discussion it was agreed that these topics have some things in common and that in some places they seemed to overlap, that is, there were some common areas in the above suggestions that seemed to be of interest to each member of the class. Obviously, it would save time and effort if these common areas could be studied on a cooperative basis. The group then agreed that the unity needed to make such cooperation possible could be secured around the larger topic of "How will the social, economic, political, and scientific trends that are apparent today affect us during our lifetime?"

It is highly probable that had this class been able to develop a unit around this larger topic, the six special interests mentioned earlier could have been included and pursued by the individuals who had suggested them. It is also probable that each member of the class sooner or later would have been led to explore sources of information, and to gain experiences in addition to those provided by conventional textbooks. In fact, the activities of such a student very likely would have taken on the characteristics of the activities engaged in by those who already have left the campus. In all fairness to the student and in keeping with the objectives of the experience unit method, the success of this learning activity ought then to be appraised not in terms of the specific subject matter covered, but rather in terms of how successfully he is able to engage in the normal activities of life.

That the unit topic selected in the above case came out of the experiences of the students in the class should be evident. The instructor could not have known in advance either the individual concerns that were expressed or the area of common concerns that was discovered when the list of suggestions was examined. For a variety of reasons, however, he might have anticipated the general area within which the interests of the class were located. He knew, for example, that the academic majors and the occupational choices of the students indicated a dominant interest in the social sciences and modern foreign languages. Similarly he knew that the class as a whole was intensely interested in the contemporary social scene, because each student was being affected very directly by the impact of events on the national and international levels. With these and other clues to guide him, he could have made advance preparations for the unit by exploring the current literature in the social studies field, following lines of thought that were receiving major attention in the public press, and accumulating or listing resources that could be made available if a need for them were to arise. With this background he could have been prepared to add to the suggestions offered by the class promising aspects of the general problem they had omitted because of limited information and experience. In other words, he could have been prepared to give direction to the group by suggesting certain lines of inquiry and action that would be educative without violating the principles of democratic group planning.

Developing and culminating a unit. Further help in learning to understand how an experience unit may be selected, developed, and brought together by means of a culminating activity, may be secured from the following description of the experiences of a group of sixth-grade pupils.

In the fall the group made up of twenty children and their classroom teacher, explored the possibilities in, and evaluated in the light of their own criteria, five topics which they had suggested as interesting "units" for a study. These five topics were (1) Electricity, (2) What Caused the Trouble in Europe, (3) Flowers, Birds, Plants, (4) South America, (5) Mechanical Things and How They Work.

The chief interest was in the European situation. Several children expressed their feeling of inadequacy in family discussions of European affairs during the week of the September Czechoslovakian crisis.

The children had to have considerable guidance to understand that in order to discuss the European situation intelligently they would have to consider problems and use materials which were to a great extent beyond their maturity level. The decision arrived at after due consideration was that the group could profitably build a background for understanding international relationships and European affairs by learning how the European people live, what they enjoy and care about, how they earn their living, what resources they have, etc. Such a study would naturally involve closely following current affairs but would shift the major emphasis to learning to understand other culture groups.

The study determined, the question of the best point of departure made the children conscious of the need for a plan. After considerable exploration and discussion, the group arrived at the following working plan. First, they would compare Europe and North America, especially the United States. Then, they would find how civilization had spread over Europe. When this was accomplished, they would plan again for the best way in which to acquaint themselves with at least those European countries which seemed to be playing leading roles in the determination of international affairs. These countries were Czechoslovakia, Germany, Italy, France, England, the Union of Soviet Russia. Soon Switzerland was added to this list for repeatedly the children had found it referred to as the international country. As the group proceeded with their plan, they found how large a part the Roman Empire had played in European history. They decided, therefore, upon Italy as the logical beginning for their intensive study.

The group began this intensive study by compiling a list of their own questions. As investigation progressed, questions gave direction to the investigation.

As the study progressed the question of a means of organization of information became a real problem. A small group initiated the idea of a book by presenting their reasons for wanting to make a book. Others could "come in on the idea" if they wished. Out of the discussion which followed a rough plan materialized for a cooperatively written group book. During later discussions definite plans were made and various children assumed responsibility for writing the different chapters.

Following investigation and discussion chapters were written, read aloud for group criticism and suggestions, then revised to the best of the writer's ability before being submitted to the typist. In a similar manner information about the several other countries was collected and organized for inclusion in the book.[4]

The above account shows how continuous planning and evaluating entered into the unit. Here again is evidence that with proper planning pupils can have the opportunity in school to practice the art of living and working together in an atmosphere of mutual respect and common concern. For those who are afraid that pupils do not have a corresponding opportunity, in this type of school, to become familiar with the social heritage or to acquire the knowledge and skills necessary for the systematic studies found on the higher academic levels, there is some comfort in the following statement taken from the same report:

Art, science, music, literature, mathematics, all functioned in this study as well as did social studies, for they all became necessary both in carrying on activities and experiments and in interpreting the culture of another people.[5]

Experience units as reported by the pupils. Another valuable source of information about the experience unit method which is available in many school and college libraries is the account written by the class of 1938 of the Ohio State University School of their own experiences.[6] The book deals with not only one unit, but with several that were planned and developed as the class moved from the seventh through the twelfth years of their secondary-school experience. For a comprehensive description of the kind of educational program that may grow out of the experience approach, the book should be read. At this point, however, the manner in which members of the class acquired greater control over their environment is of special interest, and it is described here in some detail to illustrate the continuity and order that may result for the pupil when he participates in planning his own sequence of educational activities.

In the Seventh Grade. The book begins with the class of 1938 entering the University School as seventh-grade pupils. The building was

[4] Catherine M. Williams, "Sixth Grade," *A Description of the Curricular Experiences for the School Year of 1938–1939*, pp. 19–20, The Lower School, The University School of Ohio State University, Columbus, Ohio.

[5] *Ibid.*, p. 21.

[6] Class of 1938, Ohio State University School, *Were We Guinea Pigs?*, Henry Holt and Company, Inc., New York, 1938.

new and had not been completely furnished. Nor was there an established organization or program to make the school a fixed and rigid institution. At the very outset, therefore, the class found it necessary to establish itself. An apartment similar to the apartments that are provided for home economics departments in many modern high schools, was taken over by the class to make a "home" for itself. Providing furnishings for their "home" became the point of orientation for their first experience unit. The class periods usually scheduled for the formal study of English and the social sciences were combined and made available for the unit activities. In addition to the unit, however, there were regularly scheduled classes in mathematics, physical education, science, and one elective.

Having selected their unit, the class found that it would be necessary to know something about home decorating before they could make wise decisions. This led to the study of accepted principles of home decoration, and it was learned that the first thing to do was to select a general theme or plan. After a consideration of a number of possibilities the class finally agreed upon an early American theme.

The study of furniture styles, the selection of the pieces wanted, and the actual purchase of the furniture and other material needed to carry out the theme followed in logical order. In short, the class engaged in the activities of decorating and of purchasing and arranging the furnishings in their home in a manner calculated to make them more competent to carry on similar activities in nonschool situations. The unit was brought to a close by studying the ways in which the home should be used by members of the family. A housewarming to which parents and friends were invited rounded out this phase of the study.

The class found it profitable to continue this unit for a major part of the school year. Toward the end of the year, however, the center of interest had shifted to the services and sources of supply upon which the modern home is dependent. This newer emphasis led the class into a study of the community and a new unit was developed.

In planning the new unit the class found that the home is related to the community in eight specific ways. These are:

1. Stores and markets
2. Industries
3. Welfare
4. Education

5. Transportation
6. Communication
7. Public utilities
8. Government

It was decided that each of these aspects of the community should be studied, but due to the limited amount of time that remained in the school year, only the first four were taken up at that time.

In the Eighth Year. The four aspects of the community not studied in the seventh year were to become the basis for the unit that was to be developed in the eighth year. That this plan was modified when the pupils returned to school in September is indicated in the following quotation:

At the beginning of the eighth grade our class met as a whole, discussed the values of the past year's work, and planned our program for the current year. We decided to begin with the study of transportation, continuing with communication, public utilities, and government. The teachers felt that the scientific aspects of these topics were very important, and so our schedule was set up in such a way that science, social science, and English could be one unit. This was very wise because during the first week while listing the problems we wished to investigate, we found many which dealt with the scientific phase of transportation, for example: What are the mechanical inventions of the history of transportation? and, What effect has the industrial revolution had upon the people? We broke up into small groups and studied the phases of transportation which interested us most. Some examples of things studied are: What are the different types of air transportation? What are the different types of roads? How have transportation facilities affected the development of our cities? How is energy transformed? How did the ancients travel? [7]

The class succeeded in completing the three units on transportation, communication, and public utilities during the year. There was not time, however, for the fourth unit on government which they had expected to include so this was held over for the following year.

In the Ninth and Tenth Years. In spite of organizational changes that were introduced into the school upon their return in the fall, the class was able to carry on a part of its work for the ninth year under the general topic of "Governments and Their Histories." The tenth year was devoted to a study of "important periods in the development of civilization beginning in the twelfth and thirteenth centuries." Some of the specific problems that were included are: "The Position of Women in Byzantine Civilization"; "Renaissance Art"; "The Italian

[7] *Ibid.*, p. 56.

City States"; "Religious Reformers of the Renaissance"; and "Medieval Science." The attention of the class to the need for improving group procedures is illustrated by the following description of an evaluation and planning activity engaged in during the year.

At the end of the tenth year we had a discussion on reports. Reporting back to the class on things we had learned had always been a problem. All felt that individual reports were not particularly effective. They went too slowly and could not be made interesting enough to hold the attention of the class. Furthermore, this period came late in the afternoon, and our schedule was heavy this year. These factors contributed to the ineffectiveness of the reports. Through experimenting we found that panels and small group discussions made things most clear to everyone.[8]

In the Eleventh Year. In the eleventh year the work was planned to secure a better understanding of the world today in the light of the past. For reasons that are not clear, the class was divided into two groups, one of which approached the study in the conventional, chronological manner while the second group used the problems approach. An extensive account of the experiences of the "problems" group is given below to indicate the manner in which older secondary-school pupils may react to their studies when these are organized as experience units.

After evaluating the previous study of world civilizations, we of the problems group felt that our knowledge of the background of history was greater than that of present-day environment. Therefore, we were eager to take up modern problems. We realized, of course, that we needed to know more about situations in the past which had a bearing on contemporary problems, but we wanted to begin studying these problems and to investigate only what history was relevant to them.

The instructor gave us a short introduction and then we began listing what we considered to be important national problems. These seemed to fall into three inclusive categories: the industrial system, expansion and war, and public opinion.

We started on the industrial system and subdivided the problem so that we each could study what we found most interesting and still be in the unity of the group under the major problem. Some of these individual studies were: Industrialists (Fisk, Morgan, Carnegie, DuPont, Ford, and Hearst), Corporations, Agriculture, Labor, Strikes, Distribution of Wealth

[8] *Ibid.,* p. 63.

in Columbus, How People Spend Money, Organizations with Social Aims in Columbus, Technology, The Motion Picture Industry, and Advertising.

Many of the oral reports were in the form of panel discussions. The whole class did some general reading on each subject before the reports and dis- cussion. In this way we were able to have specialization for the individual, the important general background, and still maintain historical unity for the whole class. Several of us took notes on the reports and discussion although it was not required.

By January our written reports were complete and our discussions had lasted as long as we felt was valuable. Before we started on our next unit we all wanted some kind of test on what we had just covered. We mention this because we all feel that this test was one of the fairest we ever had and about as accurate as it could be.

Each of us turned in three important questions about the subject he had reported on. To these were added other questions and some problems. We all had this complete list of possible questions about a week before the test so we could study them as much as we wanted. The day of the test we were given the final selection. There were six major questions to be explained rather than answered, and two problems to be discussed from several points of view. We could use all the notes we had, and what books we had with us. We could even have had answers written for each question on the list and then just copy those that were used. The only restrictions were that the test had to be written within the period and be our own work.

The teacher graded each answer as excellent, superior, good, fair, or poor, and at the end told each of us how well he thought we had done and what our weaknesses were. This grading was not in comparison with the rest of the class but with what he thought we could do. Those who had not done as well as they should took the test over again with different questions.

Perhaps this does not seem to be a very good test according to formal standards but it did accomplish the purpose for which it was intended: to make sure that we understood important points and could express our own ideas.[9]

In the Twelfth Year. The work of the twelfth year moved in the general direction of helping each member of the class find ways in which he might work for a better society. This involved the problem of determining what is desirable and how individuals may go about securing social changes.

One may get the impression from the sequence of units studied by the

[9] *Ibid.*, pp. 64–66.

class of 1938 as it progressed through the 6 years of the University High School that there was more than a casual interest in covering the conventional subject matter found in the social science area in a majority of American high schools. The influence the teacher had upon group planning can be detected in more instances than one. To those readers who are disturbed by this display of teacher control, it should be said that during the major part of the time the class of 1938 was in attendance, the school in question was pioneering in the use of the experience unit method. During these early pioneering days, the staff may not have felt competent or ready to stray too far from the known paths. In more recent years, however, students and staff alike have acquired the confidence and ability to rely more completely upon co-operative staff-pupil planning.

THE ROLE OF THE TEACHER

Professional preparation. It is evident that the success or failure of a unit may be determined to a considerable degree by the education and experience of the teacher. In the light of this, it is interesting to note that the certification standards in general use today for determining the eligibility of secondary-school teachers were established before the experience unit method was developed. Thus, evidence of the mastery of a given body of subject matter with some familiarity with ways in which that subject matter may be transmitted to pupils frequently is the major consideration taken into account by those who pass judgment upon the qualifications of persons who wish to teach. It is obvious, however, that when subject-matter mastery becomes merely a secondary outcome of the educative process, as it does in the experience unit, these traditional notions of what constitutes a good preparation for teaching seem to be due for revision. Limitations of space do not permit a lengthy discussion of this interesting problem at this point. However, some notion of the kind of teacher that is needed may be gained from a brief review of the functions of the teacher and the outcomes sought in the experience unit.

The major educational outcome sought in the experience unit is pupil growth in the ability to achieve a more satisfactory life. Successful living is thought to result from the skillful use of problem-solving techniques based upon or guided by the democratic social principle. It follows that the teacher who is to direct the development of problem-solving skill should be a master of the skill itself. The importance of this kind of achievement as part of the professional preparation of the teacher gains even greater significance when teaching is defined not as the transmission of subject matter, but as the guidance of pupils through successful life activities. The teacher should, therefore, be a well-adjusted individual; one who has solved for himself the kind of problems that his pupils are now attempting to solve. He should have a wealth of experience upon which the pupils may draw. He should be acquainted not only with the theoretical aspects of living but with the practical as well. For example, there is reason to question the ability of teachers who have never earned a living except as teachers, to guide pupils in making a living in the community at large. Thus, the emphasis in teacher preparation is coming to be upon the selection of capable individuals who have achieved success in the home, the school, and the community; and who are willing to expand this fund of useful experiences through summer work, travel, hobbies, and other forms of direct contact with the practical world, as well as by professional studies on a pre-service and in-service basis.

Getting acquainted with his pupils. In the light of the teacher's role as a guide, his first concern in a particular unit is not for subject matter, but for the individuals who make up the group. Therefore, he should learn to know the pupils as well as possible before the first group meeting. This can be done by examining the records kept by former teachers, studying the case history of each pupil with special attention to abilities, interests, and difficulties, by analyzing the learning activities engaged in previously, and by interviewing the pupils and their parents. From such activities the teacher may learn something of the weaknesses of each pupil that may need special attention, as well as the interests and abilities which may be drawn upon as the unit is developed. The teacher may even gather a few hints from this kind of preparation regarding the topic or problem the group may wish to pursue. This cannot be predicted with any degree of certainty, of course, but if the newspaper stories, radio broadcasts, and general conversation in the community for the period immediately preceding the initiation of a unit happen to center around a given topic, for example, a presidential election or the theft of atomic secrets, the teacher would do well to become familiar with these matters and to gather resource materials related to them.

Resource units. A recent development that is proving to be a boon to teachers who wish to use the experience unit method is the "resource unit." A resource unit is defined by one group of educators as "a systematic and comprehensive survey, analysis, and organization of the possible resources (*e.g.* problems, issues, activities, bibliographies, and the like) which a teacher might utilize in planning, developing, and evaluating a learning unit. It should be based on a major area or problem of living related to the needs of pupils. It should be designed not only to help a teacher in preplanning a learning unit but to review the significant factors of an area of living, and to suggest experiences which the teacher and the students might have to enrich living in that area." [10]

The same authors distinguish between a resource unit and a learning unit as follows:

A resource unit usually is not prepared for a particular class and includes materials for more than one grade level, while a learning unit is planned for a particular group of students. A resource unit offers material for a number of learning units, while a learning unit is for use in a specific teaching situation, and may draw upon several resource units. A resource unit is planned by a teacher or a group of teachers to be used by the teacher; a learning unit is planned co-operatively by teacher and students. [11]

Like a good road map, the resource unit provides the user with a quick overview of the entire area through which he may wish to travel. The user is then able to select from the many possibilities the particular route or combination of activities that promise to take him to the place or places he thinks he would like to go. A given resource unit may, therefore, be useful to many teachers at many different times and under different circumstances, and no two learning units developed through its use are likely to be identical.

When consulting a resource unit, the teacher may expect to find the following kinds of help:

1. A brief statement of the philosophy that gives direction to the educational effort in the society in which the school is located. In some instances, this may be supplemented by a description of the educational theories held by the individual or group of individuals who prepared the resource unit.

[10] H. B. Alberty and others, "How to Make a Resource Unit," *Educational Research Bulletin*, XXIV(3):72, College of Education, Ohio State University, Columbus, Ohio, Mar. 14, 1945.

[11] *Ibid.*, p. 72.

2. A statement of specific learning outcomes that can be sought in a unit in the area dealt with. These outcomes include ideals, values, personality traits, attitudes, knowledges, habits, and skills.

3. A survey of the whole area dealt with in the unit to give the teacher quickly and comprehensively, a working knowledge of that area. This includes issues and problems likely to be encountered as well as a list of references that may be consulted for additional information as needed.

4. A list of suggestions as to how a learning unit might be developed in this area.

5. A list of pupil activities—planning activities, developmental activities, and culminating activities—more than can possibly be dealt with in a given learning unit.

6. A list of suggestions for evaluating the outcomes.[12]

As this list shows, the resource unit gives the teacher some measure of the security formerly provided by a course outline or textbook. Because it provides lists of materials and sources of information on a large number of topics or aspects of the unit area, the teacher is spared the necessity of a frantic search for such materials whenever the interests and purposes of the class lead in an unfamiliar or unexpected direction. As a result, the teacher is free to concentrate on the process of cooperative planning and the carrying out of those plans. The resource unit thus helps inspire the confidence necessary for the group to follow its genuine interests and purposes.

Preplanning the learning unit. In the light of the discussion up to this point, it is apparent that the teacher can do relatively little by way of detailed preplanning of the learning unit without depriving the class of the opportunity to gain experience in group planning. The teacher can, however, anticipate the steps or phases through which the unit will progress and thus be prepared to help the group move from one phase to the next in an orderly manner. One secondary school has found that, *in general*, the learning units developed in that school tended to evolve by the following stages:

1. A preliminary survey of the pupil's background and needs.

2. Setting up of criteria for choice of the worthwhile group experience.

3. Examination of a range of worthwhile group experiences in the light of the criteria set up.

[12] For an excellent example of a resource unit that has these features, see Harold Alberty and others, *Science: Servant or Master*, College of Education, Ohio State University, Columbus, Ohio, 1946.

4. Cooperative choice of the best possible experience with teacher responsibility for so directing the activity as to determine whether choice fits into needs of the pupil and the culture.

5. Caring for the rights of the minority.

6. Actual division of labor and working out of experience.

7. Revision of the group working plan as needs dictate.

8. Evaluation of the group's work upon completion of the group experience or unit.

9. Transition into other units by a technique similar to that mentioned above.[13]

Familiarity with this pattern and with the kinds of activities that may be engaged in at each stage may help the teacher avoid aimless wandering or the admission into the unit of activities that may have only momentary appeal.

An example of more detailed preplanning is found in the plan used with a group of pupils of junior high-school age during the summer of 1945.[14] This plan is particularly helpful inasmuch as it was prepared to assist a group of observers to follow the unit as it was being developed. Because there were only 6 weeks available for the unit, it was necessary to curtail the stages during which the unit was selected by limiting the acceptable choices to a single, broad area. Therefore, the teacher frankly urged the pupils to think about the kind of experiences they thought might help them to understand themselves and their community better. In other words, the unit was committed to the social science area by some preliminary curricular planning. The plan as prepared in advance is as follows:

We assume that we are to gain an understanding of the United States and its growth, but beyond that initial requirement, the program is broad and free.

We (the children and the teacher) will plan the unit cooperatively. We will choose the center of interest and be guided into the scientific method of work by:

1. Formulating our problems

2. Stating our theses

[13] Commission on the Relation of Schools and Colleges, Progressive Education Association, *Thirty Schools Tell Their Story*, pp. 739–740, Harper & Brothers, New York, 1943.

[14] Prepared and used by Miss Eleanor Noyes with a group of pupils at the University of New Hampshire Summer Session, 1945.

3. Testing out our thoughts
4. Drawing tentative conclusions
5. Selecting new purposes for cooperative action

Any worthwhile activity which serves the purpose of making the group experiences vivid, will be admitted to the unit. The question as to whether or not it is an English, art, science, social studies, or spelling, etc., activity will not be approached. The requirement is merely that there is a *dominant interest* on the part of the group, that we face *real problems*, and that it contribute to a *way of working* which leads us to be maturer individuals.

The following skeleton outline is provided so that as the unit progresses cooperatively we may record procedures, thoughts, material, etc., which will, in the end, give us a picture of the complete work.

I. POSSIBLE UNIT PROBLEM

What experiences do Americans have in days when our country looks toward new frontiers?

II. POSSIBLE APPROACHES

A. Discussion of new frontiers and what has opened them.
B. Discussion of the changes the "air world" is bringing about.
C. Discussion of changes in the local community, and what brought about these. Extending this to the Eastern Seaboard.
D. Discussion of why some people moved from our community farther inland, the courage it took to face the obstacles, some of the experiences we think they met.
E. Studying maps to see how the people could have gone inland, the means of transportation usable in this undertaking.
F. Studying stereopticon slides of the barriers.
G. Enjoying
   1. Sound film—*Story of Transportation.*
   2. Silent film—*Westward Expansion—Through Transportation.*
   3. Slides—*Gateway to the West.*
H. Reading a story to entire group—*Young America*—Meigs.
I. Reading story books with this background.
J. Using reference books to find ways to the West and what land was desirable.
K. Making collections of pictures for bulletin board.

III. PROCEDURES

A. What we want to know (problems):
   1.
   2.
   3.
   4.

   B. What we think.

     (Possible solutions to the problems formulated by children in light of their experiences.)

   C. The way we shall work.

    1. More maturely and cooperatively:

      a. In a large group

      b. In a small group

      c. As individuals

   D. We will test our thoughts, broaden our knowledges and skills, and develop our creativeness, by:

    1. Having committees arrange materials.

    2. Using reference materials of all types.

    3. Keeping notebooks.

    4. Having experiences in language arts.

    5. Having experiences in creative art.

    6. Having experiences with music.

    7. Having experiences in science.

    8. Conferring:

      a. With experts

      b. With our mothers and dads

      c. With each other

    9. Taking field trips

   E. We will form tentative conclusions to our problems by:

    1. Discussions of original problems in light of our aggregate experiences and information gathered.

IV. EVALUATION

   A. Teacher and pupils plan together concerning concepts that the group should have gained from the study.

    1. Committees plan some means of measuring knowledge-growth.

   B. Discussion about our "maturer development" as revealed during the unit of work.

V. PROJECTION

   A. Plan, through discussion, ways and means of tackling our next work more efficiently and maturely.

Working with the pupils. The test of good teaching is found in the ability of the teacher to work with the pupils in reaching the desired educational goals. In the experience unit, the advancement of pupils in the ability to solve the problems of real life, the development of attitudes of respect for human personality based on understanding, and the improvement in the ability to work with others in fashioning a satisfactory social life are sought by the good teacher at every stage. It is to be expected, however, that some pupils will not be prepared to engage satisfactorily in this type of learning activity. The skillful teacher will step in to offer help at any point where it is found that pupils are incompetent or failing. Thus, in the initiation and planning stage it may be necessary to suggest a plan of organization and procedure to pupils who have had no previous experience in conducting their own affairs. Care should be exercised to avoid giving the impression that the teacher has final answers, and ultimately all suggestions should be evaluated in terms of their effectiveness and with a view to improving them for future use. In the interest of improving problem-solving ability, the teacher should encourage the careful study of possible problems for the unit before a selection is made. He should see to it that standards based on respect for the rights of individuals are set up through cooperative study and group discussion, and that these standards are used to guide the group in the selection of the unit problem. Acceptable research procedures should be suggested to make sure that the group has a sound basis for making wise choices. The attention of the pupils should be directed as needed to sources of information that are new to them or that may have been overlooked.

In the developmental stage, the teacher should be alert constantly to discover individuals or groups that are "bogging down" on their jobs. Special help will be needed in these instances to keep the unit moving ahead. Frequently difficulties of this nature arise because the pupils concerned do not possess the necessary skill or understanding for the task immediately at hand. The teacher may be able to remedy the difficulty by providing individual instruction or drill immediately. If more extensive help is needed, the pupil should be directed to remedial classes or to the courses where specialized instruction is offered.

The culmination and evaluation stage also calls for special attention. In some respects this can be the most fruitful stage of the unit in terms of encouraging pupils to give thought to the kind of life they wish to live. The self-appraisal activities frequently engaged in at this stage, which call for reorganizing the method of attack and for reevaluating the goals reached, will not come about without guidance from the teacher except in the case of experienced and quite mature students. The measurement of progress in acquiring desired skills and bodies of knowledge also requires special assistance from the teacher who has the technical knowledge necessary to use the instruments of measurement that have been designed for this purpose. Care should be taken, however, to distinguish between the knowledge and skills the pupils have chosen to acquire and those that might be looked for by teachers using the daily-assignment or the subject-matter unit methods.

Keeping the record. Finally, the teacher should keep a record of the unit as it is being developed. This record can help in keeping the group moving along in a purposeful manner if it is referred to in planning. When the group moves on, the record will indicate to new teachers and others the kind of experiences the pupils have had, the growth that has occurred, and the special abilities or weaknesses that have been observed. In this sense, the record assumes some of the functions of a course of study, for it may help in determining the nature and sequence of the experiences the pupils may be urged to undergo in subsequent units. Supplemented by other data including the records kept by the pupils themselves, the teacher's record of the unit is helpful not only in curricular planning on a school-wide basis, but also in helping the individual round out his own personal development.

SUMMARY

In conclusion it seems fair to say that the experience unit method acquires its chief characteristic from the principle that pupils can best learn to live in a satisfactory manner by carrying on real-life activities in the pursuit of ends that have significant value for them, that is, the learning activities that constitute the content of education have their source in the experiences of the pupils. To center the educative effort in the purposes, interests, needs, and concerns of the learner, the teacher functions as a guide by suggesting possibilities and considerations beyond the knowledge or experiences of the learner, and by affording a measure of security made possible by his greater experience and maturity. In this manner the teacher is merely a participant in the cooperative search for more effective controls over the environment, both physical and social.

SELECTED REFERENCES

ALBERTY, HAROLD B.: "How to Make a Resource Unit," *Educational Research Bulletin*, XXIV:72–76, Mar. 14, 1945.

ALBERTY, HAROLD B.: *Reorganizing the High-School Curriculum*, The Macmillan Company, New York, 1947.

—— *Science: Servant or Master*, A Resource Unit, College of Education, Ohio State University, Columbus, Ohio, 1946.

BLACKHURST, J. HERBERT: *Principles of Methods*, Drake University Press, Des Moines, Iowa, 1936.

BURTON, WILLIAM H.: *The Guidance of Learning Activities*, Parts II and IV, D. Appleton-Century Company, Inc., New York, 1944.

Class of 1938, Ohio State University School: *Were We Guinea Pigs?*, Henry Holt and Company, Inc., New York, 1938.

COLLINGS, ELLSWORTH: *Progressive Teaching in Secondary Schools*, Bobbs-Merrill Company, Indianapolis, 1931.

GILES, H. H., McCUTCHEN, S. P., and ZECHIEL, A. N.: *Exploring the Curriculum*, Harper & Brothers, New York, 1942.

HANNA, PAUL: *Youth Serves the Community*, D. Appleton-Century Company, Inc., New York, 1936.

KILPATRICK, WILLIAM H.: *Foundations of Method*, The Macmillan Company, New York, 1925.

MELVIN, A. GORDON: *Teaching*, The John Day Company, New York, 1944.

Michigan Department of Public Instruction: *Planning and Working Together*, Bulletin 337, Superintendent of Public Instruction, Lansing, Michigan, 1945.

Progressive Education Association: *New Methods Versus Old*, Bureau of Publications, Teachers College, Columbia University, New York, 1941.

SCHNEIDEMAN, ROSE: *Democratic Education in Practice*, Part IV, Harper & Brothers, New York, 1945.

SPEARS, HAROLD: *The Emerging High School Curriculum*, American Book Company, New York, 1940.

STRICKLAND, RUTH G.: *How to Build a Unit of Work*, Bulletin 5, U.S. Office of Education, Government Printing Office, Washington, D.C., 1946.

Chapter 14. THE EVALUATION OF PUPIL PROGRESS

IN THE EXPERIENCE UNIT METHOD

Once again, as was done in Chaps. 8 and 11 for the recitation method and the subject-matter unit method, it is desirable to approach evaluation of pupil behavior through the instructional outcomes sought and emphasized in the method under consideration. Achievement can be appraised only in terms of pupil behavior, and pupil behavior is determined largely by the degree to which educational procedures succeed in developing desired behavioral outcomes in pupils.

It is clearly brought out in Chap. 12 that behavioral changes sought in the experience unit method run the entire gamut of possible outcomes. Of the skills, knowledges, concepts, understandings, tastes and preferences, and applications under which all behavioral outcomes are classified in Chap. 5, not one is neglected in this most recently evolved of the three instructional methods. When the purpose of education is proficiency in social living and when the educational activities are real rather than artificial, the whole pupil is involved. Certainly all of the possible types of instructional outcomes are, therefore, conceived to be important. The experience unit method emphasizes the most tangible instructional outcomes, represented by knowledges and skills, relatively less and the remaining more intangible outcomes relatively more than do either the recitation or the subject-matter unit methods of instruction. This fact places more responsibility upon the teacher and other school officials for measuring the attainment of diverse types of outcomes than is true of the recitation or subject-matter unit methods.

Evaluation procedures characteristic of the experience unit method. The broad conception of instructional or experiential outcomes inherent in the experience unit method is necessarily, or at least desirably, accompanied by measurement and evaluation techniques in line with the ob-

318

jectives of instruction. Tyler's 10 steps of procedure [1] for the construction of evaluation instruments appear best to illustrate this type of approach to appraisal.

1. Formulation of course objectives
2. Definition of each objective in terms of student behavior
3. Collection of situations in which students will reveal presence or absence of each objective
4. Presentation of situations to students
5. Evaluation of student reactions in light of each objective
6. Determination of objectivity of evaluation
7. Improvement of objectivity when necessary
8. Determination of reliability
9. Improvement of reliability when necessary
10. Development of more practicable methods of measurement, when necessary

The differences in the approach to measurement of pupil achievement embodied in the above list and in the comparable procedures outlined in Chaps. 8 and 11 are tremendous. Evaluation is here approached in terms of instructional outcomes of all types and not primarily in terms of subject-matter content of courses. It is the whole child who is evaluated here, rather than the factually stocked and skilled child who is tested in the recitation method and the child possessing knowledges, skills, concepts, understandings, and tastes and preferences, who is measured in the subject-matter unit method.

Formulation of Objectives. The initial step in attempting to evaluate outcomes of the experience unit method is the determination of general objectives. Frequently these general objectives are formulated for the entire program of the school, as in those stated by the staff of the Eight-year Study of Progressive Schools.[2]

1. The development of effective methods of thinking
2. The cultivation of useful work habits and study skills
3. The inculcation of social attitudes
4. The acquisition of a wide range of significant interests
5. The development of increased appreciation of music, art, literature, and other aesthetic experiences

[1] Ralph W. Tyler, *Constructing Achievement Tests*, pp. 4–14, Ohio State University, Columbus, Ohio, 1934.
[2] Eugene R. Smith, Ralph W. Tyler, *et al.*, *Appraising and Recording Student Progress*, p. 18, Harper & Brothers, New York, 1942.

6. The development of social sensitivity
7. The development of better personal-social adjustment
8. The acquisition of important information
9. The development of physical health
10. The development of a consistent philosophy of life

Although such lists of objectives as the above are guides to effective planning of a program of evaluation, they are a source of general rather than of specific leads. It is essential for the teacher interested in the evaluation of pupil outcomes in a certain experience unit or experience area to obtain or to formulate a more specific list of objectives for the particular unit or area in question. An example of this type of analysis of objectives is that shown in the breakdown of the first general objective listed above into four major and several supplementary specific objectives: [3]

1. Development of ability to interpret data
   a. To make comparisons among data
   b. To see elements common to several items of data
   c. To recognize prevailing tendencies or trends in data
2. Development of ability to apply principles of science or social studies
   a. To make decisions concerning the probable explanation or applicable prediction
   b. To justify the explanation or prediction
3. Development of ability to apply principles of logical reasoning
   a. To examine the logical structure of an argument
   b. To distinguish between conclusions which do and which do not follow logically from a given set of assumptions
   c. To isolate the significant elements in the logical structure of an argument
   d. To recognize the application of a logical principle to explain why a conclusion follows logically from given assumptions
4. Development of certain abilities associated with an understanding of the nature of proof
   a. To analyze proofs critically
   b. To recognize the basic assumptions upon which a conclusion depends and to see the logical relationships between these assumptions and the conclusion
   c. To recognize the need for further data

[3] *Ibid.*, Chap. 2.

d. To distinguish between assumptions whose tenability could and could not be confirmed

e. To recognize possible ways for studying a problem further and to distinguish between fruitful and unfruitful methods of further study

f. To accept or reject assumptions tentatively and to test the conclusions which follow

g. To recognize that new evidence may make desirable a reconsideration of the argument and possibly a qualification of the tentative conclusions

Such a list as that above points up certain aspects of effective methods of thinking which, as desired instructional outcomes, should be measured.

Analysis of Outcomes in Terms of Behavior. The second major step involved in the evaluation of outcomes from an experience unit method is the statement of each outcome in terms of observable pupil behaviors. It is necessary to translate from objectives to outcomes, as was done in the preceding section, and then to translate outcomes into specific types of pupil behavior which will indicate the degree of attainment of the outcomes. The results of such an analysis are shown below for the second major objective above, cultivation of useful work habits and study skills, as they are listed by the staff of the Eight-year Study.[4] Subheadings are given only for the first three groups of work habits and study skills in the outline following.

1. Using study time effectively
   a. Habit of using large blocks of free time effectively
   b. Habit of budgeting his time
   c. Habit of sustained application
   d. Habit of meeting study obligations promptly
   e. Habit of carrying work through to completion
2. Establishing conditions for effective study
   a. Knowledge of proper working conditions
   b. Habit of providing proper working conditions for himself
   c. Habit of working under his own direction and initiative
3. Effective planning of study
   a. Habit of planning in advance
   b. Habit of choosing for investigation problems which have significance for him

[4] *Ibid.,* pp. 31–33.

    c. Ability to define a problem
    d. Habit of analyzing a problem
4. Selecting sources of data
5. Using various sources of data effectively
6. Determining relevancy of data
7. Recording and organizing data
8. Presenting the results of study
9. Evaluating each step in an investigation

A combination of two methods may also be used in obtaining lists of such outcomes. One, the traditional method, is that of scanning the course content unit by unit to determine the purpose of each and the types of behaviors likely to result in successful pupils. The other, and newer, method is that of analyzing the general function of a course into its subfunctions and of determining the pupil behaviors likely to result.

Construction and Validation of Evaluative Instruments. The third major step in the evaluation of pupil behavior, that of collecting situations in which pupils will reveal the presence or absence of each desired type of behavior, requires more ingenuity than does test construction with subject-matter emphases. Although the skill and knowledge outcomes present few problems, and are measurable by methods outlined in Chaps. 8 and 11, the evaluator in the experience unit method must attempt to appraise objectively the types of instructional outcomes measured only subjectively or even overlooked in more traditional measurement programs. A list of outcomes stated in terms of behavior, such as that given above, affords considerable aid in this third step. Although this question is too involved to discuss in detail here, because of the varied methods needed for different types of behavior, the discussion and illustrations to follow will furnish considerable evidence on appropriate methods.

The remaining steps in the construction of evaluation instruments are essentially paralleled by steps outlined for testing and measuring in Chaps. 8 and 11. They are concerned with the selection of situations for use in the evaluation of pupils, presentation of the situations to pupils, evaluation of pupil reactions, and improvement in the objectivity, reliability, and practicality of the technique or instrument.

It is often true in using the experience unit method that several different units will contribute to the development of a single desired outcome. It is also often true that one experience unit contributes to the development of several different desired outcomes. Therefore, it is inappropriate to attempt as direct a parallelism between measurement and instructional units in this type of program as may be appropriate where the recitation method or the subject-matter unit method is in effect. Measuring the pupils' attainment of the desired outcomes upon the completion of each unit therefore is not effective. In so far as paper-and-pencil tests are concerned, evaluation must be considered broadly and in terms of groups of related units. Emphasis should be placed upon broadly conceived tests or evaluations administered periodically, rather than upon short tests frequently administered. Evidence of this difference is found in the fact that following sections of this chapter deal with types of outcomes, whereas sections of Chap. 8 and Chap. 11 were devoted to types of measuring instruments. Outcomes treated below are work habits and study skills; such relatively intangible behaviors as are involved in ability to think, social sensitivity, appreciations, and vocational interests; personal-social adjustment; and teachers' marks.

WORK HABITS AND STUDY SKILLS

A newer and much more broadly conceived version of the traditional reading-writing-arithmetic triumvirate is that involved in the modern conception of the basic skills necessary for social living. The skills may be classified into speaking, writing, reading, and computing. The first two are in the area known as the expressive language arts and the third is in the area of the receptive language arts. Writing is concerned primarily with the expression of ideas and only incidentally with penmanship. Except for the first-mentioned skills, which must be measured by other means, these skills are subject to direct measurement by paper-and-pencil tests.

Modern techniques of measuring the three basic skills of writing, reading, and computing tend to avoid the subject-matter approach evidenced in many tests in these skill areas and to emphasize the socially useful skills apart from their source of acquisition. In so doing, they are founded upon the philosophy and method inherent in the experience unit plan. Standardized tests of these skills are most often found today for the intermediate grade and junior high-school levels, although there is evidence that concern for such outcomes is increasing at the senior high-school and even the college freshman levels.

The *Iowa Every-Pupil Tests of Basic Skills* [5] for grades 4 to 9 appear in four tests—silent-reading comprehension, work-study skills, basic language skills, and basic arithmetic skills. This battery differs significantly from most, if not all, of the other batteries for these grades by emphasizing skills to the practical exclusion of formal knowledges and by making no provision for direct measurement in the content subjects. It combines into one integrated battery types of measures often found in achievement survey tests for specific school subjects and for subject areas. The expressive English area is covered by part scores on punctuation, capitalization, usage, and spelling in the basic language skills test. Part scores for reading comprehension and vocabulary are obtained in the receptive English area from the silent reading comprehension test. Computing skills in the basic arithmetic test are measured by parts on vocabulary and fundamental knowledge; whole numbers, fractions, percentages, decimals, and denominate numbers; and problems. Somewhat different, and embodying the belief that pupils should learn how to locate information, is the test of work-study skills. Here are found part scores for map reading, use of references, use of index, use of dictionary, and reading graphs, charts, and tables.

Another test series designed for use at the high-school and college levels is the *USAFI Tests of General Educational Development*.[6] These tests were constructed for use in the educational placement of persons returning to high school or college from service in some branch of the armed forces. The purpose was to construct tests in major skill and knowledge areas which would reveal the educational level at which each person could work and which would furnish broad measures of outcomes acquired incidentally rather than narrow measures of outcomes obtained from specific and definitely patterned courses. These tests at the high-school level measure correctness and effectiveness of expression, interpretation of reading materials in the social studies, interpretation of reading materials in the natural sciences, interpretation of literary materials, and general mathematical ability.

[5] H. T. Spitzer and Ruth Fridell, *Iowa Every-Pupil Tests of Basic Skills*, Advanced Battery, Houghton Mifflin Company, Boston, 1942.

[6] Examinations Staff for the United States Armed Forces Institute, *United States Armed Forces Institute Tests of General Educational Development*, High School and College Levels, Form B, American Council on Education, Washington, D.C., 1943.

The *Iowa Tests of Educational Development* [7] constitute an integrated battery for grades 9 to 12 which appears to merge measurement of basic skills with broad measurement of other outcomes in content areas. The separate tests measure understanding of basic social concepts, background in the natural sciences, correctness in writing, ability to do quantitative thinking, ability to interpret reading materials in the social studies, ability to interpret reading materials in the natural sciences, ability to interpret literary materials, general vocabulary, and use of sources of information.

RELATIVELY INTANGIBLE OUTCOMES

The exactness of any classification of intangible outcomes, as contrasted with outcomes more definite and specific in nature, is questionable. However, certain types of behavioral changes occurring in pupils are not readily observable and are hence measurable only by means of indirect or relatively complex procedures. The purpose here is to consider such outcomes of this type as have not been dealt with in Chap. 11. Certainly the attitudes and general interests treated in that chapter may be considered as relatively intangible outcomes.

Four types of additional outcomes of relatively intangible nature will be considered in the pages following. They are ability to think, social sensitivity, appreciations, and vocational interests.

Ability to think. Teaching pupils to think has long been one of the major purposes of education. Appraisal of pupil ability to think has been a major problem, and one for which satisfactory solutions have been attained only too seldom. Some of the discussion of Chaps. 8 and 11 dealt with the development and use of tests and techniques in this behavior area. Others distinctly associated with the experience unit method rather than the recitation method or the subject-matter unit method of instruction are briefly presented here.

The ability to think is considered under the two somewhat overlapping headings of understandings and aspects of thinking, in part because two highly significant publications in the field of evaluation have dealt intensively with these outcomes. Certainly no line of demarcation can be drawn between the two. There are significant dif-

[7] E. F. Lindquist (ed.), *Iowa Tests of Educational Development,* Forms X–2 and Y-2, Science Research Associates, Chicago, 1942.

ferences represented in some of the methods of appraisal recommended, however.

Understandings. The instructional outcomes described as understandings are difficult to define exactly. Understandings certainly go beyond skills and factual knowledges in their complexity, significance, and difficulty of evaluation. They represent higher and less tangible outcomes than do formal skills and factual knowledges. Understandings are measurable by methods outlined in both Chap. 8 and Chap. 11, at some levels, but their evaluation at higher levels demands more elaborate and complex techniques than those discussed heretofore.

Findley and Scates[8] outlined levels of understanding starting somewhat above factual knowledges with abilities to discern cause and effect, to choose correct explanations of events, and to make simple judgments, ranging through abilities to draw logical inferences and to make appropriate deductions, and ending with abilities to express understanding effectively, to delimit oneself to the problem at hand, and to suspend judgment if logically necessary. These authors point out that situations used with pupils in measuring their understandings should have some but not an extreme element of novelty, should be based on reality, should provide for creative effort or originality, should be keyed to the level and kind of understanding under consideration, and should provide for pupil self-evaluation.

In view of the rather intangible nature of understandings, they may be classified in any one of many ways with equal facility. Heil and his colleagues[9] classify science understandings broadly as factual and methodological, and then list a number of desired specific behaviors of each type. Anderson and his collaborators[10] divide understandings in the social studies into those involving the acquisition of information,

---

[8] Warren G. Findley and Douglas E. Scates, "Obtaining Evidence of Understanding," *The Measurement of Understanding*, Part I, Chap. 4, Forty-fifth Yearbook of the National Society for the Study of Education, University of Chicago Press, Chicago, 1946.

[9] Louis M. Heil (Chairman), "The Measurement of Understanding in Science," *The Measurement of Understanding*, Part I, Chap. 6, Forty-fifth Yearbook of the National Society for the Study of Education, University of Chicago Press, Chicago, 1946.

[10] Howard R. Anderson (Chairman), "The Measurement of Understanding in the Social Studies," *The Measurement of Understanding*, Part I, Chap. 5, Forty-fifth Yearbook of the National Society for the Study of Education, University of Chicago Press, Chicago, 1946.

the analysis of social problems, and the practicing of desirable social relationships, and list four more specific understandings of each type. There seems to be no formula by means of which desirable understandings can be isolated easily; they must be evolved in terms of the area of pupil activity in question, the type of school, the type of pupil enrolled, and numerous other factors.

The accompanying illustration of a multiple-choice item from the *Cooperative English Effectiveness Test* represents the use of a simple item form of more than ordinary difficulty of construction in measuring an understanding of effective expression in receptive English.

EXCERPT FROM COOPERATIVE EFFECTIVENESS OF EXPRESSION TEST, B2

Directions: Read each of the following groups carefully; then decide which one of the four choices in each group is expressed most satisfactorily, and put the **number** of this best choice in the parentheses at the right of the group.

1-1 In the eighteenth century Benjamin Franklin was one of the commanding figures in science, and he was respected in the colonies and just as much in Europe for his studies in physics.
1-2 Benjamin Franklin was equally as much respected in Europe as in the colonies in the eighteenth century for his studies in physics and he was one of the commanding figures in science then.
1-3 Benjamin Franklin was one of the commanding figures in science in the eighteenth century, respected as much in Europe as in the colonies for his studies in physics.
1-4 One of the commanding figures in science in the eighteenth century being respected not only in the colonies but just as much in Europe for his studies in physics was Benjamin Franklin. . . . . .1( )

Source: Geraldine Spaulding and Miriam May, *Cooperative Effectiveness of Expression Test, B2*, Form T, Cooperative Test Service, New York, 1943.

Aspects of Thinking. In the Eight-year Study of Progressive Education, methods of thinking were classified into the four abilities: (*a*) to interpret data, (*b*) to apply principles of science and of social studies, (*c*) to apply principles of logical reasoning in general, and (*d*) to base action upon an understanding of the nature of proof.

One of the best-known and widely used types of evaluative techniques evolved in the Eight-year Study is that for ability to interpret social or scientific data. The test data presented may be in the form of tables, charts, or integrated paragraphs. From 10 to 20 statements follow each set of data, and the pupil is asked to indicate for each statement, by writing the appropriate number or marking the appropriate column of a separate answer sheet, whether the data are:

1. Sufficient to make the statement true,
2. Sufficient to indicate that the statement is probably true,
3. Not sufficient to indicate whether there is any degree of truth or falsity in the statement,
4. Sufficient to indicate that the statement is probably false, or
5. Sufficient to make the statement false.

The accompanying illustration shows a set of such data and 5 of the 15 statements following it.

EXCERPT FROM INTERPRETATION OF DATA TEST

PROBLEM I.   The graph below gives some data about hourly wages in the automotive industry and the average cost of automobiles per pound. Some additional information is given below the graph.

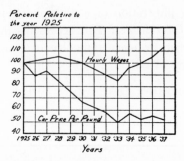

Hourly wages are given for the years after 1925 as per cents of the hourly wage of 1925.

The price per pound of cars is given for the years after 1925 as per cents of the price per pound in 1925.

Statements

1. From 1934 to 1937 hourly wages increased while car price per pound remained about the same.

2. In the airplane industry the relation of hourly wages and the price per pound of the finished products has been similar to that of the automobile industry.

3. Hourly wages will be higher in 1940 than in 1933.

4. The automobile industry made less profit in 1937 than in 1925.

5. Hourly wages were higher in 1924 than in 1937.

Source: Progressive Education Association, "Evaluation in the Eight Year Study," *Interpretation of Data Test*, 2.51, Cooperative Test Service, New York, 1939.

One other illustration from the instruments devised in the Eight-year Study for the appraisal of aspects of thinking is given here. This deals with the application of principles of logical reasoning. The illustration gives the problem, the 3 conclusions from which the pupils choose 1, and 3 of the 12 supporting statements to be marked by the pupils in one of three possible ways.

Another instrument designed for measuring this type of instructional outcome is the *Watson-Glaser Test of Critical Thinking*, which provides part scores on generalizations, inferences, discrimination of arguments, recognition of assumptions, general logical reasoning, attitudes, opinions, and applied logical reasoning. The accompanying illustration presents a test unit each from the discrimination of arguments and

EXCERPT FROM APPLICATION OF CERTAIN PRINCIPLES OF LOGICAL
REASONING TEST

PROBLEM II

An advisory commission was considering proposals for various types of super-highway to
speed up traffic and reduce accidents in a large city. The chairman of the group summarized the findings of the commission as follows: "There are just three types of super-
highway-- 1) surface (on the ground level), 2) elevated (above the ground level), 3) depressed (below the ground level). An express roadway should be free from cross traffic,
pedestrians, and parked cars. Our findings show that a surface highway will not be satisfactory. Although depressed and elevated highways both have advantages and disadvantages,
these two types will serve and are equally satisfactory except for the expense factor.
Other things being equal, the more expensive road is less satisfactory, and the elevated
highway would cost almost twice as much to build as the depressed highway."

Directions: Examine the conclusions given below. Assuming that the chairman's summary
is true, which one of the conclusions do you think is justified?

Conclusions

A. The chairman's summary proved that the depressed highway was the most satisfactory
   choice.

B. The chairman's summary did not prove that the depressed highway was the most satisfactory choice.

C. More information is needed to decide whether or not the chairman's summary proved
   that the depressed highway was the most satisfactory choice.

	A: Statements which explain why your conclusion is logical.
Mark in column	B: Statements which do not explain why your conclusion is logical.
	C: Statements about which you are unable to decide.

Statements

1. If the more expensive of two roads, which are equally satisfactory in other respects,
   is less satisfactory, then the cheaper road is the more satisfactory of the two.

2. One needs to know more about the special advantages and disadvantages of depressed
   and elevated highways.

3. One needs to understand more clearly what is meant by an elevated highway, a surface
   highway, and a depressed highway.

Source: Progressive Education Association, "Evaluation in the Eight Year
Study," *Application of Certain Principles of Logical Reasoning Test*, 5.12, University of Chicago Press, Chicago, 1940.

the applied logical reasoning parts. Pupil responses to the first are
alternate-response in form on the strength or weakness of each argument presented, while pupils react to multiple-choice item forms in the
second by choosing the most logical conclusion among those that are
given.

Social sensitivity. Social sensitivity as dealt with in the Eight-year
Study [11] was conceived to involve the following major aspects: (*a*) social
thinking, (*b*) social attitudes, beliefs, and values, (*c*) social awareness,
(*d*) social interests, (*e*) social information, and (*f*) skill in social action.
It is apparent that several of these outcomes have been dealt with in

[11] Eugene R. Smith, Ralph W. Tyler, *et al.*, *Appraising and Recording Student
Progress*, p. 161, Harper & Brothers, New York, 1942.

EXCERPTS FROM WATSON-GLASER TESTS OF CRITICAL THINKING

Discrimination of Arguments

V. In a time of widespread unemployment should relief funds be provided by the Federal government?

17. No; for individuals and localities will then lean on the Federal government rather than exercise their own efforts, initiative, and ingenuity..................... 33 Strong   34 Weak

18. Yes; for the Federal government owns billions of dollars' worth of gold now buried in the hills of Kentucky... 35 Strong   36 Weak

19. Yes; for the problem is national in scope and cannot otherwise be solved by individuals or by those localities where, due to poverty, the burden is heaviest....... 37 Strong   38 Weak

20. No; for in some regions the local officials are corrupt and use the money from Washington not to help those most in need but to reward their political supporters... 39 Strong   40 Weak

Applied Logical Reasoning

20. In an Eastern college a study of students holding radical opinions about the economic order showed that all of them scored above the average score made by college students on certain reading tests. Tom, a student at that college, was below the average score made by college students on those reading tests. We may, therefore, conclude that —

96 Tom was one of the radicals.
97 Tom did not like to read.
98 Tom might have been one of the radicals.
99 Tom was not one of the radicals.
100 None of the above conclusions properly follows from the information given.

Source: Goodwin Watson and Edward M. Glaser, *Watson-Glaser Tests of Critical Thinking*, Form A, World Book Company, Yonkers, N. Y., 1942.

Chap. 11 and previously in this chapter. However, the total evaluation of social sensitivity properly involves more than results from the appraisal of attitudes, interests, skills, and knowledges separately. The accompanying illustration shows one of the problems, 3 courses of action from which the pupils choose 1, and 3 of the 21 reasons to be evaluated by the pupils in the *Social Problems Test*.

Appreciations. In the area of appreciations, the Eight-year Study dealt primarily with those in literature and art, although music appreciation is another field in which evaluations by other than paper-and-pencil means have been made. Behaviors selected in the Eight-year Study [12] to evidence the attainment of literary appreciation are: (*a*) satisfaction in the thing appreciated, (*b*) desire for more of the thing appreciated, (*c*) desire to know more about the thing appreciated, (*d*) desire to express oneself creatively, (*e*) identification of oneself with the thing appreciated, (*f*) desire to clarify one's own thinking with regard to

[12] *Ibid.*, pp. 248–249.

EXCERPT FROM SOCIAL PROBLEMS TEST

PROBLEM VIII.   "INCOME"

There is a wide variation in incomes in America. At one extreme there are half a million
families whose yearly income is $25,000 or above. At the other extreme there are more
than two million families who earn less than $500 a year. Plans aiming at a more even
distribution of goods and services among the American people have aroused considerable
controversy.
Which of the following courses of action seems best to you?

> Directions: Choose the course (or courses) of action and fill in the appropriate spaces
>   on the answer sheet under Problem VIII.

Courses of Action:

  A. Laws should be passed establishing a minimum wage sufficient to enable all workers
     to live in moderate comfort.

  B. People with high incomes should be taxed so that the government could provide such
     services as housing and medical care for people who earn very little.

  C. There is no use trying to do anything about such great differences in income.

> Directions: Choose the reasons which you would use for your course (or courses) of ac-
>   tion and fill the spaces on the answer sheet in the column under the course
>   of action you marked at the top. If you have chosen more than one course
>   of action, and a reason supports both, mark it in both columns.

Reasons:

  1. Anyone who works should be assured at least enough pay to live on.

  2. No matter what might be done to increase the income of the poor, many of them would
     still be too shiftless to care for themselves.

  3. All people have a right to an income permitting a decent standard of living.

Source: Progressive Education Association, "Evaluation in the Eight Year
Study," *Social Problems Test*, 1.41, University of Chicago Press, Chicago, 1939.

the life problems raised by the thing appreciated, and (g) desire to
evaluate the thing appreciated. Such behaviors clearly indicate that appreciative outcomes go far beyond the knowledges, comprehensions,
and abilities to analyze and to interpret by means of which attempts
have been made to evaluate appreciations. The appreciative instruments
of the Eight-year Study are based on the assumption that pupils remember the overt behaviors, which are the ultimate criteria, and will report them accurately on pencil-and-paper instruments.[13]

Evaluative instruments used in this area were three questionnaires on
voluntary reading, the novel, and the drama, tests on literary information, a test on interpretation of literature, a test on critical-mindedness
in the reading of fiction, and a test on judging the effectiveness of written compositions. Although some of the techniques are too complex
and lengthy for presentation here, they employ testing devices very
similar to those presented elsewhere in this chapter and in Chaps. 8
and 11.

[13] *Ibid.*, p. 252.

Vocational interests. General interests inventories, as distinguished from vocational interests inventories, were discussed and illustrated in Chap. 11. Inventories designed for measuring vocational interests are dealt with here, however, because they are more in line with the ex-

EXCERPTS FROM STRONG VOCATIONAL INTEREST BLANKS

Part V. Peculiarities of People. Record your first impression. Do not think of various possibilities or of exceptional cases. "Let yourself go" and record the feeling that comes to mind as you read the item.

234 Progressive people	L	I	D
235 Conservative people	L	I	D
236 Energetic people	L	I	D
237 Absent-minded people	L	I	D

Part VIII. School Subjects. Indicate whether you liked the following or not when in school. Work rapidly. Do not think over various possibilities. Record your first impressions.

372 Algebra	L	I	D
373 Arithmetic	L	I	D
374 Art	L	I	D
375 Bible Study	L	I	D

Source: Edward K. Strong, Jr., (*top*) *Vocational Interest Blank for Men* (rev.), Form M, and (*bottom*) *Vocational Interest Blank for Women*, Form WB, Stanford University Press, Stanford University, Calif., 1938 and 1933.

perience unit method than with the subject-matter unit method of instruction.

Although inventories of this type are designed to predict future success in vocational areas or specific types of work, it should be recognized that such other factors as special aptitudes and background training are also important determiners of vocational success. In general, it is not desirable to consider results from vocational interests measurement valid for pupils below the senior high-school or college levels, inasmuch as vocational interests are quite unstable for pupils in the grade school or the junior high school.

The Strong *Vocational Interest Blank* provides separate forms for men and women. Scores are obtained, by various weightings of responses to the different questions, for 35 men's occupations and 17 women's occupations. The questions deal with occupations, school subjects, amusements, activities, comparison of interest between two items, and rating of present abilities and characteristics. The accompanying illustration shows the typical 3-point scale of response for a few items each from the parts on peculiarities of people and on school subjects. The items on peculiarities of people are from the men's form and the items on school subjects are from the women's form of the instrument.

The Kuder *Preference Record* provides scores in nine areas of study and work—mechanical, computational, scientific, persuasive, artistic, literary, musical, social service, and clerical. Although men and women take the same form of the preference record, separate norms are provided for the sexes. The example reproduced in an accompanying illustration shows items in groups of three and the manner in which pupils respond by marking the activities in which they would most like and least like to engage.

SAMPLE ITEMS FROM KUDER PREFERENCE RECORD

EXAMPLE

Put your answers to these questions in column 4.

P. Visit an art gallery

Q. Browse in a library

R. Visit a museum

S. Collect autographs

T. Collect coins

U. Collect butterflies

Source: G. Frederic Kuder, *Preference Record*, Form BM, Science Research Associates, Chicago, 1942.

PERSONAL–SOCIAL ADJUSTMENT

Appraisal in the exceedingly broad area characterized here as personal-social adjustment may well represent the ultimate in pupil evaluation. Whether such a concept as personal-social adjustment is properly to be considered a type of instructional outcome or whether it represents the sum total or ultimate in the integration of instructional outcomes in the individual pupil is not a major concern. It seems sufficient that each pupil should be aided as much as possible in his attempt to attain that optimum adjustment which is probably unique for him as an individual. Variety in human heredity and environment is so great that no two persons may be expected to have exactly the same pattern of aptitudes, backgrounds, characteristics, and goals. Hence, the attainment of adjustment is a relatively unique problem for each individual.

Emphasis upon education of the whole child in the experience unit method, supported by philosophical, psychological, and sociological evidence, is in harmony with the theory of pupil evaluation. All of the testing, measuring, and evaluating tools and techniques discussed previously in this chapter and in Chaps. 8 and 11 contribute directly to a total evaluation program. There remain, however, certain broadly evaluative procedures which appear not to be designed for measuring directly the types of instructional outcomes outlined in Chap. 5 as subject centered and activity centered. Those treated here are designed to aid in obtaining an over-all characterization of the pupil at a given time, when the results supplement those from other methods of pupil appraisal. The purpose is to obtain the best evidence available for use in pupil guidance, both present and future. Several guidance tools and techniques treated in Chap. 16 carry this concept one step further, to include provision for permanent sources of information about the pupil and for the intensive and extensive study of those individuals characterized by serious maladjustment.

Two types of evaluative approaches in this area of personal-social adjustment are appropriate for discussion here. They are observational appraisals, initiated by the teacher, and personal reports by the pupils. The major techniques of each type are outlined in the following pages.

Observational appraisals. Informal appraisals obtained through teacher observation of pupil behavior play a large part in a well-rounded evaluation program. Such appraisals of pupils differ from those which teachers have always made primarily in the background of understanding and objectivity of method the teacher brings to evaluation of pupil behavior. A teacher employing the experience unit method may be expected to have considerable understanding of pupil growth, development, and learning, and also to have clearly in mind the types of instructional objectives sought. He may also be expected to be discriminative and to apply scientific procedures in his evaluation of pupil behavior.

The teacher is constantly observing pupil behavior. Much of what he observes is of no great significance, but pupil behaviors occur fairly frequently by means of which the astute teacher may learn much concerning the degree to which desired outcomes have been acquired. Three relatively distinct techniques useful in this type of appraisal are informal observations, projective techniques, and anecdotal records. Such observations are also basic to the reliable use of rating scales, as discussed in Chap. 11.

Informal Observation. The scope of informal observations is so great that only an incomplete characterization is possible here. Pupils may well be observed with meaningful results in almost any type of school situation or activity. Answers to such questions as the following indicate the range and imply the purpose of such observational evaluations: How does the pupil use his free time? Does he ask questions to which he could learn the answers on his own initiative? Does he accept as fact all that he reads and hears? Is his behavior consistent with his expressed attitudes? Does he work cooperatively with classmates in group projects? Does he recognize the meanings and implications of end products from school activities?

Although the variety of observational situations is almost endless, the purpose in all observation is the evaluation of the whole child in life activities rather than the measurement of a segment of child behavior in artificial situations. As in any other evaluation, the teacher should seek objectivity of method in order to rule out the possibility of overinterpretation. Similar behaviors do not always represent similar causes in different pupils. Similar causes may result in varied behavior in different pupils. Hence, no rule-of-thumb procedures are effective in evaluations of this type.

Projective Methods. Techniques now designated as projective methods have had a rather brief history to date, although their forerunners are found in the free association methods evolved at least as early as the third quarter of the nineteenth century. Projective techniques at present are not tools for use by the teacher, as is also true of the individual intelligence tests treated in Chap. 16. They are still properly used only by the trained technician in psychological testing. Their brief mention here is warranted by the fact that they represent broad evaluative methods of studying personal-social adjustment.

The *Rorschach Test* and the *Thematic Apperception Test* are two of the widely used projective instruments. In various ways, they involve the presentation to the pupil of materials to which he reacts informally and largely according to his individual predispositions. The trained psychological examiner is able to analyze and synthesize these reactions in such manner that general behavioral characteristics and tendencies of the pupil are supposedly revealed. The projective method also includes such less patterned techniques as are involved in the controlled observation by trained technicians of pupil behavior when the pupil is presented a certain toy or implement or when he is placed in a particular social situation. Teacher awareness of these projective methods seems desirable, even though at present the techniques remain in the province of specialists.

Anecdotal Records. A third observational technique is the anecdotal record. Of value only when accumulated over a period of time and recorded in the pupil's permanent record, anecdotes are objective descriptions by the teacher or other school official of significant occurrences or episodes in the life of the pupil. Only those events believed by the observer to represent significant behavior tendencies of the pupil or to be of outstanding significance in some other way merit such recording, for discriminative choice of anecdotes is essential if the use of this technique is to be feasible and if the accumulated records are to be of maximum value. The anecdotal record is probably little more than an objective version of events commonly discussed by teachers in their spare time.

The anecdotal record should start with an objective and purely factual or narrative account of the event, although a sufficient part of the account should deal with the setting in which it occurred to give the anecdote meaning. If the observer's interpretations are given, as may sometimes but not always be desirable, they should be set apart from the narrative in such manner that their nature as interpretations is apparent. If the record of an event is carried to the third possible stage, that involving recommendations of the observer, the form of the record should again make clear the fact that the observer has chosen to attribute definite meanings to the behavior recorded and then to recommend procedures designed to aid the pupil.

An illustration of the anecdotal record, which shows the increased meaning to be gleaned from a series of anecdotes as they accumulate, is found in the following sequence.[14]

Date	Observer	Anecdotal Record
Sept.	Supervisor	Dorothy's stunt in the Retailing Party was highly original. Her attitude was abrupt and superior. The other girls avoided her.
Nov.	Teacher 9	She monopolized the entire group discussion today.
Dec.	Teacher 8	She told me in conference that the other students do not like her. I tried to explain that it would be desirable to be a little less aggressive and to avoid giving the appearance of feeling superior. She said little in reply and I do not know whether or not I got the idea across.
Jan.	Teacher 7	Dorothy came to me for advice on overcoming characteristics which make students dislike her. She took a difficult assignment in color and design which involved doing a costume analysis and prescription for a classmate who seemed antagonistic to her. She is doing a good job with it.
March	Teacher 7	She gave the other students opportunity to discuss and to work out their share of group assignments.
April	Teacher 7	Several students have told me that they feel she is not so much self-centered as ambitious. They said that she was gaining the cooperation and confidence of nearly all her classmates.
May	Teacher 8	In the sorority, Dorothy has become the person (next to the president) to whom people turn for suggestions, assistance, and leadership. This is true of those who first resented her.

Personal reports. Both oral and written reports by pupils are useful in the evaluation of personal-social adjustment. The informal interview is the most common method of oral reporting. The paper-and-pencil instruments filled out or responded to otherwise by the pupil, variously designated as inventories, questionnaires, check lists, rating scales, and even tests, represent the written form of personal reports. Pupil self-evaluation by the use of especially adapted check lists and rating scales

[14] Ben D. Wood, "The Major Strategy of Guidance," *Educational Record,* 15:419–444, October, 1934.

of the types discussed in Chap. 11 will not be considered directly here. Rather, attention will be devoted to the inventory or questionnaire from which results are interpreted by the teacher.

Interview. The interview may be either formal or informal. When a person is interviewed by a prospective employer, the discussion is ordinarily relatively formal and is restricted to issues pertinent to the individual's probable success in the position for which he is applying. When the teacher discusses the pupil's school activities with him, or questions him concerning his interests, attitudes, background, and other personal matters, the interview is informal. It is with the second type, often not recognized either by the teacher or the pupil as an interview, that the teacher as evaluator is primarily concerned. The interview is dealt with more extensively in Chap. 17, which is concerned with the teacher as a counselor.

Informal interviews are not ordinarily anticipated in advance by the teacher. They develop spontaneously in any well-organized experience unit method of instruction when there is an appropriate degree of rapport and mutual understanding between pupil and teacher. The pupil may come to the teacher with school or personal problems. The teacher may approach the pupil in situations where school or even personal problems of the pupil appear to exist and to merit attention. Thus, the informal interview occurs in a natural setting and in one conducive to the resolution of pupil problems. It also affords the astute teacher insights into pupil behavior which should be helpful in his future as well as his present guidance.

Inventories and Questionnaires. Personal reports of pupils on inventories and questionnaires may be designed for measuring personal-social adjustment from either of two standpoints. The first is represented by the instruments which attempt to discover how completely the pupil adapts to the pattern of conduct evidenced by the mores, customs, and laws of contemporary society. The second is represented by the instruments which are intended for the measurement of the pupil's complex pattern of feelings and behaviors in terms of its impact upon his adjustment to himself and to society.

The fact that a person who outwardly shows adjustment to the code of society may actually be poorly adjusted in his inner mechanisms illustrates a fundamental weakness of the first approach. The symptom, or overt behavior, is accepted as evidence of a condition in the individual naturally giving rise to the symptom or expression. But similar symptoms may arise from different causes, as has been pointed out previously, and similar causes may result in different symptoms. Also, circumstances or situations of vastly different types may appropriately be met by very different adjustments, and individual differences among human beings make undesirable any attempt to establish an exact pattern to which every individual should conform.

In the second approach to adjustment evaluation, the fundamental causes or conditions rather than the more incidental symptoms or behaviors are the goals. Evaluation hence becomes more complex and difficult than if the first approach were used, for there is lacking in this method any standards or patterns by means of which results can be interpreted definitely. The type of adjustment sought is that defined by Smith and Tyler [15] in their statement: "Optimum adjustment may be thought of as a compromise between the individual and the group to which he belongs, in which each party adjusts to the other to a certain extent in order to avoid conflicts within the individual or clashes between the individual and the social group."

The manner in which an adjustment inventory is used and the

Excerpt from Bell Adjustment Inventory

DIRECTIONS

Are you interested in knowing more about your own personality? If you will answer *honestly* and *thoughtfully* all of the questions on the pages that follow, it will be possible for you to obtain a better understanding of yourself.

There are *no right* or *wrong* answers. Indicate your answer to each question by drawing a circle around the "Yes," the "No," or the "?". Use the question mark only when you are certain that you cannot answer "Yes" or "No." There is no time limit, but work rapidly.

If you have *not* been living with your parents, answer certain of the questions with regard to the people with whom you have been living.

101a	Yes	No	?	Does either of your parents become angry easily?
102b	Yes	No	?	Do you sometimes have shooting pains in the head?
103a	Yes	No	?	Was your home always supplied with the common necessities of life?
104c	Yes	No	?	Do you find that you tend to have a few very close friends rather than many casual acquaintances?
105a	Yes	No	?	Was your father what you would consider your ideal of manhood?
106d	Yes	No	?	Are you troubled with the idea that people are watching you on the street?
107b	Yes	No	?	Are you considerably underweight?
108a	Yes	No	?	Has either of your parents made you unhappy by criticizing your personal appearance?
109d	Yes	No	?	Does criticism disturb you greatly?
110c	Yes	No	?	Do you feel embarrassed if you have to ask permission to leave a group of people?

Source: Hugh M. Bell, *The Adjustment Inventory*, Student Form, Stanford University Press, Stanford University, Calif., 1934.

[15] Eugene R. Smith, Ralph W. Tyler, *et al.*, *Appraising and Recording Student Progress*, pp. 353–354, Harper & Brothers, New York, 1942.

nature of norms or other bases for interpreting results are more significant in some respects than the inventory itself. Many students of mental hygiene and personality have the belief that adjustment inventories
at best serve only rather general functions, and that their results in cases
where serious maladjustment is indicated should be verified or refuted
by other evidence. Such inventories customarily provide for pupil
responses to questions on a yes-no or a like-indifferent-dislike scale.
The accompanying illustrations from the Bell *Adjustment Inventory*
and the Hayes' *Scale for Evaluating the Behavior of Children Ten to
Fifteen* represent the types of questions and provision for responses.

EXCERPT FROM HAYES SCALE FOR EVALUATING SCHOOL BEHAVIOR

Directions for Using this Scale

Following is a list of habits which children 10 to 15 years old have been found to
show. No one child could have all the habits listed, but is certain to have a considerable number of them.

Draw a circle around the T, F or U before each item to indicate: (T) you
believe the statement is true of the child being rated; (F) you believe the statement
is not true of the child being rated; (U) you are uncertain whether the statement
is true or not true of the child being rated. Be sure to draw a circle about *one* letter
and *one only* for every item in the list. Two samples are given below:

(T) F   U   usually accepts responsibility when the occasion arises

T   (F) U   often wastes time

Circle the following items in a similar manner

I

T   F   U   1. often does little things to make others happy
T   F   U   2. usually thinks of consequences both to self and others
T   F   U   3. usually accepts responsibility when the occasion arises
T   F   U   4. often shares with others
T   F   U   5. usually does his share in any group activity
T   F   U   6. often "plays hookey" from school
T   F   U   7. usually does the work expected of him
T   F   U   8. usually defends his friends only when they are in the right
T   F   U   9. usually makes friends easily
T   F   U   10. often starts fights
T   F   U   11. usually quickly forgives wrongs done to him
T   F   U   12. often uses vulgar or profane words
T   F   U   13. usually eats lunch with a group

Source: Margaret Hayes, *A Scale for Evaluating the School Behavior of Children Ten to Fifteen*, The Psychological Corporation, New York, 1933.

TEACHERS' MARKS

The marking systems outlined in Chaps. 8 and 11 as most nearly in harmony with the philosophies and procedures of the recitation method and the subject-matter unit method of instruction are those widely used in the elementary school and the college as well as in the secondary school, although colleges more widely than elementary schools have abandoned the percentage mark. However, the marking practices and related reporting practices in harmony with the experience unit method of instruction occupy a position intermediate between those deemed appropriate for the elementary school and those desirably restricted to the college and graduate school. Even though the concern here is with secondary-school practices, brief consideration of consistent practices at other educational levels seems to be warranted.

Marking problems and practices at different levels of the educational system differ to some degree in many schools and to a great degree in other schools. However, they doubtless differ less at the various educational levels than they would if adequate consideration were given to a philosophy of education based on available psychological findings. Of great significance are findings concerning individual differences in the physical, mental, emotional, and social characteristics of pupils and concerning the conditions under which optimum learning occurs. The educational levels involved go below the high school to the elementary grades and above the high school to the college and professional school.

Woodruff is more specific than most writers on marking practices in recommending methods appropriate at the various educational levels.[16] He states that elementary-school "marks should not be competitive because the objectives of elementary education do not provide for eliminating even the lowest students, but rather call for as much growth and development as each student can absorb regardless of his capacity." At the secondary-school level, he believes that emphasis logically remains on the noncompetitive aspects, although "standards beyond the capacity of the individual student begin to assume importance . . . and should therefore enter into the marks." At the college level, with some distinction between the lower and upper divisions, he believes the "emphasis shifts to competitive standards, and col-

[16] Asahel D. Woodruff, *The Psychology of Teaching*, 2d ed., pp. 254–255. Longmans, Green & Co., Inc., New York, 1948.

lege marks should therefore show some of that additional weighting." It is only at the graduate-school level where the emphasis on functional proficiency is great that he believes "rather rigid standards of performance should be demanded before an individual is entitled to recognition."

The first method of marking and reporting discussed below emphasizes self-competition rather than pupil competition, while the second method not only embodies that approach but is characterized also by evaluation of behavioral outcomes of experiential rather than of subject-matter types.

Marking achievement in terms of aptitude. Of the marking procedures based on the relationship between measures of aptitude and achievement, several are restricted to elementary-school use or are too technical and involved for ordinary use. The remaining method is one suggested by Symonds for obtaining an index of studiousness which can be used in the assignment of final marks when the purpose is to mark the pupil in terms of how well his potentialities for achievement are realized. The index of studiousness itself [17] is obtained by: (*a*) ranking the pupils in a class in terms of their scores on a test of general intelligence, (*b*) ranking them in terms of their scores on an achievement test or other quantitative measure, and (*c*) determining the amount and direction of the difference between the two ranks for each pupil. If achievement ranks are subtracted from intelligence ranks, a minus difference suggests that the pupil is making poorer than average use of his abilities, and a plus difference suggests that the pupil is making better than average use of his talents. The amount of the deviation represents his degree of deviation from the average in the use of his abilities.

This index of studiousness can be used in final marking in either of two ways. In the first method, indices of studiousness are obtained for each pupil separately on the types of appraisals used in marking, the indices for each pupil are averaged, and the resulting total indices for all pupils in the group are converted into final marks by the procedure preferred of the normal-curve systems outlined in Chap. 11. In the second method, a composite score is obtained for each pupil by the procedure outlined in Chap. 8 of weighting as desired each type of appraisal used in marking, the index of studiousness is obtained for the

[17] Percival M. Symonds, *Measurement in Secondary Education*, pp. 521–525, The Macmillan Company, New York, 1927.

composite scores of all pupils by the method outlined above, and final marks are obtained by the preferred normal-curve method.

Marking pupil achievement by evaluative methods. As conceived under the evaluative approach to assessment of pupil achievement, the purposes of marking are much broader and more fundamentally significant than are those of marking systems discussed in Chaps. 8 and 11. The purposes of marking outlined in the Eight-year Study of Progressive Schools are: [18] (a) to form a basis for understanding pupils so that effective guidance can be provided, (b) to furnish transferable information for use in guidance, (c) to provide information needed for reports to the home, (d) to provide information and methods of transferring it to others concerning pupil readiness for future experiences, and (e) to stimulate teachers to consider and decide upon their objectives, judge their relative importance, and estimate their own and pupil success in realization of the stated objectives.

Wrinkle and his colleagues at the Colorado State College of Education at Greeley experimentally tried several secondary-school marking and reporting methods and suggested several others which are in harmony with the experience unit instructional method.[19] These are parent-teacher conferences, informal letters by teachers to parents of their pupils, check forms, pupil self-evaluations, and parents' reports to the school. Some of these procedures were found to be impractical because of time requirements, possibility of misinterpretation, or for other reasons. Wrinkle favors the check form as the most practical and usable of the various departures from conventional report cards.

The questions following [20] indicate the criteria Wrinkle and his collaborators developed for use in evaluating procedures and practices for marking and reporting pupil performance.

1. Have the objectives of the educational program been identified?
2. Are the objectives clearly stated?
3. Are the objectives sufficiently analyzed so that they have specific meaning?
4. Are the objectives understood, accepted, and recognized as important by the students, teachers, and parents?

[18] Eugene R. Smith, Ralph W. Tyler, *et al., Appraising and Recording Pupil Progress,* pp. 465–466, Harper & Brothers, New York, 1942.
[19] William L. Wrinkle, *Improving Marking and Reporting Practices,* pp. 52–63, Rinehart & Company, Inc., New York, 1947.
[20] *Ibid.,* pp. 107–110.

STUDY OF THE DEVELOPMENT OF _____ IN ENGLISH

CHOOSE THE OBJECTIVES FOR WHICH YOU WISH TO RECORD JUDGMENTS, AND INDICATE WHETHER THE PUPIL IS HIGH (H), MODAL OR USUAL FOR AGE (M) OR LOW (L) BY CHECKING IN THE APPROPRIATE COLUMNS. USE ONLY HEADINGS CONCERNING WHICH YOU HAVE EVIDENCE OR AT LEAST A FAIRLY DEFINITE OPINION. MAIN HEADINGS MAY BE USED WITH OR WITHOUT THEIR SUBHEADS. AN X MAY BE USED IN THE L COLUMN TO INDICATE A SERIOUS LACK.

OBJECTIVES

WORK HABITS AND STUDY SKILLS
- PERSISTENCE
- EFFECTIVE USE OF TIME
- SKILL IN OBTAINING INFORMATION OTHER THAN FROM BOOKS

TECHNIQUES AND SKILLS
- LIBRARY SKILLS
- ABILITY TO GATHER AND RECORD INFORMATION
- ABILITY TO EVALUATE MATERIAL
- ABILITY TO ORGANIZE MATERIAL
- ABILITY TO PRESENT IDEAS OR ANOTHER THROUGH PRECIS AND PARAGRAPH

COMMUNICATION
- COMMUNICATES OWN THOUGHT — ORAL, WRITTEN
- CLEARLY AND EFFECTIVELY
- USE OF VARIOUS READING TECHNIQUES
- AURAL COMPREHENSION
- MECHANICS OF SPEECH — NOTE SERIOUS WEAKNESSES
- MECHANICS OF WRITING — IF ANY

MASTERY OF PROCESSES OF REFLECTIVE THINKING
- RECOGNIZES AND DEFINES PROBLEMS
- MAKES AND TESTS HYPOTHESES
- MAKES GENERALIZATIONS AND APPLIES PAST EXPERIENCE
- REACHES CONCLUSIONS BY LOGICAL STEPS

CREATIVE EXPRESSION
- DRAWS ON HIS OWN EXPERIENCE FOR MATERIAL
- AMOUNT OF WRITING DONE
- CREATIVE QUALITY OF THE WRITING
- WIDE VARIETY OF FORM USED — VERSE, ESSAY, STORY, ETC.

APPRECIATIONS AND UNDERSTANDINGS
- DEVELOPMENT OF PERSONAL STANDARDS
- DEVELOPMENT OF CRITICAL ABILITIES
- SENSITIVITY TO FORM, RHYTHM, SOUND OF WORDS, IMAGERY
- INSIGHT INTO MOTIVES AND OTHER IMPLICATIONS
- UNDERSTANDING OF PRESENT DAY LITERATURE
- SEES IN LITERATURE AN INTERPRETATION OF LIFE

DEVELOPING INTEREST IN THE FIELD

DEVELOPMENT TOWARD A FUNCTIONING PHILOSOPHY OF LIFE

MASTERY OF ESSENTIALS OF THE COURSE

PREDICTION OF FUTURE PROGRESS

NOTES

READING RECORD		COMMENT
BOOKS OF FICTION READ		
TYPE OF FICTION READ		
MEDIAN LEVELS OF MATURITY		
BOOKS OF NON-FICTION READ		
TYPE OF NON-FICTION READ		
MAGAZINES READ REGULARLY		
MAGAZINES READ OCCASIONALLY		
MOVING PICTURES PER MONTH		
AVERAGE PLAYS PER YEAR		

Source: Eugene R. Smith, Ralph W. Tyler, *et al.*, *Appraising and Recording Student Progress*, insert f, p. 502, Harper & Brothers, New York, 1942.

BEHAVIOR DESCRIPTION
(EXPERIMENTAL FORM)

LAST NAME — FIRST — MIDDLE — SCHOOL

THIS REPORT DESCRIBES THE CHARACTERISTIC BEHAVIOR OF THE STUDENT IN A NUMBER OF IMPORTANT AREAS. IT SHOULD NOT BE INTERPRETED AS A RATING. INSTEAD ONE SHOULD READ THE DESCRIPTIONS AND ATTEMPT TO GET FROM THEM AN UNDERSTANDING OF THE PERSON DESCRIBED, AND OF HIS FITNESS FOR PARTICULAR OPPORTUNITIES AND UNDERTAKINGS:

DIRECTIONS:

(1) IN GENERAL THE INITIALS OF SUBJECT OR ACTIVITY FIELDS ARE USED IN THE RECORDING IN ORDER TO IDENTIFY THE RELATIONS BETWEEN THE OBSERVERS AND THE STUDENT. A COMPLETE KEY IS GIVEN AT THE TOP OF THE FOLDED OVER SHEET.

(2) THE SPACES FROM LEFT TO RIGHT, BEING CHRONOLOGICAL, SHOW THE CHANGES OR CONTINUITY IN BEHAVIOR DURING THE PERIOD COVERED BY THE RECORD.

(3) WHILE AGREEMENTS IN DESCRIPTION MAY SHOW A STUDENT'S MOST COMMON BEHAVIOR, THEY MAY NOT BE MORE IMPORTANT THAN AN ISOLATED JUDGMENT WHICH OFTEN HAS GREAT SIGNIFICANCE BECAUSE OF A BETTER BASIS FOR JUDGMENT, OR BECAUSE IT INDICATES A RESPONSE TO SOME PARTICULAR CONDITION.

FIELD OR PERSONALITY	TYPE	GRADE 7	GRADE 8	GRADE 9	GRADE 10	GRADE 11	GRADE 12
RESPONSIBILITY—DEPENDABILITY							
RESPONSIBLE AND RESOURCEFUL	1						
CONSCIENTIOUS	2						
GENERALLY DEPENDABLE	3A						
SELECTIVELY DEPENDABLE	3B						
UNRELIABLE	4						
IRRESPONSIBLE	5						
CREATIVENESS AND IMAGINATION							
GENERAL	1A						
SPECIFIC	1B						
PROMISING	2						
LIMITED	3						
IMITATIVE	4						
UNIMAGINATIVE	5						
INFLUENCE							
CONTROLLING	1						
CONTRIBUTING INFLUENCE	2						
VARYING	3						
CO-OPERATING	4						
PASSIVE	5						

Source: Report and Records Committee of the Progressive Education Association, *Behavior Description*, Progressive Education Association, New York, 1938.

5. Are different objectives evaluated and reported separately?

6. Are different forms provided to serve different purposes?

7. Are different bases for evaluation utilized which are appropriate to the purposes involved?

8. Can the teacher evaluate with sufficient reliability the achievement and growth of the student with respect to the objectives which have been set up?

9. Can the reports be prepared with a reasonable expenditure of time and effort?

10. Do the evaluation procedures make provision for student self-evaluation?

11. Is provision made for the reporting of evidence and comments relative to the evaluations?

12. Are the forms so constructed as to facilitate recording?

13. Can the evaluations be easily translated into other symbols if the evaluations may have to be stated in terms of other symbols of marking?

14. Do the forms and practices serve the various functions which they are designed to serve, that is, give information, stimulate interest in improvement, facilitate guidance, provide a basis for college entrance recommendations, etc.?

Evaluative methods of marking and reporting pupil achievement often include several forms instead of the lone report card and varied procedures instead of the one procedure common when percentage or regular point-scale marking methods are used. Instruments or significant portions of instruments used in the Eight-year Study are record forms in major subject areas, a behavior description form, a form for reporting to parents, and a form for reporting to colleges.

Reports for School Subjects. The tendency to furnish reports by school subjects is the result of several realizations by teachers and other educators. Traditional percentage and letter marks fail to furnish analytical information of the type important to the teacher, the pupil, and the pupil's parents. Moreover, instructional outcomes sought in various subjects or fields differ widely. An analytical report for each individual subject prepared especially in terms of the behaviors listed as appropriate outcomes provides for the meaningful type of report desired. The accompanying illustration is from the front of the report card for use in English which was evolved by the staff of the Eight-year Study.

Behavior Descriptions. The staff of the Eight-year Study evolved a behavior description card which would, it was hoped, represent an improvement over rating scales, which would avoid comparisons of pupils, which would provide for indications of both modal and widely variable behavior of the pupil, and which would over a period of time constitute a record of behavior development in the pupil.[21] Some of the characteristics chosen for use in the behavior description and the method of using this card are shown on the accompanying illustration.

Reports to Parents. Evaluation reports to parents use marking bases fundamentally different from percentage or letter marks, especially for the reason that no marks are designated to represent failure. Rather, such designations as *high, modal,* and *low,* or *honors, satisfactory, needs to make improvement,* and *unsatisfactory* are used. Such reports often break subject areas down into the most important types of behavioral outcomes. The student evaluation report evolved in the Colorado study of marking practices is reproduced herewith.

SUMMARY

The dependence of measurement and evaluation upon the outcomes sought in the instruction of pupils is even greater in the experience unit method than in either the daily-assignment or the subject-matter unit plan of instruction. The whole gamut of outcomes must receive consideration, ranging from the tangible knowledges and skills, through the higher level concepts, understandings, and applications, and such tastes and preferences as attitudes, interests, and appreciations, to the ultimate whole-child adjustment. No type of outcome can be neglected if measurement and evaluation are to be well done.

Construction of evaluation instruments involves as a first step the determination of instructional objectives, both general and specific. These objectives must then be translated into outcomes, or those pupil behaviors which indicate that the objectives have been realized in practice. Characteristic measurable behaviors in line with the outcomes must then be sought out and subsequently presented to the pupils for their reactions. Means of evaluating the pupil reactions must next be devised. Finally, the results must be scrutinized for objectivity, reliability, and practicality. The method is such that validity should be attained as a matter of course, although evaluative techniques should be

21 Eugene R. Smith, Ralph W. Tyler, *et al., Appraising and Recording Student Progress,* pp. 471–472, Harper & Brothers, New York, 1942.

Evaluation of Student Achievement
COLLEGE HIGH SCHOOL *of* COLORADO STATE COLLEGE OF EDUCATION
at GREELEY

	1 2 3 4 5 6	
Student		, 194__
	Secondary School Year	Date of This Report
	6 8 · 12 36	2½ 5 10 15
Course or Activity	Weeks Enrolled	Regular Periods Each Week

GENERAL OBJECTIVES: The evaluation of the student's achievement of the twelve general objectives which follow is made in terms of what normally might be expected of students of similar age and school placement. O—OUTSTANDING. S—SATISFACTORY. N—NEEDS TO MAKE IMPROVEMENT. U—UNSATISFACTORY. X—INSUFFICIENT EVIDENCE OR DOES NOT APPLY, SPECIFIC BEHAVIORS ESPECIALLY RESPONSIBLE FOR O, N, OR U EVALUATIONS ARE CHECKED, SPECIFIC COMMENTS PARTICULARLY WITH REFERENCE TO O, N, AND U EVALUATIONS ARE WRITTEN ON THE OPPOSITE SIDE OF THIS SHEET.

—— 1. HE DIRECTS HIS INDIVIDUAL ACTIVITIES EFFECTIVELY ( ) begins work promptly ( ) makes good use of time ( ) requires minimum of supervision ( ) does more than the least that will be accepted ( ) meets responsibilities promptly

—— 2. HE FOLLOWS PLANS AND DIRECTIONS ( ) listens to and reads directions carefully ( ) follows and completes plans and directions which have been set up

—— 3. HE GETS ALONG WELL WITH OTHERS ( ) is considerate of rights and wishes of others ( ) is courteous and tolerant ( ) controls his temper ( ) conforms to reasonable social standards

—— 4. HE TAKES AN ACTIVE PART IN GROUP LIVING ( ) participates in group planning ( ) volunteers his services ( ) does his share in group activities

—— 5. HE SPEAKS CORRECTLY AND EFFECTIVELY ( ) speaks clearly ( ) adjusts his voice to the size of the group ( ) uses adequate vocabulary to express himself interestingly ( ) speaks with ease and confidence ( ) uses correct grammatical forms

—— 6. HE TAKES GOOD CARE OF PERSONAL AND SCHOOL MATERIALS AND EQUIPMENT ( ) shows respect for property ( ) does not waste or damage materials or equipment ( ) returns things when due ( ) reports breakage and loss

—— 7. HE OBSERVES ATTENDANCE REGULATIONS ( ) is regular and prompt in attendance except for approved cause ( ) arranges in advance for absence when possible ( ) takes initiative in making up work missed ( ) makes proper use of school health service

—— 8. HE READS WITH EASE AND UNDERSTANDING ( ) selects important ideas ( ) understands and evaluates what he reads ( ) reads with reasonable speed

—— 9. HE EXPRESSES HIMSELF CORRECTLY AND EFFECTIVELY IN WRITING ( ) expresses ideas clearly ( ) uses correct grammatical forms ( ) punctuates correctly ( ) spells correctly ( ) writes legibly

——10. HE UTILIZES AVAILABLE SOURCES OF LEARNING MATERIALS ( ) selects and uses appropriate sources of information ( ) uses library and library tools effectively ( ) effectively engages in interview and observation

——11. HE USES THE PROBLEM SOLVING METHOD ( ) recognizes problems ( ) states problems clearly ( ) collects and records appropriate information ( ) arrives at sound conclusions

——12. HE USES THE BASIC SKILLS IN MATHEMATICS ( ) uses accurately the simple fundamental combinations ( ) computes with reasonable speed ( ) uses fractions and per cents correctly ( ) selects correct processes

SPECIFIC OBJECTIVES: The specific objectives of each course and activity have been discussed with the student and used in classroom instruction and evaluation activities.

HIS ACHIEVEMENT OF THE SPECIFIC OBJECTIVES OF THIS COURSE OR ACTIVITY HAS BEEN:

☐ better than ☐ consistent with ☐ poorer than what reasonably might have been expected of him in terms of his background and ability.

☐ Such that full credit is not recommended on administrative records.

☐ Such that he cannot be recommended for admission to college courses or training programs to which this course is prerequisite.

Such as to justify encouraging him

to enroll in_____

not to enroll in_____

Supervising Teacher

This section is for record purposes and is to be detached before the report is issued to the student or his parents.

ACTUAL ACHIEVEMENT: ☐   ☐   ☐   ☐   ☐

	OUTSTANDING	ABOVE AVERAGE	AVERAGE	BELOW AVERAGE	VERY POOR*

EXPECTED ACHIEVEMENT: ☐   ☐   ☐   ☐   ☐

* Adjusted credit recommendation (to full year courses only): ¼ ½ ¾ regular credit should be allowed.

Source: William L. Wrinkle, *Improving Marking and Reporting Practices*, pp. 108–109, Rinehart & Company, Inc., New York, 1947.

under constant scrutiny concerning how well they satisfy all nine examination criteria.

Prominent among evaluative techniques are those designed to measure work-study skills, ability to think, social sensitivity, appreciations, vocational interests, and personal-social adjustment. Among the tests, techniques, and tools required are standardized and teacher-made tests, check lists, informal observations, anecdotal records, interviews, questionnaires, and inventories. Many, but probably not all, of the procedures discussed in Chaps. 8 and 11 are also applicable to the experience unit method.

Teachers' marks of a distinctly new and nontraditional type are most appropriate for use with this instructional plan. The marks involve percentages not at all and point scales very little. They appear on several types of reports designed for different purposes and for different aspects of the pupil's school career.

Just as the experience unit method of instruction represents a relatively new and unquestionably an emerging plan, the tests, techniques, and tools appropriately used to evaluate pupil attainment of the desired outcomes are also, in many cases, relatively new and unfamiliar. It behooves the teacher under an experience unit method of instruction to seek in his evaluative procedures to encompass all of the types of instructional outcomes, whether tangible and easy of measurement or intangible and difficult to measure.

SELECTED REFERENCES

BELL, JOHN E.: *Projective Techniques*, Longmans, Green & Co., Inc., New York, 1948.

BROWNELL, WILLIAM A. (Chairman): *The Measurement of Understanding*, Part I, Chaps. 3–16, Forty-fifth Yearbook of the National Society for the Study of Education, University of Chicago Press, Chicago, 1946.

BRUECKNER, LEO J., and MELBY, ERNEST O.: *Diagnostic and Remedial Teaching*, Chap. 2, Houghton Mifflin Company, Boston, 1931.

BRUECKNER, LEO J. (Chairman): *Educational Diagnosis*, Chaps. 18, 20–24, Thirty-fourth Yearbook of the National Society for the Study of Education, Public School Publishing Company, Bloomington, Ill., 1935.

FRYER, DOUGLAS: *The Measurement of Interests*, Henry Holt and Company, Inc., New York, 1931.

GRAY, WILLIAM S. (Ed.): *Reading in General Education*, Chap. 10, Report of the Committee on Reading in General Education, American Council on Education, Washington, D.C., 1940.

GREENE, EDWARD B.: *Measurements of Human Behavior*, Chaps. 13–15, 17–19, The Odyssey Press, Inc., New York, 1941.

LEE, J. MURRAY: *A Guide to Measurement in Secondary Schools*, Chaps. 3–4, D. Appleton-Century Company, Inc., New York, 1936.

Lincoln, Edward A., and Workman, Linwood L.: *Testing and the Use of Test Results*, Chaps. 6–7, The Macmillan Company, New York, 1935.

McCall, William A.: *Measurement*, Chaps. 14–16, The Macmillan Company, New York, 1939.

Mathematics in General Education, Chap. 13, Report of the Committee on the Function of Mathematics in General Education, Commission on Secondary School Curriculum, Progressive Education Association, D. Appleton-Century Company, Inc., New York, 1940.

Orleans, Jacob S.: *Measurement in Education*, Chap. 7, Thomas Nelson & Sons, New York, 1937.

Ross, C. C.: *Measurement in Today's Schools*, 2d ed., Chaps. 16–17, Prentice-Hall, Inc., New York, 1947.

Science in General Education, Chap. 9, Report of the Committee on the Function of Science in General Education, Commission on Secondary School Curriculum, Progressive Education Association, D. Appleton-Century Company, Inc., New York, 1937.

Symonds, Percival M.: *Diagnosing Personality and Conduct*, Chaps. 2, 4–5, 7–8, 12, D. Appleton-Century Company, Inc., New York, 1931.

The Social Studies in General Education, Chap. 9, Report of the Committee on the Function of the Social Studies in General Education, Commission on Secondary School Curriculum, Progressive Education Association, D. Appleton-Century Company, Inc., New York, 1940.

Traxler, Arthur E.: *The Nature and Use of Anecdotal Records*, Educational Records Supplementary Bulletin D (Revised), Educational Records Bureau, New York, March, 1940.

——: *The Use of Tests and Rating Devices in the Appraisal of Personality*, Educational Records Bulletin 23 (Revised), Educational Records Bureau, New York, November, 1942.

Wrinkle, William L.: *Improving Marking and Reporting Practices*, Chaps. 6–11, Rinehart & Company, Inc., New York, 1947.

Part 3. SOME SPECIAL ASPECTS OF

SECONDARY-SCHOOL TEACHING

Chapter 15. THE TEACHER AND THE

EMERGING CORE CURRICULUM

To this point, teaching methods have been discussed as though they were usually confined within the walls of the classroom. The impression may have been given that the teacher is free to use whatever method he may choose without concern about the effect his choice may have upon the work of his associates or upon the broader educational plans of his pupils. It is obvious, however, that modern secondary schools do not afford such convenient isolation and independence.

It was stated in Chap. 4 that the average-sized high school today has an enrollment in excess of 100 pupils. To serve the needs of a student body of this size, it is necessary to employ a staff of several teachers. The teaching assignments must be divided among the members of the staff, and as a result the pupils are required to move from teacher to teacher and from classroom to classroom as they go through the activities of the day. Even the smallest high school of which this writer has personal knowledge, a school which a few years ago boasted an enrollment of only nine pupils, employed two full-time teachers. Instruction was offered in such well-established courses as English I, English II, algebra, geometry, French I, and French II. Since each pupil took some work with each of the two instructors, some agreement had to be worked out for the equitable division of time. The resulting agreements were expressed in the daily time schedule and in the program of studies.

The modern secondary school is a complex institution. It is clear that even in small schools the choice of method must be determined in part by considerations other than personal preferences. Among such considerations, one should list the daily time schedule which governs the activities of the school as a whole, the sequence of courses, and the course of study a given class is expected to follow. The larger the school, the more rigid such administrative devices are likely to be in prescribing the amount of time the teacher can give to a particular class meeting and the specific outcomes that are to be achieved.

The limitations on the freedom of choice regarding method are the result of the division of labor upon which modern educational programs are based. It is doubtful if there is any secondary-school teacher today who is solely responsible for the total educational effort that will be made in behalf of a given pupil in a given school year. In fact, schools have become so complex and teaching responsibilities have become so specialized that one can find the elements out of which to form a suitable program of learning activities for a given pupil only by looking at the school as a whole. The education of a given pupil is the responsibility of the whole school and not that of a given teacher. If the school is to meet its responsibilities, it is necessary to coordinate the efforts of all teachers within the framework of an over-all plan.

There are many advantages that come to the teacher as a result of his participation in such a highly organized system. The present concern, however, is for the limitations that the teacher's commitments to the system place upon his freedom to choose, to plan, and to act. The administrative and instructional programs which incorporate the agreements that make a coordinated program possible tend to become cumbersome and inflexible. They do not respond to change as quickly as do the ideas and the practices of individuals. In fact, the complaint most frequently made by teachers who wish to try new procedures is that they cannot make the desired changes without throwing the entire system into confusion. It appears frequently that the only alternative is to wait until the school as a whole is willing to work out a new program that will accommodate the new procedures. This fact places a serious obstacle in the path of those teachers who are not content merely to drift along from year to year in the same old pattern of teaching.

The requests for more freedom, made by the more progressive and dynamic teachers, have been recognized in recent years by numerous administrators and other educational leaders. As a consequence, the problem of improving classroom teaching has been approached here and there on a whole-school basis. Some new types of programs that promise greater flexibility and freedom of action than that afforded by some of the older forms of organization have been developed. The beginning teacher should know about these newer trends. It is the purpose of the ensuing discussion to describe several types of administrative and instructional programs in the light of their significance for classroom method.

ADMINISTRATIVE DEVICES THAT ASSUME THE USE OF DAILY-ASSIGNMENT PROCEDURES

American secondary schools have not always been as highly systemized as they are today. The first Latin grammar schools usually employed but one teacher. His duties were to instruct the pupils in the Latin and Greek that would gain them admission to college. The colleges administered their own entrance examinations, and admission was based solely upon the applicant's performance in these examinations without reference to his record in the secondary school or the length of time he had engaged in preparatory studies. This arrangement made it possible for the teacher to employ whatever techniques or procedures he felt would prove most effective in each case. Teaching, therefore, was an individual matter, and the names of such famous teachers as Cheever, Corlett, and Lovell indicate that at least a few of them developed their art to a level that won favor with the pupils, the parents, and the colleges.[1] These men were not bound to a rigid daily time schedule—so many minutes for Caesar's *Commentaries* and so many for Greek Grammar—even though the length of the school day was prescribed in some instances.[2] Their time was spent chiefly in hearing recitations and in making new assignments. If a particular pupil required special attention, the teacher was free to give it without fear of misusing time scheduled for other purposes or of interfering with the work of another teacher.

By 1890, however, the academy and the high school had replaced the Latin grammar school. With these newer institutions a large number of new courses made their appearance, many of which were designed to serve the needs of boys and girls who had no thought of going to college. In the meantime, the colleges themselves had undergone some changes. The ability to read Latin and Greek was no longer regarded

[1] Emit Duncan Grizzell, *Origin and Development of the High School in New England Before 1865*, p. 24, The Macmillan Company, New York, 1923.
[2] *Ibid.*, p. 16.

as the only basis for determining an applicant's eligibility for admission. The technical schools in particular now demanded a foundation in the elementary branches of the sciences, and some method was needed to make sure that the right body of subject matter was mastered to the desired degree.

The high-school unit. In 1890, the New York State Board of Regents took the lead in setting uniform standards for secondary-school work by establishing the "count" as the unit for measuring instruction.[3] This agency also prescribed the number of counts in each branch or subject that might be accepted as credit for admission to college. A count was defined as "representing ten weeks' work which a pupil pursued with two other studies, and in which he recited five times a week." Shortly thereafter the count was replaced by the "unit," which is used widely even to this day, and which represents five recitations per week for 1 academic year.

It is in this manner that most secondary schools have come to require daily recitations in each subject and to make all courses run for the academic year. All courses that meet these requirements are said to be worth one unit of credit and are, therefore, of equal value in meeting graduation or college admission requirements. The occasional courses that run for one-half year only are worth only one-half unit.

The class period. For reasons of efficiency the length of the recitation period has been fixed at a given number of minutes, usually 45. This means that every 45 minutes of the day teachers and pupils alike are required to stop whatever they are doing and to move to the next scheduled activity. The period is a rigid time interval that determines the limits within which teachers must plan their work. Assignments must be long enough to occupy all of the period profitably, but not too long to be covered adequately in the time available. No activity should be engaged in that cannot be brought to an end with some semblance of having reached a logical stopping place before the period is terminated by the bell. In effect, therefore, the class period serves as the standard for measuring out the amount of ground to be covered in each class every day of the school year.

The daily time schedule. The school day consists of whatever number of periods that are thought necessary. In practice, this number varies

[3] I. L. Kandel, *History of Secondary Education*, pp. 405–406, Houghton Mifflin Company, Boston, 1930.

from school to school but it is seldom fewer than six or more than eight. The number of periods in the school day, multiplied by the number of teachers on the staff, determines the maximum number of subjects that can be offered during a given school term. This number cannot be offered without confusion and friction, however, unless there is a definite understanding as to which courses shall be recited at a given time, and all pupils who are enrolled in those courses are free to attend the class meetings. The daily time schedule arranges these matters. As such, it represents an agreement to which the entire school subscribes, and no teacher is free to change the hour of a scheduled recitation or to hold his class overtime without first securing the consent of those who will be affected. It is important to note that if a given teacher should want to use teaching procedures that cannot well be confined within the limits set by the class period and the daily time schedule, the matter calls for consideration and possibly for action by the school as a whole. This need for action on a whole-school basis must be kept in mind if one wishes to understand the curriculum changes that are taking place.

The year-long course, the 45-minute recitation, the six- to eight-period school day, and the daily assignment go hand in hand. Each is a device developed to increase the efficiency of the school that is concerned primarily with teaching subject matter. Wherever the dominant purpose of the school is "to cover the course," the rigid recitation schedule based on the fixed-time class period is looked upon as a useful if not as a necessary arrangement.

Types of curricula. Several types of curricula have grown up around the daily recitation and the rigid time schedule. The oldest is known as the single-track curriculum. It provides a single list of courses which all pupils must take in the order indicated. There is no provision for choices. Elementary schools generally have single-track curricula as do some junior high schools, particularly on the seventh- and eighth-grade levels. The single-track curriculum implies that all pupils must cover the same ground. By means of the daily assignment, the teacher controls the pace at which they shall move.

The direct opposite of the single-track curriculum is found in the free election system. As the term implies, the pupil is free under this system to take any course offered for which he has the necessary prerequisites. The logic of this arrangement is based on the assumption that each course is equivalent educationally to every other course and, therefore, the particular courses taken are of less significance than the number taken. The early academies, with their large assortment of subjects and courses and with their emphasis on utility, encouraged the free election idea. It should be remembered that these early schools served many students who had definite vocational objectives, particularly of a non-academic nature. For that reason, if for no other, these students were prepared to select from the course offerings the particular subjects that would meet their personal needs.

By the end of the nineteenth century, the secondary-school population had undergone numerous changes. Among other things, the pupils were less certain about their post-secondary-school needs. At the same time, the colleges were asking the secondary schools to teach the elementary phases of some of the college subjects, particularly the subjects in the scientific and technical areas. If left to make their own choices, these pupils could not be depended upon to select the right courses in all cases. To guard against such errors, the schools prescribed the courses that were judged to be most satisfactory in preparing for the various post-secondary-school careers. Thus there was a specific sequence prescribed for pupils who wished to prepare for classical studies in the colleges, another sequence for the scientific branches, and still other sequences for those who looked forward to the nonacademic pursuits. These sequences came to represent parallel tracks, each of which led to a different destination. A pupil might, therefore, choose the particular track he wished to travel, but having made a choice his program of studies was prescribed.

Some secondary schools continue to use the parallel-track arrangement of courses. The college-preparatory curriculum, the general academic curriculum, the fine arts curriculum, and the commercial curriculum are familiar names used to designate some of the tracks a modern high-school pupil may elect to follow at the time he enters school. Each curriculum has its prescribed sequence of studies, and each teacher is expected to pass his class on to the next teacher with the understanding that the pupils have mastered all of the subject matter that will be required of them.

There are few if any connecting points at which a pupil may transfer from one curriculum to another without suffering a discouraging loss of time. While it is true that both the student in the ninth grade of the

college-preparatory curriculum and the student in the ninth grade of
the industrial arts curriculum may be studying ninth-year English, it
frequently happens that they are dealing with an entirely different
body of subject matter. The industrial arts student, therefore, cannot
transfer to the college-preparatory curriculum at the beginning of the
tenth year because he has not had the kind of English upon which
tenth-year, college-preparatory English is based. Similar difficulties may
be encountered in other subjects.

The point is that subject matter is arranged in a definite sequence in
each curriculum. Every teacher is responsible for transmitting a particular segment in a sequence. The facts and skills in that segment are
needed for the work that is to follow. If the teacher fails to meet his
assignment, the deficiency cannot well be remedied except at the
expense of the pupils and of the other teachers.

A fourth type of curricular organization known as the constants-
with-variables has been developed to afford a larger measure of
flexibility for the pupil. The basic idea of this type was suggested as
early as 1899 by the Committee on College Entrance Requirements.[4]
The committee members recognized the need for instruction based on
the needs of individual pupils but argued that while some needs vary
due to differences in interests and vocational objectives, there are other
needs that are common to all pupils. It was recommended that the
courses that serve the common needs should appear in the program of
studies for each pupil. These courses are called the "constants." The
"variables," on the other hand, are the courses such as the commercial
subjects, agriculture, and advanced mathematics which serve special
needs and which should, therefore, appear in the programs of only
those pupils who have a special reason to elect them.

In recent years, the needs common to all pupils have come to be
interpreted as those which arise from membership in a democratic
community. The constants, therefore, are usually those courses which
are intended to develop the ability to communicate ideas, notably
English and elementary mathematics, and other courses such as general
science, history, civics, and sociology, which develop an understanding
of the contemporary physical and social environment. Since all pupils
must include the constants in their programs, there is relatively little
time lost whenever a given pupil decides to change his vocational

[4] *Ibid.*, pp. 476–478.

objective. The decision to change necessitates merely the election of a different group of variables.

Emergence of the "core" curriculum. Some schools now refer to the group of courses known as the constants as the "core." The term is meant to indicate the experiences all pupils should have in preparation for the duties of citizenship. It is important to note, however, that not all schools have the same notion of what these common experiences should be or how they should be provided. For that reason the core and the "core curriculum" mean different things to different people. The variations in these meanings will be discussed further, but for those who place their faith in the daily-assignment method, the core generally means a group of 1-year courses which are covered in daily installments. Preparation for citizenship in these circumstances means taking a certain group of courses. Where this idea prevails, the teacher of a core course is held responsible for covering a clearly defined body of subject matter and is subject to all the restrictions imposed by the fixed class period, the daily time schedule, and the division of labor implied in the course of study.

This type of core instruction involves no basic changes in the traditional concept of the class period and the daily time schedule. It demands no major reorganization of the administrative programs developed around the daily assignment. Teaching methods continue to be confined within the limits of the 45-minute class period, and the teacher must think of his obligations to the system before undertaking a modification of his teaching procedures.

Studies show that the parallel-track curriculum, the constants-with-variables curriculum, or some combination of these are the ones most commonly found in secondary schools today.[5] Prospective teachers should, therefore, be prepared to adapt their teaching procedures to conform to the school system in which they are likely to begin their professional careers. Any innovations that threaten to disrupt the existing daily time schedule or that appear to ignore the accepted subject-matter sequences will invite criticism and hostility from other members of the staff. The beginning teacher will do well to accept graciously the limitations imposed by the existing program until such a

[5] B. Lamar Johnson, "The Program of Studies," *National Survey of Secondary Education*, Monograph 19, p. 120, Office of Education, U.S. Department of Interior, Washington, D.C., 1932.

time as the staff has accepted him as an equal. From that time on he may discuss new procedures with the staff and introduce with confidence whatever modifications in his own procedures the staff is willing to tolerate. Basic changes, however, can be made safely only when the entire school has a voice in deciding upon them. It is this necessity of waiting for action by the school as a whole that tries the patience of beginning teachers who are anxious to depart from the traditional patterns of instruction.

ADMINISTRATIVE DEVICES THAT ASSUME THE USE OF SUBJECT–MATTER UNIT PROCEDURES

The most significant changes in administrative programs and teaching method have occurred with reference to the constants or core courses. There are teachers today who look upon the experiences that are to prepare for the duties of citizenship in a democracy, not merely as the taking of courses, but also as gaining practice in democratic forms of thinking and acting. It is argued that pupils must acquire skill in research, in group planning, in conducting group meetings, and in gathering valid information about the problems that are before them if they are to become competent citizens in a democracy. In many schools in the past, the extracurriculum was expected to provide these experiences, but it was soon discovered that the very pupils who had the greatest need were the ones who did not participate in the extracurricular activities. Obviously, therefore, it is necessary to provide the desired socializing experiences within the curriculum itself.

The fusion of subject matter. An early modification that was made to accommodate the varied needs of the large number of pupils enrolled in the core subjects was to change the emphasis in these courses from the mastery of subject matter to the exploration of areas of knowledge. Thus, courses in general science have been developed to provide a general introduction to the entire area of science, rather than to achieve a high degree of mastery of the system of facts that make up a given branch. In other instances, courses in history, geography, sociology, and economics have been fused into an integrated course known as "social studies." Courses of this nature were mentioned in Chap. 4 under the name of "fused" courses. Usually, the fusion has been achieved by drawing from all of the several contributing subjects the materials that pertain to a given topic or problem. Thus, a fused course may consist of a number of these topics, each one of which is so large that no pupil can learn all that is to be known about it, and is so broad that every pupil, regardless of ability or vocational objective, can find some aspect that holds special interest or value for him. A topic or problem of this nature, it will be recalled, serves very well as the point of orientation for a subject-matter unit.

The lengthened class period. A second modification in the traditional administrative pattern involves the lengthening of some of the class periods. Two trends in this direction helped prepare the way for the subject-matter unit. The first resulted in the double period for the laboratory work demanded by the emphasis on experimentation in the sciences. The double laboratory period has become a fixture in many schools because the conventional 45-minute period was not long enough to permit the pupils to conduct their experiments in a satisfactory manner.

The second departure from the conventional 45-minute period has occurred in a few schools which supervise the work of the pupils for the purpose of developing better study habits. Time for the supervision of study is provided by extending the class period to 60 minutes, only one-half of which is to be used for recitation purposes.

In the light of these developments, it is quite natural that schools that are interested in the exploration of broad areas of knowledge, possibly by means of the subject-matter unit method, should find it possible to depart from administrative patterns based on the 45-minute class period. While many teachers are using unit procedures within the traditional 45-minute period, longer periods, particularly for the fused courses, are becoming popular.

An additional device for making the schedule more flexible is noted in the practice of scheduling two related courses in juxtaposition to facilitate the correlation of subject matter. Occasionally the same teacher is asked to teach both courses in order to make possible even a higher degree of correlation. For a number of years, the Kenmore Junior High School, Kenmore, New York, has scheduled the social studies and English courses in such a manner that a pupil can devote half of his school day to these two courses alone. Furthermore, he is assigned to the same teacher and the same room for both courses. This arrangement makes it possible for a given class to be completely on its own for half of the school day, free to engage in whatever activities seem most worth while without fear of violating any obligations to other teachers or pupils.

The experiences of Kenmore and of other schools indicate that it is possible to revise the traditional administrative program to accommodate in a more satisfactory manner the work-type activities now commonly associated with the subject-matter unit method. The development of this type of program, however, is a matter that concerns the school as a whole. A progressive teacher, anxious to win greater freedom for planning and action, may try to win the school over to his point of view, but until the school is willing to introduce the desired modifications, the existing program sets the limits within which he must operate.

Finally, in schools dominated by the subject-matter approach, even though the administrative program may be changed to accommodate the work-type activities of the subject-matter unit method, the teacher will continue to be bound by the prescribed subject-matter requirements. The ground to be covered by a given class will continue to be outlined in the course of study, and the teacher will be judged primarily in terms of the facts, skills, and understandings the pupils will have acquired while under his direction.

ADMINISTRATIVE DEVICES THAT ASSUME THE USE OF EXPERIENCE UNIT PROCEDURES

It has been shown that to some educators the core means nothing more than a group of conventional, one-unit courses that each pupil must take before he can graduate. Others look upon the core as a series of fused courses, largely of an exploratory nature, one of which must appear in the program of each pupil until the required number has been taken. In either case, instruction in the core is for the purpose of developing the knowledge, skills, and understandings that a modern society demands of its members. Pupils have an opportunity to elect additional, conventionally organized courses as they may desire for purposes of specialization.

The large time block. The educators who favor the experience unit method have a different notion of the kind of experiences all pupils should have to prepare for democratic living. Subject-matter prescription in the sense of logically organized "courses" are considered to be too rigid to permit pupils to experience democratic living in a normal social setting. Furthermore, they realize that merely taking a "course" in American history will not assure good citizenship practices. These educators call for the orientation of learning activities around the purposes, interests, and needs which arise out of the experiences of the pupils themselves. An administrative organization is needed, therefore, that will allow these matters to be taken up at the time they arise rather than at the time they may have been scheduled by the curriculum makers.

The flexibility afforded by the lengthened class periods for laboratory work, supervised study, and the subject-matter unit seems to offer a solution. By adopting the expanded class period but rejecting the course prescriptions of the earlier core programs, the experience unit people have made available a block of time each day during which pupils, planning cooperatively with their teachers, may deal with whatever problems or concerns seem most significant to them. Learning to identify the important problems, to plan the attacks that are to be made on them, to carry out the plans, and to evaluate the results in terms of the objectives sought are believed to be the kinds of educational experiences each pupil should have. According to this view, the core should consist of the experiences pupils can have, under the direction of the school, which will help them grow into competent and intelligent citizens of a democratic society.

The core program. These experiences are acquired without regard for the conventional subject-matter lines and cannot be predicted with certainty. The content of a given core course, therefore, can be known only after it has been completed. After extensive study and experience, Alberty points out that this type of core program should meet the following requirements: .

1. The problems that are dealt with in the core program should provide for experiences common to large groups, that is, they should consist of a persistent or recurring concern of the society of which the school is a part.
2. The problems should cut across subject matter lines in the sense that they could not be dealt with adequately within a conventional subject matter area such as mathematics, English, science, or history.
3. The problems should call for cooperative effort on the part of pupils and teachers with respect to defining the problem and planning and executing the attack.
4. Due to the large amount of cooperation that is involved and the use

of energy resources in attacking the problems, a larger block of time should be allotted the core program than the conventional forty to sixty minute class period.

5. The problems should call for exploration of a wide range of relationships.[6]

Alberty listed such topics as "Living in the Home," "Housing," and "Community Recreation," as topics of typical problems that are suited for the core program.

The core curriculum in the secondary school of the future. In a recent publication, the National Association of Secondary School Principals recommended a curriculum built around this type of core program as the most promising line of development for secondary schools to follow in the years immediately ahead.[7] The general plan recommended by the Association identifies four major curricular areas. They are:

1. Common Learnings
2. Health and Physical Fitness
3. Personal and Individual Interests
4. Vocational Preparation [8]

The nature of these areas and the amount of time that will be budgeted for each in the daily time schedule is indicated in the accompanying diagram. As the illustration indicates, it is recommended that the core, primarily the "Common Learnings," should occupy a large share of the students' time through the ninth grade. Following the ninth grade the core should diminish in importance to provide for an increasing degree of specialization.

The program outlined by the Association is representative of several programs that have been developed by schools interested in the experience unit approach.[9]

In general, these programs provide flexibility in the daily schedule

[6] Harold Alberty, "Development of Core Curriculums," *Educational Research Bulletin*, 17:224, College of Education, Ohio State University, Columbus, Ohio, Nov. 16, 1938.

[7] National Association of Secondary School Principals, *Planning for American Youth*, Washington, D.C., 1944.

[8] *Ibid.*, p. 47.

[9] For further examples of such programs, see H. H. Giles, S. P. McCutchen, and A. N. Zechiel, *Exploring the Curriculum*, Adventures in American Education, Vol. II, Harper & Brothers, New York, 1942.

THE CURRICULUM IN AMERICAN CITY IS DIVIDED INTO FOUR MAJOR AREAS

Periods per day	GRADES							
	Early Secondary School			Middle Secondary School		Advanced Secondary School or Community Institute		
	7	8	9	10	11	12	13	14
1	Personal Interests Exploration of personal abilities and individual interests; discovery of interests in art, music, science, languages, sports, crafts, home and family problems, and leisure activities.			*Individual Interests Election by the pupil under guidance of teacher in fields of avocational, cultural, or intellectual interest.				
2				Vocational Preparation Includes the study of sciences, mathematics, social studies, literature, and foreign languages, in preparation for advanced study in Community Institute, college and universities, as well as education for industrial, commercial, homemaking, service and other occupations, leading to employment, apprenticeship or homemaking at end of grade 12, 13, or 14, and work experience.				
3								
4								
5	Common Learnings A continuous course in Social Living to foster growth in personal living and in civic competence. Guidance			of individual students is a chief responsibility of Social Living teachers.				
6	Health and Physical Fitness Includes games, sports, and other activities to promote physical fitness, together with the study of individual and community health.							

*Broken line indicates flexibility of scheduling   of these areas, depending upon their occupa-
for youth who need to spend more time in either   tional or future education plans.

Source: By permission of the National Association of Secondary School Principals.

through the use of large time blocks to replace the conventional class period, and subject-matter prescriptions are eliminated from that part of the curriculum which is designated as the core. This provides the freedom needed for teachers and pupils in cooperation to plan instruction around the problems, interests, and needs of the class.

METHODS IN RELATION TO THE CORE CURRICULUM

It must be remembered that not all of the educational activities sponsored by the modern secondary school fall within the area of the core program. At least three distinct types of learning outcomes are sought by progressive schools, each of which calls for a distinctive approach and a distinctive type of learning activity.

Developing social competence. The first of these three types of outcomes, first in the sense of its relative importance and hence in the emphasis it should receive, is the achievement of social competence. As stated in Chaps. 1, 2, and 12, this implies actual participation in the democratic social process. Pupils are expected to engage in activities that hold personal value for them in such a way that they learn to know the democratic way of life as a particular way of getting things done. The school regards it a matter of duty to provide experiences with successful group action on matters that count. Such experiences can be secured only in situations in which the action is planned and carried through in a natural, normal manner. *The experience unit method, operating within the freedom of the large time block, is well suited to this type of learning.*

Exploring the culture. The second type of outcome sought by the schools is a working acquaintance with the culture into which the child is born. The society of which the pupil is a member has had a long history. During that history much wisdom and information useful in making life more secure and satisfying, even in these days, has been slowly and sometimes painfully accumulated. This wisdom and knowledge is preserved in the literature, music, and art; is housed in the libraries, museums, and laboratories; and is known as the cultural heritage. Pupils do not have time to rediscover or to re-create all of this knowledge on their own time. They must learn to know what is already known and how it may be used. Complete mastery is neither possible nor necessary, but exploration adequate to provide a consumer's knowledge is desirable. *The subject-matter unit method is well suited for this exploratory type of learning.*

Developing special knowledge, skill, or understanding. Finally, there is a third type of outcome which involves the acquisition of specific knowledge, skills, or understanding. This kind of learning activity helps the pupil acquire the specialization his particular interests, abilities, and needs lead him to desire. While specialization suggests vocational goals, it should not be construed to mean only these. There are, for example, recreational activities including the creative arts that contribute to individual well-being. Deficiencies in the skills necessary for scholastic success, or even for social competence, also fall within this category.

When a specific goal is recognized by the pupil, it may be sought directly for its value to him and to him alone. Whether that goal is mastering the mathematics needed to gain admission to an engineering school, developing the reading skills that will enable him to keep up with his group, or learning to dance so he may have a good time at the junior prom, the school should be able to help him. *The daily-assignment method, under the direction of a competent teacher, frequently is well adapted to the realization of these specialized outcomes.*

All three methods have their place in the core curriculum. It is apparent from the preceding discussion that the core curriculum as it is now taking form, may employ not merely one, but rather all three of the major teaching methods. In the core program proper the experience unit method is most useful, for it makes possible the use of a large variety of activities including community surveys, group work, and cooperative planning and research by means of which the socializing function of secondary education may be realized. Furthermore, it makes possible the orientation of the learning activities around the interests and needs of the pupils. Since all pupils need social development, particularly in a democratic society, each pupil is required to be a member of a core group. The core program calls for a large block of time in the daily schedule when it is organized on the basis of an experience unit, and under such circumstances becomes the most prominent feature of the total school program. In some instances, as much as one-half of the school day is set aside for this purpose. It is natural, therefore, that a curriculum that has a core program as its central part should be designated as a "core curriculum."

The exploratory function of secondary education may be provided in the core curriculum by means of broad-fields courses which are taught by the subject-matter unit method. This method makes it possible to direct the attention of all the pupils in a class to a few major ideas in a conventional area of knowledge. At the same time it is possible to make provisions for some differences in individual needs and interests. All pupils may be expected to engage in this form of exploratory activity, and in some schools as much as one-fourth of the pupil's daily program is budgeted for this purpose. By requiring all pupils to register for at least one broad-fields course during each year in secondary school, each pupil will be sure to come in contact with a majority of the major fields of knowledge before graduation.

The modern secondary school is also expected to serve the special needs and interests of the pupils. The core curriculum provides for this function by means of special courses which the pupil may elect as he wishes or is convinced that he needs. These special courses may or may not be the conventional subjects of the familiar subject-matter curriculum. In many instances, however, the instruction will be teacher controlled for reasons of economy of time and effort, and may be planned on a day-to-day basis in the manner of the daily-assignment method.

The advantages of the core curriculum lie not in the fact that it utilizes the three methods of instruction, but rather in that it has been developed to provide for the complete education of the pupil. This is a complex responsibility and it demands a variety of means. The employment of the daily-assignment, the subject-matter unit, and the experience unit methods is based purely upon the fact that each method can make its own peculiar contribution to the development of the individual as that development is understood today. When experience shows that other procedures or modifications of these methods will contribute to a better type of pupil growth, appropriate adjustment in the methods as well as in the curriculum should be made. The core curriculum should not be considered as the final answer to the educational problems of the world. Rather, it is a means towards an end, to be modified or discarded when something better can be put into its place.

SUMMARY

The modern secondary school has become such a complex institution that it is necessary to divide its many functions into separate assignments. Each teacher, therefore, has a specialized function within the total school program. If the work of the school is to be effective, the efforts of everyone who has a part in that program must be directed and coordinated. The necessary coordination is achieved by means of such familiar administrative and supervisory devices as curricula, courses of study, daily activities programs, time schedules, fixed recitation periods, and testing programs.

Many of the existing administrative programs were designed on the assumption that all instruction is to be conducted by the daily-assignment method. In such cases, the 45- or 60-minute class period is the time interval on which the time schedule is built. Assignments are cut to the pattern of the class period and all curricular as well as extra-curricular activities are regulated by the clock.

In recent years some educators have projected objectives for secondary education that go beyond those which gave rise to the daily-assignment method. The rigid administrative devices introduced to make teaching by the daily-assignment method more effective have hindered the development of procedures to achieve these newer objectives. Because of these rigid programs, individual teachers have not been free to depart from the accepted teaching patterns without the consent of the school as a whole. With this fact in mind, some schools have reexamined the existing program with a view to making it more flexible.

One development that has resulted from the reexamination has been the lengthening of the class period. Sixty minutes, seventy-five minutes, or even longer periods are becoming increasingly more common in secondary schools today. A second development has brought about the coordination or fusion of subjects into broad fields of knowledge. These broad-fields courses may be explored by the subject-matter unit method. A third development is indicated by the emergence of the core program. Here the subject-matter restrictions imposed by courses of study and prescribed curricula are discarded. The class is free to deal directly with the interests, concerns, purposes, and needs that arise from the experiences of the pupils. Their attack upon such problems is guided by the teacher in such a way that the ability to solve problems is developed. This is the method that is called the experience unit.

As a result of these developments, there is emerging a form of secondary-school organizational and administrative pattern which has as its central feature this core program, and which is therefore known as the core curriculum. Although as much as one-half of the curricular activities may be included in the core program—hence one-half of the instruction is by the experience unit method—due provision is made for the exploration of the social heritage and for the acquisition of special knowledge, skills, and understandings. Broad-fields courses, taught by the subject-matter unit method, serve the exploratory needs while special instruction, possibly on a daily-assignment basis, may develop the desired forms and degrees of specialization. The emerging core curriculum, thus, may make use of all three methods of teaching, for each method serves a unique purpose each of which is necessary for a complete, well-rounded, secondary-school education.

SELECTED REFERENCES

ALBERTY, HAROLD: "Development of Core Curriculums," *Educational Research Bulletin*, 17:224, College of Education, Ohio State University, Columbus, Ohio, Nov. 16, 1938.

———: *Reorganizing the High-School Curriculum*, particularly Part II, The Macmillan Company, New York, 1947.

BOSTWICK, PRUDENCE: "A High School Core Program," *Curriculum Journal*, 9:204–207, May, 1938.

BRUBACHER, JOHN S.: *The History of the Problems of Education*, particularly Chaps. IX and X, McGraw-Hill Book Company, Inc., New York, 1947.

CASWELL, HOLLIS L. (Ed.): *The American High School*, particularly Chap. VIII, Eighth Yearbook of the John Dewey Society, Harper & Brothers, New York, 1946.

DOUGLASS, HARL R. (Ed.): *The High School Curriculum*, particularly Chap. 9, The Ronald Press Company, New York, 1947.

EVERETT, SAMUEL, and others: *A Challenge to Secondary Education*, D. Appleton-Century Company, Inc., New York, 1935.

GILES, H. H., McCUTCHEN, S. P., and ZECHIEL, A. N.: *Exploring the Curriculum*, Adventures in American Education, Vol. II, Harper & Brothers, New York, 1942.

GRIZZELL, EMIT DUNCAN: *Origin and Development of the High School in New England before 1865*, The Macmillan Company, New York, 1923.

HARAP, HENRY (Chairman): *The Changing Curriculum*, Tenth Yearbook, Department of Supervisors and Directors of Instruction, National Education Association, and the Society for Curriculum Study, D. Appleton-Century Company, Inc., New York, 1937.

KANDEL, I. L.: *History of Secondary Education*, Houghton Mifflin Company, Boston, 1930.

LORENZEN, STANLEY: "Planning a Core Curriculum: General Outline and an Illustrative Unit on Health," *Curriculum Laboratory Studies*, Bulletin 9, School of Education, University of Connecticut, Storrs, Conn., 1940.

National Association of Secondary School Principals: *Planning for American Youth*, Washington, D.C., 1944.

North Central Association of Colleges and Secondary Schools: *General Education in the American High School*, Scott, Foresman & Company, Chicago, 1942.

PETERS, CHARLES C.: *The Curriculum of Democratic Education,* McGraw-Hill Book Company, Inc., New York, 1942.

RUGG, HAROLD: *Foundations for American Education,* particularly Chap. XXII, World Book Company, Yonkers, New York, 1947.

SPEARS, HAROLD: *The Emerging High-School Curriculum and Its Direction,* American Book Company, New York, 1940.

The University School Staff: "A Proposal for a Core Curriculum in Grades Seven, Eight, and Nine," The University School, Ohio State University, Columbus, Ohio.

Chapter 16. THE TEACHER AND COMPREHENSIVE

PUPIL APPRAISAL

Measurement of the educational status of pupils, whether before teaching for inventory purposes, during teaching for diagnosis and analysis, or after teaching for determination of final status and evaluation of the school program, is only one of the aspects of pupil measurement with which teachers should be familiar. Certainly the teacher has more direct contact with and responsibility for achievement measurement than for any other type, but teacher familiarity with and ability to participate in other types of measurement are essential in modern educational practice.

The data presented in tabular form below for the use of various types of tests by 870 high schools point up the need for such understandings and abilities by secondary-school teachers. Most significant appear to be the facts that nearly nine-tenths of the schools use at least one intelligence test, seven-tenths employ at least one standardized achievement test, and one-third use aptitude, interest, and personality measures. That many of the schools have extensive measurement programs is shown by the percentages using two, three, or more tests of each type. Achievement tests were discussed in considerable detail in Chaps. 8, 11, and 14, while interests and personality measures received some attention in Chaps. 11 and 14. The remaining types of measuring devices shown in the table—intelligence and aptitude tests—are dealt with below.

INTERPRETATION OF APPRAISAL RESULTS

Two basic types of understandings seem essential to the teacher for appropriate interpretations of data concerning pupils. The first has to do with the related questions of individual differences, trait differences, and

TABLE 3. PERCENTAGES OF 870 HIGH SCHOOLS USING INTELLIGENCE, ACHIEVEMENT, AND PERSONALITY TESTS *

Number of tests given	General intelligence	Aptitude	Standardized achievement	Interest and personality
None..................	5	13	7	13
One or more.............	87	34	70	34
Two or more.............	44	20	52	20
Three or more...........	19	11	37	11
Four or more............	8	7	28	6
Five or more............	3	3	21	2
Six or more.............	....	....	16	....
Seven or more...........	....	....	13	....
Eight or more...........	....	....	10	....
Nine or more............	....	....	9	....
Ten or more............	....	....	7	....
No answer..............	8	53	23	53

* Eugenie A. Leonard and Anthony C. Tucker, *The Individual Inventory in Guidance Programs in Secondary Schools*, Vocational Division Bulletin 215, Occupational Information and Guidance Series 7, pp. 18–21, U.S. Government Printing Office, Washington, D.C., 1941.

group differences. The second is concerned with the types of derived scores and norms in terms of which measurement data are commonly reported.

Individual, trait, and group differences. Differences of three major types are significant to the teacher in the teaching and guidance of pupils. Of these, individual differences among pupils have received the most attention and are perhaps the most significant. However, trait differences within the individual seem only slightly less important in his education and guidance. Group differences between grade levels and the sexes are also of direct concern to the teacher.

Individual Differences. Mental, physical, educational, social, emotional, and other differences are tremendously great among individuals. This is true whether the group is relatively heterogeneous or quite homogeneous in some one major trait. For example, a group of children whose ages range from six years to eighteen years will differ very widely in their heights, but a group of twelve-year-old children will also differ widely in the height characteristic. It is quite typical, for example, to find that the slowest worker in a class requires from two and one-half to three times as long to do a certain set of algebraic computations as does the fastest worker. It is also common experience of teachers to find that the fastest pupil completes examinations in from one-third to one-half the time used by the slowest worker. When such differences, not restricted to speed factors by any means, exist within groups relatively homogeneous with respect to educational status, the importance of an understanding of individual differences becomes apparent.

Many of the outstandingly important characteristics of human beings are distributed along a scale or continuum from one extreme to the other in such manner that many persons are found near the center and decreasing numbers of persons are found as the distance from the center toward either extreme increases. This phenomenon is commonly known as the normal curve and is basic to many educational understandings and interpretations. Group instruction always involves heterogeneity of pupils, for homogeneity is practicable of attainment in only one characteristic, or at most two or three characteristics, at a time. Pupils who are homogeneous in one characteristic, such as chronological age, vary materially in height, intelligence, social maturity, and other important traits.

Trait Differences. Different persons grow and develop at different rates and attain differing ultimate or adult levels in any characteristics, such as height or mental ability. Somewhat similarly, a given individual grows and develops at different rates and attains differing ultimate or adult levels in his own various characteristics, such as physical height, mental age, emotional status, social status, and many others of a more highly specific nature. These variations within an individual are known as trait differences.

Although some tendency exists for similar rates of growth and development of an individual in his various traits, the differences in developmental rates are sufficiently great to have much significance educationally. For optimum effectiveness in the classroom, the teacher needs information concerning the individual pupil's level of development in the most important traits.

Group Differences. The most commonly considered group differences are those between the sexes, grade groups, age groups, racial groups, regions of the country, urban and rural groups, and groups with varying amounts of schooling. Of these, the most basically important for teacher understanding are probably sex, grade, and age differences, although some basic understandings of all such differences are desirable in the teacher.

The following quotation from Stroud [1] illustrates the great differences in school achievement between adjacent grade groups:

A fair appraisal of the various investigations places the number of pupils in the various school subjects who equal or exceed the modal achievement of the next grade above at almost a third. The percentage that falls at or below the modal achievement of the next grade below is only slightly less. About 10 per cent deviate from the mode by as much as two full grades above and two full grades below; and 2 or 3 per cent, by as much as three grades.

A sex difference of consequence, to give one further illustration, is that between boys and girls on the quantitative and linguistic factors of intelligence. On the average, boys score higher than girls on the quantitative and the situation is reversed on the linguistic scores.

A generalization of no small meaning, and one sometimes not recognized, is that group differences, *e.g.*, differences between averages for the sexes, are typically far smaller than are differences between the extremes within each group separately. For example, the difference in average linguistic aptitude of boys and girls in a tenth-grade class would be far less than that between the two girls or two boys of that class at the highest and lowest extremes of linguistic aptitude for their sex.

Derived scores and norms. A test score in itself has no real meaning. This is true even of a percentage mark, to which some teachers attach a meaning it does not intrinsically possess. A percentage mark of 83 indicates that 83 per cent of something, probably of the total test content, has been done correctly by a pupil, but exactly what that means in educational attainment no one can satisfactorily say. If the percentage mark of 83 applies to the entire content of a course, an interpretation of meaning is even more tenuous. Similarly, a score of 83 on a test having 129 scoring points means little more than a percentage of 83 on a test having 100 scoring points; the one test may merely be

[1] James B. Stroud, *Psychology in Education*, p. 397, Longmans, Green & Co., Inc., New York, 1946.

harder than the other. A test score is no more than a numerical expression of performance on the part of a pupil, so derived scores and norms are the devices by which meaning is given to such raw scores. The process is that of establishing comparability, which is discussed in Chap. 5 as one of the criteria of a good examination.

Standardized tests are usually accompanied by tables of norms which provide for the conversion of raw scores, or original scores, to some meaningful derived score basis. Some derived scores are, therefore, obtained by the use of tables of norms. Other derived scores, particularly those of the quotient type, are sometimes obtained without the use of norms. In either case, the derived measure has meaning which did not exist in the raw score from which it was obtained.

Derived Scores Based on Average Performance. Grade equivalents and age equivalents are the two types of derived scores which are based on some form of average performance, usually the median. In each instance, the pupil who has a certain equivalent score, whether it be grade or age, is thereby placed at a certain position on a growth ladder for the characteristic measured by the test.

If a pupil attains a raw score on a reading comprehension test which test norms indicate to have a grade equivalent of 9.7, his reading level is that of the average pupil who has attended the ninth grade for 7 months. The raw score is thereby given readily understandable meaning. If a total score on a standardized test battery is similarly translated by the use of grade norms for the entire test, the result is a grade equivalent of broader subject meaning. Grade norms are available for secondary-school standardized tests only in subject areas commonly studied through the high-school years, such as English, social studies, science, and mathematics, and in which growth is to be expected throughout the pupil's entire school career.

If the same pupil's raw score on the reading comprehension test is given meaning by use of a table of age norms, it may be found that his age equivalent in reading comprehension is 15–3. This age equivalent indicates that he comprehends in reading at the level characteristic of pupils who are fifteen years and three months of age chronologically. Age norms are ordinarily available only for the same types of secondary-school standardized tests as appropriately furnish grade norms, although the age norm is also applicable to intelligence tests. When a reading test score is converted to an age equivalent, the result is commonly referred to as a reading age, or RA. When a total score on a standardized achievement test battery is converted to an age equivalent, the result is known as an educational age, or EA. When a score obtained from a group test of general intelligence or mental ability is converted to an age equivalent, the result is known as a mental age, or MA.

Derived Scores Based on Variability of Performance. The percentile rank is the derived score of this type which is most commonly used at the high-school level, although several other derived scores which will not be discussed here are also based on variability of performance. A percentile rank of 63 indicates that the pupil who attained it scored higher on the test than did 63 per cent of the comparable group of pupils used in establishing the test norms. Percentile norm tables provide for the conversion of a raw score into the comparable percentile rank, and the percentile rank indicates the position of the pupil in relation to the scores made by the normative group of pupils of the same grade, who have studied the same particular course, such as plane geometry, or who have studied the same subject for the same number of semesters, as 4 semesters of French.

Percentile ranks have a range from 1 to 100. A percentile rank of 1 indicates that the pupil performance is in the lowest 1 per cent, and a percentile rank of 100 indicates it is in the highest 1 per cent. Percentile ranks should not be confused with percentage marks, for percentage marks ordinarily concentrate near the top end of a scale ranging from 0 to 100 and are seldom found below 50 or 60, whereas percentile ranks range evenly from 1 to 100. This becomes apparent when it is realized that there are as many pupils in the lowest 1 per cent as there are at any other percentile rank. Percentile ranks are most commonly used for interpreting results from achievement tests, although they are sometimes used for intelligence test results with separate norms for each grade from 9 to 12.

Derived Scores Obtained as Quotients. The third distinctive type of derived score is that obtained when one age equivalent is divided by another age equivalent. Norm tables are not directly involved in finding quotient scores. The most common types of quotient scores are the intelligence quotient and the educational quotient, but two other types, subject quotients and the achievement quotient, are sometimes used. The symbols presented in the above discussion of age equivalents and CA for chronological or life age are used in the formulas which follow. Illustrations can perhaps best be given for a certain pupil of known chronological age for whom mental age, educational age, and reading age equivalents have been determined from test scores by the use of appropriate tables of age norms.

Computations of four quotients are shown below for a pupil whose chronological age (CA) is 15–0, and for whom scores from a general intelligence test, a general achievement battery, and a reading test have been interpreted by the appropriate age norm tables to disclose that his mental age (MA) is 18–0, that his educational age (EA) is 16–6, and that his reading age (RA) is 17–3. This pupil would have an intelligence quotient (IQ) of

$$IQ = 100\,\frac{MA}{CA} = 100\,\frac{18\text{–}0}{15\text{–}0} = 100\,\frac{216}{180} = 120\,[2]$$

an educational quotient (EQ) of

$$EQ = 100\,\frac{EA}{CA} = 100\,\frac{16\text{–}6}{15\text{–}0} = 100\,\frac{198}{180} = 110$$

a reading quotient (RQ) of

$$RQ = 100\,\frac{RA}{CA} \doteq 100\,\frac{17\text{–}3}{15\text{–}0} = 100\,\frac{207}{180} = 115$$

and an achievement quotient (AQ) of

$$AQ = 100\,\frac{EA}{MA} = 100\,\frac{16\text{–}6}{18\text{–}0} = 100\,\frac{198}{216} = 91.7 \text{ or } 92$$

The IQ of 120 indicates that this pupil is mentally bright for his age. The EQ of 110 and RQ of 115 show that he is further advanced educationally than is the average pupil of his chronological age, but that his reading level is higher than his general educational level. The AQ of 92 indicates that he is at a higher level on the mental growth ladder than he is on the educational growth ladder, even though he is more advanced both mentally and educationally than is the average pupil with a CA of 15–0.

The first three quotients are similar in that they relate different types of growth to chronological age, although the first indicates mental brightness and the second and third indicate brightness in educational

[2] As the hyphens in age equivalents do not represent decimal points, the mental age of 18–0 can best be divided by the chronological age of 15–0 if both ages are converted from years and months to months. The MA of 18–0 becomes 216 months and the CA of 15–0 becomes 180 months.

achievement generally and in reading specifically. It is evident that the AQ is quite different from the other three quotients, for it differs primarily in having mental age, rather than chronological age, as the denominator of the fraction. The AQ of 92 indicates that this pupil is not achieving educationally up to expectation, for if he were his AQ would be

$$AQ = 100\,\frac{EA}{MA} = 100\,\frac{18\text{–}0}{18\text{–}0} = 100\,\frac{216}{216} = 100$$

UNDERSTANDING THE PUPIL

A teacher should possess extensive knowledge and understanding of each individual pupil if he is to contribute most effectively to the pupil's development and if he is to participate most meaningfully in the pupil's guidance. Although such extensive knowledges and understandings of individual children are dependent in large measure upon classroom and other contacts, such contacts should serve to enrich rather than to constitute the entire foundation for such background on the part of the teacher. Hence, there is a definite need for the teacher to learn much about the individual child before, and during the very early stages of, his association with him. The teacher will later have opportunity for learning from the pupil as he observes his classroom and other learning activities.

It seems advantageous to consider such knowledges and understandings of the individual pupil under the major headings of aptitudes, backgrounds, and educational status. All that the pupil is at a given moment and all that he may become in the future appear to depend upon factors appropriately dealt with in these categories. The aptitudes are those potentialities for growth and development, primarily mental and physical, which have determined in part what the child is today and which will also have a large place in determining his future. His backgrounds of experience with the physical and social environments in which he has lived have also played a large part in determining what he is today and have had cumulative effects important in determining his future. The child's characteristics at any given time may properly be considered the resultant of his heredity and environment, for what he is now depends upon the manner in which his backgrounds, or experiences contributed to the realization of his aptitudes or potentialities.

The relative contribution of heredity and environment is a question to which the answer is not greatly important here. Unless a person believes in heredity as the sole determiner of the individual's characteristics, in which case he could not logically be a teacher, recognition must inevitably be given to the environment as a potent factor in individual development. The child's heredity in its entirety and his environment in part have been determined before he enters high school. The major function of the secondary school is to provide an educational environment for each pupil which is designed to contribute most effectively to his future development in socially desirable ways. Accomplishment of this purpose is contingent upon a comprehensive knowledge and understanding by the teacher of individual pupil aptitudes, backgrounds, and characteristics.

Information concerning aptitudes of the pupil. Pupil aptitudes are considered here in the general sense of potentialities, although it will be seen later that the term is also used in a more specific sense. The aptitudes dealt with are the general intelligence, the group factors of intelligence, and the specific factors of intelligence, all in the area of mental ability, and the physical aptitudes quite definitely in the area of physical ability.

General Intelligence. General intelligence is most often defined today in terms of the individual's ability to adapt himself to new situations. Definitions more often given some years ago than today used the narrower concepts of ability to carry on abstract thinking and ability to learn. Instruments used to measure this general mental ability are variously designated as general intelligence tests, mental ability tests, general ability tests, scholastic aptitude tests, and psychological examinations. Such instruments are of three distinguishable types—individual intelligence scales, group intelligence tests, and performance tests.

The most numerous and widely used instruments for the measurement of general intelligence are group tests which can be administered simultaneously to a number of persons. Such tests first came into use during the First World War, when the *Army Group Intelligence Examination Alpha*, widely known simply as *Army Alpha*, was devised and used with army inductees for the primary purpose of selecting candidates for officer training. The *Army General Classification Test*, used much more widely in various branches of the armed services in the Second World War, is the modern counterpart. Many group tests designed for use with school children have appeared during the last three decades. Two such tests will be mentioned and illustrated in the next section of this chapter rather than here because they measure not only general intelligence but also two important group factors of intelligence.

Second in importance and widespread use to the group tests of general mental ability are individual intelligence scales. Chronologically the oldest of general intelligence measures, these scales were introduced by Binet and Simon in 1905 as the first objective measures to be devised in this area. These French psychologists published revisions of their intelligence scale in 1908 and 1911, and American adaptations of their scale have since appeared under various authorship. The American version most widely used today is doubtless the *New Revised Stanford-Binet Tests of Intelligence*, published in its latest edition in 1937. The major characteristic distinguishing these individual intelligence scales from group intelligence tests lies in the mode of administration. The former can be administered to only one person at a time and require an expert examiner, whereas the latter can be given to a group of persons simultaneously by any teacher who is reasonably skillful in test administration.

The individual intelligence scale is designed for administration only by a trained examiner. Pupil responses to questions asked orally and to pictorial materials presented to him are sometimes given verbally and are sometimes given with paper and pencil. The exercises, designed in the *Stanford Revision of the Binet-Simon* to cover persons ranging in age from two to adulthood, are scaled in level of difficulty from very easy to very hard. No one pupil is asked to take the entire scale; rather the examiner has each person start at the highest level where his success is assured and has him continue to that point on the scale beyond which he cannot succeed. The pupil's mental age is then determined by adding the years and months of mental age credit appropriate for what he has done on the part of the scale used with him to the years and months of mental age credit assigned to all portions of the scale below his starting point.

The test titles listed below for the portion of the *Stanford-Binet Scale*, Form L, appropriate for ages twelve to adulthood indicate the wide variety of abilities tested, the recurrence on several occasions of similar test situations at increasing levels of difficulty, and the general scalar arrangement of all exercises from easy to difficult.[3]

YEAR XII

Vocabulary, Verbal Absurdities II, Response to Pictures II, Repeating 5 Digits Reversed, Abstract Words II, Minkus Completion.

YEAR XIII

Plan of Search, Memory for Words, Paper Cutting I, Problems of Fact, Dissected Sentences, Copying a Bead Chain from Memory II.

YEAR XIV

Vocabulary, Induction, Picture Absurdities III, Ingenuity, Orientation—Direction I, Abstract Words II.

AVERAGE ADULT

Vocabulary, Codes, Differences between Abstract Words, Arithmetical Reasoning, Proverbs I, Ingenuity, Memory for Sentences V, Reconciliation of Opposites.

SUPERIOR ADULT I

Vocabulary, Enclosed Box Problem, Minkus Completion, Repeating 6 Digits Reversed, Sentence Building, Essential Similarities.

SUPERIOR ADULT II

Vocabulary, Finding Reasons II, Repeating 8 Digits, Proverbs II, Reconciliation of Opposites, Reading Thought of Passage—Value of Life.

SUPERIOR ADULT III

Vocabulary, Orientation—Direction II, Opposite Analogies II, Paper Cutting II, Reasoning, Repeating 9 Digits.

A third approach to the measurement of general intelligence is by means of performance tests. Such instruments require no such verbal abilities as reading and writing on the part of persons taking them, and some of them can be given largely if not solely by pantomime. Some of these are pencil-and-paper tests. Others are form-board tests which require the manipulation of apparatus and are not unlike jigsaw puzzles.

An example of a pencil-and-paper test is *Army Beta*, the nonverbal companion of *Army Alpha*, used during the First World War in measuring the general intelligence of illiterate persons and of persons literate in a foreign language but possessing serious language handicaps in English. The accompanying illustrations from one of the several modern revisions of *Army Beta* show items which request the subject to trace a

[3] Lewis M. Terman and Maud A. Merrill, *Measuring Intelligence*, pp. 110–132, Houghton Mifflin Company, Boston, 1937.

maze, to discover and mark a discrepancy, and to compare figures or numbers. The test can be given largely by pantomime.

EXCERPTS FROM REVISED BETA EXAMINATION

Mark the shortest path from each arrow at the left to the opposite arrow at the right, but do not cross any of the lines

In each square mark the thing that is wrong

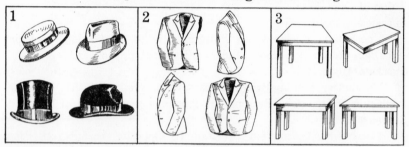

Look at each pair of drawings or numbers, and make a mark on the dotted line if they are not alike

Source: C. E. Kellogg and N. W. Morton, *Revised Beta Examination*, The Psychological Corporation, New York, 1935.

The *Pintner-Paterson "Long" Performance Scale*, for which the required apparatus is pictured in an accompanying illustration, is representative of the manipulatory type of performance test. Instructions are usually given by the examiner orally, and the pupil's success is measured by the time required, the errors made, and other types of evidence.

TESTS OF PINTNER-PATERSON "LONG" PERFORMANCE SCALE

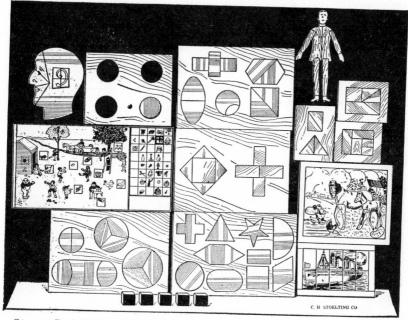

Source: Rudolf Pintner and Donald G. Paterson, *Pintner-Paterson Performance Scale*, Long Form, C. H. Stoelting Co.

Group Factors of Intelligence. One outcome of the recent attempts to determine the nature of general intelligence more exactly is what are usually called group factors of intelligence. Although the factor analysis procedure used in this attempt is still in relatively early stages of development, two group factors of intelligence have received general acceptance—a linguistic or language factor and a quantitative or non-language factor. One evidence that there are two such distinguishable factors is found in the fact that, on the average, girls possess a higher degree of linguistic ability than do boys and boys possess a higher degree of quantitative ability than do girls.

Several modern tests embody in their part and total scores not only these two group factors of intelligence but also general intelligence. The *American Council on Education Psychological Examination* provides part scores on linguistic and quantitative factors and a total score on general intelligence. The accompanying illustration shows sample items from the word completion part to represent the linguistic sections of the instrument. The language and nonlanguage part scores and total score of the *California Test of Mental Maturity* similarly distinguish two factors and a total measure of intelligence. A sample from a nonlanguage section is shown in an accompanying illustration.

EXCERPT FROM PSYCHOLOGICAL EXAMINATION FOR HIGH-SCHOOL STUDENTS

COMPLETION

Think of the word that fits the definition. Then mark the first letter of that word on the answer sheet.

---

1. The middle of the day.
    G   K   N   R   W

2. A reddening of the cheeks or face, as for shame or modesty.
    A   B   E   G   S

3. Money paid to a woman by her divorced husband.
    A   B   C   D   E

Source: L. L. Thurstone and Thelma G. Thurstone, *American Council on Education Psychological Examination for High School Students,* 1946 ed., American Council on Education, Washington, D.C., 1946.

The *Chicago Tests of Primary Mental Abilities,*[3a] based on the factor analysis work of Thurstone, provide for the measurement of seven intellectual factors designated as primary mental abilities: (*a*) perceptual ability, (*b*) numerical ability, (*c*) verbal ability, (d) spatial visualizing ability, (*e*) memory, (*f*) inductive or generalizing ability, and (*g*) deductive or reasoning ability. The length of this battery has resulted in its primary use to date for experimental and research purposes rather than in practical school measurement. A recently published battery of *Differential Aptitude Tests,*[3b] seemingly designed for more advantageous school use, provides part scores for the following intellectual factors: (*a*) verbal reasoning, (*b*) numerical ability, (*c*) abstract reasoning, (*d*) space relations, (*e*) mechanical reasoning, (*f*) clerical speed and accuracy, (*g*) spelling, and (*h*) sentences.

[3a] L. L. Thurstone and T. G. Thurstone, *Chicago Tests of Primary Mental Abilities,* Science Research Associates, Chicago, 1943.
[3b] George K. Bennett, *et al., Differential Aptitude Tests,* The Psychological Corporation, New York, 1947.

EXCERPT FROM CALIFORNIA TEST OF MENTAL MATURITY

DIRECTIONS: In each row find a drawing that is either the same drawing or different views of the first drawing. Put an X on the line under this drawing and put the number of the drawing you mark on the line to the right.

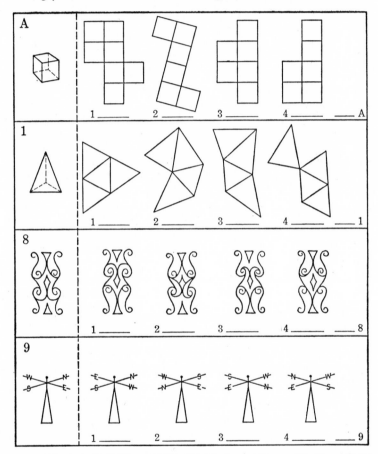

Source: Elizabeth T. Sullivan, Willis W. Clark, and Ernest W. Tiegs, *California Test of Mental Maturity*, Advanced, California Test Bureau, Los Angeles, 1942.

Specific Intelligence. Tests of specific intelligence or of academic aptitudes apparently originated more than 20 years ago with the publication of the aptitude series of the *Iowa Placement Examinations.*[3c] These and more recently published aptitude tests measure specific intelligence, *i.e.*, intelligence as it operates in fields or even in subjects of study or performance. The original *Iowa Placement Examinations* and the later revisions of these tests provide aptitude tests for English, mathematics, physics, chemistry, and the foreign languages. Other tests now provide for aptitude measurement in such professional areas as medical, legal, and educational; in such skill areas as mechanical, clerical, and stenographic; in such fine arts fields as art and music; in such other subject fields as science and physical science; and in such specific school subjects as plane geometry and algebra. The range covered by these measures of aptitude or specific intelligence is extremely broad at the professional school and college levels, somewhat more restricted at the secondary-school level, and limited to a few readiness tests, the elementary-school counterpart of aptitude tests, for the lower grades.

Physical Aptitudes. Although such physical characteristics as height, weight, and many other physical and physiological measures bear negligible relationships to mental development and general school success, some physical deficiencies and abnormalities of pupils are nevertheless important determiners of their success in special subjects and in vocations. Such different school subjects as physical education and English make different demands upon pupils; crippled children must receive special physical education instruction, if any, in the school. Similarly, such different vocations as scientist and professional athlete make different demands upon persons; a scientist need not possess the physical strength and stamina demanded of professional athletes. Tests of physical capacity and motor ability, cardiovascular tests, posture tests, and physical classification tests are useful in obtaining an adequate understanding of pupil physical characteristics.

Information concerning backgrounds of the pupil. Pupil backgrounds are important to the teacher in two ways. First, the teacher should be aware of the major influence of the individual's environment in determining how he will develop and the behavior characteristics he will acquire.

[3c] G. D. Stoddard, *et al., Iowa Placement Examinations*, Series A–2, Form M, Bureau of Educational Research and Service, State University of Iowa, Iowa City, Iowa, 1941 and 1942.

Such modern schools of psychology as behaviorism, Gestalt, the organismic, and the topological emphasize the importance of the environment. Second, the teacher should have sufficient information concerning the pupil's background to facilitate an understanding of what he is today and what environmental factors may have contributed most significantly to, or hampered him most seriously in, his development. The cumulative record commonly and the case study occasionally are sources of some information, but the use of such instruments as the *Sims Score Card for Socio-Economic Status*[4] and the *American Home Scale*,[5] both of which are filled out by the pupils, affords more information on the social, cultural, and economic status of the home.

Information concerning educational status of the pupil. The resultant of heredity and environment, or of biological inheritance and environmental influences, is found in the characteristics of a pupil at a given time. Although it is important to know what factors have operated to mold the pupil into the type of person he is today, it is only with respect to his future experiences that his growth and development may now be directed. The educational status of the pupil is here conceived to include all of those types of behavior resulting from the interaction between the aptitude and environmental factors in his past.

Physical Health Characteristics. The physical health of the pupil changes from time to time within the framework which his largely inherited physical capacities provide. Physical health has much to do with school and postschool success and with the social and emotional adjustment of the pupil, so information concerning a pupil's health is important in facilitating an understanding of him and also in pointing the way to desirable remediation or isolation on occasion.

Paper-and-pencil tests of health knowledge and health awareness are useful only in measuring acquired knowledges. Periodic examinations by school physicians and dentists, followed by any recommended remediation, and the services of a school nurse add considerably to the health measurement program of the school. However, it is a responsibility of the teacher to be conversant with the symptoms of common ailments and to be alert at all times for the presence of any such symptoms in

[4] Verner M. Sims, *Sims Score Card for Socio-Economic Status*, Public School Publishing Company, Bloomington, Ill., 1927.
[5] W. A. Kerr and H. H. Remmers, *American Home Scale*, Science Research Associates, Chicago, 1942.

pupils. Otherwise, optimum learning cannot be obtained with the pupils who are ill, and other pupils may be exposed unnecessarily to communicable diseases.

Mental Health Characteristics. The relationship between mental health and largely innate mental abilities is somewhat the same as that between physical health and largely inherited physical capacities, although diagnostic and remedial techniques in the mental health area are doubtless in earlier stages of development than are those in the field of physical health. Although mind and body are generally accepted today as merely different aspects of the whole organism, the two may be distinguished at least roughly for educational purposes.

Mental health is measured most frequently perhaps by adjustment inventories of the types discussed briefly in Chap. 14. Services of a school psychologist, clinical psychologist, mental hygienist, or psychiatrist are highly valuable in the diagnosis and remediation of disorders in mental health. Again, however, the teacher has an important place in the measurement program, for his alertness in observing and recording or reporting emotional disturbances in pupils may well be the means of revealing cases for study by those especially trained for such work. The anecdotal record is a device useful in recording such observations and over a period of time in establishing definite need for special attention to some cases.

Social Adjustment Characteristics. The social adjustment of pupils can be studied by either of two quite distinct methods. The first, treated briefly in Chap. 14, is by means of the personal report form of personality instrument. Norms make possible the determination for each pupil of his degree of social adjustment. The second, that of sociometry, measures social adjustment in terms of dynamic relationships among individuals within a group. Easily subject to use by classroom teachers, the sociometric method furnishes less definite but possibly more meaningful results.

Although teachers are often aware to some degree of social relationships within a pupil group, such as a homeroom, the sociometric method will often serve to verify and valuably supplement such impressions. Typically, each pupil is asked to list the names of the classmates he would choose first and second in such situations as the following: (*a*) as homeroom president, (*b*) as best friend, (*c*) as companion for a classroom project, or (*d*) as companion on a picnic. The variety of such situations dealing with social interrelationships among members of a group is great. If first choices are weighted two and second choices are weighted one, an index or score may easily be attained for each member of the group. The possible range of such scores is from zero, for the pupil not chosen by any classmate, to two less than twice the number of pupils, for the exceedingly rare if existent pupil given as first choice by every one of his classmates. These scores are then often divided into fourths—highest, second, third, and lowest quarters.

In the sociometric method, the results of such a tabulation are graphically represented in a sociogram. Sociograms in their simple form consist of four concentric circles, with each of the four enclosed areas constituting one-fourth of the total area enclosed. Boys and girls are often represented by special numbered or initialed symbols, such as triangles and circles, to identify the sex and individual. Straight lines, solid and dotted, drawn from figure to figure represent first and second choices. The symbols are ordinarily placed with two major ideas in mind: (a) to show score values by positions of the symbols within the circles, the inner circle for scores in the highest quarter and the remaining areas from the center outward for scores in the second, third, and fourth quarters; and (b) to show clusters of relationships, by placing the symbols so that the crossing of connecting lines and their lengths are kept to a minimum. Information concerning sex, racial, and religious factors in the dynamic social relations of the group and concerning preference for and avoidance of certain members of the group may be visualized easily from the sociogram, and the uses of such information to the teacher are widely varied.

The accompanying illustration of a sociogram shows the pattern of intergroup and interpersonal relations among the 13 boys and 23 girls in a fifth-grade class. In this sociogram, boys are shown to the left and girls to the right of the vertical line. The pupils of each sex are divided by the broken line into two racial groups. Clearly shown is evidence concerning social relations between the two racial groups, between the sexes, and among the individual members of the class.

Interest and Attitudinal Characteristics. It is well known that interests of various types, particularly in vocations, undergo great change as the child develops and matures and as societal changes occur. Interests are determined in considerable measure by the environment of the individual. Aviation, radio, television, and atomic energy represent newly developed areas of interest. It is the rare child whose vocational interests are determined early in his life, for such interests more typically mature during adolescence or even later. General interest measures of the type discussed in Chap. 11 and vocational interest measures of the

SAMPLE SOCIOGRAM

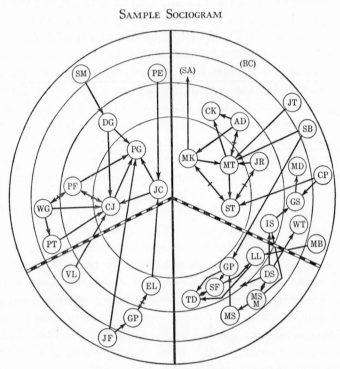

Source: Mary L. Northway and Bruce Quarrington, "Depicting Inter-cultural Relations," *Sociometry*, 9:334–339, November, 1946.

type discussed in Chap. 14, particularly the latter, should be fairly recent in their derivation if they are to be accepted as representing the pupil's present status.

Attitudes are also subject to modification as the outcome of experiences of many types. Attitudes of the American population as a whole changed markedly on prohibition between the adoption of the Eighteenth Amendment in 1920 and the adoption of the repealing Twenty-first Amendment in 1933. Attitudes of the American people on a pacifism-militarism continuum changed markedly and with exceeding rapidity on Dec. 7, 1941, when the Japanese bombed Pearl Harbor.

Hence, the attitudinal characteristics of pupils, especially where contro-versial, present-day issues are involved, cannot safely be inferred from use of the types of scales discussed in Chap. 14 several years in the past.

Educational Characteristics. Quite frequent measures of pupil attain-ment in the academic areas and subjects of study are desirable, for educational growth typically is continuous although not necessarily constant in rate. Most useful for this type of measurement are probably the standardized achievement tests of the survey type from which the results indicate pupil status in terms of age, grade, or percentile norms. However, measurement by use of performance tests in skill areas and informal objective tests in various subjects is important if steps are taken to give results the comparable meaning desirable in this situation. Much of the content of Chaps. 8, 11, and 14 is devoted to a quite ex-tended treatment of educational measurement.

TEACHING THE PUPIL

An integral part of the teaching-learning process as it is envisioned in modern schools is evaluation of pupil behavior. An interactive rela-tionship exists between teaching and measuring, for a teacher gains in his measuring insights through an adequate understanding of pupil be-havior and teaching methods, while they in turn are enriched through his increased understanding of measuring techniques. Evaluation devices and procedures may to some degree be classified by the place they most properly occupy in the teaching process—before teaching, during teach-ing, and after teaching. However, post-teaching measures obtained at the end of one school year may well be considered as preteaching measures for the following year.

Appraisals preceding teaching. Probably most significant among the measuring instruments useful just prior to or at very early stages of teaching a new pupil group are standardized tests of the prognostic and inventory types and tests in the basic skills areas. Whereas prognostic and inventory tests are treated in Chap. 11 in some detail, and whereas basic skills tests are discussed in a section of Chap. 14, the use of results from such instruments is considered only briefly here.

Prognostic tests afford evidence useful in such guidance and ad-ministrative problems as course selections by individual pupils and sectioning of classes. Inventory tests have a major function of providing evidence of those pupils' inadequacies in preparation which should receive early attention in the instructional process. Basic skills tests provide results indicative of pupil work levels in the fundamental skills of computing, receiving ideas by means of reading, and expressing ideas by means of writing. When results from the use of such specialized instruments are combined with those of more general types outlined in the section above on understanding the pupil, teachers are enabled to approach the classroom teaching situation with confidence in their understandings of individual pupils.

Appraisals during teaching. Among the measuring tools and techniques which have greatest significance during the actual teaching of a course or course unit are diagnostic and analytic tests, check lists, interviews, instructional or practice tests, and the teacher-made informal objective, essay, and perhaps even oral tests. The classroom or teacher-made tests received detailed treatment in Chap. 8, while instruments of the other types entered prominently into the discussion of Chap. 11.

Diagnostic tests directly, and analytic tests in less definite fashion, furnish evidence concerning difficulties of pupils and pupil groups useful in planning remedial instruction as needed. Check lists in skill performances enable the teacher to determine pupil progress in certain laboratory and other skills and also to diagnose and provide remediation for pupil deficiencies discovered. Interviews furnish a valuable supplementary tool in the diagnosis of weaknesses, particularly in skill performances. Instructional and practice tests are valuable in providing the drill and practice often necessary in the attainment of pupil mastery, and for individual pupils in the process of remediation.

The informal objective test particularly, of the teacher-made instruments, is valuable in the periodic measurement of pupil progress during teaching. Results from such tests may be analyzed by counting correct answers to each item and each group of related items as a basis for later remediation of class and individual pupil weaknesses. The essay and even the oral examinations may well be used as supplementary classroom testing and teaching devices if they are employed with proper precautions.

Appraisals after teaching. A wider variety of instruments and techniques appears to be suitable for use at or near the conclusion of a period of instruction, such as a school semester or year, than is true of pre-teaching or during-teaching phases of the entire process. Standardized achievement tests of the survey type, especially those designed for use in specific courses, are most appropriately used upon the completion of study of a subject. Quality and product scales and measures of such tastes and preferences as attitudes, interests, and appreciations are often most useful as the school year nears its end, and the profile chart and class analysis chart, both based on broad evaluations, appear to have much meaning at this point in the teaching process. Measures of adjustment and of such activity-centered outcomes as methods of thinking and social sensitivity are also appropriate in measuring final instructional outcomes. Instruments of these types are discussed in Chaps. 11 and 14 above.

Appraisals after teaching have at least two major uses, of which that involved in the preparation of final student reports is probably the less meaningful. The other, to afford a basis for the planning of experiences for groups of pupils and particularly for individual pupils, seems to be more highly significant. If results from standardized survey tests and scales are interpreted by means of pupil profiles and class analysis charts, if pupil attitudes, interests, appreciations, and adjustments are surveyed, and if such other less tangible outcomes as ability to think and social sensitivity are measured and the results given meaning, much of value in the planning of school activities for the next year and in the preparation for guidance of the individual pupil will be at hand.

GUIDING THE PUPIL

Pupil guidance may be considered in a number of different ways. Most broadly, education is guidance, so testing, measuring, and evaluating all contribute to pupil guidance because of their significant place in the educational process. More narrowly, pupil guidance is furnished in an educational sense when the school program and classroom activities are adapted to the abilities, interests, and needs of pupils. Another more narrow form of guidance is that involved when an attempt is made to attain for the pupil improved adjustment in his personal and social life. The content of Chaps. 8, 11, and 14 and much of the content of this chapter deal with guidance in these three senses. Again, pupil guidance is furnished in a vocational sense when course selections are made in terms of vocational goals and when the aptitudes, backgrounds, and present characteristics of the pupil are employed in vocational counseling.

The teacher as tester, measurer, and evaluator therefore has two major guidance functions: (*a*) to contribute directly to pupil guidance through his participation in school planning and in the many classroom and informal contacts with pupils where assistance and guidance are furnished, and (*b*) to contribute information concerning pupils to the guidance director or vocational counselor through record systems maintained in the school and through cooperative arrangements between the guidance and teaching personnel. Perhaps the teacher may be looked upon as a general guide and counselor to the pupil and as a contributor to the more technical guidance supplied through the office of the guidance director.

It is intended here to deal briefly with two additional measurement tools which have guidance functions. Chap. 17 is concerned with the more technical questions of teacher counseling and more in detail with the counseling uses of the many evaluative tools presented and discussed in this chapter and in Chaps. 8, 11, and 14. The tools to be presented and discussed briefly here are the cumulative record and the case study.

Cumulative records. The cumulative record constitutes not only a record of results obtained from the study of a pupil but also a means whereby the pupil may be studied. It is definitely an evaluative tool, although it is neither a test nor a technique. Its uses desirably extend through the entire educational career of the pupil and beyond his school career into his postschool life. The purposes of the cumulative record listed by Allen [6] indicate its usefulness as an evaluative tool.

1. To secure an over-all picture of the past experiences of each student.
2. To facilitate the study of exceptionally able and exceptionally handicapped children.
3. To help a teacher determine the characteristics of a group of students.
4. To aid in discovering the extent to which students are progressing toward the objectives which the school has accepted.
5. To provide data essential to an adviser when he attempts to aid students in selecting curricular and extracurricular experiences and when he endeavors to promote their social, health, educational, and vocational adjustment.

[6] Wendell C. Allen, *Cumulative Pupil Records*, pp. 4–5, Bureau of Publications, Teachers College, Columbia University, New York, 1943.

Cumulative records differ widely in the information for which they make provision and even more widely in their ways of providing for the recording of information. However, there are certain elements common to a large majority of cumulative record systems. Leonard and Tucker found in a study of the cumulative record systems in 870 high schools [7] that the following types of information were provided for most frequently: (*a*) personal data, (*b*) teachers' marks, (*c*) attendance data, (*d*) intelligence test scores, (*e*) parent's occupation, (*f*) medical data, (*g*) extracurricular activities, (*h*) achievement test scores, (*i*) dental data, (*j*) counselor's interviews, (*k*) social, personality, and interest ratings, (*l*) home and family conditions, (*m*) records of out-of-school and nongainful activities, (*n*) part- or full-time employment record, (*o*) special aptitudes, (*p*) teachers' observations and, anecdotes, and (*q*) parents' education. The significance of such information in a form readily available to the teacher is too obvious to warrant discussion.

Case studies. The attempt is made in a case study to gain such an understanding of an individual pupil and his problems as will serve for a foundation in working to attain better adjustment for him. Basic procedures are essentially similar, although vastly different in scope and in demands upon the persons making such a study, in a mild case of reading deficiency and in an acutely serious case of personality maladjustment. The problem in the first type of case is essentially that involved in diagnosis and remediation of a complex skill deficiency. The problem in the second type of case is representative of the usual broad scope of the case study. Case studies are probably most meaningful in instances where pupils are seriously maladjusted or where they may not be achieving at a level commensurate with their abilities for achievement.

A case study requires as a first step, after the cruciality of certain circumstances has made one advisable, the assembling of complete and reliable information about the pupil. This step is one of assembling and organizing the information in what is known as a case history. A complete cumulative record concerning a pupil may sometimes furnish all

[7] Eugenie A. Leonard and Anthony C. Tucker, *The Individual Inventory in Guidance Programs in Secondary Schools*, Vocational Division Bulletin 215, Occupational Information and Guidance Series 7, p. 11, U.S. Government Printing Office, Washington, D.C., 1941.

information needed for a case history, although it is often necessary to supplement cumulative record data by information gained from other sources. It may be desirable to interview the pupil's parents, his teachers, and any others who may have significant information to contribute. It may be desirable to have the pupil take certain tests, and even to interview the pupil.

When case history materials have been assembled and meaningfully organized, they should be studied carefully in the light of the pupil's problem. A tentative diagnosis should emerge from this study and serve as the foundation for a plan of treatment. It is desirable, in completing the case study proper, to prepare a written report of the case history, the tentative diagnosis, and the plan of treatment, and to submit the written report to other members of the school staff for their reactions. Revisions in the diagnosis or plan for treatment may be advisable if interpretations of others throw new light on the case.

Although the case study proper may well end with this step, the most important outcomes are those which follow. The treatment should be applied and its results evaluated over a sufficient period of time to permit of an adequate tryout. Modifications and revisions in the treatment may sometimes be desirable.

STUDYING THE SCHOOL

As democratic principles of school administration gain wider acceptance, teachers more frequently become active participants in the evaluation and planning of the school offerings. Evaluation of the school program goes beyond pupil evaluation in many ways and employs special techniques, but the point of view that the best measure of school efficiency is found in its pupil products is generally accepted today. Although the pupils and ex-pupils are used in school evaluation practices, the tendency to appraise the school mainly in terms of how pupil achievement test scores compare with norms and in terms of the percentage of its graduates who go to college is becoming less prevalent. Other and more fundamental criteria of school quality have recently been evolved.

Evaluative techniques. Two approaches to secondary-school evaluation within the last 15 years are sufficiently important to merit mention, although they by no means represent all types of secondary-school evaluative techniques. The first is the Cooperative Study of Secondary School Standards and the second is the Eight-year Study of the Progressive Education Association.

Cooperative Study of Secondary School Standards. This study of how to evaluate a secondary school, a cooperative enterprise sponsored by several educational organizations, extended over a period of some years prior to 1940. The result is an integrated set of materials recommended for use by the staff of a school and by a visiting committee of educators in evaluating the local school. Such measures of local school efficiency as are found in the postschool careers of former pupils and in the opinions of pupils and former pupils about the school supplement and aid in the evaluations of the school staff and the visiting committee. The intent is that a secondary school be studied

expressly in terms of its own philosophy of education, its individually stated purposes and objectives, the nature of the pupils with whom it has to deal, the needs of the community it serves, and the nature of the American democracy of which it is a part.[8]

Results are given meaning by the use of educational thermometers which show the position of the local school in relation to that of other schools on nine major characteristics: (*a*) curriculum and courses of study, (*b*) pupil activity program, (*c*) library service, (*d*) guidance service, (*e*) instruction, (*f*) outcomes of the educational program, (*g*) school staff, (*h*) school plant, and (*i*) school administration.[9]

Eight-year Study of Progressive Schools. This comprehensive study of 30 progressive secondary schools was carried on for some years prior to 1942. The entire study involved much which goes far beyond the direct province of evaluation, as in the development of new courses to meet broader objectives than were provided for in existing courses and in arrangements with collegiate institutions for special admissions procedures to apply for certain pupils used in the study. However, the over-all purpose was that of evaluating the program of the 30 schools, and the evaluative instruments and tools evolved in the study have con-

[8] Cooperative Study of Secondary School Standards, *Evaluative Criteria*, 1940 ed., Cooperative Study of Secondary School Standards, Washington, D.C., 1939.
[9] Cooperative Study of Secondary School Standards, *Evaluation of Secondary Schools: General Report*, Cooperative Study of Secondary School Standards, Washington, D.C., 1939.

tributed significantly to the available supply of such instruments and to the use of new techniques.

Results of the evaluative portion of the study having most pertinence in pupil evaluation by the teacher were reported by Smith, Tyler, and their colleagues.[10] Some of the material in Chap. 14 above was drawn from this source. Representative of follow-up studies of former secondary-school pupils into their postschool lives is the report by Chamberlin and others concerning the college careers of pupils involved in the Eight-year Study.[11] The 30 schools furnished still another type of over-all evaluation.[12]

Other evaluative studies. As is implied above, evaluative studies often assume the proportion and the technicalities of research studies. Although the teacher should not be expected to conduct highly technical research, for his duties and responsibilities for research are ordinarily those of a willing participant upon request, Waples and Tyler discussed nontechnical research in the study of classroom problems as a proper sphere for the teacher.[13] Many studies properly considered to be evaluative deal with classroom problems of sufficiently narrow scope to permit of comparable, nontechnical studies by teachers in the solution of their problems.

Various other quite general but extensive evaluative studies are worthy of passing mention. They range from evaluation by former pupils,[14] through evaluation in terms of the holding power of the school,[15] to comparisons of pupil performances in different types of schools.[16]

[10] Eugene R. Smith, Ralph W. Tyler, *et al., Appraising and Recording Student Progress*, Harper & Brothers, New York, 1942.

[11] Dean Chamberlin, *et al., Did They Succeed in College?* Harper & Brothers, New York, 1942.

[12] Commission on the Relation of Secondary School and College, Progressive Education Association, *Thirty Schools Tell Their Story*, Harper & Brothers, New York, 1943.

[13] Douglas Waples and Ralph W. Tyler, *Research Methods and Teachers' Problems*, The Macmillan Company, New York, 1930.

[14] University High School Class of 1938, Ohio State University, *Were We Guinea Pigs?* Henry Holt and Company, Inc., New York, 1938; and Howard M. Bell, *Youth Tell Their Story*, American Council on Education, Washington, D.C., 1938.

[15] Francis T. Spaulding, *High School and Life*, McGraw-Hill Book Company, Inc., New York, 1938.

[16] J. Paul Leonard and Alvin C. Eurich (Eds.), *An Evaluation of Modern Education*, D. Appleton-Century Company, Inc., New York, 1942; and J. Wayne

EVALUATING THE TEACHER

Teachers have long been exposed to evaluation by their pupils and the pupils' parents, by the community in general, by the school administration, and by themselves. It is doubtless true that many of the resulting evaluations have more often been founded on subjective opinion and incomplete objective evidence than on the intrinsic factors of quality in a teacher. Tendencies to rate teachers in terms of the demands they make of pupils, in terms of their conformance to local standards of conduct, and in terms of the scores made by their pupils on standardized achievement tests illustrate the arbitrary bases sometimes used in their evaluation. With proper controls and with appropriate emphasis, each of these may justifiably be included in teacher evaluation techniques, but when used casually and unscientifically they may be directly harmful to the teacher and indirectly harmful to the school.

Teachers can obtain evaluations of the degree to which they possess certain learnings and understandings deemed important in teachers by taking the *National Teacher Examinations*,[17] which include general tests in reasoning ability, English, general culture, professional information, current affairs, and specialized tests in nine secondary-school subject areas from which candidates may make appropriate selections. They may also obtain and individually use the *How I Teach* inventory,[18] which measures understanding of those aspects of child and adolescent psychology a teacher should possess. Results returned by the National Committee on Teacher Examinations for the first and scores obtained by the teacher himself on the second may be interpreted by the use of appropriate norms in obtaining a rating on these understandings important to teachers.

Case study materials designed for use in teacher education classes but also subject to use by teachers individually or in small study groups for self-evaluation are those of Mickey Murphy[19] and of Barrie Black,

Wrightstone, *Appraisal of Experimental High School Practices*, Bureau of Publications, Teachers College, Columbia University, New York, 1931.

[17] Scheduled annually, usually in February, in many examining centers throughout the country by the National Committee on Teacher Examinations, Princeton, N.J.

[18] Ida B. Kelly and Keith J. Perkins, *Purdue Teachers Examination: How I Teach*, Educational Test Bureau, Minneapolis, 1942.

[19] Warren R. Baller, *The Case of Mickey Murphy*, University of Nebraska, Lincoln, Neb., 1943.

Connie Casey, and Sam Smith.[20] These case studies measure teacher understanding of evaluative instruments and techniques, their use in diagnosis of pupil maladjustment, and the selection of appropriate remedial procedures.

Pupil ratings of teachers can be obtained by teachers themselves through the use of the *Bryan-Yntema Rating Scale for the Evaluation of Student Reactions*,[21] which requests pupils to answer 13 questions dealing with teacher practices, or even by the use of an informal questionnaire constructed by the teacher himself. It is believed by exponents of pupil ratings of teachers that judgments are obtained on highly important aspects of teacher-pupil relationships not obtainable otherwise. It is, of course, essential that pupils be granted anonymity in their responses if unbiased opinions are to be obtained.

SUMMARY

Comprehensive pupil appraisal involves much more than the selection and construction of such tests, techniques, and evaluative tools as were discussed and illustrated in Chaps. 8, 11, and 14. Those chapters were concerned primarily with means of appraising the attainment of instructional outcomes by high-school pupils taught under the daily-assignment, the subject-matter unit, and the experience unit methods of instruction.

Two types of understandings are basically important in a teacher who can participate effectively in a well-rounded program of pupil evaluation. The first is concerned with the nature and degree of those differences—individual, trait, and group—which distinguish individuals from each other, which point up variation within the individual, and which characterize groups differing in some major respect. The second is concerned with the various types of derived scores by the use of which evaluation results are given meaning.

The child comes to the school with largely predetermined mental and physical characteristics of various types. He comes also with an environmental background of experiences which cannot, of course, be

[20] John E. Horrocks and Maurice E. Troyer, (1) *A Study of Barrie Black*, (2) *A Study of Connie Casey*, and (3) *A Study of Sam Smith*, Syracuse University Press, Syracuse, N.Y., 1946.

[21] R. C. Bryan and O. Yntema, *A Manual on the Evaluation of Student Reactions in Secondary Schools*, Western State Teachers College, Kalamazoo, Mich., 1939.

modified. What he is today, and consequently what the teacher has to work with, is the resultant of his hereditary and environmental backgrounds. The teacher, in order to understand the pupil, should have an understanding of his mental and physical aptitudes, his environmental background, and his present characteristics. General intelligence and aptitude tests, measures of physical aptitudes, and measures of socioeconomic status contribute largely to this type of understanding. Evaluative techniques and tools of these types are introduced in this chapter.

In teaching the pupil, the teacher needs to employ additional tests, techniques, and tools of the types dealt with at some length in Chaps. 8, 11, and 14. In guiding the pupil, the teacher should often supplement information of the above types by that which is found in the cumulative records and by that which is evolved from use of the case study.

The teacher should also be concerned with the evaluation of the school program as a whole and with the evaluation of his success as a teacher. Various techniques and tools designed for these purposes are available for his use.

SELECTED REFERENCES

ALLEN, WENDELL C.: *Cumulative Pupil Records*, Bureau of Publications, Teachers College, Columbia University, New York, 1943.

BINGHAM, WALTER V.: *Aptitudes and Aptitude Testing*, Harper & Brothers, New York, 1937.

BRUECKNER, LEO J., and MELBY, ERNEST O.: *Diagnostic and Remedial Teaching*, Chap. 4, Houghton Mifflin Company, Boston, 1931.

DARLEY, JOHN G.: *Testing and Counseling in the High School Guidance Program*, Chaps. 2, 4, 6, Science Research Associates, Chicago, 1943.

DRISCOLL, GERTRUDE: *How to Study the Behavior of Children*, Practical Suggestions for Teaching 2, Bureau of Publications, Teachers College, Columbia University, New York, 1941.

FREEMAN, FRANK N.: *Mental Tests: Their History, Principles, and Applications*, rev. ed., Houghton Mifflin Company, Boston, 1939.

FROEHLICH, CLIFFORD P., and BENSON, ARTHUR L.: *Guidance Testing*, Science Research Associates, Chicago, 1948.

GREENE, EDWARD B.: *Measurements of Human Behavior*, Chaps. 10–11, The Odyssey Press, Inc., New York, 1941.

LINCOLN, EDWARD A., and WORKMAN, LINWOOD L.: *Testing and the Use of Test Results*, Chaps. 4–5, 12, The Macmillan Company, New York, 1935.

Mathematics in General Education, Chap. 12, Report of the Committee on the Function of Mathematics in General Education, Commission on Secondary School Curriculum, Progressive Education Association, D. Appleton-Century Company, Inc., New York, 1940.

ORLEANS, JACOB S.: *Measurement in Education*, Chap. 8, Thomas Nelson & Sons, New York, 1937.

REMMERS, H. H., and GAGE, N. L.: *Educational Measurement and Evaluation*, Chaps. 3–7, 13–16, Harper & Brothers, New York, 1943.

RUCH, GILES M., and SEGEL, DAVID: *Minimum Essentials of the Individual Inventory in Guidance*, Vocational Division Bulletin 202, Occupational Information and Guidance Series 2, U.S. Government Printing Office, Washington, D.C., 1940.

Science in General Education, Chap. 8, Report of the Committee on the Function of Science in General Education, Commission on Secondary School Curriculum, Progressive Education Association, D. Appleton-Century Company, Inc., New York, 1937.

SEGEL, DAVID (Chairman): *Handbook of Cumulative Records*, Bulletin 5, U.S. Office of Education, Washington, D.C., 1944.

TRAXLER, ARTHUR E.: *Case Study Procedures in Guidance*, Educational Records Supplementary Bulletin B (Revised), Educational Records Bureau, New York, January, 1940.

WOOD, BEN D., and HAEFNER, RALPH: *Measuring and Guiding Individual Growth*, Silver Burdett Company, New York, 1948.

Chapter 17. THE TEACHER AS A COUNSELOR

Teachers have always been counselors of pupils even though they may not have considered themselves such, and may not have performed this function well; certainly the effective teacher today and in the future must include this activity among his many duties. The question here, therefore, is not whether or not the teacher will or can serve as a counselor, but how can this function be performed effectively by all teachers.

A DEFINITION OF COUNSELING

Counseling is a dynamic, personal, and face-to-face relationship between two individuals, to which counselees bring their more or less well-defined problems for solution through mutual endeavor. The relationship, if proper for counseling success, is dynamic in the sense that both the counselor and the counselee experience growth in skills, understandings, and attitudes. The very experience of being face to face will modify the behavior of each. The relationship is personal in the sense that mutual respect, reciprocal consideration, understanding, and empathy constitute the core and set the tone of the relationship. Finally, counseling is most successful when nurtured in face-to-face situations, such as found in interviews, conversations, informal contacts, or truly democratic classrooms.

THE PURPOSE OF COUNSELING IN THE SCHOOLS OF A DEMOCRACY

The purpose of the counseling activity in the schools of a democracy is to provide opportunities for pupils to secure assistance in solving their problems in such a manner that the ability to solve problems unassisted will be developed. The counselor (teacher) and counselee (pupil) attempt more carefully to define the problem at hand and to approach its solution with mutual consideration for each other. It is a joint quest, a cooperative venture. The common goal is that the counselee will be able to arrive at a self-determined wise solution. The assistance that is given is only in the amount and of the nature necessary to enable the counselee to solve his own problems. Pupils cannot learn how to solve their own problems if counselors and other adults continue to solve them for them; in fact, they become more and more dependent upon others for the solution of future problems when they are thus freed of the responsibility for self-direction. Just enough help should be given so that pupils learn how to attack and solve problems in an intelligent manner. When this is done, the solution of one problem will add to the ability to solve other problems with less help than before.

The solution of problems involving changes in human behavior, attitudes, or understandings requires a plan of action. Such plans are most likely to be tried or carried out by the pupil if he shares in deciding what the plan will be and makes the decision himself to carry it out. If the resulting behavior provides maximum extension of the individual's freedom and provides opportunity for self-realization, then the decisions which brought about the changes in behavior are called wise decisions. If, in addition, due consideration is given to the rights of others and common problems are solved cooperatively, the process of problem solving in the counseling relationship becomes a truly democratic process.

Except for those cases in which the underlying causes are complex and deep-seated, counseling in a totalitarian society demands that the counselor dictate the solution of the problem to the counselee and insists upon blind obedience in carrying out the dictated plan of solution. It would not be desirable under dictatorships for pupils to learn how to make their own decisions and solve their own problems. Furthermore, in an aristocracy, counseling for the masses must be largely prescriptive in nature. The opportunity for making self-determined solutions to problems is reserved to persons from the higher echelons of the social structure.

In a democratic society, on the other hand, citizens have not only the privilege of making decisions for themselves, but also the responsibility for doing so, both as individuals and as members of many small and large groups.

THE ROLE OF THE TEACHER–COUNSELOR

When individuals make decisions they use habits, techniques, attitudes, interests, ideals, emotions, and experience. In a democratic society, the decisions become increasingly wiser if new facts are added to the experiences; the more facts and information, the better. This is not to exclude emotions, attitudes, ideals, and interests. The need is for a proper balance between intelligence and feeling.

The teacher in the schools of a democratic society is in a strategic position to perform the counseling function involving problems of a distributive nature and of overt, immediate behavior. Distributive problems are those in which a choice must be made regarding such things as courses, schools, vocations, and group activities. One who is well informed on sources of reliable information regarding the nature and requirements of courses of training, schools, activities, and occupations, and who can interpret the meaning of adequate cumulative data regarding individual pupils can attain a large degree of success in counseling on problems of this nature.

Such counseling to be successful presupposes a warm, friendly relationship between the teacher and the pupil. It also requires skill on the part of the teacher to carry on the process of decision making in a genuinely cooperative manner. The constant goal is that the pupil shall make wise decisions for and by himself.

If the school has the services of guidance specialists, the teacher will be extremely helpful if he furnishes all the information he has accumulated about the pupil to the guidance specialist. These guidance specialists will in turn use the data as they counsel the pupil. The teacher can also be helpful by making adjustments within the classroom so that the pupil can carry out his plan of action. Since there are about 3,000 students per trained counselor in the schools of the United States, it is quite obvious that for many years to come, teachers will have to perform most counseling functions without the help of guidance specialists.

If a teacher in a secondary school understands adolescent behavior, and has a knowledge of the abilities and desires of each pupil and of the resources for physical, social, and spiritual development in the school and community, he can attain considerable success in counseling with immediate problems of adjustment. These problems most frequently involve pupil-teacher, pupil-parent, and pupil-pupil relationships, and minor behavior difficulties.

As a teacher becomes successful in dealing with counseling problems of a distributive nature and those involving immediate behavior, he will soon find himself confronted with problems of emotional involvement which require some therapy and reeducation. If these problems are not too deep-seated, the teacher may become fairly effective in handling them, by either preceding or paralleling the counseling with in-service training activities. He could take formal counseling training in universities or agencies, read selected materials, and try different methods in working with these students on an experimental basis. When possible, cases of this level should be referred to a guidance specialist, school psychologist, or visiting teacher (psychiatric social worker).

One very popular method of working with cases of this nature is clearly defined and demonstrated in the writings of Carl R. Rogers. Dr. Rogers believes there is within each person the ability to solve his problems if a counselor can but release him from the emotional obstacles which make it difficult for him to solve them. The entire responsibility for the solutions is placed on the counselee. The following list of counseling steps, adapted by Traxler from Rogers, represents the development of this kind of counseling relationship:

1. The student asks his counselor for help and states the situation as he sees it.

2. The counselor and student discuss the situation until the problem is clearly defined.

3. The counselor leads the student to talk about the problem at length. In the beginning, the individual's statements about the problem will in all probability be negative. That is, he will talk about how difficult the problem is or how unendurable the situation, and how thoroughly disgusted he is with the whole business.

4. Instead of criticizing this attitude, the counselor accepts it as normal and logical. He does not show approval, but he avoids creating antagonism by trying to force a different attitude at this point.

5. After the individual has "talked himself out," the counselor, by means of appropriate suggestions, leads him to begin consideration of the positive side of the situation.

6. The counselor accepts the positive suggestions of the individual calmly and thoughtfully, and voices approval when the individual seems to be on the right track.

7. As the subject talks on the positive side, he begins to develop insight and to formulate a plan of action.

8. The counselor allows the individual to do most of the planning, but keeping in mind the accumulated information he has about this student, he tries to steer him into a course of action consistent with his abilities and with the problem at hand.

9. The individual puts his plan into action, thereby acquiring further understanding of the problem.

10. He develops an integrated and successful program of action, loses his need for the counselor, and terminates the guidance relationship as far as it applies to this problem.[1]

The steps above are not necessarily serial or mutually exclusive. The important element is that the pupil takes positive self-initiated steps which will insure an extension of his own personal freedom and self-realization.

As pupils bring problems which are more deep-seated and complex, and as teachers find pupils severely emotionally disturbed, they will find an increasing need for skill in recognizing cases which they do not have the skill or time to handle. A thorough familiarization with agencies in the community which can be of help will enable them to refer cases more intelligently.

COUNSELING IN INDIVIDUAL AND GROUP SITUATIONS

Counseling as defined here can take place in both individual and group situations. When students have problems of a very personal nature, and when the considerations involve fine discriminations and deep-seated emotional involvement, counseling is most effective if performed individually. The counseling relationship as presented here can also take place in groups the size of the average classroom. In fact, there are certain problems which seem to be more efficiently solved in group situations than in individual relationships. One example would be the solving of problems in which there is need for pupils to know that other pupils are confronted with the same difficulties. Generally speaking, the more common a problem is within a group, the more likely is counseling in groups to be helpful in solving the problem. A few examples of specific problems may illustrate the point. If most of

[1] Arthur E. Taxler, *Techniques of Guidance*, p. 339, Harper & Brothers, New York, 1945.

the students are emotionally disturbed regarding their outcome on a specific examination, a group attack on the problem with a resulting plan of action should reduce the emotional involvement to a considerable degree. Psychiatrists and psychologists during The Second World War found that counseling in group situations helped soldiers suffering from combat fatigue to make more rapid recovery than was possible through individual techniques alone. Another example can be taken from the field of vocational choice. If it is demonstrated in a group that certain members of the group are considering all their strengths and weaknesses in connection with the choosing and rejection of certain occupations, other members of the group may be motivated to do the same thing. Also, in solving problems of classroom behavior, there seems to be considerable evidence that role-playing [2] and feed-back [3] procedures in classroom situations are quite effective in helping students grow in the ability to make wise decisions in both school and non-school behavior.[4]

This is not to state that counseling in group activities will adequately meet the demands for counseling services in a school. There are many kinds of problems, and problems of considerable complexity and depth which cannot be solved except when individual counseling

[2] In role playing, pupils reenact behavior episodes for the purpose of studying their own behavior and learning how to control it. Suppose two pupils want a single copy of a book at the same time and the conflict results in physical blows. After the teacher resolves the immediate conflict and the emotion has subsided, either the pupils involved change roles, or other pupils may play one or both the roles, to reenact the conflict from its beginning, recalling as nearly as possible the words and actions of the episode. The class then participates in a discussion of why the conflict took place. When the motivations and causes of the conflict seem to be defined, the entire class offers suggestions as to how the conflict could have been avoided by another way of behaving. Then the two pupils are given an opportunity to practice the new way of behaving.

[3] The feed-back activity is another technique which can provide opportunities for pupils to make decisions regarding their own behavior. A rotation plan is used whereby pupils are given an opportunity to make observations of the activity of their classmates for a 15- or 20-minute period of time. At the end of this observation period, the observers "feed back" the behavior of pupils observed by reading to them a description of their behavior. All of the pupils discuss these observations from the standpoint of profitable use of time, social relationships, and other factors. The students who have been observed are then given an opportunity to suggest a better way of behaving during future classroom periods. Opportunity is also given to their fellow pupils to offer suggestions for improving the behavior.

[4] Teachers who are interested in these techniques should contact the Research Center for Group Dynamics, University of Michigan, Ann Arbor, Mich.

services are utilized. In so far as possible, individual counseling and counseling in and through group activities should be complementary to each other. In each instance there must be the type of counseling relationship and problem-solving activity which will merit the name of counseling.

SOME TOOLS OF THE TEACHER–COUNSELOR

At whatever level of counseling the teacher finds himself competent, he will become increasingly effective if he learns more and more about each individual pupil and the consequences of the choices which pupils as counselees are likely to make. This information about pupils can be secured from cumulative records (which the pupil should help maintain), tests, inventories, autobiographical data, observations, anecdotal records, rating scales, behavior descriptions, and interviews with the pupils, their peers, parents, teachers, and other professional workers.

The cumulative record. The beginning teacher is fortunate who secures a position in a school that has already developed an adequate system of cumulative records for each pupil. In situations of this kind, the teacher will want to evaluate cooperatively with the other members of the staff and administration the kinds of information which are found on the cumulative records. This evaluation should include such questions as: (*a*) Is the information being used to assist students to make wise choices and to assist teachers in their classroom teaching? (*b*) If the information found there is not being used, could it be used? (*c*) Should each kind of information be continued or dropped from the records? (*d*) What new kinds of information should be cumulated on the record which is not being recorded now?

Should the new teacher find himself in a school which does not maintain a cumulative record system, and no one has taken the initiative to bring about a discussion of the need for this indispensable tool of counseling, he should attempt to motivate the principal to provide an opportunity for staff consideration of the development of such a record. The procedure might be as follows: (*a*) Cooperative decision by the staff as to what items of information are of sufficient value to counselors and teachers to merit permanent recording. (*b*) Securing of copies of cumulative records which have been developed in many schools throughout the country. (*c*) Deciding what format would make these informations concise and quickly understandable. (*d*) Printing the final form agreed upon by all concerned. (*e*) Continuously evaluating and, if necessary, revising the form.

If all the teachers and administrators want to and are willing to do so, the data that are available could be transposed from present records to the new cumulative record forms for each pupil in the school. However, such a task is a large one and may develop negative attitudes in a staff towards the cumulative record system. If there is danger of this happening, possibly a better plan would be to start the cumulative records with the current incoming group of students. A compromise between the two plans is to start the cumulative record system with such groups as first-, fourth-, seventh-, and tenth-grade pupils. By repeating this for 3 years, the entire student body will have been accommodated.

The use of tests, inventories, autobiographical data, observations, anecdotal records, rating scales, behavior descriptions, and interviews in studying pupils and their development is presented in other chapters of this book. Since the interview is also the most important tool of the counseling process, it seems appropriate to develop it further here.

The interview. The counseling interview is a conversation with a purpose. The pupil comes to talk out his problems. The teacher listens, interprets, shares, and helps plan for the future. The teacher's behavior will change from interview to interview. He will govern his actions in relation to what he believes the counselee is thinking or feeling. Often the only help needed is that of making available pertinent information. Also, problems are sometimes solved without the interviewer saying a word. As the teacher listens, the pupil may objectify and gain insight into his worries as he talks. However, some problems require many interviews.

If possible, the teacher should plan his interviews in advance. Interviews tend to be more successful if the pupil wants them. A teacher will have to use various devices in securing this attitude. Some have arranged for test results to be given individually. Others have held group discussions on common problems and proffered individual assistance for those who desired it. As he gains a reputation for rendering valuable service to his counselees, they will seek his help.

Teachers should make every effort to hold their interviews in privacy and in pleasant surroundings. In many school buildings this presents a difficult problem. In one school the teachers gave up their lounge room for certain fixed periods of time. In another school the principal vacated his office for the use of interviewers during certain periods of the day. Personal relationships and confidences are rarely established when even a third person is present.

Furthermore, it is highly desirable that the teacher arrange the interviews so that he will not have to appear to be hurried. It is absolutely essential that the pupil feel that the counselor has sufficient time to make progress on the problem at hand. Even where large numbers of students need the service, it is quite likely that a relationship worthy of the title of counseling cannot be established when the interview period is less than 15 to 20 minutes in length. Many busy counselors seldom schedule interviews more frequently than at half-hour periods.

Finally, unless the interview is a cold interview (that is, the pupil comes for help unannounced), the teacher should read all available cumulated information before the pupil arrives. As a teacher goes over the cumulative record, he should raise such questions as these:

What are discrepancies in the record? What are the trends? Are there sudden and marked changes in achievement, health, or social behavior? Why? What does the student do best? In what area does he do the poorest work? Why does he think he wants to become an engineer? Is he aware of the science and mathematics hurdles? Do his hobbies and other activities indicate genuine interest in the field? When did he decide to become an engineer? How did he happen to choose engineering instead of one of the other professions? What do his parents think about his choice? Can he afford the training? Is he physically able to carry it out? What does he expect to get from the occupation? What evidences are present to indicate that he has a chance to realize his plan? Is his choice on too high a level in the field? Such questions as these, and many others, must "run through" the teacher's mind. While it is impossible for one to predict the content and outcomes of an interview, the teacher will be much more skillful in capitalizing on the opportunities which present themselves if he has become well oriented about the student and his probable problems before the actual interview takes place.

Ruth Strang has proposed a self-rating scale for the interview procedure which can serve both as suggested procedures for conducting the interview and as a check list for evaluating the quality of the interview. The teacher can indicate with a cross the point on the line between the two extremes where he believes his interview belongs. Most experts would agree that the more successful ones are at the left, and the less successful ones at the right. The beginning interviewer will develop a sensitivity to the poor and good features of his interviewing, if he applies the rating scale to most of his early interviews.

SCALE FOR RATING INTERVIEWS

1. What was the setting for the interview?

Plenty of time scheduled	Insufficient time
Feeling of leisure	People waiting
Privacy	People bustling in and out
Pleasant lighting, and other provisions for interviewee's comfort	Telephone to be answered
	Desk cluttered with work to do
	Glare and other discomforts

2. What was the appearance and manner of the interviewer?

Pleasant voice	Unpleasant voice
Alert and keen	Fatigued, dull
Good health	Poor health
Poise and reasonable self-confidence	Uncertain and insecure
At ease	Ill at ease, bored
Cordial	Indifferent
Genuine interest in interviewee	Patronizing

3. How did the interviewee respond conversationally during the interview?

Talked freely	Tended only to answer questions or refused to answer them
Tried to think through the problem aloud	Uncommunicative
	Unwilling to accept his responsibility in the interview

4. How did interviewer encourage the individual to get an understanding of himself and his relationships?

Successfully	Unsuccessfully
By repeating his most significant remarks	By being completely passive
	By telling interviewee what to do
By following, in a natural way clues the interviewee gave	By arguing or criticizing
By asking questions to clarify certain points	By probing
By interpreting the interviewee's remarks	By interpreting before interviewee was ready for it

5. How did the attitude of interviewee change during the interview?

Interviewee gained new and valuable insights and orientation; felt more hopeful and more confident in his ability to handle the situation; became increasingly independent of the interviewer; had a more friendly relationship	Interviewee became increasingly dependent upon the interviewer; took less responsibility for thinking through the situation himself; less self-confident; more hopeless; more resistant to counselor

6. What kind of plan resulted from the interview?

A plan worked out primarily by the interviewee—realistic and possible of being carried out	A "ready-made plan," which the interviewer imposed upon the student

7. What was the effect of the interview on subsequent relationship with interviewer?

Student was able to carry out plan; came voluntarily to the interviewer when he needed further help	No favorable change in behavior; student avoided coming to the interviewer again [5]

Facts and information in counseling. One of the skills a teacher-counselor needs is the ability to secure information about the pupil and his problem, and to interpret this information to the pupil. In vocational counseling, for example, the teacher may wish to go far beyond the cumulative record and the results of interviews to help a pupil decide his vocational potentiality in the field of chemistry. A course mark of 97 in chemistry which may be found on the pupil's cumulative record may represent many things. The teacher needs to know if the mark represents mostly the results of a standardized achievement test in chemistry or if it is a composite of the test score, classroom and laboratory activity, and general attitude. The teacher needs to know how nearly the class and laboratory activities simulated the actual work of the chemist and how adequately the course was oriented to vocational motivations. Did the pupil show a zest for learning chemistry? Did he do only the minimum assignments well, or did he perform numerous extra activities, such as belonging to the chemistry club, setting up a chemistry laboratory at

[5] Ruth Strang, *Role of the Teacher in Personnel Work*, pp. 408–410, Bureau of Publications, Teachers College, Columbia University, New York, 1946.

home, or securing part-time employment in a drugstore or a chemical factory?

The teacher must also be well informed about occupations in the field of chemistry or of the sources of information in the field which he and the pupil must tap. What characteristics are needed for success in the training and on the job? What are the advantages and disadvantages of the vocation? Are the opportunities waxing or waning? These and many other questions must be answered.

In the "traditional" school this information must be secured "outside" of the regular school activities. In the modern or life-experience school the above information becomes a part of the curriculum itself. Some "traditional" schools have introduced transitional "potpourri" group activities which are frequently misnamed group guidance classes. Needed information which is not taught in the "curriculum" is dumped into the group guidance periods. Generally included are such topics as facts about our school, social skills, citizenship, worthy use of leisure time, health, educational, and vocational information. Information of this kind should be a part of the regular curriculum and taught by teachers. These teachers will need to use films, film slides, books, pamphlets, newspapers, magazines, radio, dramatization, trips to places of work and institutions, lectures, discussions, tryout experiences, and many other teaching methods.

It is the duty of the teacher-counselor to synthesize all of the obtainable information about the pupil and about the occupation in such manner as to test the validity of the prediction of success in the occupation which the pupil is considering. Then the teacher must interpret the information to the pupil in the language of the latter in order that the pupil may be able to use the information in making the final choice.

COUNSELING IN RELATION TO INSTRUCTIONAL PROCEDURES

Consideration may now be given to the opportunities and limitations for counseling in the daily-assignment or recitation method, the subject-matter unit method, and the experience unit method. The question is not whether or not counseling can take place in schools or classrooms which use any one of these plans; the question is, rather, "What are the relative opportunities for building meaningful counseling situations in each plan?" As these plans are approached, it is well to recall again that the purpose of counseling is to assist students to make wise decisions, to develop plans of action, to enter into and progress in these plans of action in such a manner as to insure growth in the ability to carry on such activities unassisted.

Counseling in the "recitation" school. Since the counseling process takes time, one can readily see that the teacher who uses the daily-assignment or recitation method will find it extremely difficult to include adequate counseling services during his very busy day. Since he had predetermined that the pupils should "cover" a specific number of pages in each of the recitation periods of the school year, any interruptions in that schedule would naturally tend to create some anxiety and frustration on the part of both the teacher and the pupils. It should also be remembered that the teacher has worked out the objectives for each day's activity and has written them into his daily plan. The teacher also makes the assignment, provides the motivations, sets up suitable conditions for study, estimates the progress of the group, and spends some time in relating the subject matter to the personal interests of the pupils. If these are accomplished entirely by the teacher, it is obvious that the pupils have little opportunity to make decisions on their own.

Teachers as a group are highly selected and are relatively competent adults. It would be excellent if their experience and abilities could be used in helping pupils learn how to make decisions which require plans of action. The teacher who uses the recitation plan, and who wishes to help pupils learn how to make decisions, can take a few minutes from the daily class period to permit the students to suggest objectives. The teacher's comments will assist the pupils in determining whether or not they have made wise choices of objectives. These teachers will also use more thought questions than recall questions. This, too, will contribute towards developing choice-making skill on the part of the pupils in that it will give them practice in collecting, evaluating, and using facts. These teachers will also use a variety of classroom techniques, such as lectures, committee work, group discussions, audio-visual aids, and others. If the purpose in using the various techniques is made known to the pupils, they will have an opportunity to learn how to use such techniques in their own decision making.

The socialized recitation provides many more opportunities for pupils to make decisions than when they are required only to recall information they have read. They can decide what information they could contribute which would be pertinent to the subject of discussion.

They can decide how they should behave in order that all students can make a contribution, and it is quite possible that decisions by the group can be made the climax of the socialized recitation period.

Counseling in the "subject-matter" school. The subject-matter unit method provides still more opportunities for teachers to work with pupils in developing skill in making wise decisions. Generally, the teacher seems to have more time to provide these opportunities. The urge to "cover ground" is not as strong as in the daily-assignment or recitation method. Even though the objectives of the unit have been predetermined by the teacher, opportunities can be provided for pupils to make decisions regarding the feasibility of the stated objectives, their revision, and possible extension. As in the recitation method, however, decisions regarding objectives are likely to be highly controlled by the teacher because of the previous work he had spent in preparing the unit.

Opportunities for choice making are present in the selection of activities which are suggested on the guide sheet. The pupil is encouraged to discover and choose additional activities which may be of value in obtaining the objectives agreed upon. Since pupils are permitted to proceed at their own rate of learning, and are given opportunities to choose activities which they are capable of accomplishing and which challenge them, the environment of the subject-matter plan tends to stimulate the student when he makes wise decisions and to bring him dissatisfaction when he makes unwise decisions.

Opportunities for decision making are less limited and could be made available in selecting proper integration activities in the culminating phase of the subject-matter unit. This tends, however, to become a teacher-dominated choice because of the amount of training and experience needed to make these choices.

Opportunities for self-evaluation are possible in the appraisal of the outcome phase of the subject-matter unit. It is during this period that the teacher has a genuine opportunity to help students learn how to evaluate their skills, attitudes, and appreciations. The more able the student is to make objective and valid evaluations of himself, the more able he will be to make wise decisions regarding his future behaviors.

The whole procedure of the subject-matter method, particularly the pattern known as the Morrison Plan, gives the student practice in approaching his own problem solving. These activities will be more meaningful if the teacher can assist the pupil in seeing the relationship between the attack on the problem in a subject-matter unit and the attack upon real-life problems. Attack, study, integration, and evaluation are common to both. However, it cannot be assumed that the pupil's pattern of attack on the subject-matter unit will automatically transfer to life situations. The carry-over into real-life situations is almost negligible unless the teacher points out the similarity of the procedures used in the school and in nonschool situations.

Counseling in the "experience" school. Practice in problem solving that will enable students to make wise decisions in real-life situations can be implemented most effectively in the experience unit method as described in Chaps. 12 and 13. The school which uses the experience unit method provides the greatest opportunity for effective counseling by the teacher. Counseling to help pupils solve problems is not relegated to occasional opportunities or to situations outside the classroom, such as takes place in the usual after-school interview. Opportunities are found within the daily ongoing activities of the pupils. Activities are chosen for their potentiality to solve immediate problems of pupils. Objectives are worked out by the pupils and the teacher. Even evaluation is on a share basis. One can readily see that the opportunities for making choices are ever present. As each pupil or group of pupils attempts to solve problems of immediate concern, he will have need for the counsel of one who is interested, sympathetic, and willing to help find satisfactory answers. All of the activities become a joint quest or shared venture. The teacher stimulates, encourages, listens, and provides help only where it is needed and to the extent that it is needed. Teachers in such an environment find it much easier to help pupils find answers to their problems, rather than to insist upon giving a teacher's answer to the problems. The practice of choice making is concerned with real-life situations and continues to serve the individual when he leaves the school environment. The school is life; leaving school is merely an extension of this living. And here, too, is democracy; students have not only the opportunity but the responsibility to study, examine, discuss, draw conclusions about, and try the conclusions reached regarding whatever problems or concerns that may arise from their experiences.

THE FUTURE

The point of view expressed in this chapter is a transitional one. The solution of the many complex problems of student adjustment cannot be left to the classroom teacher alone. He must have skilled assistance. School administrators should work toward providing a full-time, well-trained counselor for every 300 pupils or a well-trained teacher-counselor for every 150 pupils. The teacher-counselor would serve one-half of his time in the classroom.

Counseling is a complex and highly professional skill. Estimates of the minimum training period for the school counselor range from 1 to 3 years beyond the bachelor's degree. This training should include opportunity for internship under the supervision of skilled counselors. The quality of the counseling found in a school will be strongly influenced by the personality and professional training of those who assume the counseling responsibilities, whether these people are administrators, teachers, teacher-counselors, or full-time specialists.

SUMMARY

The teacher's contacts with his pupils throughout the school day and the school year provide numerous opportunities for counseling. These contacts may range from brief, informal conversations dealing with casual things to extended and numerous interviews dealing with problems that are more deep-seated. An effective teacher can build his counseling relationship upon the rapport he has established with his pupils in the classroom, laboratory, shop, or playground. His purpose in providing counseling opportunities for his pupils is to help them make decisions, develop plans of action, and carry them out in such manner as to insure the pupils' growth in the ability of self-direction. This growth is most possible in the experience-type school but may be developed to a lesser extent in the recitation and the subject-matter unit schools. Maximum skill in the ability to make wise decisions is needed by every adult member of a democratic society.

SELECTED REFERENCES

BAXTER, EDNA D.: An Approach to Guidance, D. Appleton-Century Company, Inc., New York, 1946.

BINGHAM, WALTER V., and MOORE, BRUCE V.: How to Interview, Harper & Brothers, New York, 1941.

CHISHOLM, LESLIE: *Guiding Youth in the Secondary School*, American Book Company, New York, 1945.

COX, PHILIP W. L., and DUFF, JOHN CARR: *Guidance and the Classroom Teacher*, Prentice-Hall, Inc., New York, 1942.

DARLEY, JOHN G.: *Testing and Counseling in the High School Guidance Program*, Science Research Associates, Chicago, 1943.

DAVIS, FRANK G. (Ed.): *Pupil Personnel Service*, International Textbook Company, Scranton, Pa., 1948.

DUNSMOOR, CLARENCE C., and MILLER, LEONARD M.: *Guidance Methods for Teachers in Homeroom, Classroom, Core Program*, International Textbook Company, Scranton, Pa., 1942.

ERICKSON, CLIFFORD E. (Ed.): *A Basic Text for Guidance Workers*, Prentice-Hall, Inc., New York, 1947.

———, and HAPP, MARION C.: *Guidance Practices at Work*, McGraw-Hill Book Company, Inc., New York, 1946.

GERMANE, CHARLES E., and GERMANE, EDITH H.: *Personnel Work in High School; A Program for the Guidance of Youth*, Silver Burdett Company, New York, 1941.

HAMRIN, SHIRLEY A., and ERICKSON, CLIFFORD E.: *Guidance in the Secondary School*, D. Appleton-Century Company, Inc., New York, 1939.

JONES, ARTHUR J.: *Principles of Guidance*, 3d ed., McGraw-Hill Book Company, Inc., New York, 1945.

KOOS, LEONARD V., and KEFAUVER, GRAYSON N.: *Guidance in Secondary Schools*, The Macmillan Company, New York, 1932.

LEFEVER, D. W., TURRELL, A. M., and WEITZEL, H. J.: *Principles and Techniques of Guidance*, The Ronald Press Company, New York, 1941.

McKOWN, HARRY C.: *Home Room Guidance*, McGraw-Hill Book Company, Inc., New York, 1946.

MYERS, GEORGE E.: *Principles and Techniques of Vocational Guidance*, McGraw-Hill Book Company, Inc., New York, 1941.

REED, ANNA Y.: *Guidance and Personnel Services in Education*, Cornell University Press, Ithaca, N.Y., 1944.

ROGERS, CARL R.: *Counseling and Psychotherapy*, Houghton Mifflin Company, Boston, 1942.

RUCH, GILES M., and SEGEL, DAVID: *Minimum Essentials of the Individual Inventory in Guidance*, U.S. Government Printing Office, Washington, D.C., 1940.

SMITH, CHARLES M., and ROOS, MARY M.: *Guide to Guidance*, Prentice-Hall, Inc., New York, 1946.

State Counselors Association, New York: *Practical Handbook for Counselors*, Science Research Associates, Chicago, 1945.

STRANG, RUTH: *Educational Guidance*, The Macmillan Company, New York, 1947.

——: *Pupil Personnel and Guidance*, The Macmillan Company, New York, 1940.

——: *The Role of the Teacher in Personnel Work*, 3d ed., Bureau of Publications, Teachers College, Columbia University, New York, 1946.

TRAXLER, ARTHUR E.: *Techniques of Guidance*, Harper & Brothers, New York, 1945.

WILLIAMSON, E. G.: *How to Counsel Students*, McGraw-Hill Book Company, Inc., New York, 1939.

——, and HAHN, M. E.: *Introduction to High School Counseling*, McGraw-Hill Book Company, Inc., New York, 1940.

Chapter 18. THE CONCEPT OF DISCIPLINE

AS AN ASPECT OF METHOD

In every teaching situation it is the responsibility of the teacher to see to it that conditions prevail in which learning can take place. This is true whether the instruction is conducted by the daily-assignment method, the subject-matter unit method, or the experience unit method. As the secondary schools relax the strict classroom control, which was typical of the traditional daily-assignment method, in favor of the freedom of action found in connection with the experience unit method, there is the danger that the teacher's responsibility for maintaining satisfactory working conditions may be disregarded or improperly interpreted. Furthermore, pupils accustomed to strict control may exceed the bounds of responsible behavior when they find themselves in an atmosphere of freedom. Teachers must, therefore, be prepared to establish order and to maintain control in any classroom situation if effective learning is to take place.

The function of providing a situation in which learning can take place is frequently referred to as "discipline." In the discussion that follows the discipline problem is examined with a view to providing helpful suggestions for developing a suitable classroom atmosphere and for maintaining satisfactory control of the classroom through the democratic approach.

THE BASIS FOR DISCIPLINE

Importance of discipline. Miss Jones, teacher of general science in the seventh grade, was presenting a new unit of work to the class. She had developed a very interesting approach, one which should have appealed strongly to boys and girls at the seventh-grade level. But she was having very little success with it. In the back of the room several pupils were conversing in an undertone, apparently oblivious to the presentation by the teacher; near the front, one boy was poking another with a ruler, causing him to complain and strike back; several other pupils were reading, looking through books, or doing other assignments; only a few seemed to pay any attention to the teacher. In fact, it was difficult to hear the teacher because of the noise and confusion. Finally, in desperation, Miss Jones stopped, wrote the advance assignment on the blackboard, and asked the pupils to get to work on it.

Miss Jones came to the rear of the room, where the writer sat while observing this discouraging scene, and remarked as follows: "I can't understand it. I prepare an excellent plan, with an interesting approach. I believe I organize the materials well. I come to class all enthused about the work we are to do. But I can't keep the attention of the pupils long enough even to begin my presentation."

Miss Jones indeed had a very difficult problem. In college she was an excellent student. She was well informed in her subject, had a good command of methods of planning and teaching, and put a great deal of time in preparation. Yet she was unable to organize and control her class sufficiently well to establish those pupil-pupil and pupil-teacher relationships which are essential to effective learning. In the language of the teacher, she was not able to maintain good discipline.

The case of Miss Jones is not unique. Beginning teachers, and occasionally experienced ones as well, encounter difficulties in establishing a situation in the classroom or elsewhere in the school program that is conducive to effective learning. It is important, therefore, to examine the problem of school discipline and ascertain what approach the teacher should take to establish a situation that is desirable for carrying on the work of the school.

Purpose of good discipline. Before one can decide on the approach that should be used in establishing the disciplinary situation in the school, there must be agreement on the purposes that good discipline should serve. There are two major purposes. *First, the relationships among pupils and between pupils and teachers should be such that the most effective learning situation will pertain; and, second, the well-being and safety of the pupils must be adequately protected while they are under the supervision of the school.*

The first purpose suggests that the human relationships may vary considerably from one learning situation to another. That certainly should be true. The relationships desirable in the home economics laboratory and the shop may be quite different from those in the mathematics class; the examination period may demand different human relationships from a socialized activity; and the citizenship club should be different from the glee club, the mathematics class, or the school assembly. The subject, the size of the class, the nature of the learning activity, the maturity of the pupils, and the experience and skill of the teacher—all these have a bearing on the type of relationships between pupils and teacher which are most conducive to effective learning. The teacher's effectiveness in maintaining satisfactory discipline, therefore, will be determined in large part by his skill in developing with his pupils the most appropriate disciplinary relationships for the particular learning situation concerned.

The second purpose of good discipline, namely, protecting the safety of the pupils, is probably achieved in any situation in school when desirable learning conditions have been established. For instance, pushing and tripping other pupils, shooting spit wads, placing tacks on chairs, and similar pranks typical of the adolescent may cause serious injury to some children. Frequently more serious things occur in a classroom that is out of control. Obviously, in a classroom where a satisfactory learning situation pertains pupils have neither the time nor the inclination to engage in activities that endanger the health and safety of their classmates.

The teacher should be concerned with the safety of the pupils outside as well as within the classroom—in corridors, on the playground, in the washrooms, and on the way to and from school. The individual teacher shares in the responsibility for pupil conduct in these places in the school program, as well as in the classroom itself. He should be fully aware of his responsibility and should have some understanding of methods of obtaining desirable pupil behavior in all school situations.

Discipline and objectives of education. In the traditional American secondary school, the relationships between pupils and teachers in the classroom have been extremely formal and authoritarian. Seats are usually arranged in rows with the teacher in the front of the room. Pupils are not permitted to whisper to their neighbors except by special permission, they gain the teacher's attention by raising hands, they recite only when called upon by the teacher, and in other ways conduct themselves according to a formal pattern prescribed by the teacher. There is little variation from this formal procedure. Furthermore, this procedure is quite in harmony with the objectives of the traditional school. These schools emphasize primarily the accumulation of subject matter by the pupil; the study-recite method is employed almost to the exclusion of all others; and the teacher makes all the decisions concerning the work to be done, the activities to be employed, and the conduct to be demanded of every pupil.

The emphasis in the modern secondary school, however, is changing considerably from that of the traditional school. Today, the accumulation of subject matter has ceased to be the chief purpose of secondary education in America. Instead, attention is being directed toward preparing youth for effective life in a democratic society. Skills and attitudes in democratic living, not the memorization of facts and the accumulation of subject matter, have become the chief goal of the secondary school. This provides a much broader aim for education than that of the traditional school. For democratic living, there is concern not only with the growth of the child in subject matter, but also, and to a greater extent, with his growth in emotional stability, ability to get along with his fellows, skill in cooperative action, qualities of character and personality, and leadership ability. Obviously, the authoritarian approach to discipline, though it may have been appropriate in the traditional school, is not adequate in a school which attempts to prepare youth for effective self-direction and cooperative action in a democratic society.

Furthermore, the philosophy as well as the objectives of American secondary education has been changing. Today it is thought that the child, not the teacher, should be the "center" of the school and its program; that pupils learn best by participating in planning and carrying on the learning activities; that the pupils differ greatly from one another in their backgrounds and abilities for learning; and that pupils "learn best by doing." The relationships of pupils with each other and with the teacher are naturally affected by these newer points of view concerning education, since the human relationships in school form an essential part of the learning situation. A formal classroom situation may be very appropriate in a teacher-centered school where drill and memorization are emphasized, but it is not satisfactory if the newer points of view in secondary education are to prevail.

Principles for discipline in the modern school. It is important, therefore, to ask: What principles should guide the teacher in establishing an effective disciplinary situation in the modern secondary school? What should characterize a disciplinary situation that is appropriate as preparation for democratic living, that recognizes the child as the center of the school program, and that implements the concept that pupils learn best by participation and doing? The following principles are some of the more significant ones that should serve as a basis for discipline in a democratic secondary school:

1. *The pupils themselves should understand the purposes and the nature of the disciplinary relationships which are most appropriate for the various learning situations in which they engage.* Such understanding is essential if the school is to provide experiences in democratic living. Without it, the school situation is likely to be based on authoritarian rather than democratic principles. Furthermore, such understanding should lead to better cooperation from the pupils and a more pleasant and friendly school atmosphere.

2. *The pupils should realize that the responsibility for satisfactory disciplinary relationships in school is primarily theirs rather than the teacher's.* In a satisfactory learning situation pupils have the desire to learn. They have objectives in mind, they participate in planning the activities that lead toward those objectives, and they engage in those activities with some interest and enthusiasm. They should feel that it is their responsibility to establish an atmosphere and conditions for work that will enable them to engage in the learning activities with efficiency and effectiveness. A feeling of responsibility for their own conduct and skill in self-direction are the very foundation for human relationships in a democracy.

3. *The pupils should participate in deciding upon the nature of the human relationships that are most appropriate for the various learning situations.* This is in harmony with the current emphasis on democratic living and with the concept of pupil participation and "doing." The extent of that participation will, obviously, depend upon the maturity of the pupils, their previous experience in participating in democratic learning situations, and the skill and experience of the teacher.

4. *The precise nature of the disciplinary relationships should vary*

from one learning situation to another. In the modern secondary school there are a variety of learning situations from subject to subject and from day to day within classes. The disciplinary conditions appropriate for one learning situation are inappropriate for another. For example, in an examination period a formal situation dominated largely by the teacher may be most conducive to effective learning, while for a socialized activity an informal situation with the teacher in the background may be more appropriate.

5. *The human relationships in school should be based primarily on courtesy and consideration toward others rather than obedience to rules and regulations.* Growth in these qualities of human relationships comes not from obedience to rules, but from experiences that children have in showing courtesy and consideration toward others. This does not mean that there should be no rules and regulations, but it does mean that the emphasis should be on courtesy and cooperation. For instance, it would be more appropriate to suggest that pupils refrain from whispering and talking because it interferes with the study of their classmates, than to make a rule which prohibits whispering and imposes a penalty for breaking it.

6. *Efficiency in carrying on learning activities is desirable and appropriate in the democratic approach toward discipline.* This principle is significant because of the tendency of certain teachers to overemphasize freedom in establishing the new type of discipline. Some teachers carry this to the point where they have anarchy, not democracy, in the classroom. It is entirely appropriate, for instance, for the teacher and the class to develop orderly practices for performing certain routine activities, such as taking attendance, collecting and returning papers, and checking equipment and supplies. The democratic disciplinary situation should make adequate provision for carrying on an efficient learning situation.

7. *The teacher ultimately must be responsible for the conduct of pupils under his supervision.* That is as true in a democratic school as in an authoritarian school. But there is a difference. In the authoritarian school, the teacher assumes responsibility with no thought of permitting pupils to share in it. In the democratic school, the teacher prepares the pupils to assume responsibility for discipline. It is this leadership with pupils which is the teacher's major responsibility in establishing and maintaining good discipline.

THE PROBLEM OF GROUP DISCIPLINE

Introduction. In the previous section of this chapter some attention was given to the principles that should serve as a basis for developing and maintaining favorable conditions for learning in school. The teacher should understand thoroughly the meaning and implications of these principles. He must also, however, have some idea of how they may be implemented in practical school situations.

For discussion purposes discipline situations may be classified as follows: (*a*) situations which involve a considerable number of pupils working together as a group, such as a club, a class, or an assembly, and (*b*) situations which involve only individual pupils. In either type of situation the teacher should take a preventive approach toward discipline problems. That is, *he should try to establish such an effective working relationship with his pupils that serious disciplinary situations will not arise.* This point of view is basic to the suggestions that will be given for the teacher as he approaches his responsibility for group and individual discipline.

The teacher's personality and discipline. The most important factor in working effectively with secondary-school pupils is, no doubt, the personality of the teacher. This does not mean, as some educators believe, that there are those who can discipline and those who cannot —in other words, that skill in working effectively with pupils is largely a matter of congenital qualities which may be influenced little, if at all, by education and experience. The fact is that much can be done to shape the teacher's personality so as to improve his effectiveness in working with secondary-school youth. The personal qualities which have a bearing on this subject include the following:

1. *The teacher's appearance.* Matters of dress, style, neatness, and grooming are important in establishing the teacher's position of leadership with his pupils. This is true for the man teacher as well as the woman teacher. Pupils notice the color of the teacher's necktie, the crease in his trousers, the cut of his hair, and his personal cleanliness. Personal appearance has an influence on the extent to which he commands the respect of his pupils—and that in turn is reflected in his leadership in establishing and maintaining good group discipline.

2. *The teacher's voice.* It is not only the natural quality of the teacher's voice but the manner in which he uses it which is important.

The writer once observed a teacher who pitched his voice high as if he were shouting to a multitude—yet ordinarily there were not more than 30 pupils in his class. The pupils were worn out and irritated after listening to him for an entire period. If the teacher's voice is kept down so that it is soft and pleasing, it will be more conducive to developing a favorable group learning situation.

3. *The teacher's interest in children.* In a panel discussion by high-school pupils on the subject, "What kind of teachers do we like?" the writer heard one pupil remark: "We like teachers who are interested in what we do. We like them to come to our parties, our games, and our other activities." Such an interest must, of course, be sincere, or the pupils will soon detect the subterfuge. But certainly the teacher who has this genuine interest in his pupils will have less difficulty with discipline.

4. *The teacher's disposition.* Some teachers are pleasant, not easily disturbed, and seldom driven to anger regardless of the annoying things that may arise in school. Teachers with those qualities will find it easier to maintain effective working relationships with pupils. The teacher's disposition can be modified and controlled by those who see its importance and make an effort to do so. For instance, rest and relaxation outside school hours and during vacation periods may contribute materially to a better disposition in the teacher's relations with pupils.

5. *The teacher's decisiveness.* Some teachers find it difficult to make decisions in matters of pupil conduct. This is a serious quality indeed in meeting discipline problems. Pupils quickly sense the teacher's indecisiveness and react unfavorably to it. Teachers should develop decisiveness in their relations with pupils on matters of conduct.

There are other personality qualities, of course, that have a bearing on the teacher's ability to work effectively with secondary-school youth. The above have been mentioned particularly because they can be more readily shaped and developed than some of the others.

Teaching plans and group discipline. The second important factor in establishing and maintaining effective group discipline is the thoroughness, care, and originality with which the teacher prepares his teaching plans. If pupils are busy at a task which to them is interesting and worth while, they will not have the inclination or the time to engage in activities that interfere with the learning situation. With respect to the preparation of teaching plans, the following may be helpful:

1. The teacher should have a well-prepared unit plan and a daily plan written out and available as a guide in class.
2. The teacher should find activities which make the unit and the daily lessons of interest to the pupils.
3. The teacher should gain the enthusiastic cooperation of pupils by having them participate in the preparation of the unit and in the choice and planning of the learning activities.
4. The teacher should have reference books, study materials, work materials, maps, chalk, and other materials available and organized for use before the pupils arrive.
5. The teacher should give careful attention to the arrangements for demonstrations, audio-visual presentations, field trips, and socialized activities, so that these may proceed with efficiency from the beginning of the class period.

Establishing a favorable classroom atmosphere. Classroom "atmosphere" is difficult to define. But it is known that in some classrooms the situation is such that pupils do not think of engaging in antisocial conduct, while in others they find difficulty in conducting themselves in a courteous and cooperative manner. *Classroom atmosphere, therefore, is a third important factor in developing and maintaining satisfactory group discipline.*

The room itself is a significant element of classroom atmosphere. Some aspects of classroom construction and arrangement are beyond the control of the teacher, such as acoustical material on ceilings, proper lighting, furniture that is silent and well constructed, silent floors, adequate provision for ventilation, and size of classroom. Anything in the arrangement and construction of the room that tends to reduce noise and confusion is conducive to an atmosphere appropriate for study. Where the room conditions are not satisfactory, the recommendation of the teacher sometimes may lead to modifications that will improve the situation. The teacher should take the initiative in presenting such recommendations to the principal and superintendent.

There are many things, however, that influence classroom atmosphere which are subject to the teacher's control. The following suggestions may be helpful in improving these classroom factors:

1. *The teacher should be sure that the furniture is in good condition.* For instance, loose screws and bolts cause squeaky chairs and desks. The teacher should locate defects in the furniture and equipment and bring them to the attention of the janitor.

2. *The teacher should study the arrangement of the furniture in relation to classroom atmosphere and as it may bear on pupil conduct.* For instance, movable furniture should not only be arranged so that it is appropriate for the learning situation, but it should also present a neat and orderly appearance; it should provide adequate space for pupils to work and to pass from one part of the room to another; and it should reduce the amount of movement that is necessary to obtain reference books, use the pencil sharpener, and other items of equipment and learning materials.

3. *The teacher should give careful attention to lighting and ventilation from time to time throughout the day.* Frequently a teacher will adjust window shades in the morning, but leave them in the same position all day. Shades need to be adjusted and lights checked period by period as the position of the sun changes. The air in the room also needs to be changed frequently, or else it will become stale. In moderate weather, the windows can be kept open. In cold weather, a good plan is to open windows when classes change. This provides a change of air every period. Proper lighting and ventilation will contribute to better discipline by providing more favorable conditions for study and learning.

4. *The teacher should give attention to the neatness and orderliness of the room.* The arrangement of the teacher's desk, bookshelves, cupboards, blackboards, and bulletin boards are important in developing good atmosphere. Frequently, a room will be neatly arranged at the beginning of the day, but after a period or two the blackboards, bookshelves, and floors have become disarranged. The teacher should realize that every time a class enters his room it is the beginning of the day for that class in that room. Consequently, he should have the room neatly arranged each period. A good plan is to take the last several minutes of each class to clean the blackboards, arrange bookshelves, straighten chairs or desks, and clear the floor of paper.

5. *The teacher himself is an important factor in classroom atmosphere.* His manner in the classroom, his relations with pupils, and his attitudes of courtesy and friendliness influence the study atmosphere

of the room. Recently, the writer observed a teacher who wore hard heels that clicked sharply as she walked around the room. To make matters worse, she walked a great deal. Obviously, the noise interfered seriously with the study atmosphere that should have existed. The way in which the teacher walks around, the loudness of his voice as he helps pupils, and similar things contribute to or interfere with the study atmosphere.

Organizing classroom routine. It has already been suggested that efficiency in classroom procedures contributes to a more favorable learning situation, and therefore to more satisfactory group discipline. Routine matters in classroom organization and management have a direct bearing on the efficient use of the class period. These routines include such matters as taking attendance, collecting and returning papers, opening and closing the period, and checking out reference materials and supplies. If these matters are not efficiently organized, it may lead to confusion, waste of time, and disorderliness on the part of the pupils. Group discipline problems frequently arise as a result. *The efficient management of classroom routine is, therefore, a fourth factor in group discipline.*

From the standpoint of group discipline, the most important parts of the class period are the first few minutes and the last few minutes. The teacher should make every effort to begin the period promptly and in such a way as to gain the interest and cooperation of the pupils for the work at hand. The first few minutes may determine the atmosphere for the entire period. Pupils should take their seats and organize their materials for work upon entering the room. The teacher should immediately gain the attention of the pupils and present the objective for the period. Above all, the work of the class should begin promptly. If pupils are slow in entering the room and in settling down, it may help to have the teacher at the door and to close the door as soon as most of the pupils have entered, even though the tardy bell has not rung. A good policy is to have the class understand that they should be ready for work as the tardy bell rings—and then to begin at once.

The activities for the last few minutes of the class should be carefully planned and carried out with efficiency and dispatch. Pupils should continue to work until it is suggested by the teacher that it is time to prepare for the closing of the period. The collection of books and working materials should be made according to a well-prepared plan, the room should be arranged in order, and the pupils should remain until the teacher has indicated that they may leave. This may appear to be undue regimentation. It need not be so. Properly managed, the closing of the period should give the pupils a last favorable impression as they leave the room.

The teacher should develop, with the cooperation of the class, an efficient and orderly plan for collecting and distributing papers, study materials, and equipment and supplies needed for the learning activities. For instance, a common plan for passing out papers is to have them arranged by rows in the order in which pupils are seated. They may then be returned quietly and rapidly by passing them down the rows. Likewise, papers may be collected by having pupils pass them up the rows to the front row, and then having the teacher receive them there.

Pupils may be of considerable help in passing out and collecting reference and working materials. It is best to have certain pupils designated to help according to an efficiently organized plan. Reference books and equipment should be returned to bookshelves and cupboards at the end of the period, neatly arranged, and checked to be sure they are all returned. The importance of checking reference books and equipment each period cannot be overemphasized. The writer recalls one beginning teacher of mechanical drawing who lost several hundred dollars' worth of drawing instruments his first year of teaching because of failure to check equipment each period. Teachers are usually held responsible for equipment and books that are lost. Pupils may assist in this checking to avoid the necessity of having the teacher devote too much class time to it.

The checking of attendance should also be managed in such a way that it does not take too much time. The policy of some teachers to call the class roll, one name at a time, is time consuming and fails to establish an appropriate study atmosphere. A better plan is to check those pupils absent whose seats are vacant. This may be done by the teacher or by a pupil assistant.

There are many other items of classroom routine for which efficient and orderly procedures should be developed. These vary from subject to subject and class to class. They should be studied carefully by the teacher and the best possible procedures should be developed. The efficient management of classroom routine is a significant step toward preventing serious problems of group discipline.

Maintaining leadership in the class. From the standpoint of satisfactory group discipline, it is important that the teacher establish and maintain himself as the leader in any group of pupils. This leadership should be based, not on fear, but on mutual confidence, respect, understanding, and friendship. *The establishment of such leadership by the teacher may be considered a fifth factor in developing and maintaining satisfactory group discipline.*

The teacher's personality, which has already been discussed, is an important quality in leadership. The teacher with an aggressive, attractive, and friendly personality can more readily establish those relationships with pupils that provide the basis for democratic leadership. Other qualities which are important in establishing the teacher as a leader are command of his subject and thoroughness and resourcefulness in planning his work. These qualities have also received some attention elsewhere in this chapter.

In addition to these qualities, there are some specific things which may be of help in establishing and maintaining the teacher as a leader in a class of pupils. It should be understood that leadership is something which, once established, is retained only if an effort is made continually to retain it. That is, the teacher may do things every time he meets his class which will maintain his prestige among them. These things include the following:

1. *The teacher may stand at the door as pupils enter at the beginning of the period and as they leave at the end.* It was previously suggested that, from the standpoint of group discipline, the beginning and the end of the period are of utmost importance. Standing at the door gives the teacher an opportunity to make pupils aware of his presence during the crucial moments in the class period. He may greet them with a friendly smile, and as the occasion warrants, make an appropriate comment to individual pupils which evidences an interest in their affairs. Furthermore, pupils are more likely to be cooperative if they, as individuals, have had a brief friendly contact with the teacher as they enter the room.

2. *The teacher should be as courteous to the pupils as they are expected to be in return.* Recently the writer heard a child complain about a teacher who lectured pupils on courtesy but failed to observe

the specific suggestions that she gave. This is much too common among teachers, especially beginning teachers. No doubt, it stems from the thinking that children should show courtesy and respect toward their elders. The elders should first display the same courtesy to children—in little things and in big things. The teacher's position of leadership will be quickly jeopardized if he loses the confidence and respect of his pupils.

3. *The teacher should stand when he is in charge of the class.* For experienced teachers this is not so important, but it is very helpful for the beginning teacher, especially in a large class. This is not necessary, of course, when pupils are studying or are themselves in charge of the class activities.

4. *The teacher may better sit in the rear of the room when pupils are in charge of the class or when they are studying.* When pupils are in charge of the class activities, the teacher should temporarily relinquish his position of leadership to them by retiring to the side of the room. When pupils are studying, it is likewise best if the teacher retires to the background where pupils will not feel that they are "being watched." The basis for democratic leadership is lost if pupils feel that the teacher is a policeman.

Suggestions for improving group discipline. Up to this point, the discussion of group discipline has been concerned primarily with suggestions for developing such pupil-pupil and pupil-teacher relationships that group discipline problems will not arise. That is, of course, the ideal approach to discipline problems. There may be times, however, when the teacher is not successful in establishing or maintaining those human relationships in the classroom that are appropriate for an effective learning situation. When that happens, some measures may have to be taken to improve the situation.

The traditional way of dealing with undesirable conduct is to inflict punishment. However, in a school program that emphasizes preparation for democratic living, such an approach is an admission of failure on the part of the teacher. This does not mean that punishment should never be used. But it does mean that resort to punishment should be made only after every constructive approach has been explored and found ineffective. The following suggestions are believed to be in harmony with the democratic approach to group discipline:

1. *The teacher should examine carefully his organization of routine*

matters, preparation of teaching plans, and relationships with pupils, to ascertain if possible the reason for any unsatisfactory disciplinary situation. In other words, he should ask, "What am I doing or failing to do which may be responsible for this problem?" The suggestions given earlier in this chapter may be a source of help in making this analysis. Frequently, some change in classroom practice will lead to considerable improvement in the disciplinary situation.

2. *The teacher should solicit the help of the principal or supervisor before the situation becomes serious.* This suggestion is particularly appropriate for the beginning teacher. There are usually some early indications of difficulty which are recognized by experienced teachers, among them the following: (*a*) If pupils are slow in coming into the room and in getting ready for work, (*b*) if pupils converse too freely with their neighbors in a way that interferes with learning, (*c*) if pupils speak up in discussion without being recognized or while others are speaking, (*d*) if pupils find too many inadequate reasons for walking about the room, and (*e*) if pupils are slow in following the suggestions of the teacher with respect to conduct. When there is such looseness in the conduct of the pupils, the principal may be able to give specific suggestions for improvement.

3. *The teacher should have a talk with the group regarding the situation.* If group discipline is to be democratic, it must be based on an understanding by everyone concerned of his responsibility for developing a satisfactory learning situation. The pupils themselves will profit most from satisfactory conditions for learning—and will lose most when those conditions do not pertain. A frank discussion with the class of the need for satisfactory discipline and suggestions for achieving it may do much to gain cooperation in improving the situation.

4. *The teacher should ascertain which pupils may be the more serious problems and attempt to gain their cooperation in developing an effective learning situation.* Usually there are a few troublemakers who are the key to the problem in a group discipline situation. That is true especially in the early stages of the problem. If the teacher is able to locate these troublemakers early enough and appeal to them so as to gain their cooperation, it may relieve the group situation.

5. *The teacher may develop certain devices to improve the group discipline situation.* Such devices are likely to be effective only if they

are clearly related to the cooperation that pupils need to give if the learning activity is to continue. For instance, a teacher may just wait before proceeding with a class activity until the pupils give their attention. He may wait for several minutes without saying a word. The pupils know, of course, that work cannot be done if the class is noisy or fails to give its attention. If the class is not completely out of control, the pupils may eventually quiet down.

Another device which teachers sometimes use when pupils fail to be cooperative in a learning activity is to give a test. For instance, if a class is slow in giving its attention at the beginning of the period, the teacher may give a 5-minute drill quiz. If the class becomes unco-operative during a discussion activity, the teacher may say, "Since we cannot carry on the discussion in a courteous manner, we will write the answers to the discussion questions and count it as a test." Pupils generally accept the practice of being quiet during a test. Furthermore, it is an implementation of the idea, "The work must be done. If we can't do it courteously one way, we will do it another way." Pupils usually prefer not to have tests. It should be emphasized that devices such as these should not be employed so long as other approaches are effective. But beginning teachers—and experienced ones, too—frequently exhaust other approaches to the improvement of group discipline without success. Only then should devices such as these be employed.

Punishment of the group. Punishment is a negative approach to the problem of discipline, whether it be employed with an individual pupil or with a group. It is far more appropriate in the authoritarian than in the democratic school. Furthermore, it is difficult to employ punish-ment with a group because there will always be individual pupils who have cooperated in every way. It is difficult, if not impossible, to impose group penalties without inflicting an injustice on such pupils.

Then too, punishment places the teacher rather than the pupils "on the spot." If the teacher asks the entire class to remain after school, there is always the possibility that some of them won't do it. If only one or two pupils fail to appear, the situation may not prove too diffi-cult. But suppose that a considerable number do not report? What should the teacher do then? There is always the possibility of such a reaction when group punishment is employed.

The case against group punishment as a means of improving disci-pline is indeed a strong one. Even so, there may be occasions when such action is justified. The following suggestions should help the teacher in administering group punishment if it becomes necessary:

1. Employ group punishment only when every other approach to improving the situation is likely to be ineffective or has been exhausted.
2. Be sure that the group as a whole is involved in the misdemeanor before group punishment is used.
3. Be sure that the punishment will not lead to other complications. Keeping a class after school may interfere with bus schedules in schools where pupils are transported, with after-school activities, and with after-school jobs.
4. Be sure that the punishment is reasonable and that it is of a kind that may lead to the improvement of the situation.
5. Consult the principal or supervisor for his advice before employing group punishment. This suggestion is intended especially for the inexperienced teacher.

THE PROBLEM OF INDIVIDUAL DISCIPLINE

Introduction. There is close relationship and similarity between group and individual discipline problems. For instance, individual pupils are far more likely to be cooperative, courteous, and willing to conduct themselves in a manner that is conducive to effective learning if the group disciplinary situation is wholesome. Furthermore, some of the approaches to developing satisfactory working relationships with the group are equally effective in developing wholesome attitudes toward school on the part of individual pupils. There are certain procedures, however, which may be helpful in reaching individual pupils and gaining their cooperation which have not been discussed earlier in this chapter.

Know the individual pupil. As with group discipline, *the teacher should take the preventive approach toward individual discipline problems.* The first step is to become thoroughly acquainted with the individual pupils in one's classes—their interests, abilities, extracurricular participation, intelligence quotients, previous achievement in school, emotional stability, personality development, and school citizenship qualities. The teacher should also have some understanding of the out-of-school backgrounds of his pupils—their home and family backgrounds, after-school employment, vacation activities, and participation in such community activities as Boy Scouts, Girl Scouts, Y.W.C.A., Y.M.C.A., and church organizations. This understanding of the characteristics of individual pupils is essential if the teacher is to establish effective working relationships with them.

There are various ways for obtaining this information about individual pupils. The records in the principal's office are one source, giving such information as previous achievement, intelligence quotients, and extracurricular participation. The pupil's homeroom teacher should be able to give information concerning the personality and emotional qualities of pupils, their citizenship records, and home backgrounds. Much information can be obtained directly from the pupils themselves through questionnaires and interviews. Whatever the source of information, it is important from the standpoint of discipline that the teacher become well acquainted with his pupils early in the year. The information in the office is, of course, available when school opens. Conferences with the homeroom teachers, the pupils themselves, and with parents should be held as early as possible to obtain further information about the pupils.

Conferences with pupils and parents. One of the most effective ways of establishing a satisfactory working relationship with individual pupils is to have conferences with them to get acquainted early in the year. Only through such personal contact with pupils can the teacher establish a satisfactory basis for friendship and understanding. The personal conference gives pupil and teacher a chance to get acquainted, to find common interests, and to become friends. Teachers frequently have conferences with individual pupils after they have had some difficulty—that is, after a disciplinary situation has arisen. By that time, there may be a strained relationship between them which makes a personal conference more difficult. *For preventive discipline, the personal conference with all pupils early in the year and before situations requiring disciplinary action have arisen can be very effective.*

In a large school, it may be difficult for the teacher to have personal conferences with all his pupils. He may have 150 or more pupils in his classes, and perhaps some others in his homeroom, club, and other extracurricular activities. One suggestion is to limit the conferences to those pupils who, on the basis of their previous records, may be potential discipline problems. There is some objection, however, to such conferences if pupils suspect that they are being held primarily for disciplinary purposes. For that reason it would be unwise to limit them to selected pupils. A second plan, and perhaps a better one, is for the teacher to have conferences with those pupils with whom he has had no previous contact. In small and medium-sized schools this procedure would reduce materially the number of teacher-pupil conferences that would be necessary early in the year. For the teacher new in the school this plan would obviously not be appropriate. A third suggestion is to have conferences first with pupils in those groups where disciplinary problems are most likely to occur—but to have them with all pupils in those groups. Whatever the plan, the teacher should have such personal conferences early in the year if it is at all possible to arrange them.

Visits to the pupil's home and conferences with his parents are as helpful as the individual teacher-pupil conferences in establishing good working relations. Like the conferences with pupils, these visits should be arranged with the parents of all pupils rather than limiting them to the homes of those who are likely to be problems. The visit to the home may help to establish a friendly relationship with the pupil's parents and lead to mutual understanding between teacher, parent, and pupil. In large communities there will, of course, be difficulties in home visitation. The teacher should, however, employ this procedure when it is possible to do so.

Employing information about pupils. Up to this point, it has been urged that the teacher become thoroughly familiar with the nature and characteristics of the individual pupils under his supervision as a step toward relieving any individual discipline problems that may arise. A word should be said about the use that may be made of this information. The most obvious suggestion, of course, is to use this information to locate those pupils who are potential discipline problems. Pupils whose relationships with teachers in previous years have not been satisfactory are the first ones to study. Although these pupils may not be problems this year for every teacher, a thoroughgoing analysis of their backgrounds may be helpful in establishing relationships with them that will prevent an unsatisfactory situation.

There are other ways of locating potential discipline problems. *Previous difficulty with school work, evidence of emotional instability, and unsatisfactory home backgrounds frequently lead to pupil maladjustment in school—and in turn to discipline problems.* The teacher should exhaust every resource to assist pupils with such backgrounds to adjust to school. That is the most effective approach toward relieving individual discipline problems.

Effective planning and teaching on the part of the teacher is another direct step toward preventing discipline problems. That is fully as true with individual as with group problems. The background of information about individual pupils which the teacher acquires should be helpful for individualizing the work of the school so as to meet the needs, abilities, and interests of all the pupils. Suggestions for individualizing instruction effectively are given elsewhere in this book. At this point it should be sufficient to suggest that the teacher who succeeds in planning and teaching so as to meet the needs, interests, and abilities of each individual child should have little concern with discipline.

Working with individual problem cases. As has been suggested, the best approach to individual discipline problems is the preventive one—that is, to develop such a satisfactory learning situation that individual pupils will cooperate courteously and enthusiastically with the teacher and their fellow pupils. Few teachers have the skill, however, to achieve that ideal. In spite of all that we may do, there will be some pupils whose conduct will at times be unsatisfactory in terms of the learning situation. The teacher must have some plans for meeting such problems.

There are some educators who believe that the serious disciplinary problems among individual pupils are the result of maladjustment on the part of the child. Such maladjustment may be due to the child's home and out-of-school backgrounds, to lack of emotional stability, to personality conflicts, or to lack of ability to do the work required in school. For instance, the extremely nervous child may find it difficult to sit still much of the day; the child who has been repressed at home for years may eventually rebel against authority; and the child who consistently fails in school may develop a decided distaste for school and all it stands for. It seems desirable, therefore, to take a positive approach to improve the relationships of individual pupils with their fellows and with the teacher. The following suggestions may be helpful:

1. Review carefully all the information you can find out about the child—his home, success in school, emotional and personality record, intelligence, and interests.

2. On the basis of this information try to ascertain the reason for the child's antisocial attitudes and actions.

3. Have a conference with the child in which you discuss with him frankly his responsibility to the class, the teacher, and himself. This should not be a scolding. Rather, it should be a discussion to gain a better understanding of the child and his attitude toward school and to arrive at suggestions for improving his conduct.

4. If the teacher's conference with the child does not provide a basis for an immediate solution, solicit the aid of the school counselor, homeroom teacher, psychologist, nurse, principal, or other specialist. The teacher should continue to be primarily responsible for helping the child, but he should seek help from these specialists in understanding the child and in seeking a solution for his problems.

5. Consult the child's parents, if you are not successful in arriving at a solution at school. Solicit their cooperation and suggestions for improving the child's behavior.

6. Resort to punishment only after every effort at a positive solution has failed. Furthermore, it should be recognized that a resort to punishment is, in a sense, a failure on the part of the teacher in the use of more desirable approaches.

Punishment as a means of improving individual discipline. It has already been suggested that punishment is not a desirable means for improving individual discipline problems. Even so, there will be discipline problems for which the teacher may consider punishment the most effective approach. The nature of the punishment may vary considerably. Common devices for the less serious problems are keeping pupils after school, giving them additional work, scolding them, and depriving them of certain privileges. If more severe punishment seems appropriate, it should be administered only after consultation with the principal, the counselor, the pupil's homeroom teacher, or some other person who is responsible for assisting teachers with discipline problems.

Corporal punishment in any form should never be administered by the teacher. In most communities corporal punishment is frowned upon, and in many it is prohibited by board of education regulations. Some states prohibit corporal punishment by statute except under prescribed conditions. Furthermore, corporal punishment administered by the teacher may well defeat the very purpose it is intended to achieve. If such severe measures are demanded, the case should be referred to the principal.

Since punishment is occasionally resorted to in dealing with indi-- vidual discipline cases, it seems appropriate to offer some suggestions concerning it. The following may be helpful:

1. The child should recognize that the punishment is justified, otherwise it will not be very effective. Its value rests largely in its psychological effect on the child.

2. Punishment should be administered in private. Even a scolding publicly administered loses its effectiveness because the child is likely to be a martyr in the eyes of his classmates. This is true even though the pupils as a group recognize the justice of punishment.

3. The punishment should always be reasonable. Furthermore, it is best if it is concurred in by the pupil.

4. The punishment should not interfere with other school activities engaged in by the pupil. For instance, the teacher has no right to impose punishment which will interfere with the pupil's participation in music organizations, athletics, or clubs. Only the faculty sponsor of those activities or the principal should impose punishment which interferes with those activities.

5. The punishment should not be continued over a long period of time.

6. Once the punishment has been administered, the teacher's relations with the child should become as friendly as possible, giving him the feeling that previous misconduct will be forgotten.

7. No form of punishment should be used repeatedly, or else it will lose its effectiveness. Pupils may become accustomed to punishment much like anything else.

8. Punishment should be administered only on the assumption that it will help improve the child's behavior toward the teacher and his classmates. It must be used as one means of contributing to the total educational growth of the individual child concerned. It has no other justification. Frequently, a scolding or some other punishment finds expression for the annoyance, or even anger, of the teacher with little thought as to its probable effect upon the child's behavior.

SUMMARY

The problem of discipline in school is essentially a problem in human relationships. As such it is a difficult problem indeed. For the beginning teacher, skill in avoiding or relieving disciplinary situations will be an important factor in his success. Even for the experienced teacher it continues at times to be a problem. In summarizing this discussion on discipline the following points of view deserve particular emphasis: (*a*) The democratic approach to discipline is emphasized more today than the authoritarian approach. (*b*) A preventive approach should be taken toward discipline, with the teacher providing democratic leadership in establishing a learning situation that encourages courtesy, friendliness, and sincere cooperation on the part of the pupils. (*c*) If discipline problems should arise, a constructive approach is likely to be more effective than a hasty resort to punishment.

SELECTED REFERENCES

BAKER, FRANK E.: "Discipline," *Progressive Education,* 21:57–60, 98–99, February, 1944.

BARBOUR, RICHMOND: "What's Wrong with Corporal Punishment?", *The Nation's Schools,* 33:6, 25–26, June, 1944.

BRYAN, ROY C., and FOLEY, LOUIS: "Some False Notions about School Discipline," *Educational Administration and Supervision,* 29:16–22, January, 1943.

BURTON, WILLIAM H.: *The Guidance of Learning Activities: A Summary of the Principles of Learning,* Chap. 22, D. Appleton-Century Company, Inc., New York, 1944.

EDMONSON, J. B., ROEMER, JOSEPH, and BACON, FRANCIS L.: *The Administration of the Modern Secondary School,* Chap. X, The Macmillan Company, New York, 1948.

FOLEY, LOUIS: "Appeasement in School Discipline," *The Education Digest,* 8:44–45, February, 1943.

JENKINS, R. L.: "The Constructive Use of Punishment," *Mental Hygiene,* 29:561–574, October, 1945.

LADERER, WILLIAM C., JR.: " 'Reliant' Study Groups," *The Clearing House,* 20:480–481, April, 1946.

Michigan State Board of Education: *Youth Learns to Assume Responsibility,* Study of the Secondary School Curriculum, Leads to Better Schools in Michigan, (3): State Board of Education, Lansing, Michigan, 1944.

National Education Association and American Association of School Administrators, Education Policies Commission: *Learning the Ways of Democracy: A Case Book of Civic Education,* Chap. III, The Association, Washington, D.C., 1940.

PIERCE, PAUL R.: "Classroom Guidance of Democratic Living," *The School Review,* 51:523–529, November, 1943.

RYAN, W. CARSON: *Mental Health through Education,* Chap. IV, The Commonwealth Fund, New York, 1938.

SCHNEIDEMAN, ROSE: *Democratic Education in Practice,* Chap. 16, Harper & Brothers, New York, 1945.

SCHORLING, RALEIGH: *Student Teaching*, Chap. III, McGraw-Hill Book Company, Inc., New York, 1940.

SHEVIAKOV, GEORGE V., and REDL, FRITZ: *Discipline for Today's Children and Youth*, Department of Supervision and Curriculum Development, National Education Association, Washington, D.C., 1944.

SMITH, ELMER R.: "Perry Junior High School Improves Behavior," *The Clearing House*, 14:144–147, November, 1939.

TIEDEMAN, STUART C.: "A Study of Pupil-Teacher Relationships," *Journal of Educational Research*, 35:657–664, May, 1942.

Chapter 19. THE TEACHER USES AUDIO-VISUAL AIDS

In Part II, three general methods of teaching were identified and discussed. All three deal with materials of instruction and the communication of ideas. Although these three differ with respect to the educational outcomes that are sought, each makes use of the following types of activities and techniques:

1. Giving the pupils a general overview of an area of study before detailed assignments are made.
2. Teaching a specific fact, skill, or understanding.
3. Exploring on a wider scale an area already studied.
4. Providing drill on specific facts, skills, or understandings previously taught.
5. Reviewing materials previously studied.
6. Motivating a new assignment or unit of study.
7. Providing supplementary information.
8. Integrating that which has been learned in isolation.

Audio-visual aids are devices that help the teacher accomplish these things quickly and effectively. As such they are not identified with this or that method, but are aids to be used as needed in each method whenever they can contribute to the achievement of the outcomes sought. The present chapter, therefore, is devoted primarily to a description of the several aids now commonly available, with some attention to the merits and limitations of each. The manner in which they are to be used, as such use may bear upon method, must here be left to the discretion of the teacher.

WHAT ARE AUDIO-VISUAL AIDS?

Almost everyone is familiar with the blackboard, the textbook, the notebook, maps, crayons, reference books, etc., but only seldom are these thought of as audio-visual aids. This term is generally, though incorrectly, reserved for the host of new materials and equipment which has appeared within the past generation, particularly the materials and equipment used in the projection of pictures or associated with the radio industry.

Educational interest in the audio-visual aids has been aroused by the overwhelming evidence of their power to inform, to change individual and group behavior, and to influence the development of attitudes and opinions. The commercial development of the radio and motion pictures has placed vastly improved tools in the hands of the schools and other educational agencies to broaden the horizons of man. These two instruments alone have enabled man to transcend the limitations of the unaided human voice and the printed page and thereby to reach vast audiences instantly and simultaneously. Today the radio, motion pictures, and television may be man's most promising tools for combating ignorance and indifference. To inform, to induce changes in individual and group behavior, and to develop desirable attitudes are means to the larger educational ends. To do these efficiently and effectively is the teacher's responsibility and challenge. Properly used, audio-visual aids can help achieve these ends more quickly and effectively than most other techniques and devices.

In this chapter the following audio-visual aids will be described and the broad principles of their use discussed.

A. Visual Aids
1. Motion pictures
2. Filmstrips
3. 2″ × 2″ and 3″ × 4″ slides
4. Flat pictures and opaque projection
5. Stereographic pictures

B. Audio Aids
1. Live and transcribed radio broadcasts
2. Transcriptions and phonograph recordings
3. Public address system techniques
4. Recording equipment techniques
5. Television

Many more aids could be listed. With the exception of television, however, the above are the aids most commonly used in secondary schools today and are, therefore, the ones with which the beginning teacher should become familiar.[1]

[1] For a more detailed description of these and other aids, consult Edgar Dale, *Audio-Visual Methods in Teaching,* The Dryden Press, Inc., New York, 1947.

VISUAL AIDS

The Motion Picture. The motion picture is particularly useful as an aid in teaching facts and skills, developing attitudes and appreciations, exploring areas of study, providing information, and showing relationships. Its vivid, attention-holding qualities make it a particularly useful aid. Its chief advantages lie in its ability to portray processes in action and events in their natural sequence. A surprisingly vast body of educationally significant events, processes, and objects have been recorded which can aid young people to understand the past as well as the present. Furthermore, these events can be viewed repeatedly and in slow motion or in fixed shots. When accompanying sound is also caught on the sound track or other form of recording, the instructional setting they provide can be most realistic and vivid. Here there are no barriers of words with their many shades of meaning. The darkened room minimizes distracting influences. The motion on the screen draws attention. The ear attends the sound from the loud-speaker. Few if any other materials of instruction in current use can equal the power of the motion picture.

Since motion pictures synthesize and frequently condense information, they serve remarkably well for introducing an area of study. In some instances, however, the nature of the picture or the nature of the area to be studied is such that orientation should be provided in some other way. In such cases, the picture might better be used as a review or an integrating activity. Some pictures may serve equally well either as an introduction or as a summary of a unit of work. Teacher judgment, pupil needs, and the availability of the film must determine when and in what manner a particular motion picture is used.

The need for special equipment and a darkened room frequently poses the question of where the motion picture is to be shown. Some schools have provided a special projection room in preference to equipping each classroom with the necessary electrical outlets and darkening equipment. However, there is strong, experience-based judgment to support the showing in the classroom whenever possible. It minimizes discipline and other prejudicial attitude problems which sometimes are induced when it is necessary to move a group of pupils to the projection room.

To use motion pictures effectively, the teacher must become familiar with several pieces of equipment. He must know how to operate this equipment, whether it is of the sound or silent type, and whether it uses 8-mm., 16-mm., or 35-mm. film.

Sixteen millimeter with sound (16-mm. sound) is the film size most frequently used for classroom instruction, although there are many silent films of this size available. Thirty-five millimeter silent (35-mm.) or with sound (35-mm. sound) films are usually used in theaters and large auditoriums and are of a nature suited to these larger audiences. Many have instructional value, but their cost is usually prohibitive for classroom use. Some have been reduced to the 16-mm. size for classroom use. Eight millimeter (8-mm.) films are usually made and used by the amateur. This is the popular size for the home type of equipment and usually is without sound. Very little professionally made film is available in the 8-mm. size. Frequently, however, the amateur may have pictures of trips or of local events that have instructional value.

The motion-picture projector has a high-powered projection lamp and a lens for focusing the picture on the screen. Most 16-mm. projectors have both sound and silent film speeds, that is, films of either type may be shown with the same projector. The sound on the film is made audible by an amplifier through a loud-speaker, either built into the projector or mounted in a separate case. The volume of the sound is controlled by a special volume control and the tone quality by a tone control much as in a modern radio. Since projectors vary greatly as to the manner in which the film is threaded through the mechanism and as to the focus and sound controls, the teacher should make special arrangements to become familiar with the particular type of equipment that is available in his school before he plans to use it in an instructional situation.

Instructional motion pictures may be purchased from a producer or distributor, or rented on a short period loan seldom exceeding 3 days. Film libraries from which teachers may rent films at a nominal cost frequently are maintained by state departments of education, state universities, and some of the larger private universities and teachers' colleges. A few industries now have films describing their processes and services which may be borrowed without charge except for transportation. Many of the larger school systems have found it desirable to build up their own film libraries. It is seldom, however, that the teacher or even the school can keep films on hand for use whenever the occasion is opportune. In almost every instance it is necessary to arrange days in advance for the loan of a particular film or even for the use of the projection equipment. This lack of flexibility is one of the major disadvantages of motion pictures as instructional aids.

Available films are now catalogued like books. Most public libraries and many school libraries now keep these up-to-date catalogues on their reference shelves. *Educational Film Guide*,[2] for example, lists over 3,000 instructional motion pictures, their rental price, the film center from which they may be secured, and other pertinent information. The Guide is published periodically to keep the listings up-to-date. Some film centers publish their own catalogue which will be sent to the teacher without charge on request.

The Filmstrip. The filmstrip is a more compact and, in many respects, a more convenient form of the older "lantern slide" type of visual aid. The filmstrip is a series of still pictures mounted on one continuous strip of film which may be projected frame by frame. This affords all the advantages of a projected still picture. The class may view a particular picture long enough for each pupil to grasp all the significant details. The teacher may discuss the pictures or play a recorded lecture especially prepared to accompany that series of pictures.

The filmstrip projector usually weighs less than 10 pounds, is inexpensive, and easy to operate. Some of the more modern ones can be used satisfactorily in a semidarkened room. These features make it particularly satisfactory for classroom use. Furthermore, filmstrips can be made by the amateur photographer with the familiar 35-mm. camera, thereby enabling the teacher or members of the class to prepare instructional materials particularly suited to local needs. Commercially prepared filmstrips may be secured on either a purchase or rental basis from the film centers and producers which stock motion-picture films. Unlike motion pictures, however, the average filmstrip costs very little more than a library book. It is possible, therefore, to keep the more frequently used titles on hand for immediate use whenever the need arises. The motion-picture catalogues usually also list filmstrips.

It may be desirable to call special attention to the recorded sound that may accompany certain filmstrip titles. Generally the sound is on a 16-inch record or wax disc *which turns at transcription speed* rather than at the speed of the conventional phonograph recording. Because of its size and speed it cannot be played on the standard phonograph.

[2] *Educational Film Guide*, The H. W. Wilson Company, New York.

Therefore, accompanying sound can be used only when a special projector is used which has the pickup, amplifier, and loud-speaker built in; or when a transcription record-player is available. Since many schools are now purchasing transcription record-playing equipment to enable them to use radio recordings, it is not generally advisable for schools to purchase filmstrip projectors with built-in sound equipment.

The filmstrip can be used for many of the same purposes that motion pictures are used. They are particularly useful in supplying specific information, providing special drill, and for reviewing previously studied materials. The low cost, flexibility, and convenience of the filmstrip suggest that its popularity will increase greatly in the years immediately ahead.

Slides. The 2" × 2" and 3" × 4" Slides. Slides are still pictures mounted individually in cardboard holders or between two pieces of glass. Like all still pictures they have the advantages of clarity of detail, ample viewing time, and size of the image. All of these are important for classroom use. Since the pictures are individually mounted, they can be shown in any sequence that is desired, although they are usually available in sets and come arranged in a recommended sequence.

The 2" × 2" slide is the least expensive colored still picture for projection available today. The amateur photographer who uses a 35-mm. camera almost invariably has his color films returned to him by the commercial processor as 2" × 2" slides in cardboard mounts. Since the projector required for this size slide is inexpensive and easy to operate, it follows that this is a most popular aid for the teacher who wishes to prepare his own visual instructional materials. For these same reasons, namely, expense and convenience, the 2" × 2" slide is one of the few projected visual aids which can be used by the pupils themselves. However, slides that are to be used in this manner should be given the protection of glass covers. Sets of 2" × 2" slides may be purchased or rented from commercial producers and film centers.

The 3" × 4" slide is perhaps the oldest of the projected visual aids. Because of their size they are usually mounted between glass covers and are for that reason more bulky and more easily damaged. Also, they cost more to buy or rent. Their chief advantage lies in the fact that the projectors are inexpensive and can be used in a semidarkened classroom, even though they use only a 500-watt lamp. A major reason for their continued popularity is the ease which which teachers and pupils can prepare their own slides. Words or drawings may be put on clear cellophane, mounted between a pair of 3" × 4" cover glasses and projected on the screen in a matter of a few minutes. No photographic process is involved. Etched glass or a plastic-base material may be substituted for the cellophane thereby eliminating the need for glass covers. Ordinary pencils may be used in preparing slides, although more startling effects are produced when special colored pencils or paints are used. Because of the size of the working area the 3" × 4" slide is better suited for the preparation of nonphotographic, homemade materials than the 2" × 2" slide.

Opaque Projection. This is still another method for presenting still pictures to a group. This type of equipment can be used to project almost any type of printed materials whether in black and white or in colors. Pictures, diagrams, maps, music, or the printed word, whether it appears in a book, magazine, or on some other suitable flat surface, can be shown on a classroom-size screen on short notice. Even samples of cloth or scientific specimens, such as a butterfly, can be shown to a class without sacrificing color or structural detail. Because of these obvious advantages it is most unfortunate that the opaque projector cannot be used with satisfaction in a room that is not totally dark. This fact alone excludes it from most classrooms. Also, the area that can be projected with most present equipment cannot be larger than 6" × 6". It is amazing, though, how many large pictures have their center of interest and all pertinent detail located within a 6" × 6" area. Other larger materials can be moved around thereby permitting the projection of one section at a time. Perhaps future improvements may yet make the opaque projector one of the most popular pieces of visual aids equipment for school use.

Stereographic Pictures. Stereographic pictures, which have been associated with the old-fashioned American "parlor" for several generations, have been recognized only recently by educators as a valuable visual aid. These pictures give the effect of depth when viewed and for that reason are invaluable instructional aids whenever three-dimensional relationships are involved. They are useful not only in the branches of mathematics and sciences, such as solid geometry, physics, and anatomy, but also in developing realistic concepts of spatial relationships and environmental data with younger children. Stereographic pictures can be viewed by only one individual at a time. This places a serious limitation on their use for group instructional purposes. On the other hand, they are inexpensive and can be made a part of the classroom equipment for use by the pupils just as supplementary textbooks and other reading materials are made available.

Recognition of the educational value of stereographic pictures has stimulated the commercial production of such pictures for school use. Sets of pictures are now available mainly for use on the elementary level, although some have been prepared specifically for the more advanced courses in science and mathematics. It is generally advisable for schools to purchase sets of pictures outright and to place them in the library where they may be borrowed as needed for use in the classrooms, or used in the library by individual pupils like any other reference materials.

Several manufacturers are attempting to develop stereoscopic equipment that will project this type of picture for group instructional purposes. The time may not be far away when completely satisfactory techniques and equipment will be available. For the present, however, expense and complicated technological problems render existing equipment unsatisfactory for general classroom use.

AUDIO AIDS

Just as visual aids serve to augment the speed and thoroughness of learning through the eye, so also do the audio aids increase the effectiveness of learning through the ear. Live and transcribed radio broadcasts can multiply learning opportunities by supplying information and encouraging the development of attitudes and appreciations by stimulating the emotions. It is highly probable that children as well as adults experience the radio more commonly than any other audio or visual aid. In many ways its influence exceeds even that of the printed page.

The Live Radio Broadcast. Radio broadcasts have a scope and timeliness that cannot be matched by any other instructional aid. Within technical limits radio offers instantaneous communication with any part of the world. It can bring into the classroom the most significant problems and events of the day. Millions of Americans will never forget the day while they were in school when radio transported them into the halls of Congress to hear a President denounce ". . . a day that will live long in infamy . . . ," and to be caught up in the ground swell of feeling that committed this nation as a united force against aggression.

No other medium of communication with the possible exception of television could have duplicated this feat.

The radio has the additional advantage of validity. It is possible for the listener to catch the speaker's nuances and therefore his intended meaning rather than the erroneous inferences sometimes drawn from the printed word. The listener is also acquainted with conflicting opinions and thereby encouraged to weigh for himself the merits of the issue at stake. This has the merit of introducing the pupil, the poor reader as well as the more skilled, into the ongoing stream of life in a way that schools have never before been able to do. The general availability of radios and the common practice of installing public address systems in new school buildings has made the radio broadcast accessible in almost every classroom. This is one of the greatest forces working for the equalization of educational opportunities in America today.

Radio Transcriptions. These are broadcasts that have been recorded and which can, therefore, be heard repeatedly. The broadcasts usually are recorded on discs, 16 inches in diameter and for that reason will not fit on the standard phonograph. Furthermore, they revolve at about half the speed of the standard phonograph record. The size of the disc and the turntable speed make it necessary to have special transcription playback equipment if this type of audio aid is to be used. Such equipment is available either as a complete set, including amplifier and loudspeaker, or as a turntable and pickup which can be attached to the public address system, a sound motion-picture projector, or a standard electric phonograph. The latter arrangement is less expensive but this advantage is offset by the fact that the installation is not easily portable and therefore not as adaptable to widespread classroom use. Some transcription playbacks have two-speed motors and may, therefore, be used to play back either transcriptions or standard phonograph records.

The 16-inch transcription disc will play for 30 minutes—15 minutes of continuous playing on each side. Some national programs are recorded regularly and transcriptions of a particular broadcast may be borrowed from the sponsor without charge for classroom use. Local radio stations and university audio-visual services also make transcriptions of significant programs. Frequently they are willing to lend transcriptions to schools or even to cooperate with schools by recording special programs requested by the schools. Many of the film libraries and rental agencies now also stock transcriptions which may be borrowed in the same manner as films or slides. A few secondary schools are fortunate enough to have their own recording equipment. These, obviously, can make their own transcriptions and have them available at all times for use by the classroom teacher.

Phonograph and Transcription Recordings. These have instructional values similar to those of the transcribed radio broadcast, that is, they can be used to provide factual information and emotional color, to develop skills and understandings, and to review, summarize, or integrate materials previously encountered. The world's best music has long been made available to the teacher through phonograph recordings. Nonmusical materials, such as speeches, forum discussions, debates, and informational talks are recorded more satisfactorily by transcription. This is the same process as that used to record radio broadcasts. Children's stories, the world's finest literature, dramatizations, as well as political speeches may now be made available on call through this type of recording. The influence of the radio and phonograph in arousing interest in good music is evident on all sides. One may wonder if a similar good effect may be expected in the social and political world as a result of the increased use of transcriptions. Certainly boys and girls everywhere are being exposed to a higher standard of performance today through these media than was true of preceding generations.

Since phonograph records and transcriptions which have been prepared commercially are relatively inexpensive, they are commonly purchased by the local school. Film centers and libraries, however, have started collections to be rented to schools. Also, public libraries are establishing phonograph record loan services similar to their book-loaning programs. These, of course, are available to the pupil as well as the teacher. The alert teacher will capitalize on the fact that many homes have phonographs as well as radios and will develop out-of-school listening tastes by encouraging pupils to use these record services or to listen to well-selected radio programs.

The Public Address System. This also is a useful piece of equipment in the audio field. Several techniques have been developed involving its use for the improvement of communication skills. The system makes possible an audience situation on a moment's notice. This in itself can serve as a strong motivation for the planning, writing, and rehearsing of simulated radio broadcasts or other public performances. In preparing a broadcast that may be heard throughout the school, pupils naturally desire to make a good showing. They put forth extra effort to secure suitable materials, to organize it, and to write and speak effectively. Errors in logic, grammar, and pronunciation can be spotted quickly and corrected during rehearsals. The production is likely to be a cooperative activity, thereby setting up a natural learning situation for some of the newer approaches to citizenship education. Finally, use of the public address system may focus attention not only upon what is said, but also how it is said. Pupil attention is directed thereby to diction, enunciation, choice of words, and dramatic effect, in a way that is seldom equaled by any other means. The public address system thus can be used to provide a friendly atmosphere in which to teach functional grammar, research skills, and composition.

Recording Equipment Techniques. These are similar to those based on the use of the public address system. In this case, however, the performances are recorded and may then be played back to the performers for self-appraisal and criticism. When pupils hear their own errors, correctional steps are greatly simplified for the teacher. The value of this technique to the English or foreign-language teacher is self-evident. Less frequently recognized is the fact that individual members of an orchestra or glee club cannot hear the effect produced by the entire group except as the performance is recorded and played back. It is only in this manner that the individual can secure a realistic concept of the effect his contribution has upon the audience or how his part fits into the group effort. A recording, cooperatively prepared, may become the basis of a fruitful integrating or culminating activity for a group engaged in a unit of work. Such recordings would have the unique value of permanency to be used in the future as the opportunity or need may arise.

Various types of wire and tape recording equipment, each requiring its own unique operational technique, are now available. Some of these are cheaper to purchase and to operate than the older wax disc or cylinder methods are. It is reasonable to expect that schools will soon develop many new uses and techniques utilizing this comparatively new group of teaching aids.

Television. Television, of course, is the newest of the audio-visual aids to receive the serious consideration of the educational profession. At the present time, its use is highly restricted because of expense and the lack of technical know-how. In theory, it is the most promising of the audio-visual aids because in this one form of communication all the virtues of radio and motion picture are combined. Television makes its impression upon the consciousness of the learner through the auditory and the visual channels simultaneously. Added to this is the timeliness of the live radio broadcast and, when transmission facilities are set up, the world-wide scope of radio and motion pictures. When suitable methods for recording live broadcasts for repeated use have been developed, the educational potentialities of television will indeed be very great.

At this time numerous difficulties still limit television's effectiveness. The size of the image, for example, is much smaller than that of other projected aids. Programming is another problem that remains to be solved. The present solutions to these problems involve such large expenditures of money that they seem beyond the reach of purely educational agencies. However, if television develops as rapidly as did radio, the teacher may hope to use this new aid quite freely before 1960.

SUMMARY

It should be clear that the use of audio-visual aids does not represent a unique or distinct methodology. Rather audio-visual aids are devices for increasing the effectiveness of a variety of learning activities. They help in making the learning experience more real; they add timeliness; and they help develop interest in the content of education. These aids are particularly helpful in giving the pupil information. Therefore, whenever there is need to impart information quickly and vividly, whether that need arises in connection with a daily assignment, a subject-matter unit, or an experience unit, a well-selected audio or visual aid may be the best device the teacher can use to achieve that particular purpose.

SELECTED REFERENCES

Books

DALE, EDGAR: *Audio-Visual Methods in Teaching*, The Dryden Press, Inc., New York, 1946.

HASS, KENNETH B., and PACKER, H. C.: *Preparation and Use of Visual Aids*, Prentice-Hall, Inc., New York, 1946.

LEVENSON, WILLIAM B.: *Teaching Through Radio*, Farrar & Rinehart, Inc., New York, 1945.

McKown, H. E., and Roberts, A. B.: *Audio-Visual Aids to Instruction*, 2d ed., McGraw-Hill Book Company, Inc., New York, 1949.
Wittich, Walter A., and Fowlkes, John G.: *Audio-Visual Paths to Learning*, Harper & Brothers, New York, 1946.
Woefel, Norman, and Tyler, I. Keith: *Radio and the School*, A guidebook for Teachers and Administrators, World Book Company, Yonkers, New York, 1945.

Handbooks

DeBernardis, Amo: *The 1946 Audio-Visual Projectionist's Handbook*, *Business Screen Magazine*, Chicago, 1946.

Catalogues

Cook, Dorothy E., and Borden, Barbara: *Educational Film Guide* (formerly *Educational Film Catalogue*).
———, and Holden, Katherine M.: *Educational Film Guide, Section Two, Filmstrips*, The H. W. Wilson Company, New York, published annually.

Magazines

Audio-Visual Guide, formerly *Film and Radio Guide*, Educational and Recreational Guides, Inc., Newark, N.J.
Educational Screen, The Magazine Devoted to Audio-Visual Materials, The Educational Screen, Chicago.
Journal of the Association for Education by Radio, Chicago.
See and Hear, International Journal of Audio-Visual Education, Audio-Visual Publications, Inc., Chicago.

Chapter 20. THE PROFESSIONAL GROWTH OF

THE TEACHER

Throughout the comparatively long history of public education in this country, relatively little serious thought has been given to the teacher and his education. For example, the instructions given to Evert Pietersen, a schoolmaster employed in New Amsterdam in 1661, made no mention of the qualities a schoolmaster should possess or of the general requirements underlying the responsibilities he was about to assume.[1] There was, indeed, a long period during which teachers were largely uninstructed except as their contracts prohibited certain practices such as smoking, drinking, and swearing, and prescribed regular attendance at church. Within the past quarter century, however, a new interest has appeared in the nature and importance of good teaching, and there is considerable hope that the next decade will witness marked progress in the identification of the teacher's responsibilities as well as in the invention of more effective means for meeting them.

The growing recognition of the social value of the school. This new emphasis on the education of the teacher is due in a large measure to the impact of the last two major wars upon the "survival" thinking of men everywhere. Twice in contemporary times the American public school system has been called upon to help the world save itself from its own folly. As a result, there is a growing appreciation of the social value of good schools which is finding expression in radio forums, newspaper editorials, and dinner-table conversations. There is, also, evidence of a deep-seated faith in the public schools. This evidence is found in the demand for better teachers and better schools, and in the expanded school budgets which have been prepared and accepted in nearly every

[1] E. P. Cubberly, *Readings in the History of Education*, p. 305, Houghton Mifflin Company, Boston, 1920.

community. In this respect, the American people seem at long last to have caught up with the thinking of Horace Mann, who in 1846 as secretary to the Massachusetts State Board of Education, wrote in his Tenth Annual Report as follows:

The three following propositions, then, describe the broad everduring foundations in which the common-school system of Massachusetts reposes:

The successive generations of man taken collectively, constitute one great commonwealth.

The property of this commonwealth is pledged for the education of all its youth, up to such a point as will save them from poverty and vice, and prepare them for the adequate performance of their social and civic duties.

The successive holders of this property are trustees, bound to the faithful execution of their trust by the most sacred obligations; and embezzlement and pillage from children and descendants have not less of criminality, and have more of meanness, than the same offenses when perpetrated against contemporaries.[2]

There is strong evidence today that the citizens of this country sense the challenges so ably described by Mann and that they are now willing to invest in schools staffed by teachers who not only come well prepared, but who, also, seek continuously to improve themselves on the job. This, of course, places a heavy responsibility on the teachers themselves.

The growing recognition of the importance of the teacher. Previous chapters described the teaching found in the earlier secondary schools. As in other schools of their day the emphasis in instruction was placed on the mastery of a given body of subject matter. Since the schools were not looked upon as the sole owners of the subject matter, many bright, ambitious, "self-made" individuals prided themselves on having acquired the learning that enabled them to succeed brilliantly without the aid of schools or, in some instances, in spite of them. Schooling, therefore, may have been looked upon in some instances as the easy, or even the lazy way to acquire an education, and the teacher as one who rendered a service that fell somewhat short of respectability. The public's regard for the teacher was indicated by the type of person

[2] *Ibid.,* p. 565. Italics inserted by the present writer. See also *Teachers for Our Times,* p. 31, Commission on Teacher Education, American Council on Education, Washington, D.C., 1944.

appointed. On the elementary level, cobblers sometimes supplemented their incomes by contracting to teach a group of children to read. The sedentary nature of their work made it possible for them to "hear" the pupils recite their letters without interruption to their more important activities. Similarly, widows or other women, who for reasons of necessity could be prevailed upon, supervised the letter learning of a group of children while they gave their primary attention to household tasks. Wounded war veterans, incapable of earning a living by means of more active pursuits, also turned to schoolteaching. Thus, the teacher's salary acquired the characteristics of a dole which was distributed on the basis of the recipient's need rather than his ability.

Secondary-school teaching seems to have enjoyed a somewhat better reputation. The college student, in need of funds, quite frequently turned to teaching for a term or two. It must be remembered, however, that these temporary teachers were destined for the learned professions. They were entitled to respect, therefore, not so much for what they were, but for what they were to become, and teaching was looked upon merely as a brief pause on the road to higher things. If one continued to teach beyond the usual time needed to acquire funds, this fact was taken as an indication of a lack of ambition or of ability—a point of view perpetuated to this day in the old saying, "He who can, does; he who can't, teaches."

The importance that is now attached to teaching is clearly revealed in the new concept of the teacher's function. The old view that the teacher is primarily a crutch to aid the less able in the acquisition of a specific body of knowledge or skills has given way to the view that the teacher is a guide to better forms of living. As a guide, he is expected to be more skillful and more capable of successful living than the average adult. The ranks of the teaching profession must be filled, therefore, by the best examples of successful living and achievement that can be drawn from the adult community and not by the near failures and misfits. Thus it follows that the teacher is no longer something less than the community standard of success, but rather something higher than that to which the average citizen of the community has risen.

Just as the concept of the teacher's role has changed in recent years, so also has the concept of the teacher's preparation undergone change. As long as mastery of subject matter was the dominant objective of instruction, the teacher was generally considered to be well prepared for his job when he could submit evidence of having mastered the required subject matter himself. For a time the bachelor's degree was accepted as suitable evidence of such mastery, and until recently some states were willing to certify the possessor of such a degree to teach any subject offered by any secondary school within their jurisdiction. In more recent times, it has become the custom to require in addition to a degree a prescribed number of semester hours of college credit in the subjects to be taught before a certificate is granted. Local school administrators and boards of education, however, are now looking beyond mere ability to meet certification requirements based on subject-matter mastery, and are inquiring into the personal qualifications of the applicants. Evidence of this is found in the number of schools which require personal interviews before making appointments and in the careful and detailed inquiries that are made regarding the candidates' intelligence, reputation, and ability to succeed in group situations. Today, it is not uncommon for boards of education to look with greater favor upon successful participation in extracurricular activities and leadership experience in community service such as the Scouts, than upon a record of high scholastic achievement.

Nor are boards of education satisfied to renew appointments year after year unless the teachers give some evidence of progressive improvement. Some communities have now set up schedules of merit increments to encourage improvement. These schedules usually require evidence of advanced study before certain salary increases are granted. In a few states, the granting of permanent or life certificates is no longer looked upon with favor, and those who wish to renew their certificates are expected to present suitable evidence of professional growth.

TEACHER EDUCATION IS A PROFESSIONAL RESPONSIBILITY

It is evident that the professional preparation of teachers has two aspects. The first deals with the selection and preparation of prospective teachers before certification. This phase is generally referred to as *pre-service* education. The second aspect is that which has to do with the improvement of the teacher on the job. This phase is known as *in-service* education.

The profession must provide suitable pre-service education. As a result of scientific studies that have been conducted since 1900, the teaching profession knows much more than ever before in its long history about the nature and needs of the learner and the learning process. Local, state, and national census data indicate in a general way the magnitude of the school's job. Additional data are available about such factors as the pupil's health, cultural and economic backgrounds, the personality traits exhibited by the different age groups, and the social significance of the curriculum. Psychologists and teachers who have engaged in experimentation have shed much light upon the learner's needs and abilities, as well as upon the instructional methods by which he may best be served.

The teaching profession is well aware of the relationship between some knowledge of these things and effective service in the classroom. Under the leadership of the profession nearly every state has taken steps to require some pre-service professional preparation in psychology and the principles and methods of teaching. While not all collegiate institutions which offer pre-service courses designed to satisfy certification requirements take their professional obligations seriously, the public has shown a willingness to grant enabling powers to the profession, usually in the form of certification regulations, by means of which reluctant institutions can in time be brought into line. The responsibility for the selection and preparation of beginning teachers, therefore, is clearly up to the teaching profession.

The beginning teacher obviously has little if any voice in determining the nature of his preparation for teaching. Pre-service educational programs are generally prescribed for him either by state or by institutional authorities. However, the beginning teacher is able to determine the nature and the extent of his in-service growth. It is to this aspect of professional growth, therefore, to which the present chapter is directed.

The profession must provide for in-service growth. Much of the evidence seems to bear out the personal convictions of many leading educators that continuous in-service growth is desirable. The authors of a national publication comment as follows upon this point of view:

For all professional school personnel, no matter how adequate their pre-service preparation, there should be a continuous and systematic program to encourage growth in-service through such activities as professional reading, demonstration and firsthand observation of superior school procedures, study of individual problems in local staff workshops, independent research, travel, study at teachers' colleges or schools of education, and participation in activities of professional organizations.[3]

This list of activities gives evidence of the scope of the profession's responsibility for in-service education. The influence of the profession in planning and conducting each activity is self-evident. The degree to which they are provided as well as the measure of their success is dependent, therefore, upon the measure of responsibility members of the profession assume for them.

Modern trends in in-service education. As long as the teacher's professional qualifications were judged primarily by the evidence submitted of subject matter mastered, in-service education was looked upon as the taking of additional courses or the earning of a higher degree. Opportunities for in-service education, therefore, were available only in the geographical areas near colleges and universities or in summer-school study. The courses taken frequently had little direct bearing on the teacher's professional problems or were taught by persons who felt no personal or professional responsibility for the improvement of the public schools.

The shift in the purpose of education has brought with it new trends in in-service education. The Commission on Teacher Education [4] has described certain trends which give considerable promise of producing far-reaching changes in the ability to perform the teaching function. In brief, these may be described as follows:

1. The education of teachers, pre-service and in-service, is properly a continuous process.

2. School systems like teacher preparation institutions are striving to increase institutional unity as it applies to the more democratic participation in the program of teacher preparation.

3. Sensitivity to the importance of the human factor in teacher preparation is mounting.

4. Jobs that are commonly recognized by the teachers as needing to be done are more frequently being used as starting points for study leading to action.

[3] National Education Association, *Proposals for Public Education in Postwar America*, Research Bulletin, 22(2):55, April, 1944.

[4] Commission on Teacher Education, *The Improvement of Teacher Education*, p. 167ff., Final Report, American Council on Education, Washington, D.C., 1946.

5. The local school system itself is being used more and more as the focal center for the in-service education of teachers.

6. Increasingly system-centered programs of in-service education are being supported by budgetary allotments.[5]

7. There is a tendency to provide supervisory leadership for programs of this type.

8. There is a greater degree of functionality in the relationship between the schools and teacher preparation institutions.

9. A greater proportion of graduate study is being devoted to the professional needs of the teachers who take graduate courses.

10. Experiences of the workshop type are destined to become more common in teacher preparation.

11. In scattered instances, assistance with in-service programs is being offered by universities at reduced rates.[6]

12. Consultancy service by institutions of higher learning has a tendency to eliminate credit barriers as far as earning graduate credit for participation in in-service programs is concerned.

13. The promotion of in-service programs by school systems tends to make for clearer and more continuous relations between those systems and the cooperating colleges or universities.

14. Finally, there is some ground for hope that a new degree of cooperation between colleges and universities will develop as the result of an attempt to meet with adequate effectiveness the growth needs of particular school systems and their teachers.[7]

Further evidence of the new trends in in-service education is found in the nature of the supervisory services provided in many school systems. At one time the supervisor was held responsible for stimulating teachers to improve on the job. In-service growth was thought to begin with the supervisor's visit to the classroom and to take its direction from the recommendations offered the teacher in the light of that which had been observed. Today, there is a tendency to spread the responsibility for bringing about improvement to the staff as a

[5] The West Hartford Schools, Conn., have a new item of $2,200 in the 1948–1949 budget for this purpose.

[6] The University of Connecticut charges a flat fee of $100 for candidates admitted to graduate study for the first graduate degree and an additional $125 for the doctoral degree.

[7] An ever-increasing number of first-rate colleges and universities are recommending the pursuit of special area training with facilities and personnel at other than their own institutions.

whole. The improvement of instruction, therefore, is regarded in a more democratic light, and the improvement process may be initiated by:

1. A curriculum study
2. A study of ways to improve and extend supervisory services
3. The formation of study groups
4. A locally sponsored workshop
5. Teacher-administration cooperation in planning and carrying out some group activity
6. Teacher participation as citizens in the community [8]

Some notion of the kind of in-service education opportunities that are now available may be gained from the following table.

TABLE 4. OPPORTUNITIES FOR PROFESSIONAL GROWTH OF TEACHERS IN SERVICE REPORTED BY 1304 CITIES *

Type of opportunity	No.	Per cent
Professional courses	925	71
Committees	847	65
Faculty and departmental meetings	212	16
After-school or summer workshops operated locally	143	11
Study conferences, research groups, study groups, forums	163	13
Lectures by outside speakers brought in by school system; teacher's institutes	85	7
Extensive professional library; guided professional reading	78	6
Other opportunities	50	4

* Adapted from National Education Association, *Teacher Personnel Procedures: Employment Conditions in Service*, Research Bulletin, 20(3):92, May, 1942.

From the above data it will be seen that course instruction continues to be the most prevalent form of in-service education. It should be stressed, however, that the modern courses most frequently are of a professional rather than a subject-matter nature, and are offered in extension by persons primarily interested in the improvement of classroom practices. The prevalence of committee activities gives further evidence of the present trend toward the orientation of in-service

[8] Adapted from Commission on Teacher Education, *Teachers for Our Times*, p. 21, American Council on Education, Washington, D.C., 1944.

activities around the professional problems of the teacher. It may be said that professional growth begins with the teacher himself, and it occurs to the extent that he takes steps to deal more effectively with the problems he encounters from day to day.

Attitudes of teachers toward in-service education. So much unfavorable comment has been heard in the past about professional courses and teachers' meetings that one may wonder what is the attitude of teachers toward these newer developments. On the whole, this attitude has been encouraging and one that gives promise of productive results. Numerous studies have been conducted in this area and there is ample evidence available to support the claim that teachers move to those school systems which offer the better opportunities for professional growth, whether measured in terms of increased responsibility, greater freedom to plan, or improved working conditions.[9]

The kind of in-service educational opportunities judged to be most helpful is indicated by one study in which 170 high-school teachers were asked to rate the following in-service offerings:

1. Professional courses
2. Courses and lectures in secondary education
3. Faculty meetings
4. Supervision
5. Professional readings in secondary education
6. Participation in educational experiments
7. Membership on professional committees
8. Professional association membership
9. School visitations

The accompanying charts present graphically the reactions of these teachers to three types of opportunities, namely, professional courses, courses and lectures in secondary education, and school visitation. The enthusiasm of these teachers for school visitation is apparent at once. Similar enthusiasm was expressed for professional reading and for experimental work of the type described in the study. In contrast, professional courses, lectures, county meetings, and faculty meetings were regarded as not more than moderately helpful, and a few teachers regarded them as having no value whatsoever.

[9] Report of the Committee on Tenure, *The First Five Years of Teaching Experience*, p. 19, National Education Association, Washington, D.C., May, 1939.

TABLE 5. TEACHER REACTION TO IN-SERVICE OFFERINGS *

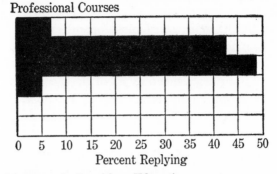

Professional Courses

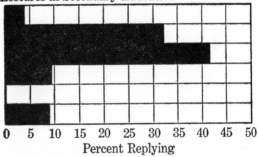

Courses and Lectures in Secondary Education

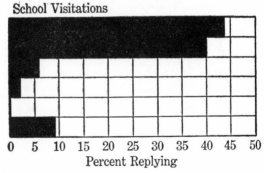

School Visitations

* Adapted from data compiled by M. N. Woodring, "An Evaluation of the Contribution of Secondary Education to the In-Service Training of High School Teachers During the Last Decade," *Educational Administration and Supervision,* 22:641–52, December, 1936.

One may properly ask: "Why do so many teachers shun faculty meetings?" "Why do teachers feel that professional courses and state meetings fail in their purposes?" The answer to both questions seems to be the same, *i.e.*, limited opportunity for teacher participation in planning and executing these activities and, therefore, limited application to the teacher's daily work. If teachers could attend meetings and institutes planned by all of the members of their group, their attitude might be different.[10] Faculty meetings, for example, can be made more acceptable if certain principles are followed. Pitts[11] has recommended four such guides as follows:

1. The program for each meeting should grow from the needs of the teachers as these needs are recognized and expressed by them.

2. Each program should provide the opportunity for the cooperation and the participation of the teachers in each phase of it.

3. The work should be planned so that each teacher may have the opportunity to secure the greatest amount of growth possible from the meeting which he attends.

4. No teachers' meeting can be successful unless the teachers feel that they have made some progress toward their goal.

In many instances where the staff is large, small informal group meetings provide greater opportunity for cooperation and participation than do general faculty meetings. However, each faculty member should participate in at least one group meeting, and no momentous decisions involving the school as a whole or all of the teachers should be made at a group meeting where all teachers have not had equal representation. Doubtless if teachers were given the opportunity of planning their own meetings, there would be increased interest in them. Teachers, like others, need to join in the educational experiences that accompany planning for group action.

At the Rochester, New York, Athenaeum and Mechanics Institute, it was found that the interest and attendance were better when faculty meetings were scheduled at regular, predetermined intervals with a definite, though flexible, topic of discussion; that the use of outside specialists as discussion leaders tended to inhibit the participation of

[10] Roy E. Learned, "More Acceptable Faculty Meetings," *The Education Digest*, 8:24–26, September, 1942.

[11] Clara L. Pitts, "Characteristics of a Good Teachers' Meeting," *Educational Method*, 16:241–247, February, 1937.

certain instructors, but that when these specialists attended and participated as one of the group, the others were much more active and exhibited a greater interest in the interplay of ideas.[12]

The changing administrative attitude toward in-service education. Teacher participation in the formulation of educational policies or even in the direction of professional meetings is a relatively recent development. Many administrators still believe that these are their prerogatives exclusively. This attitude became current because the administrative function in education was differentiated from the teaching function and developed in imitation of the management function in industry. Thus, as the schools grew in size and expanded their services, they copied the plan of organization and the division of responsibilities found in some of the more successful industrial enterprises. A sharp distinction came to be drawn between the administrator and the teacher, with the managerial responsibilities so frequently implied in the phrase, "final authority and final responsibility," placed securely in the hands of the administrator. While this arrangement made possible certain fiscal economies and the development of integrated school systems, it also encouraged the view that administrators possess a unique type of intelligence or wisdom that makes their judgments on all, or nearly all, educational matters superior to those of the teachers. The school programs, therefore, took form in the minds of the administrators. Supervisors were employed to help put those policies into action, and in-service education was introduced to inform the teachers what the administration expected them to do. When teachers attended faculty meetings, teachers' institutes, or conferences, they usually were "talked to" about matters relating to administrative policy. Only seldom were they given opportunities to discuss the problems that arise in the minds of all serious-minded teachers as they work directly with pupils. It is small wonder, therefore, that these earlier in-service activities acquired unpleasant connotations in the minds of many of the older teachers.

Recent years have witnessed the introduction of a change in attitude with reference to the administrator's role in education. It is now generally agreed that the success or failure of the school cannot be measured by the same fiscal standards used to determine the success or failure of a business enterprise. Schools are not run to show a profit, and the management methods of profit enterprises are not necessarily good

[12] Leo Smith, "Faculty Seminars," *School Executive*, 60:20–21, April, 1941.

in the field of educational administration. It is becoming increasingly clear that schools are expected to do whatever can be done in the classroom and elsewhere to help boys and girls achieve to the fullest possible extent of their potentialities. The test of success is found primarily in what happens to the pupils, and only secondarily in how cheaply the schools have been operated to achieve those ends. Administration, therefore, is coming to be regarded as a service function rather than as a control function; a service function in the sense that through the administrator the resources of the school and the community are made available to the teacher for his use in the all-important pupil-teacher relationship. The focal point in education thus is shifting back to the teacher-pupil situation with the teacher as a key person in originating policy discussions.

Evidence of this shift was found in a study conducted under the auspices of the North Central Association in which more than 300 schools participated. The conclusions are based on the opinions expressed by both teachers and principals. The 10 most useful techniques for in-service education, listed according to rank, were found to be the following:

1. Organizing teachers into committees to study problems
2. Organizing studies of special topics—general staff meetings
3. Providing a professional library and browsing-room for teachers
4. Having teachers (not administrators) give reviews of articles in current educational magazines
5. Giving special financial awards for participation in programs of in-service education
6. Engaging cooperatively in a systematic evaluation of the school using the criteria of the Cooperative Study of Secondary-school Standards
7. Carrying out a well-planned attack upon the problems of curriculum development
8. Holding forums where parents, pupils, teachers, and board members participate
9. Attending summer workshops
10. Visiting teachers in one's own school or in other schools [13]

It is a significant fact that in the case of each of the above techniques there is opportunity for teacher participation and cooperation. They are not techniques of the "administrator-domination" type.

[13] C. A. Weber, "Promising Techniques for Educating Teachers in Service," *Educational Administration and Supervision*, 28:691–695, December, 1942.

IMPLICATION OF IN–SERVICE EDUCATION FOR THE TEACHER

In this and preceding chapters attention was called to a changing educational atmosphere. Learning is now coming to be identified with increased ability on the part of the learner to deal satisfactorily with the problems that confront him from day to day. The teacher is now looked upon as a guide or coach skilled in solving problems rather than as one who already has all the answers. The curriculum is now determined by the pupil's need for the information and the skills that will help him deal with his problems of adjustment and adaptation to his physical and social environment. Today, the administrative and supervisory personnel increasingly strive to make available in the learning situation resources and experiences that are not available to the teacher alone. All of these changes present a challenge to the teacher. Few persons today expect the young teacher, recently graduated from college, to be as successful during his first year or two of teaching as he will be later. Consistent growth can be expected from year to year and frequently is expected, as indicated by the salary schedules which provide for the highest earnings during the years immediately preceding retirement.

Such growth, however, is not inevitable. There is a significant difference between a teacher who has had 20 years of experience and one who has had 1 year of experience 20 times. Growth begins with a recognition of a need for improvement, and this recognition can bear fruit only when it occurs in the mind of the teacher himself. As in the case of the pupil, the teacher learns as he consciously seeks to improve his relationships with those with whom he must live and work. Opportunities for growth appear in the form of cooperative ventures with the pupils, other teachers, and the members of the community. Unfortunately, pre-service education is still largely concerned with individualistic information-getting as distinguished from the acquisition of experience in cooperative group living. The beginning teacher, therefore, must learn on the job to identify himself with such groups and to participate in the common search for solutions to the problems peculiar to that group and possibly to no other. As a member of a group he must assume a share of the responsibility for identifying problems and for bringing them into the open where they may be dealt with on a group basis. Professional growth is now identified more and more with the development of skill in identifying problems related to pupil growth and of working with others in finding satisfactory solutions.

In-service education today is an open attempt to promote such professional growth. Committees, staff meetings, study groups, panel discussions, and other in-service techniques are instrumentalities by which staff and community resources can be marshaled for more effective attacks upon the problems of instruction than would be possible if the teacher were left to his own resources. Frequently, special information or a new perspective is desired which can be provided most economically by a special course or a lecture by someone particularly well qualified in that area. The school, through the efforts of those in leadership positions, may provide in-service opportunities, but only the teacher can decide to make use of them. Appointments to committees, invitations to staff meetings or to local study groups can be viewed either as unnecessary annoyances or as opportunities for professional growth. As in any democratic enterprise, the opportunities and the responsibilities rest with the individual.

SUMMARY

The professional growth of the teacher is achieved by a program of pre-service studies and by a variety of activities designed to help him grow on the job. While there is no intention here to minimize the importance of pre-service education, it is the latter or in-service program over which the teacher has the most direct control and which can be directed to serve his needs once he is in a position to know what they are. It is the in-service program, therefore, to which the present chapter is directed.

In-service growth implies continuous learning, experimentation, a spirit of open-mindedness, a sense of self-criticism, and a willingness to capitalize upon the strength of the multiple mind. There must be an inner desire on the part of the teacher to be professional and to work for higher standards and goals expressed in terms of pupil growth.

On the basis of the many studies made of the many promising in-service techniques, it is reasonable to conclude that a good in-service program will embody the following characteristics:

1. It will provide for intelligent leadership which will encourage and enlist the initiative of all of the teachers and supervision which will promote

self-interest and self-activity on the part of all teachers for professional improvement. It will provide a program based upon well-formulated objectives derived from a study of the needs of individual teachers in individual learning and teaching situations, recognizing that individual teachers differ in teaching ability and in their needs and potentialities. It will aid in the development of a feeling of security and professional status in the school community.

2. It will provide ample opportunity for teachers to assume responsibility for leadership in staff activities, to share responsibilities, and to develop respect for the ideas and opinions of colleagues.

3. It will provide aids to in-service training right within the teacher's own school system. Every school should have a professional library-reading-workroom complete in every detail as to new books on educational theory and practices, educational periodicals, daily newspapers, bulletins, and courses of study from various state departments of education, a typewriter, mimeograph machine, etc. Teachers should share responsibility in the maintenance and upkeep of the room. *Materials should not be kept in the superintendent's office or in the faculty room,* but in a special staff library-reading-workroom. It should provide "workshops" right within the school —using the services offered by state departments of education, state universities, and the ideas and services of the local staff members.

4. It will encourage the study and discussion of problems based upon local classroom situations and experiences. It will seek to develop a school program based upon the needs of the school community—in other words, the training program should not be separated from the educational needs of the pupils for whom the teachers have responsibility.

The most ample program of in-service activities, however, cannot force growth upon a reluctant and uncooperative teacher. Professional growth can occur only as the teacher seeks to improve himself. Having taken the initiative, in-service aids are means to his self-improvement. Professional growth can be initiated only by the teacher.

SELECTED REFERENCES

American Association of School Administrators: *Paths to Better Schools,* Chap. VI and p. 166, Washington, D.C., 1944.

American Council on Education: *Teachers for Our Times,* Commission on Teacher Education, Washington, D.C., 1944.

BARR, A. S., BURTON, W. H., and BRUECKNER, LEO J.: *Supervision, Principles and Practices in the Improvement of Instruction,* D. Appleton-Century Company, Inc., New York, 1938.

CHRISTENSEN, HELEN: *Techniques of Secondary School Supervision*, unpublished master's project, University of Connecticut, Storrs, Conn., July, 1945.

CUBBERLY, E. P.: *Readings in the History of Education*, Houghton Mifflin Company, Boston, 1920.

HADSALL, L. F.: "The Extension Activities of Certain Publicly Supported Institutions in Assisting Teachers in Service in Elementary Science or Nature Studying," *Science Education*, 20:7–11, 1936.

KINDRED, L. W.: "Your Teachers' Institutes Can Be Improved," *Nation's Schools*, 30:19–20, August, 1942.

KYTE, GEORGE C.: "The Elementary School Principal as a Builder of Teacher Morale," as quoted by Norman Forest in "The Good in Part-time Supervision," *American School Board Journal*, 96:16, January, 1938.

LEARNED, ROY E.: "More Acceptable Faculty Meetings," *The Education Digest*, 8:24–26, September, 1942.

National Education Association: *The First Five Years of Teaching Experience*, Report of the Commission on Tenure, Chicago, May, 1939.

———: *Teacher Personnel Procedures: Employment Conditions in Service*, Research Bulletin, Washington, D.C., 20 (3):92, May, 1942.

———: *Proposals for Public Education in Postwar America*, Research Bulletin, Washington, D.C., 22 (2):55, April, 1944.

———: *The Teacher Looks at Personnel Administration*, Research Bulletin, Washington, D.C., 23 (4):122, December, 1945.

PITTS, CLARA L.: "Characteristics of a Good Teachers' Meeting," *Educational Methods*, 16:241–247, February, 1937.

Professors of Education Administration: *Developing Leaders for Education*, A Report of a Work Conference, Endicott, N.Y., 1947.

SMITH, LEO: "Faculty Seminars," *School Executive*, 60:20–21, April, 1941.

TEAD, ORDWAY: *The Art of Leadership*, McGraw-Hill Book Company, Inc., New York, 1935.

WEBER, C. A.: "Promising Techniques for Educating Teachers in Service," *Educational Administration and Supervision*, 28:691–695, December, 1942.

WILLIAM, O. S.: "Teacher and Democratic Administration," *The Clearing House*, 18:515–518, May, 1944.

WOODRING, MAXIE N.: "An Evaluation of the Contribution of Secondary Education to the In-Service Training of High School Teachers during the Last Decade," *Educational Administration and Supervision*, 22:641–652, December, 1936.

VISUAL AIDS

The following list of visual aids can be used to supplement some of the material in this book. This list is selective in terms of the authors' experience. Undoubtedly there are many more films because new productions are being released constantly. We suggest that each film be previewed because it may contain information either too advanced or too elementary for some classes.

These films can be obtained from the producer or distributor listed with each title (addresses are given at the end of the bibliography). In many cases these films and filmstrips can be obtained from your local film distributor; also, many universities have large film libraries from which they can be borrowed.

The running time is given in minutes (min). All are sound and in black and white. The motion pictures are 16 millimeter and the filmstrip is 35 millimeter single frame.

Listed with each film are the chapters to which it is applicable. You may find other chapters where it will also be appropriate for your class.

MOTION PICTURES

Antioch College, Ohio (19 min—1942, Antioch, Chap. 12). Shows this college's program of combining work experience with college classroom study.

Assignment: Tomorrow (26 min—1945, NEA, Chaps. 1, 2, 20). Shows the role of the National Education Association.

A Broader Concept of Method—Developing Pupil Interest (13 min—1947, McG-H, Chaps. 12, 13, 15, 17). Shows principles and techniques of securing student interest in learning.

A Broader Concept of Method—Teachers and Pupils Planning and Working Together (19 min—1947, McG-H, Chaps. 12, 13, 15). Shows principles and techniques of guiding pupils to participation in their learning experiences.

Democracy (11 min—1945, EBF, Chaps. 1, 2, 15). Shows that a democracy is based on shared respect and shared political power.

Despotism (11 min—1945, EBF, Chaps. 1, 2, 15). Shows that despotism is based on restricted respect and concentrated power.

Film Tactics (20 min—1943, Castle, Chap. 19). Shows the proper presentation of visual materials, especially motion pictures.

Learning to Understand Children—A Diagnostic Approach (21 min —1947, McG-H, Chap. 3). Shows how a good teacher uses diagnostic measures to analyze a maladjusted student.

Learning to Understand Children—A Remedial Program (23 min— 1947, McG-H, Chaps. 3, 9, 10, 12, 13, 15). Shows how the teacher in the above film helped the child to better adjustment by a good remedial program.

Maintaining Classroom Discipline (15 min—1947, McG-H, Chap. 18). Shows how teacher attitude and good techniques of teaching secure the cooperation of the class.

Principles of the Art and Science of Teaching (47 min—1942, Iowa, Chaps. 9 and 10). Shows teaching principles and techniques.

Teaching (10 min—1945, Voc G, Chap. 20). Explains the teaching profession, qualifications, training required, working conditions, and rewards.

Using the Classroom Film (11 min—1945, EBF, Chap. 19). Shows principles and techniques of using classroom motion pictures.

Willie and the Mouse (10 min—1942, TFC, Chaps. 9, 10). Shows psychological learning principles.

Wilson Dam School (21 min—1942, TVA, Chaps. 12, 13, 15). Shows an improved rural school and its program.

FILMSTRIPS

Designing Examinations (Jam Handy; Part I—Chap. 8; Part II— Chaps. 8, 11).

LIST OF PRODUCERS AND DISTRIBUTORS

Antioch—Antioch College, Yellow Springs, Ohio.

Castle—Castle Films, Inc., 30 Rockefeller Center, New York 20.

EBF—Encyclopaedia Britannica Films, Inc., 20 N. Wacker Dr., Chicago.

Iowa—Department of Visual Instruction, University of Iowa, Iowa City, Iowa.

Jam Handy—Jam Handy Organization, General Motors Bldg., Detroit, Michigan.

McG-H—McGraw-Hill Book Company, Inc., 330 W. 42 St., New York 18.

NEA—National Education Association, Washington, D.C., or Executive Secretary of your state association.

TFC—Teaching Film Custodians, 25 W. 43 St., New York 18.

TVA—Tennessee Valley Authority, Knoxville, Tennessee.

Voc G—Vocational Guidance Films, Inc., 2718 Beaver Ave., Des Moines, Iowa.

INDEX

A

Ability, 382
  creative, 205
  deductive, 386
  differences in, 47–50
  generalizing, 386
  inductive, 386
  linguistic, 385
  mental, 381
  numerical, 386
  perceptual, 386
  physical, 381
  quantitative, 385
  reasoning, 386
  spatial visualizing, 386
  to think, 323, 325–330
    evaluation of, 325
  types of, 49
  variations in, 48
  verbal, 383, 386
Ability grouping, 71, 76
Ability patterns, individual, 50
Ability tests, general, 381
  mental, 381
Academies, 22, 24, 45, 74, 76, 123, 355, 358
Academy movement, 122
Achievement, composite measures of, 189, 265
Achievement measurement, 373
Achievement quotient (*see* AQ)
Achievement test rating scale, standardized, 108
Achievement test scores, 397
Achievement tests, 138, 374, 398
  high school, Sones-Harry, 249
  Metropolitan, 261

Achievement tests (*Continued*)
  progressive, 252
  standardized, 237, 259, 373, 393, 395
Action, cooperative, 17, 287
Activities, 217, 232, 278, 284
  cooperative, 33, 80, 222, 457
  cooperative venture, 473
  culminating, 222–224, 226, 233, 301, 457
  developmental, 222
  effort in, 215
  extraclass, 65, 80
  extracurricular (*see* Extracurricular activities)
  integrating, 211, 233, 449, 457
  learning, 206
  real-life, 206, 279
  records of, 397
  social, 206
    pupil participation in, 212
  study, 280
  supplementary, 279
  work-type, 363
Activity movement, 270–281, 287
Activity program, 27, 28
Adjustment, 112
  personal-social, 323, 333
Adjustment characteristics, social, 390–391
Adjustment inventories, 340
Administration, 3
Administrative devices, 78
  using daily-assignment procedures, 355–361
  using experience unit procedures, 363–366
  using subject-matter unit, 361–363
Administrative function, 471

Departmentalization of instruction, 133
Development, emotional, 51
  physiological, 51
Devices, 6, 7
  administrative (*see* Administrative devices)
De Voss, James C., 237
Dewey, John, 26, 204, 206, 213, 282–284
Diagnosis, 163, 373
Dickens, Charles, 155
Differences, in ability, 47–50
  group, 375
  in home background, 53–54
  individual, 47, 60–61, 86, 87, 90, 134, 202, 225, 234, 237, 254, 341, 368, 373, 374
  in personal and social problems, 56–60
  physiological and emotional, 50–53
  in pupil attitudes and work habits, 55–56
  trait, 375
Discipline, 13, 27, 231, 423–445, 449
  formal, 78
  group (*see* Group discipline)
  individual, 439–444
    punishment in, 443
  as maintaining leadership in class, 435
  mental, 45, 46, 119, 122, 123
  and objectives of education, 425–427
  principles for, 427–428
  purpose of, 424–425
Donatus, 119
Douglass, Harl R., 67, 160
Drill, 153, 232, 315

E

EA, 378–379
Economics, 25
Education, comparative, 3
  democratic, 10, 66, 69, 206, 282, 283, 285, 288, 292, 293, 361, 363, 405, 406, 472
  as experience, 206
  history of, 3
  objectives of, 234, 293, 426
    and discipline, 425–427
  as participation in democratic way of life, 27–28
  professional, 3

Education (*Continued*)
  purpose of, 6, 122, 204–206, 234, 279, 294, 448, 461, 472
  secondary (*see* Secondary education)
Educational characteristics, 393
Educational Film Guide, 451
Educational goals, 63
Educational objectives, 100, 216, 320
Educational opportunity, equality of, 44, 46, 50
Educational outcomes, 213, 236, 308, 361
Educational Policies Commission, 32
Educational psychology, 3
Educational theory, 3
Educators, objectives of, 212
Effort in activities, 215
Eight-year Study of the Progressive Education Association, 77, 96, 100, 319, 321, 327, 329–331, 343, 344, 399, 400
Election system, free, 357
Elections, 17
Electives, 70, 74, 87
Electricity, 122
Elliott, Edward C., 164, 165
Ely-King Tests in American History, 250
Emile, 272
Emotions, 407
Employment record, 397
Environment, 380–381, 389
  physical, 7
  school, 206
  social, 7, 33
Erasmus, 119
Essay examinations, 161, 164–171
  construction of, 166–168
  improvement of, 166
  scoring of, 169–170
Ethical character, 24
Evaluation, 95–97, 109, 161, 298, 303, 307, 393, 395, 396
  (*See also* Pupil evaluation)
Evaluation activity, 212
Evaluation instruments, 95–101, 331, 399
  construction of, 319
Evaluation techniques, 95–101
Evaluative instruments, 237
  construction of, 322
  validation of, 322
Evaluative procedures, 334

4.00